The **AA** **KEY**Guide
Vietnam

Contents

KEY TO SYMBOLS

- Map reference
- Address
- Telephone number
- Opening times
- Admission prices
- Bus number
- Train station
- Ferry/boat
- Driving directions
- Tourist office
- Tours
- Guidebook
- Restaurant
- Café
- Shop
- Bar
- Toilets
- Number of rooms
- Parking
- No smoking
- Air conditioning
- Swimming pool
- Gym
- Other useful information
- Shopping
- Entertainment
- Nightlife
- Sports
- Activities
- Health and beauty
- For children
- Cross-reference
- Walk/tour start point

HOW TO USE THIS BOOK

Understanding Vietnam is an introduction to the region, its geography, economy and people. **Living Vietnam** gives an insight into Vietnam today, while **The Story of Vietnam** takes you through the country's past.

For detailed advice on getting to Vietnam—and getting around once you are there—turn to **On the Move**. For useful practical information, from weather forecasts to emergency services, turn to **Planning**.

Out and About gives you the chance to explore Vietnam through walks and tours.

The **Sights**, **What to Do**, **Eating and Staying** sections are divided geographically into five regions, which are shown on the map on the inside front cover. These regions always appear in the same order. Towns and places of interest are listed alphabetically within each region.

Map references for the **Sights** refer to the atlas section at the end of this book or to the individual town plans. For example, Hanoi has the reference ✛ 283 D3, indicating the page on which the map is found (283) and the grid square in which Hanoi sits (D3).

UNDERSTANDING VIETNAM

Vietnam is a seductive place—an intriguing mix of a country steeped in Marxist creed yet embracing capitalist economic reform. The country has worked hard to shake off its reputation as a war zone and has worked hard, too, on building up a name for itself as an unusual and offbeat visitor destination. In both respects it has won much success.

The busy streets of Ho Chi Minh City (above left). Fishing on the Mekong River (above). Mountains on the Chinese border between Cao Bang and Lang Son (above middle). Fixing a jeep on the roadside

CONTEMPORARY LIFE AND CULTURE

Many Westerners go to Vietnam to see and experience a completely different way of life that contrasts strongly with their own. Here is a society where family loyalties and obedience to parents are paramount, but where a city café culture is emerging; where some people make do on next to nothing and endure backbreaking work day after day under a cruel sun, knee-deep in mud, yet retain enormous pride and dignity.

Discovering at first hand something of the interesting history and culture of this ancient civilization is a priority for many visitors. Few histories have been rewritten as many times as Vietnam's, as each victor reinterprets the events of the past to portray himself in the most flattering light. But some events are beyond distortion by propaganda, and some facts are visible for all to see. Historic towns, scarred battlefields, dusty museums, ransacked palaces, vernacular architecture, junk shops, venerable places of worship and elderly people with long and vivid memories provide vital repositories of Vietnam's history and culture.

Vietnam's fight against poverty has made dramatic strides in the past decade. The Vietnam development report *Attacking Poverty*, published in 2000 (funded by non-governmental organizations), reported that households below the poverty line had dropped from 58 percent in 1992–93 to 37 percent in 1997–98. Social indicators such as access to education and health care also improved sharply. School enrolment rates rose, and evidence of malnutrition among children under five declined sharply from 51 percent to 34 percent. However, the pattern of economic growth and reduction of poverty has not been even. While agriculture grew by a healthy 4.5 percent a year over the five years under study, the industrial sector grew by a massive 13 percent. Rural Vietnam improved, but nowhere near as fast as urban Vietnam. The findings resulted in the *Comprehensive Poverty Reduction and Growth Strategy*, published in 2003, which outlined plans for health care, rural clean water supply and sanitation, as well as the National Action Program for Vietnamese Children, and National Strategy for the Advancement of Women.

CUISINE

Vietnam is a fertile country, and food is plentiful, though malnutrition through poverty is still a problem. It is not regarded as a sin to enjoy the fruits of the land and sea, and restaurants tend to place greater emphasis on food than on decor. The culinary tradition is a fusion of Vietnamese, Chinese and French cuisine (▷ 206–210), and meals are likely to be of good quality whether they're served in luxury hotels, floating restaurants, workers' cafeterias or streetside eateries, or at noodle carts or seaside barbecues.

LANGUAGE

Jesuit Alexandre de Rhodes (▷ 31) romanized the Vietnamese script in the 17th century, so although Westerners may find the language daunting, it is a fairly straightforward matter to read the names of hotels and streets. English is learned and spoken by many young Vietnamese, and French is spoken to a lesser degree among the older generation. This applies mainly to the cities and visitor resorts; neither language is likely to be an aid to communication anywhere remote. Many Vietnamese face similar problems when traveling within their own country, as the northern, central and southern dialects and accents are mutually almost incomprehensible.

RELIGION

Vietnamese people are generally open-minded and pragmatic on spiritual and metaphysical matters. Many people are animist, seeing living spirits in the objects and landscapes around them. Respect for, and even worship of, ancestors is a way of life instilled by the elderly in the young. Buddhism and Christianity are widely represented; Buddhism was brought over from China and Roman Catholicism from France. Cao Daism, Vietnam's homegrown system of belief (▷ 14), borrows ideas from all the major religions, hoping one day to transcend borders and become the one true global religion.

Potentially, tourism can be a serious threat to the minorities' way of life. Any visitors to minority villages should be aware of the extent to which they contribute to this process. Traditional means of livelihood can be quickly and understandably abandoned when a higher living standard can be obtained from the tourist dollar. Long-standing societal and kinship ties can be weakened by the intrusion of outsiders. Young people may question their society's values and traditions, which may seem archaic and anachronistic by comparison with those of the modern visitor, and dress and music are in danger of losing all cultural significance if they become mere tourist attractions.

Fruit and vegetable baskets at the Temple of Lady Chua Xu, Sam Mountain (above left). Mother and child near Hoa Binh (above). Fishing boats, Nha Trang (above middle); Bobla waterfall near Dalat (above right)

ETHNIC MINORITIES

Vietnam is home to 54 ethnic groups, including the Vietnamese (Kinh) themselves. Groups vary in size from the Tày, with a population of about 1.3 million, to the O-du, who number only 100 individuals. Ethnic groups belonging to the Sino-Tibetan language family, such as the Hmông and Dao, and the Tibeto-Burman language group, such as the Ha Nhi and Phu La, are more recent arrivals, having migrated south from China within the past 250 to 300 years. These people live almost exclusively on the upper mountain slopes, practicing swidden agriculture (clearing land for cultivation by slashing and burning vegetation) and posing little threat to their more numerous lowland-dwelling neighbors, notably the Thai.

Life has been hard for many of the minorities, who have had to fight not only the French and Vietnamese but often each other in order to retain their territory and cultural identity. Traditions and customs have been eroded by outside influences, although some alien ideas have been successfully accommodated. Centuries of Viet population growth and decades of warfare have taken a heavy toll on minorities and their territories; increasingly, population pressure from the minority groups themselves poses a threat to their way of life.

The highland areas of Vietnam are among the most linguistically and culturally diverse in the world. In total, the highland peoples number just over 8 million. The generic term for these diverse peoples of the highlands is Montagnard (from the French for "mountain people") or, in Vietnamese, *nguoi thuong* (highland citizen). The highland peoples themselves identify with their village and tribal group, not as part of a wider "highland citizens" grouping.

CIVIL UNREST

Tensions between citizens and the government have come to a head on several occasions. In May 1997 there were disturbances in the poor northern province of Thai Binh, when local farmers staged demonstrations complaining of corruption and excessive taxation. Eventually, a report appeared in the army newspaper *Quan Doi Nhan Dan* detailing moral decline and corruption in the province's Communist Party. A few months later riots broke out in Roman Catholic Dong Nai, in response to the seizure of church land by a chairman of the People's Committee. In 2001, thousands of ethnic minority people rioted in Gia Lai and Dac Lac provinces. The army was called in to reimpose order and all foreigners were banned from this Central Highlands area. In April 2004 violence between ethnic minorities and the government again flared up in the Central Highlands.

HUMAN RIGHTS

Human Rights Watch has condemned Vietnam for its treatment of those trying to spread information about democracy via the internet. Several internet dissidents are in prison on charges of espionage and disseminating propaganda against the state. In 2003, physician Dr. Nguyen Dan Que was sentenced to two-and-a-half years' imprisonment after sending an email on state censorship to the US; Dr. Pham Hong Son was sentenced to 13 years' imprisonment plus three years' house arrest also in 2003 for, among other charges, translating an article on democracy from the US Embassy website in Vietnam. According to Human Rights Watch, "Harsh prison sentences and vaguely worded charges of spying appear designed to intimidate not only government critics, but everyone in Vietnam who uses the internet."

VIETNAM'S REGIONS

The name Vietnam derives from the name adopted for the country by Emperor Gia Long in 1802: Nam Viet. This means, literally, the Viet (the largest ethnic group) of the south (Nam), and replaced the country's previous name, Annam.

The country is "S" shaped, covers a land area of 127,246 square miles (329,565sq km) and has a coastline of 2,157 miles (3,471km). The French subdivided Vietnam into three regions, administering each separately: Tonkin or Bac Ky (the northern region); Annam or Trung Ky (the central region); and Cochin China or Nam Ky (the southern region). Although these administrative divisions have been abolished, the Vietnamese still recognize their country as consisting of three regions, distinct in terms of geography, history and culture. Their new names are Bac Bo (north), Trung Bo (center) and Nam Bo (south). Today, there are 58 administrative provinces (see map, left).

The most important economic zones, containing the main concentrations of population, are focused on two large deltaic areas. In the north, there are the rice fields and settlements of the Red River, and in the south is the fertile alluvial plain of the Mekong. In between, the country narrows to less than 31 miles (50km) wide, with only a thin ribbon of fertile lowland suited to intensive agriculture. Much of the interior, away from the coastal belt and the deltas, is mountainous. Here, minority hilltribes (Montagnards), along with some lowland Vietnamese resettled in New Economic Zones since 1975, eke out a living on thin soils. The rugged terrain means that only a quarter of the land is cultivated. Of the remainder, somewhere between about 20 and 25 percent is forested, although some of this is heavily degraded.

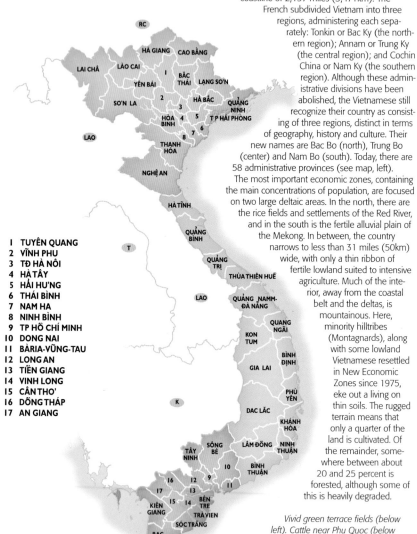

1 TUYÊN QUANG
2 VĨNH PHU
3 TĐ HÀ NÔI
4 HÀ TÂY
5 HẢI HU'NG
6 THÁI BÌNH
7 NAM HA
8 NINH BÌNH
9 TP HỒ CHÍ MINH
10 DONG NAI
11 BÀRIA-VŨNG-TAU
12 LONG AN
13 TIỀN GIANG
14 VINH LONG
15 CẦN THO'
16 ĐỒNG THÁP
17 AN GIANG

Vivid green terrace fields (below left). Cattle near Phu Quoc (below middle). Lily pads in the Plain of Reeds in the Mekong Delta (below right)

The Northern Highlands In the far north are the Northern Highlands, which ring the Red River Delta and form a natural barrier with China. The rugged mountains on the west border of this region—the Hoang Lien Son—exceed 9,800ft (3,000m) in places. The tributaries of the Red River have cut deep, steep-sided gorges through the Hoang Lien Son, which are navigable by small boats. The eastern portion of this region, bordering the Gulf of Tonkin, is far less imposing; the mountain peaks of the west have diminished into foothills, allowing easy access to China. The principal towns and cities of the region are Lao Cai and Dien Bien Phu in the northwest and Haiphong and Halong in the east.

The Red River Delta This region lies in the embrace of the hills of the north, with Hanoi at its core. The delta covers almost 5,800 square miles (15,000sq km) and extends 150 miles (240km) inland from the coast. Rice has been grown on the alluvial soils of the Red River for thousands of years. Yet despite the intricate web of canals, dikes and embankments, the

A tourist boat in Halong Bay; Ho Chi Minh City traffic; Cai Rang floating market, Can Tho

Vietnamese have never been able to tame the river completely, and the delta is the victim of frequent and sometimes devastating floods. The area is very low-lying, rarely more than 10ft (3m) above sea level, and often less than 3ft (1m). Although the region supports one of the highest agricultural population densities in the world, the inhabitants have frequently had to endure famines—most recently in 1989.

The Central Region South of the Red River Delta region lie the central lowlands and the mountains of the Annamite Chain. The Annam Highlands, now known as the Truong Son Mountain Range, form an important cultural divide between the Indianized nations to the west and the Sinicized cultures to the east. The northern rugged extremity of the range is in Thanh Hoa Province. From here the Truong Son stretches more than 750 miles (1,200km) south, to gradually end 50 miles (80km) north of Ho Chi Minh City (formerly Saigon). The Central Highlands form an upland plateau, occupied by the hill resorts of Buon Me Thuot and Dalat. On the plateau, plantation agriculture and hill farms are interspersed with stands of bamboo and tropical forests. To the east, the Annamite Chain falls off steeply, leaving only a narrow and fragmented band of lowland suitable for settlement—the central coastal strip. In places the mountains advance all the way to the coast, plunging into the sea as dramatic rockfaces and making north–south communication difficult. At no point does the region extend more than 40 miles (64km) inland, and in total it covers only 2,605 square miles (6,750sq km). The soils are often rocky or saline, and irrigation is seldom possible. The main centers of population are Vinh, Hué, Danang, Hoi An, Nha Trang and Vung Tau.

The South The Mekong Delta is not as prone to flooding as the Red River Delta, and consequently rice production is more stable. The reason for this less severe flooding is the regulating effect of the Great Lake of Cambodia, the Tonlé Sap. During the rainy season, when the water flowing into the Mekong becomes too great for even this mighty river to absorb, rather than overflowing its banks, the water backs up into the Tonlé Sap, which quadruples in area. The Mekong Delta covers 25,900 square miles (67,000sq km) and is drained by five branches of the Mekong, which divides as it flows toward the sea. The vast delta is one of the great rice bowls of Asia, producing nearly half of the country's rice, and over the years has been cut into a patchwork by the canals that have been dug to expand irrigation and hence the area given over to cultivation. The region was largely forested until the late 19th century, when the French supported its settlement by Vietnamese peasants, recognizing that it could become enormously productive. The deposition of silt by the rivers that cut through the delta means that the shoreline is continually advancing—by up to 260ft (80m) each year in some places. To the north of the delta lies Ho Chi Minh City (HCMC or Saigon). The main towns of the delta itself are My Tho, Can Tho, Rach Gia, Ha Tien and Chau Doc. Offshore is the large unspoilt island of Phu Quoc, while farther south is the protected marine environment of the Con Dao archipelago.

THE BEST OF VIETNAM

BEST HISTORIC SITES

Cu Chi Tunnels (▷ 149) This extensive tunnel complex was the home of some 16,000 resistance fighters during the Vietnam War.

Dien Bien Phu (▷ 82–83) The Vietnamese victory over the French here in 1954 heralded the collapse of their Indochinese empire.

Hoa Lo, Hanoi (▷ 63) This legendary prison housed American POWs during the Vietnam War.

Ho Chi Minh's Mausoleum, Hanoi (▷ 66) The mausoleum houses the preserved body of Ho Chi Minh.

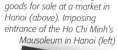

My Son (▷ 123) The glories of the Champa kingdom are immortalized in stone here at what was the empire's core spiritual seat.

Old City, Hanoi (▷ 68–71) Markets, flower-sellers, restaurants, traders' quarters and decaying shop houses are crammed into the most vibrant part of the capital.

Reunification Hall, Ho Chi Minh City (▷ 140) One of the most historically significant buildings in Vietnam.

A young woman carrying her goods for sale at a market in Hanoi (above). Imposing entrance of the Ho Chi Minh's Mausoleum in Hanoi (left)

BEST RELIGIOUS SITES

Cao Dai Great Temple, Tay Ninh (▷ 146–147) A fantastical building, dedicated to an indigenous Vietnamese religion that combines elements of other world religions.

Perfume Pagoda (▷ 91) This popular pilgrimage spot is dedicated to the guardian spirit of mother and child, and is built amid caves peppered with hundreds of incense sticks.

BEST MUSEUMS

B-52 Museum, Hanoi (▷ 62) The downed machinery of the American fighting machine has found its final resting place in the yard of this curious museum.

Museum of Champa Sculpture, Danang (▷ 104–105) Admire sculptural body art and depictions of Hindu deities in some of the most perfect examples of Champa creativity.

Vietnam Museum of Ethnology, Hanoi (▷ 78) The museum is dedicated to Vietnam's 54 ethnic minorities.

War Remnants Museum, Ho Chi Minh City (▷ 142) This collection of Vietnam War military equipment and photographs presents a graphic account of the conflict.

The impressive Cao Dai Great Temple, Tay Ninh (above). An exhibit displayed in the War Remnants Museum, Ho Chi Minh City (above left). Carved wooden elongated heads on display in the Vietnam Museum of Ethnology, Hanoi (left). Vietnam is home to a number of minority groups (right)

BEST SCENERY

Cuc Phuong National Park (▷ 84) Walk here in April or May to be encircled by thousands of green and yellow butterflies.

Halong Bay (▷ 86–89) Sail out on a boat to enjoy the jade-green, silken waters of this UNESCO World Heritage Site, studded with thousands of limestone outcrops.

Highland walking (▷ 91, 95, 96) Around Mai Chau, Sapa, Son La and other areas of northwest Vietnam, you'll see stilted houses, terraced emerald-green paddies, and the vibrant tones of the ethnic minority dress.

Sapa (▷ 92–95) Home to the Hmông ethnic minority, Sapa is surrounded by some stunning scenery.

Tam Coc (▷ 97) Glide down the Ngo Dong River through magnificent limestone scenery.

THE BEST OF VIETNAM

A vibrant oriental dragon (right)

The Hanoi Opera House—one of the finest colonial-style buildings in the city (above).
Selling vegetables at Hoi An market (right)

Ceramic Buddhas

A tasty dish in Saigon

Beach Villa, Nha Trang

BEST EVENINGS OUT

Ben Thanh Market, Ho Chi Minh City (▷ 135) Slip down to the night market and slurp on a bowl of *pho* (noodle soup) while watching the world go by.

Lam Son Square, Ho Chi Minh City (▷ 137) If you're feeling brave, mount a motorbicycle, either as a driver or passenger, and cruise around the square at night in the balmy air amid the roar of thousands of other motos.

Opera House, Hanoi (▷ 67) Step out for an evening performance inside the elegant, iconic Opera House.

Sky drinking, Ho Chi Minh City (▷ 250–253) Take to one of the city's skyscraper hotels for a nighttime drink and marvel at the energy of this new powerhouse, with its glittering nightscape.

BEST BROWSING

Can Tho Market (▷ 144) Motor up the river from Can Tho and enter the busy world of the floating market—brightly painted boats crammed with fruit and vegetables on the Mekong River.

Hanoi shopping (▷ 168–170) Duck in and out of the hundreds of clothing, handicraft and souvenir stores in Hanoi, indulging in a riot of bright patterns and varied textures.

Ho Chi Minh City shopping (▷ 181–183) Head for Dong Khoi Street and District 1 to pick up silk souvenirs, trinkets and other unmissable purchases.

Hoi An (▷ 108–113) Wander around the silk emporiums and Chinese temples and indulge in glorious food in this quaint mercantile town.

Hué (▷ 114–117) Absorb the atmosphere of this imperial capital, its tombs and its setting on the Perfume River.

BEST PLACES TO EAT

Fusion Cuisine, Hanoi Step out for an elegant dining experience at Bobby Chinn (▷ 211), where there's good food, wine, fresh rose petals, a comfortable lounge area and a chic, glass-fronted interior; or sample any of the multitude of excellent restaurants that fill Hanoi's streets (▷ 211–215).

Ho Chi Minh City restaurants (▷ 223–228) Some of the most exquisite, tasty, sensuous and indulgent dishes in the world are served in the numerous eateries of Ho Chi Minh City.

Moca Café, Hanoi (▷ 214) Sip coffee in a window seat and watch the locals pull up onto the sidewalks with their motos. Follow the wisps of exhaust smoke as they curl skyward in the rain.

BEST RESORTS

Dalat (▷ 242–243) Inhale the mountain air at this highland retreat, a former French colonial hill station and now the Vietnamese honeymoon capital.

Mui Ne (▷ 246–247) Wind down in luxury resorts with plenty of facilities on a perfect strip of palm-studded sand.

Nha Trang (▷ 248–249) The pleasures of travel can be found at this beachside hangout, with restaurants, bars and cafés, plus diving, watersports and spas for pampering.

Phu Quoc (▷ 256–257) Sunbathe, snorkel, eat and drink in one of the small number of resorts on this unspoilt island off the Cambodian border.

THE BEST OF VIETNAM

TOP EXPERIENCES

Bargain with the ethnic minority vendors in Sapa (▷ 93–95), who dangle their charms and souvenirs under your nose, with calls in French of *"jolie, jolie!"*.

Be dazzled by the verdant greens of a Mekong paddy; in spring, the young rice shoots up through the murky waters and transforms the landscape.

Bicycle around the paddy fields of Mai Chau (▷ 91), an attractive small town surrounded by Thái ethnic minority villages.

Boating on the Suoi Yen River with a dramatic backdrop of densely forested hills

Emperor Minh Mang's tomb, Hué (left)

Dine in a French restaurant in Saigon (▷ 223–228), and sample the fine legacy of French cooking.

Drive a motorcycle around Saigon—not for the faint-hearted but a novel way to see the sights.

Women of the Miao minorities in Sapa trying to strike a deal with a passing tourist

Eat fish on the quayside in Hoi An (▷ 108–113)—some of the tastiest around.

Eat *heo quay* and *com tam* (anywhere)—broken rice with barbecued pork makes a delicious breakfast, lunch or dinner.

Eat *pho bo* in Hanoi (▷ 211–215); this beef noodle soup is warming, nourishing and tasty.

Have Sunday champagne brunch in Le Beaulieu at the Metropole Hotel in Hanoi (▷ 212), one of the country's top hotels—but get there early; champagne is served for a limited time.

Kayak around the island-studded waters of Halong Bay (▷ 86–89), exploring caves and deserted beaches.

Pamper yourself with a body massage at a luxury spa, a relatively new concept in Vietnam.

Relax in a resort at Mui Ne (▷ 246–247), the sandy peninsula near Phan Thiet, with Vietnam's best selection of beach resorts.

Swim at China Beach (▷ 105), one of Vietnam's most spectacular beaches, with golden sand, wonderful surf and clear, blue water.

Take a boat on the Perfume River (▷ 114–117), which connects many of the historical sites of enchanting Hué.

Take an early evening boat ride on the Thu Bon River in Hoi An (▷ 108–113) while swallows dip over the water and the ancient town's lights twinkle in the distance.

Treat yourself to a piece of original art: Contemporary Vietnamese art is making a serious impression on the international scene.

Visit Minh Mang's Mausoleum in Hué (▷ 119), for gardens, pavilions, gatehouses and statues.

Walk around Hoan Kiem Lake (▷ 64–65); as the sun sets in Hanoi, couples come here to huddle on the benches, and walkers come to enjoy the fresh air.

Warm yourself by a log fire on the cold winter nights in Sapa (▷ 92–95), an especially memorable experience at Christmas.

Flooded paddy fields beneath mist-covered mountains in the Mai Chau Valley

A beach massage is a great way to relax

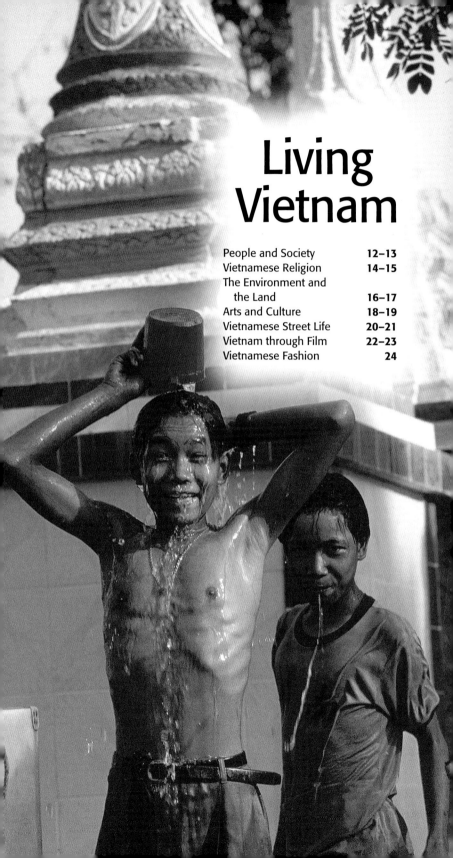

Living Vietnam

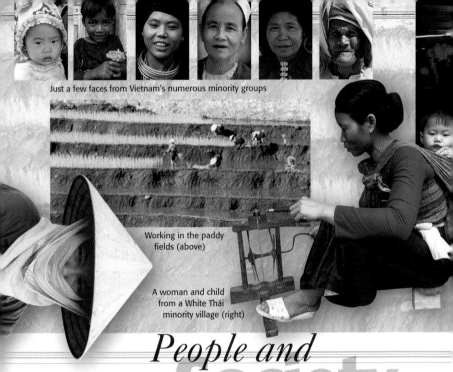

Just a few faces from Vietnam's numerous minority groups

Working in the paddy fields (above)

A woman and child from a White Thái minority village (right)

People and Society

Granny Rules, OK?

The family is all important in Vietnamese society. To some extent, poverty has kept families together, with three generations typically living under one roof. Nearly every house has an ancestral altar where photos of great-grandma and grandpa are propped up among the food and sometimes alcoholic offerings. Vietnamese families often have very traditional values, a legacy of Confucianism: the ideal of children's loyalty to their parents. This means that even grown-up children bring their earnings home to the family, and very often the grandmother controls all. If a son needs to take a course, everyone in the family contributes, and spouses are also drawn into the network of interdependence and support.

Vietnam is changing fast. Apart from China, it has the fastest annual growth rate in Asia—a leap forward that came of bleak necessity. When the war ended in 1975, Vietnam was starving. In 1986, a desperate government announced a policy of *doi moi* (renovation): decollectivizing agriculture and encouraging small private businesses. The constitution of 1992 announced privatization of state-owned enterprises, and in 2000 a trade agreement was signed with the US. Subsidies on consumer goods were reduced, wages increased and foreign investment was actively encouraged. Vietnam is now the world's second-largest exporter of both rice and coffee, while garments and seafood are other major exports. Electrical appliances spill out of shops, and for the first time many Vietnamese are taking jobs outside the family. Meanwhile, the limits of political reform seem to have been reached. There is no open political debate, and official disapproval makes it difficult to get the police reference required for a university place, a passport or a job. The future is uncertain. The population is growing rapidly, and the rural poor—75 percent of the population—resent the cities' economic gains. While the economies of Hanoi and Saigon grow at about 20 percent a year, the countryside lags far behind.

Delivering kumquat trees for the *Tet* festival

Dividing the day's catch in Mui Ne

Playing chess in the streets of Hanoi's Old Quarter (below)

A group of children from a Muong minority village near Hoa Binh

Lucky Bids

The popularity of gambling is evident in the informal credit circle known as *Hui*. The scheme lasts as many months as there are participants. Members agree to put in a fixed amount, say 100,000d each month, and bid in a blind auction, entering a zero bid if they need no cash. If, in month one, a father needs money for his daughter's wedding, he will bid maybe 25,000d. If this is the highest bid, he will receive 75,000d from each member (100,000d less 25,000d). In future months he cannot bid again but must pay 100,000d to whoever collects that month's pot. Towards the end, those who have taken nothing out but have paid in 100,000d (minus the winning bids) per month can enter a zero bid and get the full 100,000d from all participants. The risk is that participants may artificially raise the stakes, raking in a lot of interest for non-bidding participants that month.

"If You Loved Me…"

Karaoke is a national pastime, and karaoke parlors abound in every town. This is one place where mixed groups can meet in private for courtship, singing romantic songs to one another. This is a modern echo of a mountain tradition still in practice, whereby the young men of a village go to visit the young women of another village and sing impromptu love songs, to which the girls improvise a sung reply, sometimes full of licentious puns. There's a strong element of romance and sentimentality in Vietnamese culture, and a long tradition of poetry-writing. Emperors used to hold poetry competitions for their ministers, and examinations for aspiring mandarins included writing poetry to a strict form—within the examination time!

First Milestones

Infant mortality levels in Vietnam have fallen dramatically, but remain high by Western standards. Not surprisingly, Vietnamese families celebrate two important milestones in the early lives of their children. *Day thang* (full month) is celebrated one month after birth. Traditionally, after staying in bed with her baby for the first month, the mother would go out to introduce her baby to the village. Today, parents hold a small party for friends and neighbors. *Thoi noi* is celebrated at the end of the first year. At the party the baby is presented with a tray holding items such as a pen, a mirror, scissors, soil and food. Whichever item the baby takes first indicates its character and likely job: scissors for a tailor, pen for a teacher, soil for a farmer and so on.

Kumquats and First-footers

A few weeks before *Tet*, Vietnam's important New Year festival, bicycles with mini-orchards of kumquat trees bound to the back begin to appear on the streets. Choosing a kumquat tree is a serious matter. It must have ripe fruit, unripe fruit and buds to represent the three generations of a family; it must have dark green leaves, bright new leaves and leaf buds. During *Tet* visitors call to appraise and admire one another's trees. Another *Tet* tradition is first-footing, where the first person to call by in the new year determines the household's luck. To be sure of a good outcome, families invite their first-footers, who must be distinguished and preferably rich, and must not be divorced or have lost a member of the family in the past year.

Seated worshipers inside Cao Dai Great Temple, at Tay Ninh

Buddhist offerings at a pagoda in Hanoi (left)

Vietnamese
Religion

Historically, the Vietnamese have taken a pragmatic view toward religion. Whenever a new one comes along, they simply fuse it with what they have and carry on. Even Ho Chi Minh has been added to the pantheon, his statue appearing in a village temple just outside Hanoi. For a time, Communism frowned on all religions and statues were hidden away, but now they are reappearing. This fusion of faiths means that temples may hold the statues of deities of several religions, all of which still influence the Vietnamese psyche. From animism, possibly the oldest, come the goddesses of heaven, forests and waters, revered in villages where small spirit houses hang in the trees. The black and white S-shaped designs on "worry balls" for arthritic hands are taken from the yin (passive) and yang (active) symbols of Taoism. Confucianism's structure of loyalties—of ministers to emperor, of children to parents, of wives to husbands—is still a strong influence in Vietnamese filial piety and respect for elders. Buddhism is an important religion in the country. Christianity, imported by Portuguese and French priests, has left a legacy of temple-like churches. Hinduism has also made an impact, and there are pockets of Islam.

A Jarai spirit effigy from Kontum

Asian Spectacular

Officially titled The Third Great Universal Religious Amnesty, Cao Daism has grown from a vision witnessed by one man in 1919 to a religion with more than 5 million followers, making it the third biggest faith in Vietnam. Cao Daism synthesizes elements from other world religions, and by 1948 had fostered a 10,000-strong army that fought against both the French and the Communists. Since independence, the Cao Dai church has peacefully struggled against the government, which seized all its assets in 1997 as part of "official recognition." Cao Daists today continue to practice their visually spectacular rituals openly and to petition the authorities with demands for religious freedom.

The decorative exterior of a pagoda in Soc Trang (below)

The Temple of Lady Chua Xu, Sam Mountain (above).
A memorial at Dalat Cathedral (right)

Muslim Cham village elders (above)

Monks at a pagoda in Soc Trang

Hypnotic Festivals

Buddhism is an enigma in Vietnam—the largest organized religion in the country and a cultural constant that means different things to different people. Many Buddhists' beliefs are heavily influenced by Taoism and Confucianism. Vietnamese Buddhism is subdivided into various groups, the biggest belonging to the Mahayana vehicle, which easily conforms to the Vietnamese idea of religion, combining folklore with the veneration of enlightened beings. Temples began to decline after 1975 owing to a state policy discouraging people from becoming monks or nuns. However, attendance at festivals and pilgrimages is now climbing, and about half of all Vietnamese practice some form of Buddhism. Urban temples often have electronic music, powerful incense and hypnotic light shows, providing an entrancing atmosphere during major festivals.

Popular Beliefs

Formal religions had to build on the foundations of ancient animist beliefs to get a foothold in Vietnam, and old traditions are still running strong and even blossoming as society changes. Since the late 1980s, village pagodas have undergone a frenzy of refurbishment. In a village near Hanoi, a local woman who lived 200 years ago is revered for instigating the now prosperous pharmaceutical industry; another village temple is devoted to a princess who developed the silk industry. One village faith features the courtship ritual of grabbing eels from a jar: A young man and woman try to catch the eel without looking into the jar. The young man has to keep one hand on the young woman's breast while a committee of judges watches closely, along with fellow villagers who call out and tease the couple.

Christian Troubles

Roman Catholicism has been a political force in Vietnam ever since the French missions of the early 19th century. Catholics have played a part in many national events, creating the national script, for instance. There are more than 6 million Roman Catholics in Vietnam, mainly in the south, where the former government was Catholic dominated. Evangelical Christianity is less tolerated, and some priests who spoke against the authorities have been jailed. Nevertheless, the government has said it regards Christianity as a "positive force," and in 2004 introduced its Ordinance Regarding Religious Beliefs and Religious Organizations, proclaiming freedom of belief for all faiths that cooperate with the state.

Other Beliefs

The doctrines of Confucius pervade every aspect of Vietnamese life, stressing the importance of family and lineage, and the worship of ancestors, but they do not constitute an organized religion. Likewise Taoism, while having several temples and sects devoted to its principal historical figures, has no formal clergy or church, but still exerts its influence on national culture, particularly through pilgrimages. Famous Taoist temples by the West Lake and on Hoan Kiem Lake in Hanoi continue to be popular. Cults such as Tran Hung Dao and Chu Vi feature blood and mutilation rituals and female spiritmediums. Hoa Hao is a Buddhist sect that has grown into a major religion in its own right, its leaders now joining Christian and Buddhist clergy in opposition to government controls. Small Muslim, Hindu and Bahai communities also exist.

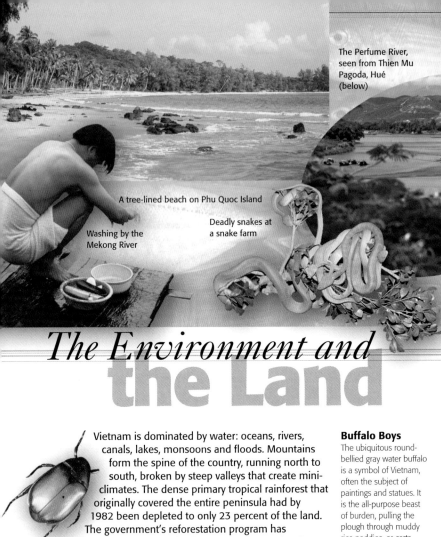

The Perfume River, seen from Thien Mu Pagoda, Hué (below)

A tree-lined beach on Phu Quoc Island

Washing by the Mekong River

Deadly snakes at a snake farm

The Environment and
the Land

Vietnam is dominated by water: oceans, rivers, canals, lakes, monsoons and floods. Mountains form the spine of the country, running north to south, broken by steep valleys that create mini-climates. The dense primary tropical rainforest that originally covered the entire peninsula had by 1982 been depleted to only 23 percent of the land. The government's reforestation program has increased this to 28 percent, but just 10 percent is primary rainforest. Scientists and overseas conservation agencies are enumerating, cataloging and protecting Vietnam's flora and fauna, with some remarkable success—such as the rescue of the U-Minh forest in the Mekong Delta from the damage of wartime defoliants. The Javan rhinoceros, one of the rarest large mammals in the world, thought to survive only in West Java, Indonesia, was discovered here in 1989, and an even more astonishing discovery followed: two completely new species of mammal. In 1992, the Vu Quang ox, known to locals as *sao la*, was the first new large mammal species to be found in 50 years. In 1993, a new species of deer, the giant muntjac, was spotted in the Vu Quang Nature Reserve. Since 1962, when Cuc Phuong National Park was created, 87 nature reserves have been established in all, covering 3.3 percent of Vietnam's land area.

Buffalo Boys

The ubiquitous round-bellied gray water buffalo is a symbol of Vietnam, often the subject of paintings and statues. It is the all-purpose beast of burden, pulling the plough through muddy rice paddies, or carts laden with bags of rice or farm produce along dirt tracks or even into Hanoi and Ho Chi Minh City. Every young country boy must do his stint as a buffalo boy, minding the creature, which is often a family's most precious possession. The image of a boy on the back of the water buffalo, or a white bird perched on its back plucking insects, is a familiar one.

Paddy fields near Lai Chau (above)

You'll never forget it— an elephant ride in Ban Don

Cloud-topped peaks towering over the Tam Ton Pass, Lao Cai Province (far right)

A beautiful lotus flower

The Scrap Economy

Scavenging for metal and other recyclable materials is an activity undertaken by many of the poorest Vietnamese to boost their incomes. According to a report by Michael DiGregorio, of Hawaii's East-West Center, some 6,000 people in Hanoi earned a living scavenging for scrap in 1992, this figure rising to 8,000 in 1996. As a result, 275 tons of "garbage" from the waste economy were fed back into the productive economy every day—more than a third of the capital's daily refuse. In the 1990s, an itinerant junk buyer could earn US$1.41 a day—five times more than comparative agricultural wages. However, nearly 40,000 people have died while scavenging since 1975 after "discovering" some of the 35 million landmines and 300,000 tons of unexploded ordnance that remain scattered across the country.

Pulling Up Poppies

Opium poppies have long been a significant source of income for Vietnam's poorer ethnic minority areas. However, the extent of plantation is a matter of dispute. Vietnam's official estimate is that only 778 acres (315ha) are used for poppy cultivation; the Ministry of Agriculture and Rural Development claims that in Sơn La 9,419 acres (3,812ha) out of 9,884 acres (4,000ha) of crop have been destroyed. The UN Office of Drugs and Crime believes there to be 5,683 acres (2,300ha) of poppies, a reduction from the 1993 figure of 31,876 acres (12,900ha). Whatever the actual figures, the state has invested over 38 billion dong in alternative crops such as fruit trees, rice, maize and tea.

The Mekong

The Mekong River is one of the 12 great rivers of the world and is the source of much of Vietnam's agricultural wealth. It stretches around 2,800 miles (4,500km) from its source on the Tibet Plateau to its mouth in the Mekong Delta, where it deposits fertile silt. The first European to explore the Mekong was French naval officer Francis Garnier. His Mekong Expedition (1866–68) followed the river upstream from its delta in Cochin China (southern Vietnam). Of the 6,188 miles (9,960km) that the expedition covered, 3,144 miles (5,060km) were charted for the first time. The river is navigable only as far as the Laos– Cambodian border, where the Khone rapids make it impassable.

Trekker's Delight

Vietnam's forests provide great trekking opportunities and unusual sights. The mountain slopes of Nghe An Province on the Laos border harbor some of the rarest animals in the world, notably the Saola antelope, discovered in the 1990s. Although you have to get really lucky to spot a wild elephant or gibbon, there is still plenty of breathtaking forest to walk through. Serious work is now going on to try to preserve and regenerate the woodland of this densely populated country. Dr. Nguyen Van Sinh, of Hanoi's Institute of Ecology and Biological Resources, takes visitors around Cuc Phuong National Park, where he is running a project to restock the area with local plant life. Restoring native tree species will take the pressure off remaining primary and secondary forests, benefiting wildlife and the Vietnamese people.

A film poster (left)

A group of *cai luong* actors (below)

Wearing a vivid dragon mask

Woodcarving repairs at Thay Pagoda, Hanoi

Arts and Culture

Before *doi moi* (▷ 12), the arts in Vietnam were state-funded and censored. Since 1987 there has been a relaxation of control; two-way cultural projects have been launched between Vietnam and the US, limitations on movie production have been lifted (though film scripts are still monitored) and art galleries, once forbidden, flourish in Ho Chi Minh City and Hanoi. However, sources of funding can prove elusive in the newly liberalized economy. One initiative that has emerged to fill the gap is a government program, assisted by international agencies, to train staff in arts and heritage management. Traditional arts such as carving are encouraged, as in Kim Bong village, near Hoi An, where UNESCO supports a master sculptor and 15 apprentices. Other cultural traditions have survived—such as *cai luong* theater and water puppetry, Hué's court dances, and the traditional music performed on Vietnam's unique instruments, the *danh ba*, a huge bamboo-tube xylophone, and the vertically strung bamboo xylophone.

A girl takes part in the religious procession to Ngoc Son Temple in Hanoi

Cai Luong Theater

Performed in Hanoi and Ho Chi Minh City, *cai luong* (reform) theater is madcap musical farce. "Reform" merely means a newer incarnation of *cheo*—comic folk theater that originated in villages of the south a century ago. The plots originally made fun of feudal mandarins—feudalism persisted until 1945 and the abdication of Vietnam's last emperor (▷ 29). Dialog, mostly sung, is now updated to make fun of contemporary powers, in one of the few venues where such criticism is tolerated. Costumes are bright, wildly elaborate and outrageous, there are pretty women and dancers, and it is clear even to foreigners who the good guys and the bad guys are, making this an unforgettable experience even to those without a word of Vietnamese.

A billboard promoting HIV awareness (left)

Bicycling past an eye-catching government poster

Bobby Chinn has found culinary success since coming to Vietnam

Be sure to catch a water puppet show (left)

Water Puppetry

Green bamboo blinds serve as curtains behind a watery "stage." Shiny gilt dragons, spouting water, pop up from beneath the surface, bobbing up and down as dragons do. A fisherman comes rowing along. The puppets, 15in (38cm) high, are so engaging that it is easy to forget the puppeteers manipulating them from behind the blinds, using strings passed through underwater bamboo poles. Best known of the water puppet troupes is the Thang Long in Hanoi, which has made numerous tours abroad. To join the Thang Long theater troupe—a much coveted position, as puppeteers are well paid and have a chance to travel abroad—boys and girls go through a four-year course at Hanoi's College of Arts, then serve an apprenticeship in one of three villages.

Pictures of Vietnam

Recognized by both the Vietnamese Association of Photographic Artists (VAPA) and the International Federation of Photographic Art (FIAP), photographer Long Thanh from Nha Trang is one of the most distinguished in his field. Working only in black and white, he takes many of his famous images in and around his native Nha Trang. The city lies in the old kingdom of Champa, and the Cham villages and people provide most of the subject matter. Long Thanh first started taking pictures at the age of 13, and has since collected some 18 international awards, including a gold medal in Austria's International Photographic Competition. His pictures have been shown around the world, and are exhibited and sold in Nha Trang (▷ 180) and shown on his website (www.vnn.vn/vnn3/nhiep anh/LongThanh.htm).

Poster Art

Vietnam's countryside and towns are peppered with propaganda and health and safety billboards, where posters have been elevated to an art form. They cover a range of subjects, including government policy, elections, road safety, the danger of HIV, while some commemorate historical events. The Mekong Delta, in particular, is littered with boards expounding the dangers of intravenous drug use and sex without condoms. In the north, remarkable billboards depict the Vietnamese victory at Dien Bien Phu in 1954. At election time, the country is covered in images of the Viet Kinh, ethnic minorities and military at the ballot box. Luong Anh Dung, an official government painter for 30 years, produced many of the nationalist images. Today, propaganda and advertisement painting is taught at fine arts schools as part of an applied graphic arts program.

Bobby Chinn Makes Waves

Restaurateur Bobby Chinn has been making waves ever since he came to Vietnam in 1995. Born in New Zealand, Chinn is half Egyptian, half Chinese, was educated in England and grew up in the US. Inheriting an interest in food from his Chinese and Egyptian grandmothers, Chinn learned his culinary trade while working in restaurants in San Francisco before going on to apprentice in France. He settled in Saigon, where he ran Joe's and the renowned Camargue Restaurant. He has also run the Red Onion Bistro in Hanoi Towers and Miro. His attempts at running a successful restaurant in Vietnam were almost defeated by bureaucracy and business practices, but, unwilling to give up, he opened the eponymous restaurant (▷ 211), with its great position overlooking Hoan Kiem Lake in Hanoi. He has plans to open another in Saigon

ARTS AND CULTURE 19

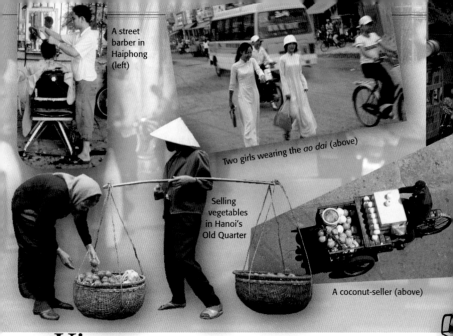

A street barber in Haiphong (left)

Two girls wearing the *ao dai* (above)

Selling vegetables in Hanoi's Old Quarter

A coconut-seller (above)

Vietnamese
Street Life

You need to keep your wits about you when strolling the streets of Vietnam's cities. The sidewalks are crowded with people seeking relief from the heat in any trifling breeze. Add the areas stringed off for parking bicycles and motorcycles, the clutter of "dust cafés" and pedestrians ambling arm in arm, and the squatting itinerant vendors selling lottery tickets, cigarettes, oranges or mangoes, and there's little chance of getting anywhere in a hurry. On any blank wall a barber might hang a mirror and a limp towel and unfold a chair, while a corner bicycle repair shop may advertise itself by displaying an inner tube and a bottle of motorcycle oil. As you stroll along, a scooter may come zooming out of a house across the sidewalk in front of you at any moment, its driver looking neither right nor left. And shouts from hawkers waft through the air as they approach, either doing the rounds or on the way to a spare patch of shade.

A souvenir shop on two wheels

Coffee Cabaret

Forget Starbucks or the Left Bank in Paris: Vietnam is the place to find café culture. The country is now a major coffee exporter and overflows with an amazing variety of cafés. Some offer 30 gourmet varieties, including fox coffee—apparently, the beans are collected from fox dung. There is a haven of bohemian cafés near Hanoi's small lake, thick with goatee beards and the international editions of famous newspapers. Almost anywhere in Vietnam you can wander into a café, take a wooden chair with a view of the street and choose a hot or iced coffee. Hot coffee, served in a traditional drip filter, takes so long to drip through that your glass stands waiting in a bowl of hot water. This keeps the coffee warm—and it's well worth the wait.

Traffic at Nha Trang's market (left)

A young saleswoman at Ben Thanh Market, Ho Chi Minh City (right)

A bustling tree-lined street in Hanoi (right)

Mopeds are a popular form of transportation

Cult of the Honda

Every aspiring chic miss and smart lad in Vietnam's cities yearns for a Honda Dream—the more expensive the model, the better. Vietnam's sea of gently moving bicycles has evolved into a noisy cacophony of motors, as riders race through the streets, around Hoan Kiem Lake in Hanoi or up and down Dong Khoi Street in Ho Chi Minh City, wearing the latest Western fashions and sunglasses. During weekends, the Vietnamese youth come out in force to show off their steeds. But as with cellphones, television sets and air-conditioners, the fashionable edge has already begun to fade, as many buyers settle for less expensive Chinese models.

The Other Side

Crossing the street in Vietnam's cities is an extreme sport. One popular story goes that the wife of a foreign visitor refused to leave the hotel throughout her husband's two-year contract because she couldn't cross the street outside their hotel. Traffic lights are more or less obeyed—except by bicycles, which go anywhere, anytime. Pedestrians are marooned on the curb while the light turns yellow, red and green, and the bicyclists carry on their journeys regardless. Cautious beginners position themselves on the off-traffic side of Vietnamese pedestrians for protection; veterans stride slowly into the oncoming traffic, looking straight ahead. The traffic weaves around them, all eye contact is avoided, and it's everyone for him or herself!

Bia Hoi

Walking around Vietnam's cities is great fun, but when the sensory overload starts to bite, take a rest in a *bia hoi* bar. The Vietnamese are never shy of passing a few minutes with a visitor who's not afraid to mingle, and the famous *bia hoi* bars are some of the best places to mix and pick up some real local tips. *Bia hoi* (fresh beer) is the mildly alcoholic local draft brew, sold at prices as low as 800d for a half-pint glass in thousands of tiny street bars across the country. It's brewed overnight and is served in stylish bottle-green jugs. The cheaper and dingier the bar, the better it often is, and side dishes of dog or shots of snake whiskey add some spice.

Dust Cafés

Vietnam's city sidewalks are full of small cafés, where tiny, low plastic stools are set around equally low tables. The Vietnamese call these "dust cafés," and they are the talking shops of the country. Even when most people should be working, dust cafés are busy. The usual order is a beer or tea, sometimes coffee, or the standard Vietnamese fast food for breakfast, lunch, supper or a late-night snack—a bowl of *pho* (noodle soup). Nothing discourages the customers. Come the monsoons, when city streets are awash with mud, or the bitterly cold winter months of the north, the cafés are still going strong and the *pho* is consumed as eagerly as ever.

A tense scene from *Full Metal Jacket* (left)

Michael Caine in *The Quiet American* (above)

Fire burns in *Apocalypse Now*

Vietnam through
Film

Few countries have provided so much material for celluloid tales as has Vietnam. In the post-Vietnam War era, US film studios made some of the most harrowing, soul-searching and cinematically exciting films of the 20th century, focusing on the nation's involvement in the war. In the 1990s, French-made films covered the colonial era in Vietnam before the French withdrawal in 1954. Vietnamese-made films, however, have suffered arrested development. After World War II, Ho Chi Minh encouraged the production of propaganda documentaries. In 1959, the first film was released—*On the Same River*—about a couple who were divided when the border along the 17th parallel was created in 1954.

Post-1975, when the country was reunified, all Vietnamese films were state-funded and monitored at the script stage by the Ministry of Culture. In 2002, however, the ministry relaxed its rules, though Vietnamese film directors are still not fully at liberty to criticize the Vietnamese regime through the medium of film.

Don Duong (right) angered national censors after starring in *We Were Soldiers*

Divided Opinions

Don Duong, a Vietnamese film actor, angered national censors in 2002 by appearing in what the Vietnamese government regarded as a movie with a pro-US stance. Duong starred in Hollywood's *We Were Soldiers* (directed by Randall Wallace), which depicts the Battle of Ia Drang in 1965—the first major battle of the Vietnam War. During the battle, 400 US troops, led by Lieutenant-Colonel Harold Moore (Mel Gibson), and 2,000 North Vietnamese soldiers, commanded by Nguyen Huu An (Duong), met in bloody hand-to-hand combat, leaving severe casualties on both sides.

Vietnamese authorities claimed that the movie distorted history, and the National Film Censorship Council moved to ban the actor from appearing in productions, and to fine him. Duong emigrated to the US in 2003.

The 1950s version of *The Quiet American* (above).
Robert de Niro in *The Deer Hunter* (left)

Robin Williams plays a radio DJ in *Good Morning Vietnam*

Catherine Deneuve in *Indochine*

Saigon Stars

The 2001 film version of *The Quiet American*, Graham Greene's novel of love, war, murder and betrayal set in 1950s Saigon, was filmed in Vietnam—the first Hollywood blockbuster made in the country since the end of the war. It stars Sir Michael Caine as journalist Thomas Fowler, Brendan Fraser as American aid worker Alden Pyle and Do Thi Hai Yen as Fowler's lover, Phuong. The Hotel Continental, the social pivot of the time, is replicated on screen by the Hotel Caravelle (▷ 137), which faces the real thing across Lam Son Square (Place Garnier). The La Fontaine milk bar on Dong Khoi Street (rue Catinat), frequented by Phuong, is now the Givral café and patisserie. The infamous double bomb scene in front of the Opera House and La Fontaine used hundreds of Vietnamese extras.

Crossing Boundaries

Director Le Hoang's film *Gai Nhay* (*Bar Girls*), about sex, drugs and HIV, has rocked cinema audiences since it was released (in Vietnam only) in 2003. HIV and drugs are serious social problems in Vietnam, with 80,000 reported HIV cases at present and rates as high as 65 percent among intravenous drug-users. Produced by Ho Chi Minh's Liberation Studios, which is run by the army, the film tackles such contemporary social taboos as prostitution and drug addiction. It is a disturbing portrayal of the grim lives of two prostitutes, Hoa (My Duyen) and Hanh (Minh Thu), with scenes of gang rape and murder. The film cost US$78,000 to make but raked in more than a million dollars in box office sales and is Vietnam's biggest grossing movie to date.

Cinematic Century

Vietnam has undergone a cinematic revolution in the 21st century. With the help of an American donation of US$100,000, 13 Vietnamese directors took a cinematography course in the US and visited Hollywood studios to learn more about moviemaking. Filmmakers are also keen to improve sound quality to boost international sales. Since 2002 the Ministry of Culture has reversed much of its policy on censorship and has encouraged private film studios to open up. The 2003 movie *Bar Girls* (▷ left), about drug abuse and HIV, was one result; another was *Luoi Troi* (*Heaven's Net*), directed by Phi Tien Son and tackling corruption and crime. Its subjects are Nam Cam, executed in 2004 for a 15-year killing spree in Ho Chi Minh City, and the party officials and local police officers indicted during his trial.

New Perspectives

American filmmakers' attempts to come to terms with their country's involvement in Vietnam have produced some classic movies. Francis Ford Coppola's *Apocalypse Now*, substituting Vietnam for the Africa of Joseph Conrad's novel *Heart of Darkness*, won two Oscars in 1979. *The Deer Hunter* (1978), starring Robert de Niro, charts the horrors into which three tough steelworkers are plunged in Vietnam; it won five Oscars. Stanley Kubrick's *Full Metal Jacket* (1987) followed GIs to the Tet Offensive, and *Good Morning Vietnam* (1987) starred Robin Williams as a disc jockey working for the armed services radio. Oliver Stone's trilogy, *Platoon* (1986), *Born on the Fourth of July* (1989) and *Heaven and Earth* (1993), deals with the war and its aftermath, in the first two from a US soldier's perspective, and in the third from the viewpoint of a Vietnamese woman.

A fashion show of local styles (above)

Saigon fashion (left)

Modeling a Vietnamese hat at an Armani show in 2004 (right)

Vietnamese Fashion

The new entrepreneurial streak in Vietnam has proved a catalyst for fabulous fashion design and ingenuity. Although known for the beautiful *ao dai*, the classic-cut trouser tunic of local women, Vietnam was not previously renowned for its haute couture. Nowadays, fashionistas flock here to see the latest in desirable clothes, bags, shoes and other accessories from the country's own designers. From the inception of ideas to fabrication, and to the clothes racks, this has been fashion development on steroids. Since economic liberalization, designers have gained national and international fame, some selling to such halls of sartorial fame as Harrods and Henri Bendel.

Asian Fusion

Most fashion designers using Vietnam as their creative hub are women. The exception to this rule is the maitre d' of the ubiquitous Khaisilk empire, Hoang Khai. His label is synonymous with silk and seduction, and his creativity now spans restaurants and hotels, as well as his silk empire. Christina Yu, a lawyer from Hong Kong, created glitzy label Ipa-Nima. Her bags and sequinned shoes fill two shops in Hanoi (▷ 169) and in Ho Chi Minh City. Frenchwoman Valerie Gregori-McKenzie produces ethereal clothes, embroidered cushions and bags under the label Song. She has two shops, in Hanoi (▷ 170) and Saigon (▷ 182). Sylvie Tran Ha set up SXS in Saigon, specializing in suede. Many designers combine native materials with ideas, methods and motifs of the ethnic minority communities.

The Silk Road to Success

Khaisilk began as a work-shop in Hanoi in 1980. Since then the empire has expanded, with shops in Hanoi, Saigon and Hoi An. Owner Hoang Khai's entrepre-neurialism seems limitless. His stylish restaurants and hotels exhibit interior design that is among the most glamorous in Vietnam. Mr Khai, who dresses in black, wins award after award for his silk output and uses intriguing advertisements showing a glance of a bag or silk shoe-clad foot, to ensure Khaisilk's place as the number one boutique.

Top Tunic

Vietnam's national women's costume, the *ao dai*, has been successfully exported worldwide and is worn by hotel receptionists and office workers in humid Saigon. The name means long dress, and the costume consists of a long, flowing tunic of diaphanous fabric worn over a pair of loose-fitting white pants; the tunic has splits from the waist down. It dates to the mid-18th century, when both men and women wore trouser suits buttoned at the front. The modern design was created by the literary group Tu Luc Van Doan in 1932, and is based on ancient court costumes and Chinese dresses. In traditional society, decoration and complexity of design indicated the wearer's status; gold brocade and dragons were for the sole use of the emperor.

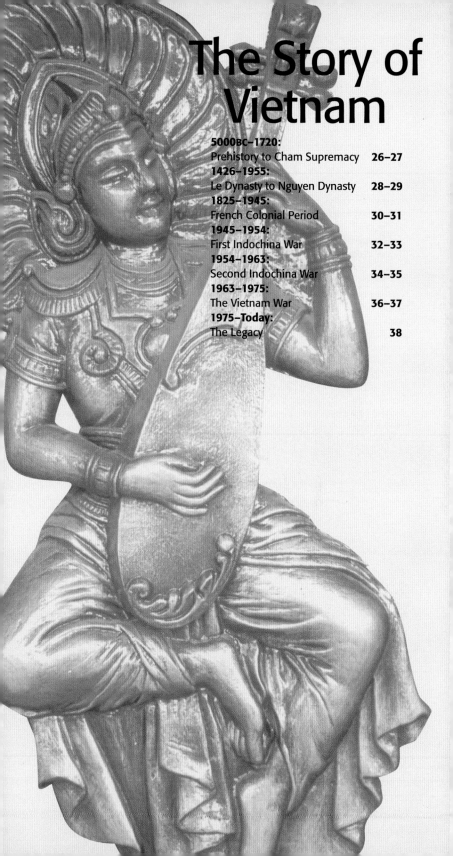

The Story of Vietnam

Prehistory to Cham Supremacy

Between 5000 and 3000BC, two Mesolithic cultures occupied north Vietnam: the Hoa Binh and Bac Son. The Vietnamese trace their origins to 15 tribal groups known as the Lac Viet, who settled in north Vietnam at the beginning of the Bronze Age. Chinese cultural influence over the north began in the second century BC, and the Chinese dominated Vietnam for more than 1,000 years, until the 10th century. The Ly Dynasty (1009–1225) was the first independent Vietnamese dynasty, based at Thang Long, now Hanoi, and following the Chinese Confucian model of government and social relations. In south Vietnam, where the dynastic lords achieved hegemony only in the 18th century, the most significant power was the kingdom of Champa (AD200–1720), focused on the lowlands running down the Annamite coast. Champa built its power on the maritime trading route through Southeast Asia, and for more than 1,000 years the Cham resisted the Chinese and the Vietnamese. Finally, in 1471, the Cham were defeated by the Vietnamese, and the kingdom shrank to a small territory around Nha Trang until 1720, when surviving members of the royal family and many subjects fled to Cambodia.

Dong Son Drums

Dong Son (Bronze Age) culture thrived on the coast of Annam and Tonkin between 500 and 200BC, and its craftsmen produced an iconic instrument now seen all over Vietnam: the squat, bronze Dong Son drum, which can measure more than 3ft (1m) in height and width. Decoration is both geometric and naturalistic, notably on the finely incised drum head. Most excavated drums are associated with human remains and other precious objects, and may have symbolized power and prestige. Some are surmounted with bronze figures of frogs, and may have been used to summon rain.

5000BC

Top of an ornately decorated Dong Son drum (above)

Champa ruins at My Son (right)

A Champa tower at Po Klong Garai (below)

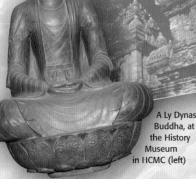

A Ly Dynasty Buddha, at the History Museum in HCMC (left)

Female Warriors

The Trung sisters are among the most revered of Vietnamese heroines. In AD40, the Lac Lords of Vietnam agitated against Chinese control, encouraged by Trung Trac, wife of Lac Lord Thi Sach, and her sister, Trung Nhi. Both did battle while pregnant, having donned gold-plated armor over their bellies.

Although there was an independent kingdom for a short time, the uprising proved fruitless. A large Chinese army defeated the rebels in AD43, captured the two sisters, executed them and sent their heads to the Chinese Han Dynasty court at Lo-yang. An alternative version of events describes the sisters throwing themselves into the Ha Giang River to avoid capture, and turning into statues, which were washed ashore and taken to Hanoi's Hai Ba Trung Temple (▷ 62).

The Trung sisters repel a Chinese invasion in the first century AD

The Battles of Bach Dang River

In AD938, unable to confront the powerful Chinese fleet on equal terms, the Vietnamese General Ngo Quyen sank sharpened iron-tipped poles into the bed of the Bach Dang River. When the Chinese fleet appeared off the mouth of the river, Quyen sent shallow-draft boats to taunt the enemy into attack. As the tide fell, the heavy ships were impaled on the stakes, and more than half the Chinese were drowned.

Legendary warrior Tran Hung Dao (1225–1300) repeated the trick centuries later (see right). In 1283 he was appointed commander of the Dai Viet forces and twice faced Mongol invasion from the north, under Kublai Khan's command. In 1284, a 500,000-strong Mongol army was warded off with superior tactics, and withdrew. Three years later a Mongol Chinese fleet of 400 ships appeared off the coast, and Tran Hung Dao copied the 10th-century strategy of laying stakes beneath the water—with equally devastating effect.

Champa Customs

An anonymous manuscript compiled in Manila about 1590–95 described a gruesome custom apparently followed during the tiger hunt that marked the last of the Champa year's six seasons. It was possibly part of the documentation assembled by Don Luis Perez Dasmariñas in justification of his scheme for the conquest of Indochina. According to this account, the king and his wife would send out 100 or more highland people along the roads with the express order that they should not return without filling two gold basins with human gall, which was to be from people of their own nation and not foreigners. Anyone caught on the road was tied to a tree, where their attackers would cut out the gall bladder. The king and his wife would then bathe in the human gall to cleanse away their sins.

Tran Hung Dao, victor of the second Battle of Bach Dang River

Wily Warrior

The name of legendary warrior Tran Hung Dao is etched on the memory of all Vietnamese and is inscribed on street names across the land. He was born in Nam Dinh, nephew to King Tran Thai Ton of the Tran Dynasty, and in 1283 became commander of the Dai Viet forces. The expansionist policies of the Mongols posed a constant threat to Vietnamese security, and twice on his watch, Kublai Khan invaded Vietnam from the north. In 1284, the Mongols crossed the border at Lang Son. General Tran Hung Dao evacuated the capital and called for national unity in the face of the attack. The military trounced the Mongols and forced them to withdraw. The Mongols again invaded in 1287. This time the general devised a copy-cat tactic similar to that used in the 10th century (see left).

Kublai Khan, leader of the Mongol invasion of Vietnam

1720

Champa towers at Phan Thiet (below) and Duong Long (right)

Le Dynasty to Nguyen Dynasty

After 1,000 years of Chinese domination and centuries of dynastic squabbles, one man harnessed nationalistic sentiment and molded the country into a powerful fighting force. In 1426 Le Loi, together with tactician Nguyen Trai, led a campaign to remove the Chinese from Vietnamese soil and, following victory against the Ming Dynasty (1368–1644), claimed the throne in 1428. Between 1460 and 1497 his successor, Le Thanh Ton, established the system of rule that was to guide Vietnamese emperors for 500 years. However, an ambitious extension of territories, all ruled from distant Hanoi, eventually led to the disintegration of imperial rule. Noble families, locally dominant, challenged the emperor's authority, and the Le Dynasty gradually dissolved into deadly conflict and regional fiefdoms: Trinh in the north, Nguyen in the south. There were numerous peasant rebellions, of which the most serious was the Tay Son rebellion of 1771. Eventually, in 1802, the Nguyen Dynasty was established when Emperor Gia Long ascended to the throne in Hué.

1426

Nguyen Trai

Nguyen Trai, mandarin, poet and nationalist, rose to prominence as an adviser to Le Loi during the 10-year campaign to eject the Ming. His counsel "better to win hearts than citadels" was heeded by Le Loi, who aroused patriotic fervor in his countrymen to achieve victory on the battlefield. It was on Nguyen Trai's suggestion that 100,000 defeated Ming troops were given food and boats to make their way home. After the war he accepted a court post, although later resigned. He was a prolific composer of verse, which is considered some of the finest in the national annals. On an overnight visit to Nguyen Trai, Emperor Le Thai Tong (Le Loi's son and heir) died unexpectedly. Scheming courtiers blamed Nguyen Trai, who in 1442, along with three generations of his family, was executed, a punishment known as *tru di tam tôc*.

A statue of Trung Truc, of the Nguyen Dynasty, in Rach Gia

The emperor's clothes in Hué's Imperial Museum

Hué Citadel (right), built during the reign of Gia Long

The poet Nguyen Trai (above)

A wealthy Chinese couple in Saigon, in 1872 (right, inset)

Tay Son Rebellion

In 1771, the famine-stricken peasantry rallied to the three Tay Son brothers, whose army of clerks, farmers, hill people and scholars swept through the country fighting Trinh and Nguyen lords. Through brilliant strategy the brothers extended their control south to Saigon and north to Thang Long. Taking advantage of this disorder, the Chinese sent a 200,000-strong army south in 1788. In the same year, one of the brothers, Nguyen Hue, proclaimed himself emperor Quang Trung, and on the fifth day of *Tet* in 1789 the brothers attacked and defeated the Chinese near Thang Long. Quang Trung introduced policies of land reform, wider education and fairer taxation, but died in 1792, failing to provide the dynastic continuity necessary for Vietnam to survive the impending French arrival.

Pigneau de Behaine, a missionary during the rebellion

Eunuch Intrigue

Eunuchs were key members of the Nguyen Dynasty court in Hué. They were the only men allowed inside the Purple Forbidden City, to serve the "Son of Heaven"— the emperor—and his wives and concubines. These castrated men, who wore green and red floral gowns and flat, oval hats, arranged the emperor's nightly activities and took bribes from concubines in exchange for choosing them as the night's favored companion. In 1836, Emperor Minh Mang limited the eunuchs' powers, preventing their rise to the powerful position of mandarin, and graded their services. Premier eunuchs (clerks) were paid six times more yuan and four times more rice than the lowly errand boys. The employment of eunuchs was abolished in 1914 by Emperor Duy Tan (reigned 1907–16).

Emperor Minh Mang, who reigned from 1820 to 1840

Death of the Son of Heaven

The death of the Nguyen Dynasty emperors was always accompanied by elaborate burial rites. After the death of the penultimate emperor Dai-Hanh-Hoang-Khai-Dinh in 1925, seven diamonds were placed in his mouth and his red and gold lacquered coffin was covered with young tea leaves. Official mourning began with animal sacrifices and lasted 60 days. When Emperor Gia Long died in 1820, a three-year mourning period was inaugurated. It is said that three days after his death, a messenger was sent to the Hoang Nhon Pagoda to tell the Empress, who was already dead, that her husband was deceased. Ten days before his funeral, the tomb was opened, and a week later the dead king was informed of his imminent burial.

Emperor Bao Dai, in the glowing robes worn for his coronation in 1926

Last Emperor of Vietnam

Bao Dai, born in 1913, was the 13th and last emperor of the Nguyen Dynasty, crowned in 1926 while the French still ruled Indochina. During World War II, Japanese occupiers declared Vietnam independent under Bao Dai, but he was forced to relinquish his role in favor of Ho Chi Minh, leader of the nationalist Viet Minh. After his abdication on August 25 1945, Bao Dai was made an adviser in the new Hanoi government, but subsequently left the country. He returned, with French backing, in 1949, as emperor and leader of the southern government in Saigon. In 1955, a republic was established and Bao Dai was deposed. He lived out the remainder of his days in exile, and died in Paris in 1997.

1955

Young women of the 19th century in traditional dress

Elephants are still used on ceremonial occasions

French Colonial Period

1825

In 1825, Emperor Minh Mang (reigned 1820–40) issued an imperial edict outlawing the dissemination of Christianity. The Christian faith had a large following among the poor peasantry and, fearing revolt, his successor Emperor Tu Duc (reigned 1847–83) ordered a mass execution of Catholics between 1848 and 1860. In response, the French attacked and captured Saigon in 1859. In 1862, Tu Duc signed a treaty ceding the three southern provinces; subsequently the French conquered the north, hoping to control trade routes to China. In 1883 and 1884, the French forced the Emperor, and after his death his officials, to sign treaties making Vietnam a French protectorate, and in 1885 the Treaty of Tientsin recognized the French protectorates of Tonkin (North Vietnam) and Annam (Central Vietnam), to add to the colony of Cochin China (South Vietnam).

Colonial rule was opposed by nationalists such as Phan Boi Chau (1867–1940) and Phan Chau Trinh (1871–1926). Vietnam Quoc Dan Dang (VNQDD), founded in 1927, was the country's first nationalist party, and the first significant Communist group was the Indochina Communist Party (ICP), established by Ho Chi Minh in 1930. Both organized resistance. Japan occupied Vietnam from August 1940, although the French remained in administrative control. After Japan's surrender in 1945, Ho Chi Minh declared himself president of the Democratic Republic of Vietnam (▷ 32).

Emperor Tu Duc (above).
The martyrdom of Father Marchand, 1835 (right)

From Servant of Christ to Saint

François-Isidore Gagelin of Les Missions Etrangères de Paris (the Paris Foreign Missions Society) was the first European priest to be executed in Vietnam. The 32-year-old was strangled by six soldiers as he knelt on a scaffold in Hué in 1833. Three days later, having been told of the Christian belief in resurrection, Emperor Minh Mang had the body exhumed to confirm the man's death. Between 1848 and 1860, 25 European priests, 300 Vietnamese priests and 30,000 Vietnamese Roman Catholics were executed. Ten missionaries, including Gagelin, known as the martyrs of Vietnam, were canonized by Pope John Paul II in June 1998.

Hanoi's French colonial architecture (below)

Preacher and Translator

Even before the 19th century, the French had an influence on Vietnam. Alexandre de Rhodes, one of the Jesuit founders of the Paris Foreign Missions Society, was based in Cochin China and Tonkin between 1624 and 1645. He converted the Vietnamese writing system from Chinese characters (*Chu Nom*), as it had existed since the 13th century, to Romanized script, building on the work of Portuguese missionaries. Rhodes' Vietnamese–Portuguese–Latin dictionary was published in Rome in 1651, but the conversion was not fully in use until it was officially adopted by the French in the early 20th century. De Rhodes was expelled four times from Vietnam: The final, permanent expulsion was in 1645, when Rhodes left for Macao.

Alexandre Yersin

Alexandre Yersin was born in Switzerland in 1863. He completed his medical education in Paris, becoming assistant to Louis Pasteur, and took French citizenship in 1888. As a ship's doctor, he traveled to Vietnam, where he recommended the temperate Dalat Plateau for development as a hill resort. In 1894, on a visit to plague-stricken Hong Kong, Yersin identified the causative agent of the plague, the bacillus now called *Yersinia pestis*. In 1895 he set up a laboratory in Nha Trang that, in 1902, became the first Institut Pasteur outside France. Here, he developed a plague treatment, and at Suoi Dau, 16 miles (25km) south, established a cattle farm to produce serum and vaccines and to improve breeding stock. He died in 1943.

Ho Chi Minh

Ho Chi Minh (He Who Enlightens) was born in 1890 to a poor scholar-gentry family. In 1911, while in France, he converted to Communism, and in 1923 he moved to Moscow to train as an activist. From there, Ho traveled to China to help form the Vietnamese Communist Movement, culminating in the creation of the Indochina Communist Party in 1930. In the following years, he was a Buddhist monk, served six months in Hong Kong for subversion, traveled to China several times and, in 1940, returned to Vietnam—his first visit in nearly 30 years. Ho went on to declare Vietnamese independence in 1945 (▷ 32), but took on a largely ceremonial role after the country split in 1954. He died in 1969.

The Japanese in Vietnam

In June 1940, France fell to Nazi Germany. From August of that year the Japanese occupied Vietnam, and were granted full access to military facilities in exchange for allowing continued French administrative control. In March 1945, the Japanese seized power from the French and forced Emperor Bao Dai to declare independence. Between March and September 1945, a famine struck Tonkin, killing 2 million people. The Viet Minh stepped in to attack rice stocks and to rally support for liberation from Japanese and French control. The Japanese surrendered in 1945 and the Viet Minh seized power before the French could regain control. The First Indochina War (▷ 32) soon followed.

Cartoon of Emperor Bao Dai

Alexandre de Rhodes

Alexandre Yersin

...e seraient les foux qui pensent à la résistance aux Japonais!

...anese propaganda leaflet, distributed during ...orld War II (above).
...e arrival at Saigon of French ...vernor-General Beau, 1902 (left)

1945

Vietnamese prisoners in French stocks in 1907

CHỦ TỊCH
HỒ CHÍ MINH VĨ ĐẠI

A huge statue of Ho Chi Minh at Can Tho (left)

First Indochina War

The First Indochina War started in September 1945 in the south and in 1946 in the north. These years marked the onset of fighting between Ho Chi Minh's Viet Minh and the French. The Viet Minh proclaimed the creation of the Democratic Republic of Vietnam on September 2 1945, when Ho Chi Minh read out the Vietnamese Declaration of Independence in Hanoi. In the south, British troops fought the Viet Minh. When 35,000 French reinforcements arrived, Ca Mau, at the southern extremity of the country, fell on October 21. From that point on, the war in the south became an underground battle of attrition, with the north providing support to their southern comrades.

In February 1946, the French and Chinese signed a treaty leading to the withdrawal of Chinese forces, and in March, Ho concluded a treaty with France recognizing Vietnam as a free state within the French Union and the Indochinese Federation.

The French controlled the cities, but the Viet Minh were dominant in the countryside. By the end of 1949, with the success of the Chinese Revolution and the establishment of the Democratic People's Republic of Korea (North Korea) in 1948, the US was offering support to the French in an attempt to stem the "red tide" of Communism.

The Viet Minh

The Viet Minh, or Doc Lap Dong Minh Hoi (League for the Independence of Vietnam), was imported from China by Ho Chi Minh in 1941. The group took control of Hanoi when the Japanese withdrew in 1945, with the initial support of the Office of Strategic Services (the wartime precursor to the CIA). In the north, the Viet Minh had to deal with 180,000 Nationalist Chinese troops, while preparing for the imminent arrival of a French force. Unable to confront both at the same time, and deciding that the French were probably the lesser of two evils, Ho Chi Minh decided to negotiate with France.

Torture of Vietnamese Prisoners sculpture, Hanoi

1945

Anti-aircraft fire at Dien Bien Phu (above)

Vietnamese forces advance against the French at Dien Bien Phu

Haiphong Customs Incident

One episode is usually highlighted as the flashpoint that led to resumed hostilities after the March 1946 treaty with the French. The French seized customs control in Haiphong in November 1946; the Vietnamese resisted and fighting broke out. The port city was bombarded by French naval guns, air bombing ensued and tanks rolled into the streets. After a few days, the French had control of the city, harbor and airport. They claimed 5,000 Vietnamese casualties and five French; the Vietnamese put the toll at 20,000 Vietnamese dead. In December, the Viet Minh attacked the French garrison in Hanoi justifying it by citing the earlier French bombing. For the French, this December incident marks the beginning of the First Indochina War.

Dien Bien Phu

The decisive battle of the First Indochina War was at Dien Bien Phu. At the end of 1953, the French, led by Colonel Christian de Castries, with American support, parachuted 16,000 men into the area in an attempt to protect Laos from Viet Minh incursions. The narrow valley surrounded by steep, wooded peaks was thought by French strategists to be impregnable. But Vietnamese General Vo Nguyen Giap moved his 55,000 men into the surrounding area, manhandling heavy guns (with the help of 200,000 porters) up the mountainsides until they had a view over the French forces. From the surrounding highlands, Giap had the French at his mercy. On May 7 1954, the French surrendered—one of the most humiliating of French colonial defeats—marking the end of the French presence in Indochina.

American Assistance

US involvement in Vietnam began when the Office of Strategic Services (OSS) sent the Deer Mission from its southern China base to Vietnam in the last days of World War II, to help the Viet Minh resist the Japanese and to assist American airmen who had been shot down. Between 1950 and 1954, however, a shift in American policy saw a substantial increase in financial, military and advisory aid to the French, in an effort to prevent the spread of Communism in Asia. During this time about US$2.6 billion was spent by the US, and from July 1954 military and economic aid was also pumped in to support the newly formed southern government of Vietnam.

General de Castries, inside a bunker in Dien Bien Phu (below)

Geneva Conference

After their defeat at Dien Bien Phu, the French sued for peace in Geneva. On July 20 1954, Vietnam was divided along the 17th parallel into the northern Democratic Republic of Vietnam (DRV) and South Vietnam—with a view to reunifying elections in 1956. These were never held. The border was kept open for 300 days and about 900,000 Vietnamese traveled south, while nearly 90,000 Viet Minh troops and 43,000 civilians went north. A provision under the Geneva Accords to honor the dead of both sides in an ossuary was never fulfilled. During nine years of war between the Viet Minh and the French, between 250,000 and a million civilians, 200,000 to 300,000 Viet Minh and 95,000 French colonial troops had been killed.

General Vo Nguyen Giap

Lt. Col. Peter Dewey of the OSS was killed by Communist guerillas in 1945

Ho Chi Minh awards medals for bravery (left)

The Dien Bien Phu War Memorial (right)

1954

The Viet Minh flag

QUYẾT CHIẾN QUYẾT THẮNG

ĐIỆN BIÊN PHỦ

An evocative mural at Hoa Lo Prison Museum

Second Indochina *War*

In 1954, Vietnam was split in two, with the Communists in control in the north. The Communists, under Ho Chi Minh, were confident that their sympathizers in the south would soon overthrow the government there. This changed with the rise of Ngo Dinh Diem, President of the Republic of South Vietnam, who undermined the strength of the Communist Party in the south. From 1959, the north shifted its strategy toward military confrontation, leaving armed resistance largely to guerrillas belonging to the Cao Dai religion and the Hoa Hao Buddhist millenarian sect. The establishment of the National Liberation Front (NLF) of Vietnam in 1960 was an important development in creating an alternative to Diem. Its military wing was the Viet Cong. The conflict intensified from 1961 when armed forces under the Communists' control were unified under the People's Liberation Armed Forces (PLAF). The north infiltrated 44,000 sympathizers into the south between 1959 and 1964, while the number recruited in the south was between 60,000 and 100,000. The election of US President John F. Kennedy in 1961 coincided with the Communists' decision to widen the war in the south. Kennedy dispatched 400 special forces troops and 100 military advisers to Vietnam—in contravention of the 1954 Geneva Accords—and began arming the Army of the Republic of Vietnam (ARVN). By the end of 1962, there were 11,000 US personnel in the south, but the US had so far avoided large-scale, direct confrontation with the Viet Cong.

1954

Ngo Dinh Diem

Ngo Dinh Diem was born in 1901 to a Roman Catholic, Confucian family and held a post at the court of Emperor Bao Dai. In 1946, Ho Chi Minh offered him a post in the DRV government, which he declined. Eight years later, Diem returned from self-imposed exile in the US to become Premier of South Vietnam under Bao Dai's government. After two rigged elections, Bao Dai was deposed and Diem became President of the Republic of South Vietnam in 1955. He proceeded to suppress all opposition in the country and refused to hold elections for reunification. Security forces led by his brother, Ngo Dinh Nhu, terrorized much of Vietnamese society. On November 2 1963, Diem and his brother Nhu were both assassinated during an army coup.

The dictator Ngo Dinh Diem

Old shells on display at Vinh Moc (left)

A US soldier near Cu Chi in 1966 (right)

The Ho Chi Minh Trail

The Ho Chi Minh Trail (Truong Son Trail), along which supplies and troops were moved by the North Vietnamese Army from the north to the south via Laos, was established in 1959. There were, in fact, eight to ten roads, camouflaged in places and maintained by 300,000 full-time and 200,000 part-time workers. Initially, supplies were carried on bicycles; later, trucks were used, provided by China and the Soviet Union. By the end of the conflict the trail comprised 9,544 miles (15,360km) of all-weather and secondary roads. One hero of the People's Army is said, during the course of the war, to have carried and pushed 60 tons of supplies a distance of 25,491 miles (41,025km)—roughly the circumference of the world.

Ho Chi Minh

Strategic Hamlets

An important element in Ngo Dinh Diem's military strategy in 1962 was the establishment of "strategic hamlets," a plan designed by his brother, Ngo Dinh Nhu, and modeled on British antiguerrilla warfare during Malaya's Communist insurgency (1948–60). The aim was to deny Communists rural support bases, and involved surrounding villages with barbed wire and forcing many peasants to relocate from their ancestral lands. By September 1962, more than 4 million people (34 percent of the population) had been moved. Of the 7,000 to 8,000 villages sealed in this way, only a fifth could ever have been considered watertight.

The Battle of Ap Bac

In January 1963 at Ap Bac, not far from the town of My Tho in the Mekong Delta, the Communists scored their first significant victory in the south. Facing 2,000 well-armed troops of the Army of the Republic of Vietnam (ARVN), a force of just 300 to 400 People's Liberation Armed Forces (PLAF) inflicted heavy casualties, killing 63 ARVN and three Americans, wounding 109 ARVN and three Americans, and downing five helicopters. American advisers were scathing about the performance of their South Vietnamese allies, and it was this defeat that led them to conclude that the ARVN needed the direct intervention of US troops.

Self-immolation and Discontent

On June 11 1963, 66-year-old Thich Quang Duc from Hué became the first of several monks to commit assisted suicide in protest at the regime and US involvement in Vietnam. Companions poured gasoline over him and set him alight as he sat in the lotus position. Pedestrians prostrated themselves at the sight, and the next day pictures of the monk in flames filled the front pages of newspapers around the world. Some 30 monks and nuns followed Thich's example. Fifteen thousand demonstrators gathered at the Xa Loi Pagoda in Saigon on August 1963 to hear speakers denouncing the religious discrimination of the Diem regime. Two nights later ARVN special forces raided the pagoda, wounding 30 and killing seven people. Soon afterward Diem declared martial law, and the pagoda became a focus of discontent.

Monks protest against suppression in 1963

1963

Murals at a war graves site near Danang

Huynh Tau Phat, President of the NLF, talks to journalists at Cu Chi

The Vietnam War

According to US government files, President Lyndon B. Johnson (in office 1963–69) was a reluctant warrior, who doubted the wisdom of intervention but who believed the US must honor its pledge to help South Vietnam. In March 1965 he launched aerial war against the north, and by June there were 74,000 troops in Vietnam. By mid-1967 the Communist leadership in the north escalated hostilities in the south in an attempt to regain the initiative. During the early morning of February 1 1968—New Year (*Tet*)—84,000 Communist troops, almost all Viet Cong, simultaneously attacked targets in 105 urban centers. The Tet Offensive concentrated American minds. The costs by that time had been vast, and thousands of men had been killed for a cause that, to many, was becoming less clear by the month. Negotiations began in Paris in 1969 to try to secure an honorable settlement for the US. Against the wishes of South Vietnam's President Nguyen Van Thieu, the US signed a treaty on January 27 1973; the last combat troops left in March 1973. The North's Central Committee formally decided to abandon the Paris Accord in October; by the beginning of 1975 they were ready for the final offensive. On April 30 the Communists achieved total victory.

1963

Gulf of Tonkin

Two American destroyers, the USS *Maddox* and USS *C. Turner Joy*, were attacked—reportedly without provocation—by North Vietnamese patrol craft in international waters on August 2 1964. The US responded by bombing shore installations, and the Gulf of Tonkin Resolution, requesting greater military involvement, was presented to Congress for approval. Only two Congressmen voted against the resolution, and President Johnson's poll rating jumped from 42 percent to 72 percent. In 1971 Pentagon papers were leaked to the New York Times. According to these, the USS *Maddox* had been involved in intelligence-gathering, while supporting clandestine raids by South Vietnamese mercenaries well inside North Vietnamese territorial waters.

Nguyen Van Thieu (above and left)

A scene from Francis Ford Coppola's film *Apocalypse Now*, set during the Vietnam War

Operation Rolling Thunder

Operation Rolling Thunder, the most intense bombing campaign any country had yet experienced, began in March 1965 and ran through to October 1968. In three and a half years, twice the tonnage of bombs was dropped on Vietnam (and Laos) as during the whole of World War II. At the campaign's peak in 1967, 12,000 sorties were being flown each month; a total of 108,000 were flown throughout 1967. North Vietnam claimed that 4,000 out of its 5,788 villages were hit. B-52s dropped their bombs from such altitude—55,700ft (17,000m)—that the attack could not be heard until the bombs hit their targets. By the end of the war in 1973, 15 million tons of all types of munitions had been used in Indochina, an explosive force representing 700 times that of the atomic bomb dropped on Hiroshima in Japan in 1945.

After the Tet Offensive

Although the Tet Offensive was a strategic victory for the Communists, it was also a tactical defeat. They may have occupied the US embassy in Saigon for a few hours but, except in Hué, Communist forces were soon repulsed by US and ARVN troops. However, US Forces commander General William Westmoreland's request for more troops was turned down, and US public support for the war slumped further, as people grew dismayed by the scale and intensity of the offensive. The aim of the Viet Cong incursion into Saigon was, in fact, not to take the embassy but to make a psychological gesture—and indeed from that date the Johnson administration began to search seriously for a way out of the conflict.

The Phoenix Program

The Phoenix Program was established in the wake of the Tet Offensive with the aim of destroying the Communists' political infrastructure in the Mekong Delta. Named for the Vietnamese mythical bird the Phung Hoang, which could fly anywhere, the program sent CIA-recruited and trained Counter Terror Teams into the countryside to capture Communist cadres. By 1971, the program was estimated to have led to the capture of 28,000 members of the Viet Cong Infrastructure, the death of 20,000, and the defection of a further 17,000. By the early 1970s, the Mekong Delta towns, previously strongholds of the Viet Cong, had reverted to the control of the local authorities.

My Lai Massacre

On March 16 1968, Charlie Company, under the command of Lieutenant William Calley, was dropped into the village of Son My. In the hamlet of My Lai, 504 unarmed villagers were massacred. Some of Calley's men refused to participate. The story of the massacre was filed by Seymour Hersh, but not until November 1969. In 1971, a court martial convicted Calley of the murder of 22 people. No one else was convicted. His life sentence was commuted to house arrest, and three years later President Nixon granted a pardon. In 1998, Lawrence Colburn and Hugh C. Thompson Jr., who stopped the massacre, were awarded the highest medal for bravery not involving enemy conflict.

Lyndon B. Johnson

Ho Chi Minh

The poignant My Lai massacre memorial

1975

Frederick Hart's Vietnam Memorial in Washington D.C., US

Taking cover in a destroyed US tank, in Cu Chi, 1968

The Legacy

The Socialist Republic of Vietnam was established on July 2 1976 when Vietnam was reunified. It was the beginning of a collective struggle to come to terms with the war, build a nation, reinvigorate the economy, and exorcize the ghosts of the past. Thousands of South Vietnamese were sent to re-education camps; many fled, first illegally and then legally through the Orderly Departures Program. In 1986, at the sixth party congress, the Vietnamese Communist Party launched its economic reform program, *doi moi*. Under this program, much of the economy has been freed up, while the party has ensured that it retains ultimate political power. The Asian economic crisis of 1997 to 1998 slowed the pace of change, but—while political tensions have come to the fore—economic growth in Vietnam since the 1990s has been unprecedented.

Entente Cordiale

From 1975 the US imposed a trade embargo on Vietnam and blocked its attempts to gain membership to the International Monetary Fund and similar agencies. The former countries of the Eastern Bloc filled the gap, providing billions of dollars of aid and technical expertise, but in 1990 the Soviet Union halved its assistance to Vietnam, making improved relations with the West a matter of urgency. In 1991, the US opened an official office in Hanoi to assist in the search for MIA (Missing in Action) personnel; three years later the trade embargo was lifted, and in 1995 fully normalized relations were resumed. In 1997, Douglas "Pete" Peterson, the first post-war American ambassador to Vietnam—and a former POW—took up his post in the capital. The National Assembly finally ratified the trade treaty in 2001, heralding a substantial increase in bilateral trade. In 2003, the US imported US$4.5 billion worth of Vietnamese goods, roughly four times more than it exported to Vietnam.

Vietnamese Exodus

After reunification many political refugees fled Vietnam in boats—some paying between US$500 and US$3,000 to secure a place—in the hope of reaching other Southeast Asian countries. Of those who embarked it is estimated that at least a third died at sea, from drowning, dehydration or at the hands of pirates. Despite the risks, Vietnamese continued to leave in huge numbers: By 1980 there were 350,000 awaiting resettlement in refugee camps. Soon the process became semi-official. From 1982 there was an exodus of economic refugees, and more than 40,000 refugees moved into camps in Hong Kong. A program of forcible repatriation, instigated at the end of 1989, was suspended in the face of international protests. More than 1 million Vietnamese have been resettled since 1975, the majority in North America, Australia, France, the UK and Germany.

A Pepsi ad in Hanoi (left)

1975...

Cutting up old shells in Danang

Poster for Hamrong Tourist Mountain

Many Vietnamese fled the country in boats after reunification

On the Move

ARRIVING

ARRIVING BY AIR
Vietnam is relatively well served by international airlines, although at the time of publication only United Airlines offered direct flights from the United States. Paris is the main departure point from Europe, with code-shared Vietnam Airlines/Air France flights. Hong Kong and Bangkok are often used as stopover points. International airports are: Tan Son Nhat Airport (SGN) in Ho Chi Minh City, Noi Bai Airport (HAN) in Hanoi and Danang Airport (DAD), where some international flights from the region land.

The principal national and international carrier is Vietnam Airlines, which has a virtual monopoly on domestic routes. Other major international carriers are Air France, Cathay Pacific, KLM, Lufthansa, Malaysian Airlines, Qantas, Singapore Airlines, Thai International and United Airlines. The only other domestic carrier is Pacific Airlines.

AIRPORTS
Tan Son Nhat Airport is 4 miles (7km) north of downtown Ho Chi Minh City, or Saigon, the economic powerhouse of the country and its largest city. It is well connected with the wider world—indeed, more airlines fly here from more places than do to Hanoi. The air-

The terminal building at Phu Quoc's airport

port is in the process of being upgraded: A new international terminal was completed in 2006.

Airport facilities in the arrivals lounge include visitor information, branches of Vietcombank and First Vinabank, and a post office. Inside the departures area there is a branch of Vietindebank, a post office, a first-aid office and a telephone service. There are duty-free shops both on arrival and departure.

International departure tax is US$12 for adults and US$6 for 2- to 16-year-olds. Pay at the

GETTING DOWNTOWN FROM THE AIRPORT		
FROM	**TAN SON NHAT AIRPORT TO SAIGON**	**NOI BAI AIRPORT TO HANOI**
TAXI	There is a taxi rank outside both terminals. Airport taxis are metered; a tip is requested on payment. Journey time: around 20–30 min. Price: US$5–7	Official airport taxi company, Noi Bai Taxis, lines up outside the terminal and has a booth close to the Vietnam Airlines airport minibus service on Quang Trung Street in central Hanoi. Journey time: 45 min–1 hour. Price: Chartering a taxi to a hotel from the airport should cost no more than around US$10 (150,000d). Metered taxis may cost more than US$15 and charge an additional road toll of 10,000d
AIRPORT BUS	Number 152 runs from the airport to Ben Thanh market. Frequency: every 15 min between 5.20am and 8.55pm. Price: US$0.12 (2,000d)	The Vietnamese Airlines Minibus (tel: 04-8250872) runs from outside the Noi Bai Airport main terminal. There are two stands—one on the far left and one on the far right of the exit behind the airport information desk. Passengers are delivered to the Vietnam Airlines office on 1 Quang Trung Street. The minibus runs in both directions daily 5am–6.20pm (5, 5.30, 6, 7.30, 8, 8.30, 9, 9.30, 10.20, 3, 4, 5.30, 6.20) Frequency: daily from airport every 30 min or when full. Journey time: 45-min–1 hour. Price: US$2.

desk to the right of the Vietnam Airlines check-in.

The small domestic airport terminal is the building on the far right in the complex. There are toilets, a shop and a small seating area. Vietnam Airlines closes check-in 30 minutes before departure. Pacific Airlines also uses this terminal.

In the departure lounge there is a shop and a magazine stall, a telephone booth, toilets and a Sasco restaurant selling fresh juices, breakfast, lunch and dinner. There is a 5,000d premium for taxis to enter the airport area.

Noi Bai Airport, Hanoi's modern airport, is 22 miles (35km) from the city, about a 45-minute drive. There are toilets inside the arrivals halls and in the main terminal building, which also has two snack bars, the Aerocafé (daily 6am–11pm), a bank of telephones, a post office, a pharmacy, a first-aid unit, two currency exchange desks and a Vietcombank branch with an ATM accepting Visa, MasterCard, JCB, Amex, Cirrus, Maestro and Diners Club. The Agribank branch accepts foreign exchange and travelers' checks and has an ATM accepting Visa only. Both are open Mon–Fri 7.30–4. The Incombank branch accepts Visa and MasterCard only and is open daily 6am–midnight.

There is a visitor information desk (with scant information), open daily 7–5, and an airport information desk (6am–11pm, tel 04-5844427).

International departure tax from Noi Bai is US$14 for adults and US$7 for children (2–12).

Transfers
If this is your first trip to Vietnam, the easiest way of reaching your final destination is to contact your hotel or tour operator and ask them to meet you at the airport. You are guaranteed a price that will not fluctuate at the whim of

the taxi driver, and for the sake of a few dollars more it is well worth it. Self-drive car rental is not available in Vietnam, but cars with drivers can be rented ($\triangleright$ 53).

ARRIVING BY TRAIN
International rail connections exist only with China. There are connections with Beijing via Nanning to Hanoi crossing at Lang Son, and from Kunming to Hanoi via Lao Cai. The lines are slow and distances are great.

ARRIVING BY ROAD
There is a road crossing at Moc Bai on Highway 1 connecting Phnom Penh in Cambodia with Ho Chi Minh City. A second route to Phnom Penh via Chau Doc includes a boat crossing. A further

road crossing into Cambodia is at Tinh Bien, approximately 14 miles (22km) south of Chau Doc. The road crossing at Lao Bao, north of Hué, allows travel through to Savannakhet in Laos, and there is a road crossing to Laos from Dien Bien Phu, though few people take it. There are three land crossings between China and Vietnam: at Lao Cai, Dong Dang and Mong Cai.

ARRIVING BY SEA
There are no regular sea crossings into Vietnam although an increasing number of cruise ships sail into Vietnamese waters. The only other international connection by boat is the Mekong River crossing from Chau Doc to Phnom Penh.

Breakfast with a view after a night in a sleeper service from Hanoi

USEFUL TELEPHONE NUMBERS AND WEBSITES		
VIETNAM AIRLINES		
Ho Chi Minh City	116 Nguyen Hue Boulevard, tel 08-8320320, fax 08-8230273; open Mon–Fri 7.30–6, Sat 8–12, 1.30–4.30, Sun and hols 8.30–12.30; www.vietnamairlines.com	
Hanoi	1 Quang Trung Street, tel 04-8320320, fax 04-9349666, open daily 7am–6pm; www.vietnamairlines.com	
AIRPORTS		
Ton San Nhat, Saigon	tel 08-8485383/8320320	
Noi Bai, Hanoi	tel 04-8866527	
Danang	tel 0511-830339	
TAXIS		
Airport taxi, Ho Chi Minh City	tel 08-8446666	
Noi Bai Taxis, Quang Trung Street, Hanoi	tel 04-8865615	

GETTING AROUND

Vietnam is a large country and some patience is required when trying to get around. If you plan to visit for two weeks or less and want to cover a lot of ground, it's important to factor in some flights; Open Tour buses are also a useful and inexpensive way of bridging important towns. Local bus services are for hardy travelers, who want to get right off the beaten track. Overnight train journeys are another good way of covering long distances.

HOW TO GET AROUND

Because of the lack of self-drive car rental, the slow speed of public transportation and the remoteness of some areas, many visitors use tour operators (▷ 202–204) to take them on day- and week-long trips. This option has the benefit of an English-speaking guide and safe vehicles, and some of the most popular trips include week-long journeys around northwest or northeast Vietnam or into the Mekong Delta. Getting around within cities generally involves renting cyclos (bicycle carriages), *xe ôms* (pronounced "shay oms;" motorcycle taxis), metered taxis and buses.

The entire country is on the move over *Tet* (Vietnamese New Year, ▷ 167), and transportation —both international and national—is reserved for a week either side. Christmas, Easter and the Western summer vacation are also popular with visitors, and all travel during these times is best reserved in advance.

An overview of the road to Reunification Hall, Ho Chi Minh City

ON THE ROAD

The main highway is Highway 1, a single-lane road that runs from Lang Son, near the Chinese border, down to Hanoi, then all the way down the coast to Ho Chi Minh City. Highway 5 is another major route—a two-lane highway to Haiphong. Roads in Vietnam are notoriously dangerous. According to Vietnam's National Committee for Traffic Safety, 6,327 people were killed in 9,470 traffic accidents in the first six months of 2004. However, there are signs of growing attention to road safety. There are far more traffic lights, road dividers and traffic police on the intersections ready to pounce on offenders.

Open Tour buses connect the main cities and visitor centers in Vietnam on a daily basis for a reasonable fare. There's also a network of public buses, but journeys are slow and uncomfortable and can be dangerous. Minibuses ply more regular routes, but are often alarmingly overladen.

CROSSING THE ROAD

Vietnam's streets, especially in Saigon and to a lesser extent in Hanoi, may look anarchic but in fact a strict code of conduct applies. Unlike Westerners, the Vietnamese do not wait for a lull in the traffic, but launch themselves straight into the flow, eyes ahead so as to avoid

walking into a passing bicycle. Responsibility for their safety rests entirely with the oncoming bicyclists. In order to make it easier for bicyclists to avoid them, they walk at a steady, even pace with no deviation from a clearly signaled route, as any slight change in trajectory or velocity would spell certain disaster. The only vehicles that will not maneuver their way around pedestrians are buses.

Rush hour is generally all day in Vietnam, but peaks between 6.30am and 9.30am and between 4pm and 6.30pm. In Ho Chi Minh City the roads are only really quiet between about 2am and 5am.

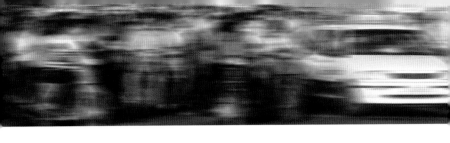

FLIGHTS

Domestic flight coverage is good in Vietnam, with regular flights to many destinations. Prices are reasonable considering the distances covered, and flights may be altered without penalty. The dominant carrier is Vietnam Airlines, serving 15 destinations. Pacific Airlines serves three cities and Vasco Airlines serves four; there is a possibility of more routes opening up in the south.

Vietnam Airlines flights cannot be reserved direct; however, a schedule is available online at www.vietnamairlines.com. Pacific Airlines' website invites reservations through an agent but does not have real-time availability or direct reservation: www.pacificairlines.com.vn.

TRAINS

The Vietnamese rail network is run by Vietnam Railways and extends from Hanoi to Ho Chi Minh City. Its branch networks include Hanoi to Haiphong, Hanoi to Dong Dang in the northeast and Hanoi to Lao Cai in the northwest. It is an economical and comfortable way to travel if you opt for first-class tickets. Take care not to leave luggage unattended on the train, and if possible lock it away.

BOATS

Boat services in Vietnam include connections between Ho Chi Minh City, Can Tho and Chau Doc; between Ha Tien and Chau Doc; between Ha Tien and Phu Quoc; and between Rach Gia and Phu Quoc. Ho Chi Minh City is connected by boat to Vung Tau and there is a ferry service between Halong Bay, Haiphong and Cat Ba Island.

VIETNAMESE ADDRESSES

Odd numbers on Vietnamese houses usually run consecutively on one side of the street, evens on the other; "bis" after a number, as in 16 bis Hai Ba Trung Street, means that there are two houses with the same number; "ter" after the number means that there are three houses with the same number.

Hitching a ride in Ho Chi Minh City

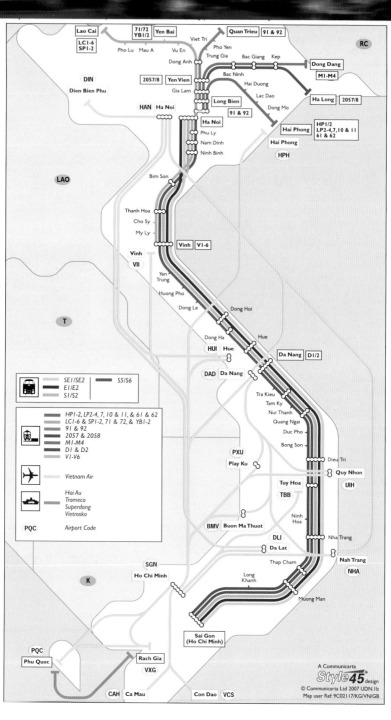

Getting Around Ho Chi Minh City

Ho Chi Minh City, or Saigon as it is still sometimes called, has abundant transportation—which is fortunate, because it is a hot, large and frenetic city. Metered taxis, motorcycle taxis and cyclos compete for business, and many visitors who prefer some level of independence opt to rent (or even buy) a bicycle or motorcycle.

ON THE MOVE

BICYCLE AND MOTORCYCLE

Bicycles and motorcycles can be rented from some of the low-budget hotels and cafés, especially in Pham Ngu Lao Street. Bicycles should always be parked in the roped-off compounds (*gui xe*) that are all over town; they will be looked after for a small charge (500d by day, 1,000d after dark, 2,000d for motorcycles; always get a ticket).

BUS

The bus service in Ho Chi Minh City (HCMC)/Saigon has become more reliable and frequent in recent years. Buses are green or yellow and are a safer, less expensive and, in some cases, more convenient alternative to other modes of transportation in the city. They run at intervals of 10 to 20 minutes, depending on the time of day. In rush hours they are jammed with passengers and can run late. There are bus stops every 550 yards (500m). The same price applies to all routes: 2,000d per person. All these buses start from or stop by the Travel Information Center opposite Ben Thanh Market (tel 08-8214444). A free map of all bus routes can be obtained here.

CYCLO

Cyclos (bicycle carriages) are a peaceful way to get around the city. They can be rented by the hour (approximately US$2 per hour) or to reach a specific destination. Some drivers speak English, and each tends to have his own patch, which is jealously guarded. Expect to pay more outside the major hotels—you can save some of the fare by walking around the corner.

Cyclos are being banned from more and more streets in the

USEFUL BUS ROUTES

No. 1 Saigon–Chinatown; from the bus stop you can walk to Cholon Coach Station (*ben xe Cho Lon*); runs 5am–9pm.

No. 2 Saigon–Eastern Coach Station (*ben xe mien dong*); from here buses go to provinces in the Mekong Delta; runs 4.45am–7pm.

No. 26 Ben Thanh Market–Western Coach Station (*ben xe mien tay*); from here buses go to all provinces in other parts of Vietnam; runs 5am–6.40pm.

No. 28 Ben Thanh Market–Tan Son Nhat Airport (stops beside SuperBowl, near the airport); runs 5.30am–6.40pm.

No. 152 Ben Thanh Market–Tan Son Nhat Airport (straight to the airport—very often empty); runs 5.15am–8.55pm.

center of Saigon, and as a result some journeys are becoming longer and more expensive—a frequent reason cited for extra money, whatever the agreed fee.

MOTORCYCLE TAXI

Motorcycle taxis (Honda or *xe ôm*) are the quickest way to get around town and are less expensive than cyclos; agree on a price and hop on the back. *Xe ôm* drivers can be recognized by their baseball caps and tendency to chain smoke; they congregate on most street corners, and often shout "moto" to attract custom. Prices vary according to distance; a short journey should not cost more than 10,000–15,000d. Try to haggle the fare down a little if you can.

When you dismount, do so on the side without the exhaust pipe, to avoid being scalded by the fumes. Keep all belongings on the bicycle (hold your bag in front of you, resting behind the driver); flapping baggage is dangerous and is a target for thieves. If targeted, do not resist as you may be pulled off and the

A cyclo driver waits for his next fare to show up

result may be far worse than losing a camera or bag.

TAXI

Saigon has quite a large fleet of meter taxis. There are more than 14 taxi companies and competition has brought down prices, so that a taxi ride for two or more is less expensive than a cyclo or *xe ôm*. The standard of vehicle and service vary widely, and some companies are more expensive. Ensure that the meter is set after you get in. All taxis are numbered; in the event of forgotten luggage or other problems, ring the company and quote the number of your taxi.

TAXIS	
COMPANY	TELEPHONE
Airport Taxi (white or blue)	08-8446666
Mai Linh Taxi (green and white)	08-8226666
Festival (gray)	08-8454545
Saigon Tourist (red)	08-8222206
Vinataxi (yellow)	08-8111111
Mai Linh Deluxe (white)	08-8262626
Vinasun (white)	08-8272727

Getting Around Hanoi

Hanoi is getting more frenetic by the minute as its growing wealth is invested in the internal combustion engine, but its elegant tree-lined boulevards make walking and bicycling a delightful experience nonetheless. If you like the idea of being pedaled, then a cyclo is the answer, but be prepared for some concentrated haggling. There are also motorcycle taxis (*xe ôm*), self-drive motorcycles to rent, and a fleet of metered taxis.

Cyclos (left) and bicycles (above) are a great way to travel in Hanoi

BICYCLE

Bicycling is the most popular form of local mass transportation and is an excellent way to get around the city. Bicycles can be rented from most visitor cafés and hotels; expect to pay about US$1 per day. For those staying longer, it might be worth buying a bicycle.

CYCLO

● Hanoi's cyclo drivers charge twice the price of a taxi journey, and consequently most cyclo journeys are for leisurely rides rather than as a mode of transportation from A to B.
● Drivers also have a tendency to forget the agreed fare and ask for more; some travelers ask that the price be written down if communication is a problem.
● Some drivers will ask for more if it is raining; tip at your discretion.

● A trip from the railway station to Hoan Kiem Lake should not be more than 15,000d. The same trip on a *xe ôm* would be 10,000d.

MOTORCYCLE

● Renting a motorcycle is a good way of getting to some of the more remote places. Visitor cafés and hotels rent a variety of machines for around US$6 to US$8 per day. Note that rental shops insist on keeping the renter's passport. As hotels also want to keep visitors' passports it can be hard to rent other than at your hotel.
● Cuong's Motorbike Adventure (40 Luong Ngoc Quyen Street, tel 04-8266586) buys, sells, rents and repairs Minsks only.

A Hanoi cyclo driver takes a rest between pedaling fares around

RACING

A recent trend in contemporary society has manifested itself in the form of young male Hanoians racing each other on powerful motorcycles around the city streets. Up to 400 racers take part, and the more reckless cut their brake cables. A number of racers and spectators have died, and police have so far been unable to prevent the clandestinely organized events. A team of police riders equipped with fast bikes, guns and electric cattle prods has at least been assembled to maintain order. The Hanoi People's Committee also put forward the suggestion of building a special racetrack, presumably with the hope that the legalization and management of the "sport" will help to control it.

TAXI COMPANIES	
There are plenty of metered taxis in Hanoi.	
City Taxi	tel 04-8222222
Hanoi Taxi	tel 04-8535252
Mai Linh Taxi	tel 04-8222666
Airport Taxi	tel 04-8733333/
	091-3211902

Domestic Flights

DOMESTIC CARRIERS

Vietnam has three domestic carriers:

Vietnam Airlines
www.vietnamairlines.com.vn

Pacific Airlines
www.pacificairlines.com.vn

Vasco Airlines
e-mail vasco-heas@hcm.vnn.vn

AIRLINE PRICES

AIRLINE	CLASS	ONE WAY (US$)
Vietnam Airlines		
Hanoi–Danang	B	82
Hanoi–Hué	B	82
Saigon–Danang	B	82
Saigon–Haiphong	B	154
Saigon–Hanoi	B	154
Danang–Buon Me Thuot	E	37
Danang–Nha Trang	E	42
Danang–Pleiku	E	30
Danang–Quy Nhon	E	27
Hanoi–Danang	E	60
Hanoi–Dien Bien Phu	E	35
Hanoi–Hué	E	60
Hanoi–Nha Trang	E	95
Rach Gia–Phu Quoc	E	19
Saigon–Buon Me Thuot	E	30
Saigon–Dalat	E	30
Saigon–Danang	E	60
Saigon–Haiphong	E	110
Saigon–Hanoi	E	10
Saigon–Hué	E	60
Saigon–Nha Trang	E	42
Saigon–Phu Quoc	E	38
Saigon–Pleiku	E	42
Saigon–Quy Nhon	E	38
Saigon–Rach Gia	E	37

Key: B = business E = economy
Round-trip fares are double the figures shown.

Pacific Airlines

Prices range from US$88 to US$95 one way from Hanoi to Saigon and vice versa, depending on the class and type of aircraft.

Vasco Airlines

Ca Mau	26–29
Can Tho	22
Con Dao Island	45
Rach Gia	25

● Pacific Airlines is less expensive than Vietnam Airlines but does not fly as many routes. The main hubs are Hanoi in the north, Ho Chi Minh City (Saigon) in the south and Danang in the middle. There are air connections to: Hanoi, Haiphong, Na San (Son La) and Dien Bien Phu in the north; Vinh, Hué, Danang, Pleiku, Quy Nhon, Buon Me Thuot, Dalat and Nha Trang in the central region; and Saigon, Phu Quoc, Rach Gia, Ca Mau, Can Tho and Con Dao in the south.

● Tickets for all domestic flights should be reserved as soon as possible after arrival, but during low season it is perfectly possible to secure seats just a few days before flying or even the day before. Flights can subsequently be altered at no cost at Vietnam Airlines booking offices, seat availability permitting. Domestic departure tax is now included in the price of the flight ticket.

● Vietnam Airlines changes its timetable and ticket prices every six months. A comprehensive timetable booklet can be picked up in all offices. Following the Phnom Penh Tupolev crash in 1997, the fleet of Soviet aircraft has been replaced by Airbuses and Boeings.

● As well as all the standard materials now banned from aircraft around the world, note that Vietnam Airlines also prohibits the carriage of fish sauce and durian (a smelly tropical fruit).

The Antonov An-38 is used by Vasco for services to Con Son

BOOKING OFFICES

AIRLINE	TELEPHONE
Vietnam Airlines	
Buon Me Thuot: 67 Nguyen Tat Thanh Street	50-954442
Can Tho: 20 Hai Ba Trung Street	71-824088
Dalat: 40 Ho Tung Mau Street	63-822895
Danang: 35 Tran Phu Street	511-821130
Dien Bien Phu: Dien Bien Phu Airport	23-825536
Haiphong: 30 Tran Phu Street	31-921242
Hanoi: 25 Trang Thi Street	04-8320320/9349630
Ho Chi Minh City: 116 Nguyen Hue Boulevard	08-8320320/8244482/8230695
Hué: 7B Nguyen Tri Phuong Street	54-824709
Nha Trang: 91 Nguyen Thien Street	58-826768
Phu Quoc: 291 Nguyen Trung Truc Street	77-980778/846086
Pleiku: 55 Quang Trung Street	59-823058/824680
Quy Nhon: Nguyen Tat Thanh Street	56-825313
Rach Gia: 180 Nguyen Trung Truc Street	77-861848
Son La: 419 Chu Van Thinh Street	22-858199
Vinh: 2 Le Hong Phong Street	38-847359
Pacific Airlines	
Danang: 35 Nguyen Van Linh Street	0511-583583
Hanoi: 36 Dien Bien Phu Street, Ba Dinh District	04-7339999
Ho Chi Minh City: 177 Vo Thi Sau Street, District 3	08-2907349
Vasco Airlines	
Ho Chi Minh City: B114 Bach Dang Street, Ward 2, Tan Binh District	08-8489134/9971707

Buses

ON THE MOVE

Although distances are great, journeys are uncomfortable and roads are dangerous, the majority of visitors to Vietnam travel overland. It is possible to travel the length of the country in this way, by both train (▷ 50–52) and bus. Since Highway 1 is dangerous and public buses are slow, most visitors opt for the inexpensive and regular Open Tour bus, which runs from Saigon to Hanoi and back, stopping off at several towns en route.

PUBLIC BUSES

Public buses, in general, are slow, old and cramped, but they usually arrive at their destination. It is not uncommon to see buses being totally disassembled at the side of the road, and it is rare to travel through the country by public transportation without experiencing several breakdowns or punctures. Speeds average no more than 22mph (35kph); public road transportation can be a long and tiresome (sometimes excruciating) business, but it is also fascinating and the best way to meet Vietnamese people.

A bewildering array of contraptions pass for buses, from old French jalopies to Chevrolet, Ford and DMC vans and Soviet buses. Many have ingenious cooling systems, in which water is fed into the radiator from barrels strapped to the roof;

along the route there are water stations to replenish depleted barrels (look for the sign *nuoc mui* or *do nuoc*).

● Most bus stations are on the outskirts of town; in bigger places there may be several stations.

● Long-distance buses invariably leave very early in the morning (4am to 5am).

● Buses are the least expensive form of transportation, although sometimes foreigners are asked two to three times the standard price.

● Prices are normally prominently displayed at bus stations.

OPEN TOUR BUSES

One of the best and most popular ways to travel by road is by traveler-café minibus, also known as the Open Tour bus. Almost every tour operator or travelers' café listed in the tour operators section (▷ 202–204) runs a minibus service or acts as an agent. Operators match their rivals' prices and itineraries closely; indeed, many operate a clearing system to consolidate passenger numbers to more profitable levels.

● The popular Open Tour bus ticket is a flexible, one-way ticket from Saigon to Hanoi or Hanoi to Saigon. Buses run daily and include the following stops:

Going by bus (above and below) offers quite an experience

SHORT DISTANCES	
JOURNEY	**PRICE**
Hanoi–Ninh Binh	US$4
Hanoi–Hué	US$7
Hanoi–Saigon	US$27
Hué–Hoi An	US$3
Hoi An–Nha Trang	US$8
Nha Trang–Dalat	US$8
Dalat–Saigon	US$6

OPEN TOUR BUS TIMETABLE			
HANOI–SAIGON	**MILES (KM)**	**DEPARTS**	**ARRIVES**
Hanoi–Ninh Binh–Hué	435 (700)	6.30pm	11.30am
Hué–Hoi An	75 (120)	8am	4pm
Hoi An–Nha Trang	330 (530)	6am	5pm
Nha Trang–Dalat	133 (214)	8am	3pm
Dalat–Saigon	191 (308)	8am	3pm
SAIGON–HANOI	**MILES (KM)**	**DEPARTS**	**ARRIVES**
Saigon–Dalat	191 (308)	7.30am	2.30pm
Dalat–Nha Trang	133 (214)	8am	3pm
Nha Trang–Hoi An	330 (530)	6am	5pm
Hoi An–Hué	75 (120)	8am	4pm
Hué–Ninh Binh–Hanoi	435 (700)	6.30pm	10.30am

Vendors try to sell their wares to bus passengers at Can Tho

● There is also a bus station in Cholon, which serves destinations such as Long An, My Thuan, Ben Luc and My Tho.
● Minibuses for Vung Tau depart from Ham Nghi Street; hop in quickly as they are not meant to pick up passengers in town (30,000–40,000d).

HANOI BUSES
● The Southern bus terminal is out of town, but linking buses run from the northern shore of Hoan Kiem Lake. The terminal serves destinations south of Hanoi: Saigon, Buon Me Thuot, Vinh, Danang, Thanh Hoa, Nha Trang and Dalat.
● Express buses usually leave at 5am; reserve seats in advance.
● Buses to Haiphong depart from Gia Lam bus station (across Chuong Duong Bridge); journey time is 2.5 hours, and the cost is 20,000d.
● Other routes such as Hoa Binh, Son La and Dien Bien Phu go from My Dinh bus station, some miles to the west of Hanoi.
● Buses can be flagged down on Tran Quang Khai Street before they cross the bridge.
● Ha Dong station, in the southwest suburbs, has buses to Hoa Binh. Get to the station by local bus or *xe ôm*.
● Giap Bat station on Giai Phong Street serves destinations south.

Everyone is on the move at Ho Chi Minh City's bus station

Saigon, Mui Ne, Nha Trang, Dalat, Hoi An, Hué and Hanoi. You can join at any stage of the journey, paying for one trip or several as you go.
● The Hanoi to Hué sector and vice versa is an overnight trip.
● Open Tour buses depart and arrive at their own offices. They often take passengers to their own or associated hotels; if you do not want to stay there, be firm about it.
● Buses also stop at tourist destinations along the way, such as Lang Co, Hai Van Pass, Marble Mountains and Po Klong Garai.

SAIGON BUS STATION
● Since the completion of a new road around Saigon, long-distance public buses, unless specifically signed "Saigon" or "*ben xe* Mien Dong," do not come into the city. Instead, passengers are dropped off on the ring road at Binh Phuoc bridge. From here it is a 45-minute *xe ôm* journey into town.
● There are two main bus stations and a fleet of air-conditioned buses connecting central Saigon with the bus terminals (2,000d). These leave the bus station opposite Ben Thanh Market.
● Buses north to Dalat, Hué, Danang and all points on the road to Hanoi leave from the Mien Dong terminal, north of town on Xo Viet Nghe Tinh Street.
● Buses south to the Mekong Delta (Ca Mau, Rach Gia, Ha Tien, Long Xuyen, My Tho, An Long, Can Tho and elsewhere) leave from the Mien Tay terminal, some distance southwest of town on Hung Vuong Boulevard.

Trains

Vietnam Railways (www.vr.com.vn) runs the 1,615-mile (2,600km) national network. The website lists timetables and fares across the land and is easily navigable. The rail link between Hanoi and Saigon passes through many of the towns and cities worth visiting, including Hué, Danang and Nha Trang. Other than going by air, the train is the most comfortable way to travel—but this applies only to first-class seats. With overnight stays at hotels along the way to see the sights, a rail sightseeing tour from Hanoi to Saigon, or vice versa, should take a minimum of 10 days, but you need to buy tickets for each separate journey.

FARES
Fares are inexpensive, and foreigners now pay the same price as locals. The difference in price between first and second class is small, and it is worth paying extra. Children under five travel free, and children between five and nine years of age pay 50 percent of the ticket price.

TRAINS
There are three seating classes and four sleeping classes on the network:
● First class: air-conditioned soft seat; long-distance tickets include meals.
● Second class: soft seat.
● Third class: hard seat.

For overnight trips there are four classes:
● Hard-berthed cabin sleeping six.
● Air-conditioned hard-berthed cabin for six.
● Soft-berthed cabin for four.
● Air-conditioned soft four-berthed cabin.

● Prices vary according to the class of cabin chosen, the berth (lower berth is more expensive than top berth) and the time the train leaves.
● The slow local trains are entertaining if you have the time and want to enjoy the company of local people.
● The kitchen on the Hanoi to Saigon route serves soups and simple, but adequate, rice dishes (it is a good idea to take additional food and drink on long journeys).

HANOI TO SAIGON
● Six trains daily leave Hanoi for Saigon and vice versa.

● Odd-numbered trains—SE1, SE3, SE5, TN1, TN3, TN7—travel south.
● Even-numbered trains—SE2, SE4, SE6, TN2, TN4, TN8—travel north.
● The SE9 and SE10 run for the *Tet* festival and peak public holidays, stopping at important destinations along the way such as Vinh, Dong Hoi, Hué, Danang, Nha Trang and Saigon.
● The express trains (known as the Reunification Express) take between 29 and 39 hours, but delays are possible.
● The SE1 from Hanoi to Saigon takes 29 hours and the SE3 takes 39 hours. The chart below details fares for these trains, which cover the length of the country.

HANOI TO SAPA
● Sapa can be reached by overnight train from Hanoi to Lao Cai in a journey lasting between 8.5 and 10 hours.

● A fleet of minibuses ferries passengers from Lao Cai rail station to Sapa.
● There are numerous classes of seat or berth on the trains, and the Victoria Sapa Hotel and Royal Hotel have their own private cars. Another company, Tulico, also operates a sleeping car.
● If you travel with Ratraco (part of Vietnam Railways), you can only buy a one-way ticket in Hanoi and need to book the return trip as soon as you get to Lao Cai or Sapa. If you book for Ratraco through a tour operator you can buy a round-trip ticket. If not, a rail office in Sapa (open 7.30–11.30, 1–4) sells tickets for the journey back to Hanoi (use their minibus to Lao Cai; 25,000d).
● The Victoria Express, for hotel guests only, runs four times a week, leaving Hanoi Monday, Wednesday, Friday and Saturday at 10pm (Train LC5), arriving in Lao Cai at 6.30am.

HANOI TO SAIGON: TRAIN FARES		
TYPE OF SEAT/CABIN	TRAIN SE1	TRAIN TN3
Hard seat	473,000d	460,000d
Soft seat	525,000d	510,000d
Air-conditioned soft seat	571,000d	556,000d
Hard-berthed cabin for six (bunk 1, i.e. lower level)	769,000d	748,000d
Hard-berthed cabin for six (bunk 2)	702,000d	682,000d
Hard-berthed cabin for six (bunk 3)	579,000d	562,000d
Air-conditioned hard-berthed cabin for six (bunk 1)	846,000d	822,000d
Air-conditioned hard-berthed cabin for six (bunk 2)	771,000d	750,000d
Air-conditioned hard-berthed cabin for six (bunk 3)	636,000d	619,000d
Soft-berthed cabin for four (bunk 1)	859,000d	835,000d
Soft-berthed cabin for four (bunk 2)	844,000d	820,000d
Air-conditioned soft-berthed cabin for four	948,000d	922,000d
Air-conditioned soft-berthed cabin for four	931,000d	905,000d

• It returns from Lao Cai on Tuesday at 7pm (LC2), arriving 4am; Thursday and Saturday at 10.20pm (LC4), arriving 8.10am; and Sunday at 9.15pm (LC6), arriving at 6am.
• There are two cars, each with five superior cabins (four berths) and two deluxe cabins (two berths with a bedside table and ample luggage rack). All are air-conditioned, with wood paneling.
• It can accommodate 48 people and includes a restaurant car, Le Tonkin, with upholstered banquettes and table lamps, seating 40 people (open 9pm–midnight and 5.30am–6am).
• Prices vary from US$90 to US$220 for a round trip. One-way tickets are available (US$75–95) but not on Friday or Sunday.

• The Royal Train (04-8245222) has soft, air-conditioned, four-berth and six-berth sleepers in two cars (US$16 one way and

Passengers on this overcrowded train to Lao Cai, via Sapa, spill out onto the roof

AIR AND RAIL JOURNEY TIMES

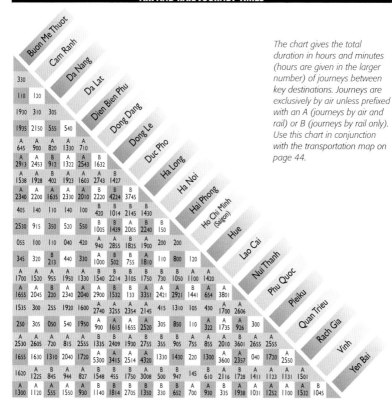

The chart gives the total duration in hours and minutes (hours are given in the larger number) of journeys between key destinations. Journeys are exclusively by air unless prefixed with an A (journeys by air and rail) or B (journeys by rail only). Use this chart in conjunction with the transportation map on page 44.

To \ From	Buon Me Thuot	Cam Ranh	Da Nang	Da Lat	Dien Bien Phu	Dong Dang	Dong Le	Duc Pho	Ha Long	Ha Noi	Hai Phong	Ho Chi Minh (Saigon)	Hue	Lao Cai	Nui Thanh	Phu Quoc	Pleiku	Quan Trieu	Rach Gia	Vinh
Cam Ranh	330																			
Da Nang	110	120																		
Da Lat	1930	310	305																	
Dien Bien Phu	1935	2150	555	540																
Dong Dang	A645	A900	A820	A1330	710															
Dong Le	A2913	2453	B912	A1322	A2543	B1632														
Duc Pho	A1538	1928	B402	A1923	1603	2743	1427													
Ha Long	A2340	A2200	A1635	A2330	2010	B2220	B4224	B3745												
Ha Noi	405	140	110	140	100	B420	B1014	B2145	1430											
Hai Phong	2530	915	350	520	550	B1005	B1439	2005	2240	150										
Ho Chi Minh (Saigon)	055	100	110	040	420	A940	A2855	1825	1900	200	200									
Hue	345	320	B213	440	330	A1000	B502	B755	1810	110	800	120								
Lao Cai	A1700	A1520	955	A1950	1330	A1540	B2214	B3105	1750	730	1050	1100	1420							
Nui Thanh	A1655	2045	B220	A2340	2040	2900	1532	B133	3351	2421	2921	1441	654	A3801						
Phu Quoc	1535	300	255	1920	1600	2740	3255	2354	2145	415	1310	105	430	A1700	2606					
Pleiku	250	305	050	540	1950	A900	1615	1655	2520	305	850	110	A322	1735	926	300				
Quan Trieu	2530	2605	720	815	2555	B1335	2409	1930	2755	355	905	755	A2010	3601	2655	2555				
Rach Gia	1655	1630	1310	2040	1720	B5300	3415	2514	4320	1330	1430	220	1300	A3600	2357	040	1720	A2550		
Vinh	1620	A1225	845	944	827	1548	455	1750	3008	500	947	145	610	2116	1728	1411	1123	1131	1501	
Yen Bai	A1300	1120	A555	1550	930	1140	1814	2705	1350	330	652	700	930	335	1938	1031	1252	1100	1532	1045

Young visitors line up at the ticket office at Hanoi station

US$13 one way, respectively). It leaves on the daily SP1 train from Hanoi at 9.30pm, arriving in Lao Cai at 6am, and returns at 9.15pm (LC6), arriving in Hanoi at 6am.

● Tulico cars (tel 04-8287806) leave Hanoi on the daily LC5 at 10pm, arriving in Lao Cai at 6.30am (US$16 for a first-class cabin, US$13 for a second-class cabin). The return is on the LC6 at 9.15pm, arriving at 6am.

● Ratraco (tel 04-9422889, fax 04-9422893, ratraco@hn. vnn.vn; www.ratracogroup.com) offers three classes of seating between 59,000d and 75,000d and a soft, four-berthed cabin for 210,000d one way.

● Children under five who share their parents' berth are not charged. Those over five and using an adult berth are charged the full price.

● Prices include a drink, a snack, and a Kleenex. If you enter through the Mango Hotel, 118 Le Duan Street, staff there will direct you to the right train.

HANOI TO HAIPHONG

● There are four trains daily to Haiphong: one from the central station, and three from Long Bien station, at the western end of Long Bien Bridge near the Red River. Get there by taxi or *xe ôm*.

BUYING TICKETS

● All tickets must be bought in advance.

● Most ticket offices have some staff who speak English.

● Lines can be long and sometimes confusing, and some offices keep unusual hours. If you are short of time and short on patience it may well pay to get a tour operator to reserve your ticket for a small fee.

● All sleepers should be reserved three days in advance.

● You may also telephone; tickets will be delivered in Hanoi only (tel 04-8253949/8252770).

HANOI STATION

● 120 Le Duan Street, Hanoi, tel 04-9423697.

● The central station (*ga* Hanoi) is at the end of Tran Hung Dao Street (a 10-minute taxi ride from the middle of town).

● For trains to Saigon and the south, enter the station from Le Duan Street; for trains to Haiphong, Lao Cai and China, enter from Tran Quy Cap Street.

● Platform tickets are 1,000d.

HO CHI MINH CITY (SAIGON) STATION

● Thong Nhat Railway Station, 1 Nguyen Thong Street, Ward 9, District 3, Ho Chi Minh City, tel 08-8436528.

● The station (*nha ga*) is 1 mile (2km) from the middle of the city at the end of Nguyen Thong Street.

● Facilities for the visitor include an air-conditioned waiting room, post office, bank (no travelers' checks) and toilets (best avoided).

● The ticket office is open daily 7–7, tel 08-9310666/9318952.

● There is a Train Booking Agency at 275c Pham Ngu Lao Street, open daily 7.30–11.30, 1.30–4.30, tel 08-8367640, which saves an unnecessary journey out to the station.

● Alternatively, for a small fee, most travel agents will obtain tickets.

Two police officers sharing one moped outside Hanoi's central station

OTHER PRINCIPAL STATIONS

● Danang Station, 122 Haiphong Street, Danang, tel 0511-823810.

● Hué Station, 2 Bui Thi Xuan, Hué, tel 054-822175.

● Nha Trang Station, 17 Thai Nguyen Street, Nha Trang, tel 058-822113.

Rented Transportation

Self-drive car rental is not available in Vietnam. It is, however, possible to rent cars with drivers, and this is a good way of getting to more remote areas with a group of people. Prices vary across the country and according to the period of rental. Motorcycles can be rented easily and are an excellent and exhilarating way of getting off the beaten track. Bicycles can also be rented by the day in the cities and are useful for getting out into the countryside. Within cities, cyclos (bicycle carriages), *xe ôms* (motorcycle taxis) and metered taxis will all be used at some point in your trip to get around large areas or, in the case of a cyclo, for a leisurely ride.

CAR RENTAL

Cars with drivers can be rented for around US$40 to US$70 per day, depending on distance traveled and which company rents out the car. It pays to shop around. Many of the tour operators and travelers' cafés listed on pages 202–204 will rent out cars with drivers.

Note that car rental prices increase by 50 percent or more during *Tet*. Some companies rent by the day or by the day plus distance covered. Others charge by the kilometer. Prices vary according to whether a four-seat car or a minibus is rented. Cars are usually four- and seven-seaters. All are modern and air-conditioned.

● A standard, air-conditioned modern car including the driver, gasoline, tolls and food, and accommodations for the driver in and around Hanoi and the north costs around US$420 for one week. A larger car with seats for seven costs around US$75 a day or US$490 a week.

● Tolls are applicable where motorists cross new bridges or new roads. A four-seater car is charged 10,000d.

● For driving the length of the country from Hanoi to Saigon, the cost for an air-conditioned, standard car rises to around US$1,200 for a week, including gas and driver, and food and accommodations for the driver. A discount may be offered for a one-way service where a company has multiple branches throughout the country.

● A round trip works out as a less expensive option. For example, Hanoi to Hué and back within four days costs around US$250.

BICYCLE AND MOTORCYCLE

In cities and towns often the best (and least expensive) way to get around is to rent a bicycle or motorcycle. There has been some tightening up of regulations regarding motorcycle driver's licenses, but for the time being, the police and the rental agencies do not apply them to foreigners (but check before you rent). Take time to familiarize yourself with road conditions and ride slowly. Most towns are small enough for bicycles to be an attractive option, but if you are taking in a sweep of the surrounding countryside (touring around the Central Highlands, for example) a motorcycle allows you to see more. Bicycles are pretty hard work in Dalat and Kontum.

● Hotels often have bicycles to rent, and there is usually someone willing to lend their machine for a small charge (10,000–15,000d per day).

● Many travelers' cafés rent out bicycles and motorcycles, the former for around 12,000–15,000d a day, the latter for around 90,000–120,000d per day.

● Motorcycles are rented out with helmets and bicycles with locks. Some longer-stay visitors buy bicycles (around US$50), which they then sell on or give to Vietnamese friends.

Motorcycles lined up and for rent in Ho Chi Minh City

INFRINGEMENTS AND FINES	
INFRINGEMENTS	**FINE (DONG)**
Bicycle	
Not moving in the right-hand lane	10,000
Three riders bicycling shoulder to shoulder	20,000
Clinging to automobiles or motorcycles, carrying cumbersome luggage or veering through traffic in the street	50,000
Illegal racing and fleeing after causing accidents	500,000
Protesting about police officer's decision	bicycle confiscation + 1 million
Organizing illegal races	2 million
Motorcycle	
Not moving in the right-hand lane	50,000
Speeding	100,000
Riding an unlicensed vehicle	200,000
Riding when drunk	500,000
Fleeing the scene of an accident	up to 2 million
Illegal racing	5 million
Illegal racing and protesting about police decisions	50 million

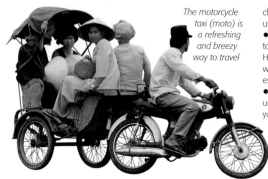

The motorcycle taxi (moto) is a refreshing and breezy way to travel

cheap meal. Taxi drivers are unlikely to do this.

● The cyclo is a wonderful way to get around the Old City of Hanoi, and is ideal for anyone with plenty of time to spare, especially in smaller towns.

● Do not take a cyclo after dark unless the driver is well known to you or you know the route.

● A cyclo from the New World Hotel to the Zoo in Saigon should be around 10,000d, but is often more; a cyclo tour of Cholon could cost as much as 200,000d.

● Always park your bicycle or motorcycle in a guarded parking place (*gui xe*). Ask for a ticket (2,000d).

● It is possible to book bicycles on to trains, but this must be done at least two days in advance. The cost from Nha Trang to Danang, for example, is US$4.

● Foreigners do not currently need a driver's license or proof of motorcycle training to rent a motorcycle in Vietnam.

FINES AND REGULATIONS

● Traffic police stand on every street corner collecting fines for supposed breaches of traffic law, and may confiscate your motorcycle keys.

● The government tried to introduce a law making the wearing of crash helmets compulsory, subject to a 20,000d fine. However, the public opposed the law, and it is now compulsory only for motorcyclists riding on highways.

● In some cities you can turn right on a red light. Pedestrians, especially, need to know this.

MOTORCYCLE TAXI (HONDA ÔM OR XE ÔM)

Ôm means to cuddle, which gives some idea of the style of this ubiquitous and inexpensive transportation. Motorcycle taxis are found on most street corners, outside hotels or in the street. With their uniform baseball caps and dangling cigarettes, *xe ôm* drivers are readily recognizable. If they see you before you see

them, they will shout "moto" to get your attention. In the north and upland areas the Honda is replaced with the Minsk, that Russian workhorse of the hills. A *xe ôm* from the middle of Saigon to the airport costs around 20,000d (tourist rate); the shortest journeys cost at least 5,000d, but fares are always open to bargaining.

CYCLO

Cyclos are a slow and leisurely form of transportation. Cyclo drivers charge double a *xe ôm*, which, when multiplied by the premium levied on foreign visitors, makes the journey more expensive than a drive in an air-conditioned taxi, especially if there are two or three of you. A number of streets in the central areas of Saigon and Hanoi are one-way or out of bounds to cyclos, necessitating lengthy detours that add to the time and cost. Many cyclo drivers regale their passengers with their life stories, give potted histories of all the pagodas visited and then pedal them to a little diner for a wonderful and

TAXI

Taxis ply the streets of Hanoi and Saigon and other large towns and cities. If you are new to the country your best bet is to go to a hotel wherever you may be and take one of the taxis waiting there, or ask the hotel to call you one. Although they are found in virtually every large town in the country, taxis sometimes need to be summoned by telephone.

● Fares are inexpensive—around 12,000d per kilometer—and the drivers generally know their way around and speak some English.

● You will probably need to know the right *quan* (district) for your destination if you are traveling some way.

● Always keep a varied selection of notes with you so that when the taxi stops you can round the fare up to the nearest small denomination. Normally, short trips earn a tip of between 2,000 and 5,000d.

● At night use the better known taxi companies rather than the unlicensed cars that often gather around popular nightspots.

Hard to miss, a bright taxi cab in Ho Chi Minh City

Boats

Boats and hydrofoils make important crossings and journeys in several parts of Vietnam (▷ 44). Boats run regularly and are less expensive (although slower) than flying where plane routes also exist. There are four principal sea crossings—one in the north and three in the south—and two main river journeys in the Mekong Delta, plus some short crossings linked by regular ferry services throughout the Mekong Delta.

The ferry that crosses to Anh Binh from Vinh Long

HALONG CITY, HAIPHONG AND CAT BA ISLAND

● Ferries depart for Haiphong from Hon Gai (Halong City) at 6am, 8.30, 11 and 4pm, price 60,000d, duration 3 hours. The trip itself is worthwhile: The ferry is packed with people and their produce, and threads its way through the limestone islands and outcrops that are so characteristic of the area, before winding up the Cua Cam River to the port of Haiphong. For Cat Ba take the Haiphong ferry to Cat Hai and either transfer to the Haiphong–Cat Ba ferry or hop over to Phu Long and take a *xe ôm* from there.

● The air-conditioned Greenlines hydrofoil from Haiphong to Cat Ba departs once a day, price 100,000d, duration 1 hour. The timings vary slightly depending upon season, but usually there is one boat in the morning, at 9am, returning at 4pm or 3.15pm in winter. If it is not running late, the 6am train from Hanoi will get you to Haiphong just in time to take a *xe ôm* across town for the morning boat.

● The ferry from Haiphong via Cat Hai (usually crowded) to Cat Ba departs 6.30am and 1pm, price 80,000d, duration 2 hours 30 minutes, and from Cat Ba

departs 5.45am and 1pm. Alternatively, take the Hon Gai ferry at 9am, stopping off at Cat Hai; from there, take a small boat to Phu Long on the west of Cat Ba Island and a *xe ôm* or bus (erratic service) to Cat Ba town.
Contact details: Greenlines, 4M Tran Hung Dao Street, Hong Bang District, Haiphong, tel 031-747370.

HO CHI MINH CITY (HCMC) TO CAN THO AND CHAU DOC

The Victoria hotel chain operates a service to Can Tho from HCMC and from Can Tho to Chau Doc, but it is only for guests of the Victoria Can Tho and the Victoria Chau Doc.

● Daily: Chau Doc to Can Tho at 7.30am, Can Tho to Chau Doc at 1.30pm, price US$30 per person, minimum two people, duration 3 hours. Chartered boat US$300.

● By request: HCMC to Can Tho at 8am, Can Tho to HCMC at 11am, price US$55 per person, minimum five people, duration 5 hours. Chartered boat US$550.

● HCMC to Chau Doc at 8am, Chau Doc to HCMC at 8am, duration 8 hours, price US$80 per person, minimum five people. Chartered boat US$800. Rates include taxes, a bottle of water and a piece of fruit or a

cookie. The luggage limit is 66lb (30kg) per person.
Contact details: Victoria Hotels and Resorts, 2nd Floor, 101 Tran Hung Dao Street, District 1, Ho Chi Minh City, tel 08-8373031; www.victoriahotels-asia.com

HA TIEN TO CHAU DOC

The ferry wharf is just to the northeast of the pontoon bridge on Nguyen Van Hai Street in Ha Tien. Ferries to Chau Doc depart at 6am, price 80,000d, duration 7–10 hours. You should take food and water with you.

HA TIEN, HON CHONG AND RACH GIA TO AN THOI TOWN, PHU QUOC

● The ferry to and from An Thoi to Ha Tien takes 4 hours, price 43,000d.
Contact details: Ha Tien Ferry, Nguyen Cong Tru, tel 77-863242; An Thoi Port, tel 77-851092.

● An express vessel (adults 160,000d on top floor of boat, 130,000d on ground floor; children half price) leaves Rach Gia at 8.30am and returns from An Thoi, Phu Quoc, at 1.30pm, duration 2 hours 15 minutes.
Contact details: Haiau, 16 Trang Hung Dao Street, Duong Dong, Phu Quoc, tel 88-981000; taucaotochaiau@hcm.vnn.vn.

● An express vessel from Rach Gia to An Thoi, Phu Quoc, leaves at 8am and returns at 1pm, adult 130,000d (child 70,000d), duration 2 hours 35 minutes.
Contact details: Superdong, Duong Dong, Phu Quoc, tel 77-846180; An Thoi at the dock, tel 77-990368; superdongexpressship@yahoo.com.

● A high-speed boat service from Rach Gia sails at 1.30pm, returning from An Thoi, Phu

Beautiful dragon boats take visitors along the Perfume River

Quoc, at 8.30am, duration 2 hours 10 minutes, adult 130,000d (child 70,000d).
Contact details: Trameco, Khu Pho 1, Duong Dong, tel 77-980666.

● High-speed hydrofoil from An Thoi, Phu Quoc, to Hon Chong departs at 6.30am, duration 4 hours, returning at 1.30pm, duration 3 hours 30 minutes, adult 130,000d (child 65,000d).

Contact details: Vietrosko, tel 77-980444; vietrosko@ yahoo.com.

HO CHI MINH CITY TO VUNG TAU

Two or three competing companies operate hydrofoils from the wharf at the end of Ham Nghi Street, District 1, in Saigon to Halong Street jetty in Vung Tau. Crossings take about 1 hour 15 minutes.

● The first Petro Express service is at 6.15am and then on the hour from 7am–5pm, except 1pm. The return from Vung Tau is at 6.15am and then on the hour 8am–5pm. Price US$10 adults, US$5 children, one way. Ticket office open daily 5.30–5.
Contact details: Petro Express, on the Saigon jetty, tel 08-8210650; in Vung Tau, tel 064-810625.

● The Greenlines service has the same departure times and prices as Petro Express. Children aged under 6 travel free. Booking office open daily 7am–8pm.
Contact details: Greenlines, office on the jetty and at 1A Ham Nghi Street, tel 08-8218061; Vung Tau, tel 64-810202.

● The Vina Express operates from 6am to 4.30pm both ways, with eight departures daily. Price 145,000d adults, 75,000d children. Booking office open daily 6–5.30.
Contact details: Vina Express, on the jetty, tel 08-8215609; Vung Tau tel 064-856530; vinaexpress@hcm.vnn.vn.

VISITORS WITH A DISABILITY

There are very few amenities in Vietnam for visitors with disabilities. City streets are cluttered with vendors, motorcycles and street furniture, and the poor paving presents even more obstacles to anyone with restricted mobility. Generally, however, restaurant and hotel staff are accommodating and helpful.

AROUND TOWN

● Wheelchair access is improving, and more shopping malls, hotels and restaurants provide ramps for easy access, although most sites are still some way behind.

HOTEL ROOMS

● Some of the more well-heeled hotels have designated rooms for guests with disabilities; these are listed in the individual entries (▷ 234–258). These are few and far between, so it's advisable to reserve early.
● Wheelchair-designated rooms can be found at the Hilton Hanoi Opera, Nikko Hanoi, Sofitel

Metropole, Sofitel Plaza Hanoi and Sunway Hotel in Hanoi; at the Furama Resort in Danang; at Lang Co Beach Resort, Lang Co in the central region; at the Caravelle, Legend, Renaissance Riverside, Rex and Sheraton in Saigon; and in the Saigon-Phu Quoc Resort on Phu Quoc in the south.

TOURS

● High-quality tour operators can arrange tours with suitable transportation for those with a disability. Wheelchair-users, however, can be accommodated only in hotels with designated rooms.

This chapter is divided into five regions, which are shown on the map on the inside front cover. Places of interest are listed alphabetically within each region. Major sights are listed at the start of each region. To see where the sights are located, turn to the atlas on pages 281–287.

The Sights

HANOI

Hanoi's name, which means "within a river bend," accurately describes its position on the Red River. Vietnam's capital is a city of broad, tree-lined boulevards, lakes, parks, weathered colonial buildings, elegant squares and some of the newest office blocks and hotels in Southeast Asia. In an age of urban sprawl it remains small and compact, historic and elegant.

MAJOR SIGHTS

Hanoi

283 D3 ■ Vietnam Tourism, 30A Ly Thuong Kiet Street ☎ 04-8264154 ⏰ Mon–Fri 7–11.30, 1.30–5
www.vietnamtourism.com • Comprehensive coverage of Vietnam life and attractions; English-language site option

HOW TO GET THERE

✈ Noi Bai Airport, 22 miles (35km) from city; taxi and minibus service
🚂 Ga Hanoi (central station), 120 Le Duan Street
🚌 Southern bus terminal (destinations south) out of town, with links from northern shore of Hoan Kiem Lake; Kim Ma station (destinations northwest), Nguyen Thai Hoc Street; Gia Lam station (Haiphong), over Chuong Duong Bridge; Giap Bat station (destinations south), Giai Phong Street; served by Open Tour buses from the south

The Opera House (right) dominates the busy city streets

The view across Hoan Kiem Lake to the Thap Rua (Tortoise Tower)

SEEING HANOI

Several districts, each with its own distinctive atmosphere, make up the city. At its heart is Hoan Kiem Lake, north of which is the Old City (or Thirty-Six Streets/36 Pho Phuong), densely packed and bustling with commerce. The French Quarter, still largely containing French buildings, is south of the lake. Here are the Opera House and the grandest hotels, shops and offices. A large block of the city west of Hoan Kiem Lake (Ba Dinh District) represents the heart of government and the civil and military administration of Vietnam. To the north of the city is the West Lake, Tay Ho District, fringed with the suburban homes of the new middle class. It's easy to get around the city with xe ôms, cyclos, taxis or just walking.

BACKGROUND

The origins of Hanoi as a great city lie with a temple orphan, Ly Cong Uan. Ly rose through the ranks of the palace guards to become their commander and in 1010, four years after the death of Emperor Le Hoan, was enthroned, marking the beginning of the 200-year-long Ly Dynasty. On becoming emperor, Ly Cong Uan moved his capital from Hoa Lu to Dai La, which he renamed Thang Long (Soaring Dragon)—present-day Hanoi. During the period of French expansion into Indochina, the Red River was proposed as an alternative trade route to that of the Mekong. Francis Garnier, a French naval officer, was dispatched to the area in 1873 to ascertain the possibilities of establishing such a route. When negotiations with Emperor Tu Duc failed in 1882, and despite having only a modest force of armed men, Garnier attacked and captured the citadel of Hanoi under the dubious pretext that the Vietnamese were about to attack him. From 1882 onwards Hanoi, along with the port city of Haiphong, became the focus of French activity in the north. Hanoi was made capital of the new colony of Annam, and the French laid out a residential and business district, constructing mansions, villas and public buildings incorporating both French and Asian architectural styles.

TIPS

• Spring, when it's pleasantly warm, is a good time to visit Hanoi. From May until early November it's hot and humid, and from November to February it can be very chilly.
• On December 31 Chinese lanterns are released above Hoan Kiem Lake, filling the air with rainbow flutterings.

DON'T MISS

OLD CITY
Hanoi's historic and commercial heart (▷ 68–71).
HOAN KIEM LAKE AND ENVIRONS
An oasis of calm in the maelstrom that surrounds it (▷ 64–65).
HO CHI MINH'S MAUSOLEUM
File past Ho Chi Minh's body, laid out for eternal rest and viewing (▷ 66).

THE SIGHTS

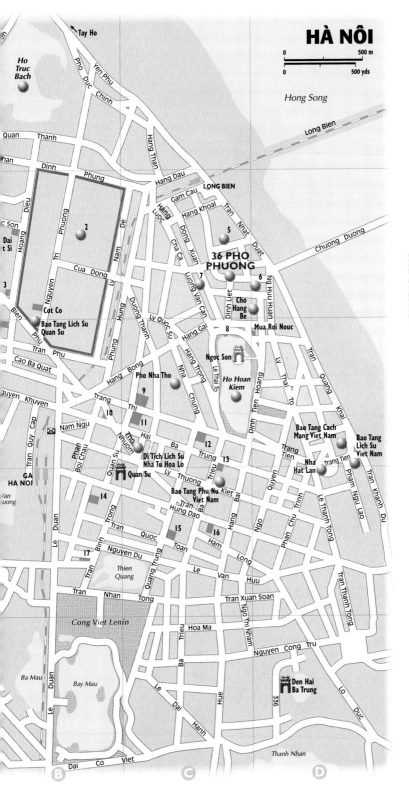

HÀ NÔI

0 ——————— 500 m
0 ——————— 500 yds

Ho Truc Bach

Tay Ho

Hong Song

Long Bien

Pho Duc Chinh

Yen Phu

Quan Thanh

han

Dinh

Phung

Hang Than

Hang Dau

LONG BIEN

Gam Cau

Hang Khoal

Tran Nhat Duat

Dieu

c Son

Dai t Si

Phuong

Tri

Nam

De

Cua Dong

Ly

Hang Luoc

Dong Xuan

Cha Ca

5

Chuong Duong

36 PHO PHUONG

Luong Van Can

7

6

Ng Huu Huan

Nguyen

Cot Co

Bao Tang Lich Su Quan Su

Hung

Duong Thanh

Ly Quoc Su

Dinh Liet

Cho Hang Be

Bien

Phu

Tran Phu

Cao Ba Quat

Phung

Hang Gai

8

Mua Roi Nouc

uyen Khuyen

Hang Bong

Pho Nha Tho

9

Trang

Thi

Nha

Hang Trong

Chung

Ngoc Son

Ho Hoan Kiem

Le Thai To

Dinh Tien Hoang

Ly Thai To

Tran Quang Khai

Tran To

Tran Quy Cap

Nam Ngu

10

11

Hai

Nhuom

Ly Quoc Su

Ba

Di Tich Lich Su Nha Tu Hoa Lo

12

Trung

13

Trieu

Bao Tang Cach Mang Viet Nam

Bao Tang Lich Su Viet Nam

Phan Boi Chau

GA HA NOI

/an uong

Le Duan

14

Quan Su

Ly Thuong

Bao Tang Phu Nu Viet Nam

Kiet

Ba

Tran Hung Dao

Trang Tien

Nha Hat Lan

Trang Tien

Pham Ngu Lao

Tran Khanh Du

Tran Binh

15

16

Ham

Hang

Long

Quang Trung

Quoc Toan

Le

Van

Huu

Ngo

Phan Chu Trinh

Le Thanh Tong

17

Nguyen Du

Thien Quang

Tran

Nhan

Tong

Tran Xuan Soan

Ngo Thi Nham

Tran Thanh Tong

Cong Viet Lenin

Ba Mau

Bay Mau

Le Duan

Le

Dai

Trieu

Ba

Hoa Ma

Hue

Hanh

Nguyen Cong Tru

336

Den Hai Ba Trung

Lo

Duc

Dai

Co

Viet

Thanh Nhan

THE SIGHTS

Interesting works of art adorn the Ambassadors' Pagoda

Ho Chi Minh Museum entrance, and huge statue of Uncle Ho

Ho Chi Minh's House shows his relatively modest lifestyle

AMBASSADORS' PAGODA

⊞ 61 B4 • 73 Quan Su Street
☎ 04-8252427 ⏰ Daily 7.30–11.30, 1.30–5.30 🎟 Free

In the 15th century, a guesthouse for visiting Buddhist ambassadors stood on the site of the Ambassadors' Pagoda (**Chua Quan Su**), hence its name. Today's pagoda was built between 1936 and 1942 and contains stone sculptures of past, present and future Buddhas. Scholars, pilgrims, incense-sellers and beggars crowd into this hub of Buddhist learning; at the back is a school room that's in regular use. A short distance south of the pagoda are Thien Quang Lake and Lenin Park (**Cong Vien Lenin**), which contains a statue of Vladimir Lenin (admission to the park is between 1,000d and 10,000d, depending on the entrance you use and how wealthy you look). Nearby, on Le Duan Street south of the train station, stands sell an array of US, Soviet and Vietnamese army surplus kit.

B-52 MUSEUM

⊞ 60 A2 • 157 Doi Can Street 🎟 Free

US B-52 Stratofortress bomber plane remains have been hawked around Hanoi over many years, but some have found a final resting place at the B-52 Museum (**Bao Tang Chien Tang B-52**). At this curious place visitors can walk over the wings and tail of a shattered B-52 in the yard. The size and strength of the B-52 is incredible—with a capacity to hold 60,000lb (27,000kg) of explosives in its undercarriage, it is, in capability terms, still the world's biggest bomber aircraft.

As in most Vietnamese museums, enemy objects are literally heaped up while native pieces are painted, tended and carefully signed with the names of their heroic units. These include anti-aircraft guns, the devastating SAMs that wreaked so much havoc on the US Air Force, and a MiG-21.

HAI BA TRUNG TEMPLE

⊞ 61 D5 • Tho Lao Street 🎟 Free

The Hai Ba Trung Temple (**Den Hai Ba Trung**) overlooks a lake and is dedicated to the Trung sisters, Trung Trac and Trung Nhi, who are said to have drowned themselves in the first century AD, rather than surrender to the Chinese. The temple was built in 1142 and has been restored a number of times. It contains crude statues of the sisters, which are carried in procession each year during February (▷ 172).

HOA LO PRISON

See page 63.

HOAN KIEM LAKE AND ENVIRONS

See pages 64–65.

HO CHI MINH MUSEUM

⊞ 60 A2 • 3 Ngoc Ha Street ☎ 04-8463752 ⏰ Tue–Thu, Sat, Sun 8–11.30, 2–4 🎟 Adult 10,000d 📷 ❓ Labeling in English and French

This innovative museum (**Bao Tang Ho Chi Minh**) is an architectural monument in its own right. Large, white and modernist, it was opened in 1990 in celebration of the centenary of Ho Chi Minh's birth. Stairs lead from the foyer to a bronze statue of Ho Chi Minh against a background of sun and trees. Displays trace Ho's life and work from his early wanderings around the world to his final victory over the south and his death. Exhibits show the Vietnamese plight versus colonial life, juxtaposing straw huts and bowls and a French officer uniform, carved screen and upholstered cyclo. Interpretive work also includes a totem pole, which symbolizes the power of the global national liberation movement. **Don't miss** A thermos and cigarette case made from plane debris are shown in the 1954–75 corner.

HO CHI MINH'S HOUSE

⊞ 60 A2 • Presidential Palace Memorial Site, 1 Bach Thao ☎ 04-8234760 ⏰ Tue–Thu, Sat, Sun, 7.30–11.30, 2–4 🎟 10,000d

The residence of the governors general of French Indochina, now a Communist Party guesthouse, was built in the compound of the former Presidential Palace between 1900 and 1908. In 1954, when North Vietnam achieved independence, Ho Chi Minh declined to live here, saying it belonged to the people. Instead, he stayed in what is said to have been an electrician's house in the same compound from 1958 to 1969. This modest, wooden house (**Nha San Bac Ho**) is airy, personal, and immaculately kept. Ho conducted meetings under the house, which is raised on wooden pillars, and slept and worked above (his books, slippers and telephones remain). Behind the house is Ho's bomb shelter and the hut where he died in 1969.

A group of ethnic minority women in traditional dress

HOA LO PRISON

Vietnamese and American prisoners of war were incarcerated and tortured in this notorious, French-built prison. Infamous cell conditions, punitive equipment and escape features are displayed.

Hoa Lo (**Di Tich Lich Su Nha Tu Hoa Lo**), better known as the Hanoi Hilton, is the prison where US POWs were incarcerated, some for six years, during the Vietnam War. Up until 1969 prisoners were also tortured here. Rather than face torture, two US Air Force officers, Charles Tanner and Ross Terry, concocted a story about members of their squadron who had been court-martialled for refusing to fly missions against the north. Thrilled with this piece of propaganda, the prison authorities told visiting Japanese communists the story and it filtered back to the US. Unfortunately for Tanner and Terry, they had called their imaginary flyers Clark Kent and Ben Casey (both TV heroes). When the Vietnamese realized they had been fooled the two prisoners were again tortured. The Hilton's final prisoners were not released until 1973, some having been held in the north since 1964.

THE MUSEUM
In 1992, a US mission was shown around the prison where 2,000 inmates were housed in cramped and squalid conditions. Despite pleas from war veterans and party members, the site was sold to a Singapore-Vietnamese joint venture and is now a hotel and shopping complex, Hanoi Towers. As part of the deal, the developers had to leave part of the prison for use as a museum and, now dwarfed by the modern towers, it is an eternal witness to the horrors of torture.

Maison Centrale is the legend over the main gate that leads to the museum. Conditions under colonial rule, when the French incarcerated patriotic Vietnamese, are replicated; by 1953 they were holding 2,000 in a space designed for 500. Cell reconstructions, with the fetters control on the outside, are still in place, and parts of the sewers used by escapees can be seen, as can female torture equipment.

Less prominence is given to the holding of US pilots (although there are propaganda displays of good treatment, clean clothes and POWs exercising), but Douglas "Pete" Peterson, the first post-war American Ambassador to Vietnam (in office 1997–2001), who was one such occupant (imprisoned 1966–73), has his mugshot on the wall, as does John McCain (imprisoned 1967–73), now a US senator.

Don't miss In the first outdoor passageway is an almond tree with a hollow in which political prisoners left messages.

Relief mural (top) showing French mistreatment of Vietnamese prisoners. A cell exhibit (above) at Hoa Lo

RATINGS	
Cultural interest	●●●●●
Historic interest	●●●●●
Walkability	●●●●

BASICS
✚ 61 C3 • 1 Hoa Lo
☎ 04-8246358
⏰ Tue–Sun 8–11.30, 1.30–4.30
💷 Adult 10,000d
📖 Pamphlet included in admission price
❓ Labeling in English

TIPS
● One block east of the prison is the Cho 19–12, a market selling fresh fruit, vegetables and meat.
● Photography is forbidden in the prison.

Hoan Kiem Lake and Environs

The serene focal point of central Hanoi is framed by branches and cloaked in a filmy haze after the clarity of the dawn light. Dominating the lake is the elegant, red Sunbeam Bridge.

Bright columns frame a shrine in the Jade Hill Temple

Sticks of incense give off an atmospheric aroma at Jade Hill

An incense burner emits scented smoke at the Jade Hill Temple

RATINGS		
Cultural interest		● ● ●
Good for kids		● ●
Historic interest		● ● ●
Photo stops		● ● ● ●

BASICS

✚ 61 C3 • Dinh Tien Hang
◎ Daily 7.30–6
💲 3,000d to enter Ngoc Son Temple

TIPS

● Get up at dawn to see the locals practicing *tai chi* around the lake.
● Photography is also better very early in the day, when there are few visitors and the light is clearer.
● To the side of the Jade Hill Temple is a room containing a preserved tortoise and a collection of photographs of the creatures in the lake.

Crossing the Sunbeam Bridge on Hoan Kiem Lake (opposite). Pagoda buildings around the lake (inset)

A Socialist Realist statue at the northern end of the lake

Hoan Kiem Lake (Lake of the Restored Sword), or **Ho Guom** (and Ho Hoan Kiem), as it is more commonly known in Hanoi, is named after an incident that is said to have occurred during the 15th century. Following a momentous victory against an army of invading Ming Chinese, Emperor Le Loi (Le Thai To, reigned 1428–33) was sailing on the lake when a golden turtle appeared from the depths to take back the charmed sword with which he had secured the victory and restore it to the lake from whence it came. Reminiscent of the story of the sword in the stone, of British Arthurian legend, Le Thai To's sword assures the Vietnamese of divine intervention in times of national crisis. It is a story that is graphically portrayed in water puppet theaters (*mua roi nuoc*) across the country. On a small island in the southern part of the lake there is a modest and somewhat dilapidated tower (the Tortoise Tower, Thap Rua), which commemorates the event.

In actual fact, the lake does contain some very large tortoises. One that was captured in 1968 is reputed to have weighed 550 lb (250kg). The creatures that inhabit the lake are believed to be a variety of the Asian softshell tortoise.

JADE HILL TEMPLE AND SUNBEAM BRIDGE

When the French first set foot in Hanoi in the latter part of the 19th century the lake was an unhealthy lagoon surrounded by so many huts that it was impossible to see the shore. Today, the lake is encircled by an attractive park—a beauty spot that is much loved by city residents and used by them every morning for jogging and the practice of *tai chi*.

In the northeast corner of the park is the Jade Hill (**Den Ngoc Son**) Temple, which was built in the early 19th century on a small, tree-shrouded island, on the foundations of the old Khanh Thuy Palace, which itself was built in 1739. The temple is dedicated to Van Xuong, the God of Literature, but the 13th-century hero Tran Hung Dao, the martial arts genius Quan Vu and the physician La To are also worshiped here. Local people can usually be seen playing board games in the temple precincts. The island is linked to the shore by a red, arched wooden bridge—the Sunbeam Bridge (The Huc), constructed in 1875.

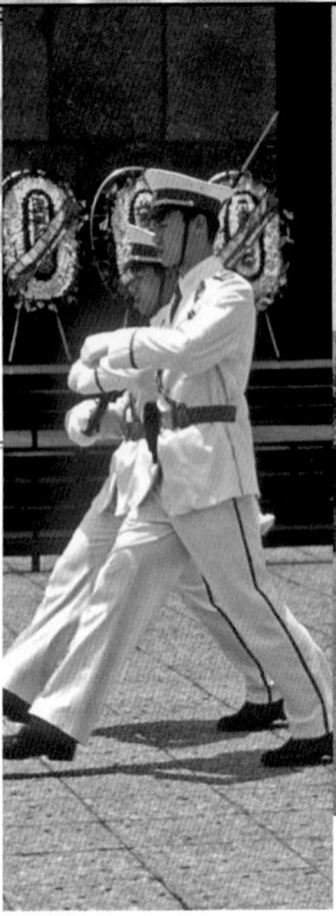

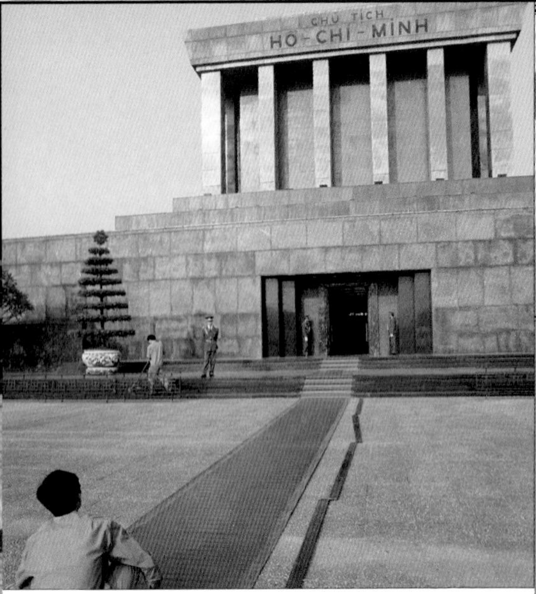

Changing the Guard at the Ho Chi Minh Mausoleum (above). The mausoleum (above right) is reminiscent of Soviet architecture

HO CHI MINH'S MAUSOLEUM

This monolithic marble memorial houses the body of the revered father of the nation. At this place of solemn pilgrimage the Vietnamese line up to view their dead leader—a Communist ritual now practiced in few nations.

RATINGS

Cultural interest	●●●●●
Historic interest	●●●●●
Walkability	●●●●

BASICS

60 A2 • Hung Vuong Street

04-8455128

Apr 1–Oct 31 Tue–Thu 7.30–10.30, Sat, Sun, public holidays 7.30–11; Nov 1–Mar 31 Tue–Thu 8–11, Sat, Sun, public holidays 8–11.30

4,000d

No photography allowed

TIPS

- Before entering the mausoleum you must leave possessions at the office (*ban to chuc*) on Ong Ich Khiem Street, to the south.
- If you take your camera you will be ushered to a drop-off point and you can collect it from a kiosk at the exit, saving the trip across Ba Dinh Square before visiting Ho Chi Minh's house, the One Pillar Pagoda and the Ho Chi Minh Museum.
- Do not take anything into the mausoleum that might be construed as a weapon, such as a pocket knife.
- Dress neatly, walk solemnly and do not talk.

The Vietnamese have made Ho Chi Minh's place of rest a site of pilgrimage, where visitors march in file to see his embalmed corpse inside the mausoleum (**Lang Chu Tich Ho Chi Minh**). This is contrary to his wishes. Ho wanted to be cremated and his ashes, placed in three urns, to be left on three unmarked hills in the north, center and south of the country. He once wrote: "Cremation is not only good from the point of view of hygiene, but it also saves farmland."

The mausoleum, built 1973 to 1975, is a huge, square, columned and forbidding structure and must be among the best constructed, maintained and air-conditioned (for obvious reasons) buildings in Vietnam. Ho lies in a low-lit glass coffin, dressed in simple clothes, and a guard stands at each corner of his bier.

PRESERVATION

The embalming of Ho's body was undertaken by the chief Soviet embalmer, Dr Sergei Debrov, who tended to many other Communist leaders. He was flown to Hanoi from Moscow as Ho lay dying, bringing with him two transport planes packed with air-conditioners and other equipment. To escape US bombing, the team moved Ho to a cave, where it took a full year to complete the embalming process. Russian scientists still check up on their handiwork. Their embalming methods and fluids are still a closely guarded secret; in an interview, Debrov once noted the poor state of China's Chairman Mao's body, which was embalmed without Soviet help.

BA DINH SQUARE

From Ho Chi Minh's Mausoleum walk north up Hung Vuong Street then onto Ba Dinh Square, where Ho read out the Vietnamese Declaration of Independence on September 2 1945. Subsequently this date became National Day—and it was also the date on which Ho died in 1969, although the announcement was postponed so as not to mar people's enjoyment of National Day in the beleaguered north.

Don't miss In front of Ho Chi Minh's Mausoleum on Bac Son Street is a memorial to those who died fighting for Vietnam's independence.

The Museum of the Vietnamese Revolution is in a colonial building

Illumination enhances the already fine Hanoi Opera House

Inspirational decoration is a feature of St. Joseph's Cathedral

MUSEUM OF THE VIETNAMESE REVOLUTION

🕂 61 D3 • 216 Tran Quang Khai Street
☎ 04-8254151 ⏰ Tue–Sun 8–11.45,
1.30–4.15 💰 10,000d ❓ Labeling in English and French

This museum (**Bao Tang Cach Mang Viet Nam**), housed in a beautiful old French villa next to the Opera House, traces the struggle of the Vietnamese people to establish their independence. It leaves the impression that American involvement in Vietnam has been just one episode in a centuries-long struggle against foreign aggressors.

The 3,000 dryly presented exhibits are arranged throughout 29 rooms, and cover the struggle for independence, 1858–1945 (halls one to nine); the national independence movement, 1945–75 (halls 10–24); and modern Vietnam (halls 25–27). Of most interest are photos of opium smokers and beggars in Hanoi at the turn of the 20th century; displays relating to the founding of the Vietnamese Communist Party; a French guillotine, chains and clubs used to beat nationalists jailed at Hoa Lo (▷ 63); and exhibits relating to the formation of the Viet Minh and those connected to Dien Bien Phu (▷ 82–83). The final rooms illustrate a reunified country of bountiful harvests, large civil engineering projects and smiling peasants. Presents given to Ho Chi Minh and various congresses of the Vietnamese Communist Party—including a zebra cloth and an elephant tusk—are also on display.

The roofline of the One Pillar Pagoda in Hanoi

OLD CITY

See pages 68–71.

ONE PILLAR PAGODA

🕂 60 A2 • Ong Ich Kiem Street 💰 Free

This tiny and exquisitely formed pagoda (**Pho Chua Mot Cot**) was built in 1049 by Emperor Ly Thai Tong (reigned 1028–54); it has since been rebuilt several times, most recently in 1955 after the French destroyed it before withdrawing from the country. Smoking stalks of incense sitting in a giant red bowl at the top of the small staircase create a peaceful atmosphere. The Emperor built a little lotus-shaped temple in the center of a water-lily pond after dreaming of the Goddess of Mercy, Quan Am (Vietnam's equivalent of the Chinese goddess Kuan-yin), sitting on a lotus and holding a young boy, whom she handed to him. Shortly afterwards his wife gave birth to a son.

As the name suggests, the pagoda is supported on a single (concrete) pillar with a brick and stone staircase running up one side. Dragons run along the apex of the elegantly curved tiled roof, but the ungainly concrete pillar and the pond of green slime in which it is embedded detract from the enchantment of one of Vietnam's most revered monuments.

OPERA HOUSE

🕂 61 D4 • 1 Trang Tien Street
☎ 04-9330113 ⏰ During performances only 💰 Depends on performance; average 120,000d–150,000d

The grand, art nouveau Opera House (**Nha Hat Lan**) is an iconic symbol of Hanoi. It was built between 1901 and 1911 by François Lagisquet and is one of the finest French colonial buildings in the capital. Shutters, wrought-iron work, balconies, and a tiled frieze cover the exterior, and the upper balustrade is topped with griffins. Below, some 35,000 bamboo piles were sunk into the mud to provide foundations. After years of neglect, the Opera House saw a lavish US$14 million restoration in time for the Francophone Summit in 1997. Original drawings were consulted and experts brought in to supervise craftsmen. Slate was carried from Sin Ho to retile the roof, Italians oversaw the relaying of the lobby's mosaic floor, and French artists repainted the auditorium.

ST. JOSEPH'S CATHEDRAL

🕂 61 C3 • 40 Nha Chung Street ☎ 04-8285967 ⏰ During Mass (daily 5–7am, 5–7pm); at other times (5am–10pm) ring at side door for entry 💰 Free

West of Hoan Kiem Lake in a little square, the twin-towered neo-Gothic St. Joseph's Cathedral (**Pho Nha Tho**), built in 1886, was one of the first colonial buildings in Hanoi, completed just one year after the Treaty of Tientsin gave France control over Vietnam. Some fine stained-glass windows remain. On holy days the building is covered in billboards depicting the subjects of the commemoration. The square in front is dominated by a sculpture of the Virgin Mary, ringed by a wrought iron fence.

Old City

Hanoi life is at its most vibrant in this beautiful, busy maze of old shops, houses and temples. Small streets are packed with popular restaurants and interesting stores in this shabby, chic district.

Tiny houses in the Old City are seemingly squashed together

The home of a bicycle-rider, perhaps, in the Old City

The wares of Old City vendors spill brightly onto the streets

SEEING THE OLD CITY

Hanoi's Old City, also known as the Thirty-Six Streets (36 Pho Phuong), is a delightful warren of lanes inhabited by tinkers, tailors, shoemakers, stone engravers, florists and innumerable other traders, though the crafts and trades of the past have given way in large part to karaoke bars, video rental shops and souvenirs. Nevertheless, this is still the city's liveliest area, humming to the sounds of birds, cyclo drivers, revving motorcycles and women selling their wares from baskets balanced on their shoulders. Forming its boundaries are Hoan Kiem Lake to the south, the Citadel to the west, the Red River to the east, and to the north the vast indoor Dong Xuan Market, devastated by fire in 1994 but rebuilt and operating again within two years. Cyclos are available to take visitors around the Old City, but by far the best way to explore it is on foot.

HIGHLIGHTS

TUBE HOUSES

Narrow dwellings known as *nha ong* (tube houses) are characteristic of this whole area. Although they may have shop fronts only 10ft (3m) wide or less, the main body of the houses can be up to 160ft (50m) long. Whereas in the Vietnamese countryside the dimensions of houses were calculated on the basis of the owner's own physical dimensions, in urban areas no such regulations existed, and tube houses evolved so that each house owner could have an area—albeit very small—of shop frontage facing onto the main street. Traditionally built of bricks stuck together with sugar-cane juice, the tube houses tend to be interspersed by courtyards or "wells" to allow light inside and provide some space for outside activities such as washing and gardening. Houses also have a natural air-conditioning system, a consequence of the air flow created by the difference in ambient temperature between the inner courtyards and the street outside. The longer the house, the greater the velocity of the flow. It's still possible to see a shared wall in between some of the tube houses. These shared walls were built in a step-like pattern and not only marked

RATINGS	
Cultural interest	●●●●●
Historic interest	●●●●●
Photo stops	●●●●●
Walkability	●●●●

BASICS
✚ 61 C2
🛈 30A Ly Thuong Kiet Street, tel 04-8264154; Mon–Fri 7–11.30, 1.30–5
🍴 Restaurants serving Vietnamese, Chinese, French and international food
☕ Many cafés serving Vietnamese and international food; some also provide tour information
🍸 Lively bars with music, pool, dancing and long opening hours

www.sinhcafe.com
This Hanoi-based tour company offers a Hanoi city tour as well as tours farther afield.

Bicycles and conical hats are two ubiquitous items on the streets of Hanoi (opposite)

This Old City shop sells bamboo in all forms, shapes and sizes

---

TIPS

● Don't be put off by shops with only a solitary mannequin in the narrow window. These are tube houses—enter the shop and walk down the passageway into much larger showrooms at the back, where there is plenty of stock.

● Many budget cafés offer reasonably priced tours and places to stay, and are also a good way to meet other travelers. Tours of Hanoi and the Old City are offered by Sinh Café, 52 Luong Ngoc Quyen, tel 04-9261568 (▷ 203).

● For a walk in the Old City ▷ 191–193.

---

land boundaries but also acted as fire breaks. House frontages were not given regulated positions until the early 20th century and as a result some streets have a wonderfully irregular appearance.

Older houses tend to be lower, as commoners were not permitted to build higher than the emperor's own residence. Other regulations prohibited attic windows looking down on to the street (a precaution against assassination attempts, and a means of preventing residents from looking down on a passing king). Purple and gold were shades strictly reserved for royal use, as was the decorative use of the dragon.

FRENCH HOUSES
✠ 61 C2 • Nguyen Sieu Street and nearby

By the early 20th century, inhabitants of the tube houses had started replacing their traditional dwellings with buildings inspired by French architecture. Many fine structures from this era remain, and these can best be appreciated by standing back and looking upward. Shutters, cornices, columns, wrought-iron balconies and balustrades are common decorative features. An ornate facade sometimes conceals the pitched roof behind.

Some conservationists fear that this unique area will be destroyed as residents who have made small fortunes in the wake of the liberation of the economy redevelop their houses without reference to the traditional surroundings. However, the desire to build new homes is understandable, as the tube houses are cramped and squalid, and many have no facilities.

MEMORIAL HOUSE MUSEUM
✠ 61 D2 • 87 Pho Ma May ☎ 04-9285604 🕐 Daily 8–5.30 💰 5,000d ❓ Much of the explanatory text is in French only

The house at 87 Ma May Street is a splendidly preserved example of an original shop house, and is now open to the public. The house was built in the late 19th century as a home for a single family, and given the restricted space available it soon becomes clear that the shop houses' miniature interior courtyards, giving light and fresh air, and their little gardens were of fundamental importance. The wooden upper floor and pitched, fish scale-tiled roofs are typical of the style once followed by most of the houses in this area. From 1954 to 1999 no fewer than five families shared the building on Ma May Street as the urban population rose and living conditions declined.

MUSEUM OF INDEPENDENCE

⊞ 61 C2 • 48 Hang Ngang Street ⏰ Mon–Sat 8–5 💲 Free

Ho Chi Minh lived at 48 Hang Ngang Street, at the north end of Hang Dao Street (before it becomes Hang Duong Street), and this is the spot where he drew up the Vietnamese Declaration of Independence in 1945, modeled on the US Declaration of Independence. The modern building now houses a small museum with black and white photographs of Ho.

HANG BE MARKET

⊞ 61 D2 • Gai Ngu Street ⏰ Daily 5–5

A walk through Hang Be Market (**Cho Hang Be**) reveals just how far Hanoi has developed over the past decade. There is a wonderful variety of food on sale—live, dead, cooked and raw. Quacking ducks,

newly plucked chickens, saucers of warm animal blood, pigs' trotters, and freshly picked and pickled vegetables are among the produce whose quality is a remarkable testament to the rapid strides made by Vietnamese agriculture. There are also beautiful cut flowers on sale in this market and the surrounding streets.

Woven mats for sale (above left). A shop display of brightly painted Tet festival masks (above center). This statue of a white horse, draped with embroidered silk, is in the Bach Ma Temple (right)

BACKGROUND

The original Old City grew up as a squalid, dark, cramped and disease-ridden labyrinth of streets to the east of the Citadel, where the emperor had his residence. This part of Hanoi has survived surprisingly intact, and today is the most beautiful area of the city. By the 15th century there were 36 short lanes here, each specializing in a particular trade and representing one of the 36 trade guilds. Among them, for example, were the Phuong Hang Dao (Dyers' Guild Street) and the Phuong Hang Bac (Silversmiths' Street). The 36 streets have interested European visitors since they first started coming to Hanoi. In 1685, Samuel Bacon noted that "all the diverse objects sold in this town have a specially assigned street," remarking how different this was from "companies and corporations in European cities." The streets in question not only sold different products, but were usually also populated by people from different areas of the coun-

A sturdy bicycle is an invaluable means of transportation for this Old City clothing merchant

try—even from single villages. They would live, work and worship together because each of the occupational guilds had its own temple and its own community support networks.

Some of this past is still in evidence. At the south end of Hang Dau Street, for example, is a mass of stalls selling nothing but shoes, while Tin Street is still home to a community of tinkers.

Temple of Literature

Almost a thousand years ago, this tranquil complex was established and dedicated to learning. Stone stelae record the names of scholars who passed its exacting examinations.

RATINGS	
Cultural interest	● ● ● ● ●
Historic interest	● ● ● ● ●
Photo stops	● ● ● ●
Walkability	● ● ●

SEEING THE TEMPLE OF LITERATURE

The peaceful complex of the Temple of Literature (Van Mieu Pagoda)—the largest temple in Hanoi—is set in a walled garden containing a number of graceful buildings and bordered by Nguyen Thai Hoc, Tong Due Thang, Van Mieu and Quoc Tu Giam streets. The temple and its compound are arranged north–south, and visitors enter at the southern end. Walls divide the

Two graceful bronze storks, standing on tortoises, guard this sumptuous red and gold Confucian sanctuary (above). Using the Temple of Literature for what it was intended (right)

five courtyards, which are linked by paths and gates originally reserved for the emperor; walkways to each side were used by administrators and mandarins. From the main gate a path leads through the Cong Dai Trung to the Van Khue Gac Pavilion, built in 1805 and dedicated to the Constellation of Literature; beyond lies the Courtyard of the Stelae. North of here is the Great Success Gate (Dai Thanh Mon), leading to a courtyard flanked by two 1954 buildings whose predecessors (destroyed in 1947) were reserved for 72 disciples of the Chinese philosopher and teacher Confucius. Facing it is the Great House of Ceremonies, and adjoining this is the Great Success Sanctuary (Dai Thanh), which contains a statue of Confucius.

HIGHLIGHTS

VAN MIEU GATE
On the sidewalk approaching the main gate, two pavilions house stelae bearing the inscription *ha ma* ("climb down from your horse"), a reminder that even the most elevated dignitaries had to proceed

BASICS
✚ 60 A3 • Pho Van Mieu, corner of Pho Quoc Tu Giam
⏱ Summer daily 7.30–5.30; winter daily 7.30–5
🎫 Adult 5,000d, child under 15 free
📷 Guided tour (45 minutes) in French or English 50,000d
🏬 Small gift shop inside temple
📖 Brochure 3,000d

on foot. Van Mieu Gate (**Cong Van Mieu Mon**) is adorned with 15th-century dragons; traditionally, the large central gate was opened only on ceremonial occasions.

COURTYARD OF THE STELAE

At the heart of the Courtyard of the Stelae is a rectangular pond, the Well of Heavenly Clarity (**Cieng Thien Quang**). Arranged around it are the stelae themselves, on which are recorded the names of 1,306 scholars who passed the temple's triennial examinations (*tien si*). Of the 82 that survive (30 are missing), the oldest dates back to 1442 and the most recent to 1779. Each stela is carried on the back of a tortoise, symbol of strength and longevity, but they are arranged in no specific order. Three chronological categories can, however, be identified. There are 14 from the 15th and 16th centuries—recognizable as

The entrance to the Temple of Literature (above). Stelae at the temple (above right) bear the names of centuries of graduates of this, Vietnam's first university

A richly hued image of Confucius (opposite) in the Temple of Literature

Traditional Vietnamese music is played at the Temple of Literature

the smallest in the courtyard and embellished with floral motifs and yin-yang symbols. These have a noticeable lack of dragon emblems, which at the time were a royal preserve. Dragons were permitted by the 17th century and can be seen on the 25 stelae from that period, along with pairs of phoenix and other creatures mythical or real. The remaining 43 stelae are of 18th-century origin; they are the largest and are decorated with pairs of stylized dragons, some merging with flame clouds.

Passing the temple examinations was not easy. In 1733, out of some 3,000 entrants, only eight passed the doctoral examination (*thai hoc sinh*) and became mandarins—a feat that took 35 days. The practice of recording the successful doctoral entrants' names was begun in 1484 on the instruction of Emperor Le Thanh Tong (reigned 1460–98), and continued through to 1878, during which time 116 examinations were held. The Temple of Literature was not used only for examinations, however: Rice was also distributed to the poor and infirm, in rations of 18oz (500g). In 1880, French Consul Monsieur de Kergaradec recorded that 22,000 impoverished people came to receive this meager handout.

GREAT HOUSE OF CEREMONIES

Although the Great House of Ceremonies (**Dai Bai Duong**) was built relatively recently—in the 19th century—it was designed in the far earlier style of the Le Dynasty. Inside is an altar on which sit statues of Confucius and his closest disciples. The carved, wooden friezes inside it are a riot of ornament, with dragons, phoenix, lotus flowers, fruits, clouds and yin-yang disks vying for attention. All are symbolically charged, depicting the order of the universe and by implication reflecting the god-given hierarchical nature of human society, each in his or her place. Not surprisingly, the Communist government held reservations for a long time about preserving a temple that extolled such heretical doctrine.

BACKGROUND

The temple was founded in 1070 by Emperor Ly Thanh Tong (reigned 1054–1072), dedicated to the Chinese philosopher Confucius (who had a substantial following in Vietnam), and reputedly modeled on a temple in Shantung, China, the birthplace of the sage. Some researchers, while acknowledging the date of foundation, challenge the view that it was built as a Confucian institution, pointing to the ascendancy of Buddhism during the Ly Dynasty. Confucian principles and teaching rapidly replaced Buddhism, however, and Van Mieu subsequently became the intellectual and spiritual center of the kingdom as a cult of literature and education spread among the court, the mandarins and then among the common people. At one time there were said to be 20,000 schools teaching the Confucian classics in northern Vietnam alone.

The Fine Arts Museum has some superb lacquer works

One of the larger exhibits at the Vietnam Military History Museum

The 13th-century Kim Lien Pagoda stands by West Lake

THE SIGHTS

VIETNAM FINE ARTS MUSEUM

➕ 60 A3 • 66 Nguyen Thai Hoc Street ☎ 04-8233084 🕙 Tue–Sun 8.30–5, Wed, Sat 8.30–9 💰 20,000d 🚩 Tours in English or French, 8.30–5, 70,000d; audio tours 5,000d per person. Tour office right of main entrance 🏷 Labeling in French and English

The Fine Arts Museum (**Bao Tang My Thuat**) has some 20,000 items, more than 2,000 of which are on show at any one time. The first-floor galleries display pre-20th century art, including Dong Son bronze drums, particularly fine stone Buddhas, and Nguyen Dynasty art. Folk art, on the next floor up, includes works from the Central Highlands, delicate lacquer paintings and woodblock prints. On the top floor is a range of 20th-century Vietnamese work, including excellent watercolors and oil paintings by contemporary artists who are now building a significant reputation. There is also a large collection of overtly political work, posters and propaganda. A comprehensive collection of ethnic minority clothes is exhibited in an annex.

VIETNAM HISTORY MUSEUM

See page 77.

VIETNAM MILITARY HISTORY MUSEUM

➕ 61 B3 • 28 Dien Bien Phu Street ☎ 04-8234264 🕙 Tue–Thu, Sat, Sun 8–11.30, 1–4.30 💰 20,000d, cameras 5,000d 📷 🏷 Random translation of exhibit labels into English and French

Battles and episodes in Vietnam's fight for independence are illustrated in the Military History Museum (**Bao Tang Lich Su Quan Su**), from the struggles with China to the French defeat at Dien Bien Phu and the Vietnam War. It's also worth seeking out the striking new propaganda poster images commemorating the 50th anniversary of Dien Bien Phu, by Le Hoang Anh; overall, the political poster work is the museum's most interesting element, and includes commemorations of every anniversary since the battle of Dien Bien Phu in 1954.

An untouched MiG-21 stands at the museum entrance, while the wrecked remains of B-52s, F1-11s and Q2Cs are piled up in courtyards at the back. Some of the wreckage belongs to a plane shot down in Halong Bay on August 5 1964. The pilot, Everett Alvarez Jr, was the first US aviator captured in the Vietnam War and was sent to Hoa Lo prison for eight-and-a-half years.

In the precincts of the museum is the Cot Co, a flag tower raised on three platforms. Built in 1812, it is the only substantial remaining part of a citadel built by Emperor Gia Long (reigned 1802–19); it was destroyed by the French in 1894–97. There are good views over Hanoi from the top, but other parts of the citadel are in the hands of the Vietnamese army and are out of bounds to visitors.

VIETNAM MUSEUM OF ETHNOLOGY

See page 78.

VIETNAM WOMEN'S MUSEUM

See page 79.

WEST LAKE

➕ 60 A1

Sprawling along the northwestern fringe of the city is West Lake (**Ho Tay**), once a meander in the Red River. On its eastern shores a walkway leads from the causeway to the Tran Quoc Pagoda, Hanoi's oldest pagoda, which was originally built on the banks of the Red River in the sixth century AD. The existing building, including the triple gate, largely dates from 1815, but contains a stela dated 1639 recounting its unsettled history. A few miles north, on the tip of a promontory, stands Tay Ho Pagoda, dedicated to Thanh Mau, the Mother Goddess, and notable chiefly for its setting. It is reached along a narrow lane lined with stands selling fruit, roses and paper votives, and a dozen restaurants serving giant snails with noodles (*bun oc*) and fried shrimp cakes.

As development has spread northward this area has become a middle-class suburb, with new houses in an unplanned and uncoordinated sprawl. The lake has shrunk by 20 percent, from 1,200 acres (500ha) to 1,000 acres (400ha), as residents and hotel and office developers have reclaimed land. The lake is also suffering encroachment by water hyacinths, which are fed by organic pollutants from factories and untreated sewage. The view from Nghi Tam Road, which runs along the Red River dike, presents a contrasting spectacle of sprawling houses interspersed with the remaining plots of land, currently intensively and attractively cultivated market gardens that supply the city with flowers and vegetables.

Artillery exhibits, such as this SAM (surface-to-air) missile launcher (left), fill the courtyard of the Vietnam Military History Museum

VIETNAM HISTORY MUSEUM

Vietnam's foremost history museum, in a former French colonial institute, houses Dong Son drums, sculpture from the creative powerhouse of the Champa Empire and other relics.

The History Museum is in an imposing French colonial building (above)

Ernest Hébrard, responsible for many colonial-era structures, designed the building housing the History Museum (**Bao Tang Lich Su Viet Nam**) in 1931 as the home of the École Française d'Extrême-Orient, a distinguished archeological, historical and ethnological research institute. He employed a distinctly Indochinese style appropriate to the building's original and, indeed, its current function. The École Française d'Extrême-Orient played an important role in the preservation and restoration of ancient Vietnamese structures and temples, many of which were destroyed or threatened with demolition by the French to enable the growth of their colonial city. Today, the museum remains a center of cultural and historical research, and its collection spans Vietnamese history from the Neolithic Age to the 21st century.

MUSEUM LAYOUT

On the second floor, galleries trace the country's past from the Neolithic Age (Bac Son), represented by stone tools and jewels, through the Bronze Age (Dong Son), with finely engraved ceremonial bronze drums (▷ 26), symbolizing wealth and power. Wooden stakes used to impale invading Chinese forces in 1288 were found in 1976 at the confluence of the Chanh and Bach Dang rivers, and a giant oil painting depicts the famous battle. A replica of the country's oldest Buddha Amitabha statue dominates the far end. Amitabha is the Buddha of Infinite Light, and the original, from 1057, was from Phat Tich Pagoda in Bac Ninh Province. Facing the statue are the country's oldest minted coins, Dinh Dynasty currency from AD968. In contrast is a collection of outsized paper currency from 1875.

The next floor up spans the 15th century to the present day. Champa (▷ 26–27) is represented by some remarkably well-preserved stone carvings of *apsaras* (mythical dancing girls) and a head of Garuda, found at Quang Nam. There are relics such as 18th-century bronze pagoda gongs and urns of successive royal dynasties, but some are reproductions.

Don't miss A giant turtle, symbol of longevity, supports a vast stela praising the achievements of Le Loi (reigned 1428–33), founder of the Le Dynasty, who harnessed nationalist sentiment and drove back the Chinese.

RATINGS
Cultural interest	●●●
Good for kids	●●●
Historic interest	●●●●●

BASICS
✚ 61 D3 • 1 Pham Ngu Lao Street
☎ 04-8242433/8241384
🕐 Tue–Sun 8–11.30, 1.30–4.30
💰 Adult 15,000d, child (5–15) 2,000d, camcorder 30,000d, camera 15,000d
💬 Occasional personal tours given by curators for a small gratuity
❓ Individual exhibit labels in English and French; larger, introductory text in Vietnamese

TIPS
● Avoid classroom hours, as this is a popular venue for school trips.
● If you can, take a personal tour, as exhibit descriptions are brief.

A 13th-century statue exhibit

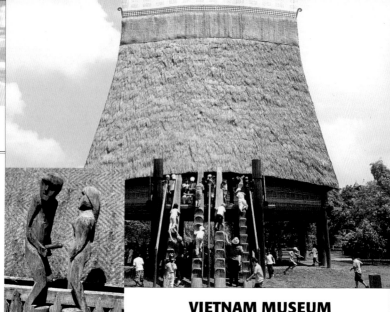

VIETNAM MUSEUM OF ETHNOLOGY

A replica Bahnar house (top).
An explicit fertility symbol (inset)

Outstanding collections here span the ethnographic spectrum that makes up the Vietnamese nation. Displays include clothes, cultural implements, social rites and full-size model ethnic houses in the grounds.

RATINGS

Cultural interest	●●●●●
Good for kids	●●●●●
Historic interest	●●●
Photo stops	●●●

BASICS

🔲 60 A2 • Nguyen Van Huyen Street, Cau Giay District
☎ 04-7562193
🕐 Tue–Sun 8.30–5.30. Discovery Room: Tue–Sun 8.30–11.30, 1.30–4.30
💷 20,000d, cameras 20,000d, camcorders 30,000d
🚌 Minibus 14 from Dinh Tien Hoang Street to Nghia Tan, a few blocks from the museum
🎧 Guided tours in French and English 30,000d
🏪 Postcards, metalwork, lacquerware and fabric gifts
🥤 Water, soft drinks and snacks
❓ Labeling in English and French; wheelchair access

TIPS

● Plan to spend at least a couple of hours here if you want to watch the absorbing videos recording cultural rites and see the house recreations in the grounds.
● In the Discovery Room children are taught to make such objects as accessories used to decorate houses for the dead.

This wonderful collection of items and photographs reflecting Vietnam's 54 ethnic minorities is presented in an informative, interesting and lively manner. The museum (**Bao Tang Dan Toc Hoc Viet Nam**) was established in 1981 and now contains some 25,000 objects and 15,000 photographs, arranged on two floors and beginning with an overview of the majority Kinh people and the other designated minority peoples. Exhibits include functional items—hats, baskets, fishing implements—and other intriguing objects, such as water puppets and paper toys. Pictures and quotes are used to explain how and why things are made.

On the museum's upper level displays concentrate on the hill tribes of Vietnam and its borders. Elaborately decorated and vibrantly dyed costumes are on show, including a very impressive bamboo vest, as well as everyday tools and illustrations of the villages themselves.

PAST AND PRESENT

Much of the work on display is historical, but the museum is also attempting to build up its contemporary collection, and there is a particular focus on craftwork—lacquerware, woodcarving and pottery. Perhaps the most memorable items, though, are the ordinary possessions—a Vietnamese pig counter, a money counter, a bamboo lunar calendar from the Muong, or the bicycle belonging to a man who somehow used it to carry more than 800 fish traps at a time.

Fascinating videos show buffalo sacrifice ceremonies, Bahnar and Hmông funerals and Tày shaman rituals. In the grounds is the open-air section, still under development. Here, alongside the modern, purpose-built museum, replicas are being created of ethnic buildings to illustrate their remarkable range of styles. There are steeply pitched roofs of tile, thatch or local timber, walls of bamboo or no walls at all, a long house from the Ede community, a Tày stilt house, a half-raised, half-grounded Dao house, and a burial ground of the Gia-rai people.

Regular performances of folk singing and dancing are laid on at the museum, and there is often a craftsperson at work there producing traditional items on the spot.

Pedal-boating across the calm waters of White Silk Lake

VIETNAM WOMEN'S MUSEUM

Tribute is paid here to the role of ordinary women in war, motherhood, nationbuilding and day-to-day life. Sculpture, photographs and everyday items illustrate their lives and there are research and education facilities for the women of today.

➕ 61 C4 • 36 Ly Thuong Kiet Street ☎ 04-8259935
🕐 Tue–Sun 8–4 💰 20,000d
❓ Labeling in French and English

RATINGS			
Cultural interest	●	●	●
Historic interest	●	●	●

Thousands of items were collected over a decade from families and women's union offices to furnish this unusual museum (**Bao Tang Phu Nu Viet Nam**). Domestic dishes, weapons, clothes and all sorts of other memorabilia were gathered together and housed in the green building, designed by female architect Tran Xuan Diem and opened in 1992.

The entrance hall ensemble alone is worth the entry fee—a marble-floored space dominated by a statue of the Mother of Vietnam by sculptor Nguyen Phu Cuong. The dome lighting above the sculpture graphically symbolizes a mother's breast, with a giant nipple inverted and producing milk, represented by droplets of sparkling stones.

PUBLIC AND PRIVATE LIVES

Spread out over four floors, the displays juxtapose tributes to women's success in public life and to their role in the family and home life. The chronological display starts with a piece of stone from Nghia Linh Mountain (Pho Tho province), where, according to legend, Mother Au Co gave birth to her children (▷ 90). It continues with a bas-relief of the popular uprising against foreign aggression led by the two Trung sisters in the first century AD (▷ 27). This dual approach is carried on throughout, with accounts of the role of women at Dien Bien Phu, pictures of women in tiger cages on Con Dao Island, and models and reconstructions of women in the Cu Chi Tunnels (▷ 149). One floor up from ground level are exhibits on peasant women and on the part played by women in national defense; on the next floor posters help illustrate the development and activities of the Vietnam Women's Union. Also included, elsewhere in the museum, are ethnic costumes and contemporary dress—complete with photographs of beauty queens.

Don't miss A display of conical hats is accompanied by photos of those no longer in use. Other pictures show village women with baskets, and Kinh women wearing palm-leaf raincoats.

Stylish, elegant 12ft (3.6m) gold statue of the Mother of Vietnam

THE SIGHTS

WHITE SILK LAKE

➕ 61 B1 • Thanh Nien Street 💰 5,000d

White Silk Lake (**Ho Truc Bach**) was created during the 17th century with the construction of a causeway across the southeast corner of West Lake (**Ho Tay**). This was the site of an 18th-century royal palace that had, so it is said, a hundred roofs; all that is left now is the terrace of Kinh Thien, with a dragon staircase, and a number of stupas, bridges, gates and small pagodas. The palace was subsequently used as a prison for concubines who had transgressed the rules. While in custody the women were obliged to weave a fine silk fabric, whose beauty was well known and gave the area its name.

At the southwest corner of the lake is the very beautiful Quan Thanh Pagoda, originally built during the early years of the Ly Dynasty (1010–1225) in honor of Huyen Thien Tran Vo, the Northern God, whose emblems are the tortoise and the snake. The pagoda has since undergone many alterations and now houses a large bronze statue of General Tran Vo and a bell dating from 1677. The Taoist temple is a famous martial arts school, and students can sometimes be seen practicing their skills in the courtyard.

Across the causeway is West Lake (▷ 76), a popular recreation area, with opportunities for shoreline bicycle rides, boat rentals and birdwatching—notably egrets and cranes. A number of privately owned luxury villas line the lakeshore, and further development for tourism seems to be inevitable.

THE NORTH

The mountainous northern region is punctuated with limestone peaks and fertile valleys of paddy fields, tea plantations, stilt houses and rivers cloaked in water hyacinths. There are real riches to discover in this mostly remote area—Sapa, a former French hill station and home of the Hmông people; Dien Bien Phu, site of an historic battle; national parks full of butterflies and primates; and the sparkling waters of Halong Bay.

MAJOR SIGHTS

Dense forests cloak the hills of the Ba Be National Park

Local produce on sale at the roadside near Bac Can

An immense rockface broods over the Bich Dong temples

BA BE NATIONAL PARK

➕ 283 C1 • 27 miles (44km) west of Na Phac on Highway 279 ☎ 0281-894026 💲 10,000d plus 1,000d insurance per person and 10,000d per car 🚗 Range of English-language guided tours. Private tours arranged from Hanoi

Vietnam's eighth national park, Ba Be (**Vuon Quoc Gia Ba Be**), designated in 1992, covers 57,674 acres (23,340ha) on the eastern shore of beautiful Ba Be Lake. Another 19,964 acres (8,079ha) provide an encircling buffer zone. It protects about 417 plant species, 100 butterfly species, 23 amphibian and reptile species and 110 bird species. Of 50 species of mammal, 10 are seriously endangered, including the Tonkinese snub-nosed monkey (*Rhinopitecus avunculus*) and the black gibbon (*Hylobates concolor*). The park has a number of villages inhabited by the Tày, Red Dao, Dao Tien (Coin Dao) and White Hmông ethnic minorities.

BAC CAN

➕ 283 D2 🚌 Bus station on Duc Xuan Street. Connections from Ha Giang, Cao Bang and Hanoi 🍴 Vietnamese food 🚗 Private tours from Hanoi

The market town and capital of Bac Can Province lies on the River Cau and attracts all the region's main ethnic minority groups to its daily market—the Tày people and local branches of the White Hmông and Red Dao, in addition to Dao Tien (Coin Dao) and Dao Quan Chet (Tight Trouser Dao). Bac Can acquired enormous strategic significance during the First Indochina War as the westernmost stronghold of the Cao-Bac-Lang battle zone. It was captured by the Viet Minh in 1944 and retaken by the French in 1947, but frequent guerilla attacks forced them to abandon the town after two years.

BAC HA

➕ 282 B1 🚗 Connections from Lao Cai and Pho Lu 🚆 From Lao Cai or Hanoi (10 hours) to Pho Lu 🚐 Minibus tours from some Sapa hotels

Hundreds of local minority people flock in from the surrounding districts to shop and socialize at Bac Ha's Sunday market (7am–1pm). Among the regulars are the Flower Hmông, wearing embroidered linen; Phu La, in square aprons embroidered with motifs; La Chi, in turbans (men) or four-paneled dresses (women); and Tày, Vietnam's largest ethnic minority, dressed in black. While the women trade and chat, the men drink rice wine. There are several walks to outlying villages. Pho village of the Flower Hmông is around 2.5 miles (4km) north; Thai Giang Pho village of the Tày is 2.5 miles (4km) east; and Na Hoi and Na Ang villages, also Tày, are 1 mile to 2.5 miles (2km to 4km) west.

BAC SON

➕ 283 D2 🚗 Connections from Hanoi, Lang Son 🚗 Private tours from Hanoi

Settled mainly by members of the Tày and Nung ethnic groups, this small market town has two claims to significance in the nation's history. The first derives from the very large number of prehistoric objects unearthed here by archeologists. The Bac Son period (5000–3000BC) was characterized by the development of pottery and the widespread use of refined stone implements, including distinctive axes, with polished edges.

The second is the Bac Son Uprising of September 1940, when revolutionaries escaped here from Lang Son prison and established the first revolutionary power base in the Viet Bac. The following year French forces launched a campaign of terror, forcing the leaders of the uprising to retreat into the mountains, but the tide subsequently turned steadily against the French throughout the region.

The road into town passes a stilted white building, in which the Museum of the Bac Son Rebellion (daily 7–4) has prehistoric tools and weapons, letters and other documents relating to the uprising, and personal effects.

BICH DONG

➕ 283 D3 ℹ️ Tran Hung Dao Street, Ninh Binh, tel 030-881958; Mon–Fri 7–11.30, 1.30–5 💲 31,500d plus 23,500d per person for boat ride 🚗 Leave Highway 2 9 miles (14km) south of Ninh Binh; Bich Dong is 3 miles (5km) farther west 🚗 Private tours from Ninh Binh and Hanoi

Bich Dong consists of a series of temples and caves built into, and carved out of, a limestone mountain during the reign of Le Loi (reigned 1428–33). A trail leads up from the lower temple past Buddha's footprints embedded in the rock to the middle temple and a cave with rock forms. There's also a rock that's said to help choose the sex of a baby. The highlight is a scramble to the peak for glorious views over the area.

Off to Bac Can market to sell corn

Dien Bien Phu

A crushing defeat inflicted on the French forces here in 1954 heralded the collapse of their Indochinese empire. Historic battle sites, a dazzling bronze commemorative statue and war cemeteries mark the event.

THE SIGHTS

Rusting (above), but still proudly proclaiming the 1954 victory

RATINGS

Cultural interest	● ● ●
Historic interest	● ● ● ● ●
Photo stops	● ●
Walkability	● ● ●

BASICS

✚ 282 A2
🏠 Highway 12, near middle of town. Connections with Hanoi, Son La, Lai Chau, Sapa
✈ Airport 1 mile (2km) north; connections with Hanoi
🍴 Near Vietnamese cemetery, market and Airport Hotel; local food
🚗 Private tours from Sapa and Hanoi
www.dienbienphu.org
Official version of the battle and the political background.

TIPS

● Visit the Victory Monument in the late afternoon for the best pictures of the valley and the glowing statue.
● A 15-minute video in the museum uses live footage and a large model to make sense of the battle.

SEEING DIEN BIEN PHU

Dien Bien Phu is a bland, modern town deep in the highlands of northwest Vietnam, close to the border with Laos. Unremarkable though the town may be, its surroundings are impressive. It sits in the Muong Thanh valley, a heart-shaped basin 12 miles (19km) long and 8 miles (13km) wide and crossed by the Nam Yum River. It's a majestic landscape, with Thái stilt houses nestling around the edges of lusciously green paddy fields. The town itself is quite easy to negotiate on foot, but the battlefield sites are well spread out, most to the west of the Nam Yum River, and are best visited by car or by motorcycle.

HIGHLIGHTS

HILL A1

🕐 Daily 7–11, 1.30–6 💵 5,000d ❓ Explanations in Vietnamese only
This small hill, known as Eliane 2 to the French, was the scene of the fiercest fighting of the hostilities of 1954, when it formed the foremost French stronghold in the area. It still holds reminders from the decisive battle in which the Viet Minh forces prevailed, marking the end of French influence in the whole of Indochina. These relics include a bunker and a French tank, or bison, named *Gazelle*. There's also a war memorial, dedicated to the Vietnamese who died on the hill, and nearby is the entrance to a tunnel that was excavated by coal-miners from Hon Gai and ran beneath French positions several hundred yards away. The tunnel was subsequently filled with 2,200lb (1,000kg) of high explosives, which were detonated at 11pm on May 6 1954 as a signal for the final assault. The huge crater that resulted still scars the landscape.

HISTORIC VICTORY EXHIBITION MUSEUM

✉ 7 Thang 5 Street ☎ 023-826298 🕐 Daily 7.30–11, 1.30–4.30 💵 5,000d 📶
❓ All labels in English and French
In the grounds of the Historic Victory Exhibition Museum (**Nha Trung Bay Thang Lich Su Dien Bien Phu**) is a wide collection of assorted Chinese, American and French weapons and artillery, ground vehicles and aircraft. Inside, the museum illustrates national resistance from 1945 to 1953, then goes on to cover the 1954 battle, with a comprehensive range of photographs and illustrations and a display that includes a "packbike" with a carrying capacity of 816 lb (370kg) that was used to support the troops. There are also displays relating to the battle in Hanoi's Museum of the Vietnamese Revolution (▷ 67).

REVOLUTIONARY HEROES' CEMETERY

✉ 7 Thang 5 Street 🕐 Daily 7.30–11, 1.30–4.30 💵 Free
The Revolutionary Heroes' Cemetery (**Nghia Trang Liet Sy Dien Bien Phu**) contains the graves of some 15,000 Vietnamese soldiers killed during the course of the Dien Bien Phu campaign. A large bas-relief runs along its main front wall; look closely and you'll see Ho Chi Minh flanked by Viet Minh General Vo Nguyen Giap to the left and Hoang Van Thai, Giap's deputy, on the right. Sitting next to Hoang Van Thai is Pham Van Dong, who later became premier of North Vietnam.

VICTORY MONUMENT

✉ Off 7 Thang 5 Street

Dien Bien Phu's newest sight towers over the town. The Victory Monument (**Tuong Dai Chien Dien Bien Phu**), erected at a cost of US$2.27 million, is an enormous, 132-ton (120-tonne) bronze sculpture—the largest monument in Vietnam. It was sculpted by former soldier Nguyen Hai, and depicts three Vietnamese soldiers standing on top of General de Castries' Bunker. Engraved on the flag is the motto "Quyet Chien, Quyet Thang" (Determined to Fight, Determined to Win). One of the soldiers carries a Thái child. The work was commissioned to mark the 50th anniversary of the 1954 victory.

GENERAL DE CASTRIES' BUNKER

✉ Off Highway 12 🕐 7–11, 1.30–5 💵 5,000d

The command bunker of French General Christian de Castries has been rebuilt on the site of the battlefield as it would have looked in 1954. Eight of the ten French tanks are scattered over the valley, along with numerous US-made artillery pieces.

BACKGROUND

Settled from an early date, Muong Thanh valley was an important trading post on the caravan route between China and Burma for 2,000 years. Over the centuries many fortifications were constructed in and around Muong Thanh, the best known being the fabled Citadel of the Thirty Thousand (Thanh Tam Van), built during the 15th century. The town of Dien Bien Phu itself came into existence only in 1841 when, in response to continued Lao, Siamese and Chinese banditry in the area, the Nguyen Dynasty ordered the establishment of a royal district governed from a fortified settlement at Muong Thanh. Dien Bien Phu was occupied by French forces during their major northwest campaign of 1888–89, and it was subsequently maintained as a garrison town, with fluctuating fortunes. The last, calamitous battle between the occupying French and the forces of Ho Chi Minh's Viet Minh was waged here from March to May 1954. The French, who under Vichy rule had accepted the authority of the Japanese during World War II, attempted to regain control after the Japanese surrender. Simultaneously, Ho had declared independence on September 2 1945, and after nearly a decade of war the French finally gave up the fight after their catastrophic defeat in the 1954 Battle of Dien Bien Phu.

Immortalized in gold (top)—a monument at the Revolutionary Heroes' Cemetery.
A tank at the Historic Victory Exhibition Museum still looks ready for action (above)

MORE TO SEE

FRENCH WAR MEMORIAL

✉ Off Highway 12

A white obelisk surrounded by a gray concrete wall and black iron gates sits on a bluff overlooking the Nam Yum River near de Castries' command bunker. This is the French War Memorial (**Nghia Trang Phap**), inaugurated on July 5 1994 on the initiative of the French Foreign Legion.

ĐIỆN BIÊN PHU

Trang Dang Ninh

0 — 500 m
0 — 500 yds

7 Thang 5

Tuong Dai Chien (Dien Bien Phu)

Nha Trung Bay Thang Lich Su (Dien Bien Phu)

Muong Thanh 8

Nghia Trang Liet Sy (Dien Bien Phu)

Nghia Trang Phap

Nam Rom

1	Machine Gun Post
2	*Gazelle* (French Tank)
3	Hill A1
4	Crater
5	General de Castries' Bunker
6	Artillery Pieces
7	Tank

Majestic mountains along the Chinese border, near Cao Bang

Hang Kenh communal house is renowned for its carvings

CAO BANG

➕ 283 D1 ℹ️ Phong Lan Hotel, 83 Be Van Dan Street, tel 026-852245; Mon–Fri 7–11.30, 1.30–5 🚌 Kim Dong Street

Cao Bang, set in a narrow valley, has some late-19th-century French buildings. The Exhibition Center (Hoang Nhu Street, tel 026-852616, open Wed, Sat 7.30–11, 2–5) records the fight for independence. Ho Chi Minh's headquarters was at Pac Bo, 35 miles (56km) north of Cao Bang; his old staff car has pride of place at the museum.

CUC PHUONG NATIONAL PARK

➕ 283 C3 ℹ️ Ninh Binh Tourism Administration, Tran Hung Dao Street, Ninh Binh, tel 030-881958. Park office: 030-848006 🎟️ Adult 40,000d, child 20,000d. Rescue Center: 10,000d

This area of deeply cut limestone (**Vuon Quoc Gia Cuc Phuong**) reaches peaks of 2,600ft (800m) and is covered by 54,300 acres (22,000ha) of tropical forest. In April and May the park is cloaked in swarms of green and yellow butterflies. The Endangered Primate Rescue Center (tel 030-848002, daily 9–11.30, 1.30–4) has langurs, lorises and gibbons.

DIEN BIEN PHU

See pages 82–83.

HA GIANG

➕ 282 C1 ℹ️ Tran Hung Dao Street, tel 019-867054; Mon–Fri 7–11.30, 1.30–5 🚌 Nguyen Trai Street

You can get permits here (at the tourist company) to visit the far northern Dong Van-Meo Vac region. Archeological treasures have been unearthed here, and it also saw a flowering of Bronze Age culture—the most beautiful Dong Son bronze drums (▷ 26) originate from and are still made here. There's a daily market.

HAIPHONG

The third-largest city in Vietnam, where a customs house incident triggered the First Indochina War, retains an attractive heart with colonial-style architecture.

➕ 283 D3
ℹ️ 57 Dien Bien Phu Street, tel 031-842432; 15 Le Dai Hanh Street, tel 031-842669; Mon–Fri 7–noon, 1.30–5
🚌 Tam Bac station, connections with Hanoi; Binh station, connections with Bai Chay; Lach Tray station, connections with Do Son
🚢 Central and Long Bien, connections with Hanoi 🚢 Connections with Cat Ba, Hon Gai ✈️ Airport 4 miles (7km) from city; connections with Saigon 🚐 Private tours from Hanoi

RATINGS	
Historic interest	◕ ◕
Walkability	◕ ◕ ◕

TIP

● The streets around the theater support the greatest concentration of food stalls and shops.

In the heart of town, where Tran Hung Dao and Quang Trung streets meet, is the 1904 Great Theater, where, in November 1946, 40 Viet Minh fighters died in a pitched battle with the French. The Haiphong Museum at 66 Dien Bien Phu Street (Tue, Thu 8–10.30am, Wed, Sun 7.30–9.30pm) contains records of the city's turbulent past. On Me Linh Street is the early 20th-century Nghe Pagoda, dedicated to heroine General Le Chan, who fought with the Trung sisters (▷ 27) against the Chinese. The 1672 Du Hang Pagoda, south of the center on Chua Hang Street, contains fine woodcarving, and farther south, at 51 Nguyen Cong Tru Street, is Dinh Hang Kenh, a communal house (*dinh*), built in 1856 and now serving as a temple.

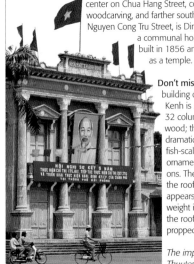

Don't miss The main building of Dinh Hang Kenh is supported by 32 columns of ironwood; the roof is dramatic—decorated in fish-scale style and ornamented with dragons. The corners of the roof turn up and it appears that the sheer weight is too much, as the roof is now propped up with bricks.

The imposing Great Theater (left)

HOA LU

Vietnam's 10th-century capital sits in stunning scenery of rocks towering over rice paddies. Kings once inhabited the now half-ruined citadel of temples.

Hoa Lu was the capital of Vietnam from AD968 to 1010, during the Dinh and early Le dynasties. Its strategic location, in the narrow valley of the Hong River, provided easy defense of passes and views over the northern plains in case of Chinese incursions. Its temple art and architecture is primitive in form and massive in conception, dominated by huge stone carvings of elephants, rhinoceros and horses.

Much of this former capital, which covered more than 494 acres (200ha), has been destroyed, although archeological excavations have revealed a great deal of historical and artistic interest. The two principal temples at Hoa Lu are those of Dinh Bo Linh, who took the title King Dinh Tien Hoang (reigned AD968–80), and Le Hoan, who became King Le Dai Hanh (reigned AD980–1009).

DINH TIEN HOANG

The 11th-century Temple of Dinh Tien Hoang, reconstructed in 1696, is a series of courtyards, gates and buildings. An ancient inscription on one of its pillars—*Dai Co Viet*—is the derivation of the name Vietnam. The back room is dedicated to Dinh Tien Hoang, whose statue occupies the central position. In the AD960s, Dinh Tien Hoang pacified much of the Red River plain, but banditry continued to plague the kingdom. A large kettle and a caged tiger were placed in the palace courtyard, in which law-breakers were to be boiled and gnawed. In the ensuing uneasy calm, Dinh Tien Hoang promoted Buddhism and geomancy, arranged strategic marriages and implemented reforms. But in AD979 his infant son, Hang Lang, made heir to the throne, was killed by his adult son, Dinh Lien, and soon afterward both father and surviving son were killed as they lay drunk in the courtyard. They say the assassin's flesh was fed to the citizens.

LE DAI HANH

The Temple of King Le Dai Hanh is dedicated to the founder of the Le Dynasty, who seized power after the regicide of Dinh Tien Hoang. Le Dai Hanh also took the throne of his wife, Duong Van Nga, and there are representations of her, Le Dai Hanh and Le Ngoa Trieu (Hanh's eldest son), each occupying its own altar, in the rear temple.

Don't miss Next to Dinh Tien Hoang's temple is a small hill, and at the top is Dinh Tien Hoang's tomb, reached via 265 steps.

Heading home (top) after a day in the fields. The Temple of Dinh Tien Hoang (above) is set in a pretty walled garden

RATINGS				
Cultural interest	●	●	●	
Historic interest	●	●	●	●
Walkability	●	●	●	

BASICS

✚ 283 D3

🛈 Tran Hung Dao Road, Ninh Binh, Hoa Lu District, tel 030-881958

💰 15,000d

🚌 Ninh Binh, then car or motorcycle

🍴 At Van Xuan hotel, off Highway 1

📍 4 miles (6km) north of Ninh Binh, 4 miles (6km) west of Highway 1; follow signs to Truong Yen

🚐 Private tours from Ninh Binh and Hanoi

TIPS

● Ninh Binh is the base for visits to Hoa Lu; it has rail connections with Hanoi and Ho Chi Minh City and is served by Open Tour buses.

● Guides are available, but the easiest option is to charter a car and driver.

Halong Bay

Halong is a sparkling, emerald-green bay dotted with sailing junks and thousands of forested limestone towers. Cat Ba, home to the rare white-headed langur, is the largest island in an archipelago of hundreds.

A tourist boat's carved dragon figurehead leads the way

Rock formations in rainbow shades at Hang Dau Go

A peaceful sunset scene on the calm waters of Halong Bay

RATINGS					
Good for kids	●	●	●	●	●
Outdoor pursuits	●	●	●	●	●
Photo stops	●	●	●	●	

BASICS

✚ 283 E3

ℹ Information and Tourist Guide Center, Halong Bay portside, tel 33-824867; Bai Chay Tourist Wharf, tel 33-846592

🚉 Bai Chay station, Halong City; connections with Hanoi

🚢 Haiphong; then bus or ferry

🍴 Range of restaurants in Halong City

🚤 Boat tours from Halong City, Cat Ba Town; tours include caves. Private tours from Hanoi

www.halong.org.vn
Website of the bay's management committee, with comprehensive information on the area.

SEEING HALONG BAY

Spectacular Halong Bay (Vinh Ha Long) and its 3,000 islands cover 580 square miles (1,500sq km), spreading to the Chinese border. At dusk the stars and lights of moored junks ripple across the deep blue water in unearthly silence. There are two bases from which to explore the bay—Halong City or Cat Ba—but many opt for all-inclusive trips from Hanoi, where tourist cafés and operators also offer tours of the bay with one night in Bai Chay. This is the prettier, western side of town (officially Halong City West), which is divided in two by the bay waters. Halong City East is the main port and ferry dock. Full- or half-day trips of the bay can be taken from Cat Ba. The islands of the bay are separated by a broad channel. East are the smaller outcrops of Bai Tu Long, and west are the larger islands, with caves and secluded beaches.

HIGHLIGHTS

CAVES

🎟 All caves 15,000d

Vietnamese poets and artists have long drawn inspiration from the crooked islands, seeing the forms of monks and gods in the rock faces, and dragon's lairs and fairy lakes in the depths of the caves. The more spectacular of these are Hang Hanh, 1 mile (2km) long and full of stalagmites and stalactites. Hang Luon is another flooded cave, which leads to the hollow core in a doughnut-shaped island. It can be swum or navigated by coracle. Hang Dau Go is where a famous Vietnamese general, Tran Hung Dao, stored wooden stakes in 1288, prior to studding them in the bed of the Bach Dang River to destroy a 400-strong Mongol-Chinese invasion fleet (▷ 27). Hang Thien Cung is a hanging cave, a short 165ft (50m) haul above sea level, with dripping stalactites, stumpy stalagmites and solid rock pillars.

CAT BA ISLAND

🚢 Service to Phu Long 🚤 Connections from Haiphong 🍴 In Cat Ba Town

Cat Ba (**Dao Cat Ba**) occupies a stunning setting in the south of Halong Bay. Much of the island and the seas around are designated a

River dwellers' boats (opposite) dot the waters of the main harbor at Cat Ba Island

national park (see below) and, while perhaps not quite teeming with wildlife, it is pleasantly wild and green. Cat Ba's remoteness has been steadily eroded (it only got electricity in 1999) and it is now a handy weekend break for many Hanoians. Despite the growth of karaoke-loving weekenders, it remains an attractive place. Best of all it is a springboard into the surrounding waters of Halong Bay and an increasingly popular alternative to Halong City. Outside the town there are only a few small villages, and perhaps the greatest pleasure is to rent a motorcycle and explore. The islands around Cat Ba are larger than the outcrops of Halong Bay and generally more dramatic.

Brightly painted sailing boats (below) alongside Halong City pier. Tourists can enjoy a cruise of the bay on board a traditional junk (below right)

CAT BA NATIONAL PARK

🕐 Park office: daily 7–5.30 🎫 15,000–25,000d depending on distance covered
📷 Park guide: US$5 for half a day, US$10 for full day. Guide for single (one-way)

trips to sites of interest in the park: 20,000–30,000d depending on distance Roughly half of Cat Ba Island is a national park (**Vuon Quoc Gia Cat Ba**), established in 1986. Of this area a third consists of coast and inland waters. The park is home to 109 bird and animal species, and of particular importance is the world's last remaining troop (about 200) of white-headed langur. These elusive monkeys are rarely spotted, and then only from the sea, as they inhabit wild and remote cliff habitats. There are also several types of rare macaque (rhesus, pig-tailed and red-faced) and moose deer. Vegetation ranges from mangrove swamps in sheltered bays and densely wooded hollows to high, rugged limestone crags sprouting caps of hardy willows. The marine section of the park is no less bountiful; the high economic value of its fish and crustacea populations keeps the local fishing fleet hard at work and prosperous.

ĐAO CÁT BÀ & VINH HA LONG

0   5 km
0   5 miles

BACKGROUND

Halong means "descending dragon," a reference to the enormous beast that is said to have careered into the sea at this point, cutting the bay from the rocks. According to another myth, the islands are dragons, sent by the gods to impede the progress of an invasion flotilla. The area was, in fact, the site of two famous sea battles, in the 10th and 13th centuries (▷ 27). It is now a UNESCO World Heritage Site.

Geologically the tower-karst scenery of Halong Bay is the product of millions of years of chemical action and river erosion working on the limestone to produce a pitted landscape. At the end of the last ice age, when glaciers melted, the sea level rose and inundated the area, turning hills into islands.

Tools and bones indicate that Cat Ba Island was occupied by humans 6,000 to 7,000 years ago. The population is now about 12,000 and is concentrated in the south.

The landscape is enticing on both land (above) and sea (top)

The Top Temple (above) is guarded by stone lions and gaudily painted warriors, which bear close scrutiny (below) for their detail and expressions

RATINGS	
Cultural interest	● ● ●
Historic interest	● ● ● ● ●
Photo stops	● ● ●

BASICS

✚ 283 C2 • 62 miles (100km) north-west of Hanoi 🎫 Free 🚗 Turn off Highway 2 about 7.5 miles (12km) north of Viet Tri, Vinh Phu Province 🚌 Private tours from Hanoi

TIP

● The temples are particularly busy during the Hung Kings' Festival, a two-week celebration on the 10th day of the third lunar month.

HUNG KINGS' TEMPLES

Myth and history intertwine in this striking hillside site. This was an ancient royal capital and, legend has it, the birthplace of the Viet people.

An almost perfectly circular hill rises unexpectedly from the monotonous Red River floodplain, with two lakes at the bottom. This is the legendary home of the Viet people, and the site chosen by the Hung Vuong kings as their capital.

The stories say that the Viet people are the product of the union of King Lac Long Quan, a dragon, and his fairy wife, Au Co, who gave birth to 50 boys and 50 girls. Half the children followed their mother to the highlands and half remained with their father on the plains, giving rise to the Montagnards and lowland peoples of Vietnam. Historically easier to verify is the story of the Hung kings (**Den Hung**), who built a temple in order to commemorate the progenitors of the Vietnamese people.

WHAT TO SEE
The Hung Kings' Museum, at the foot of the hill (daily 8–11.30, 1–4) displays pottery, jewelry, fish hooks, arrowheads and ax heads (dated 1300–1000BC) excavated from the province, as well as bronze drums dating from around the fifth to the third centuries BC.

A track climbs the hill to a memorial to Ho Chi Minh and the Low Temple, dedicated to Au Co, mother of the country. At the back is a statue of the Buddha of a Thousand Arms and a Thousand Eyes. In the Middle Temple, farther uphill, Prince Lang Lieu was crowned seventh Hung king; here, too, kings would play chess and discuss pressing affairs of state. Prince Lang Lieu's most enduring creation is a pair of cakes, *banh trung* and *banh day*, which are still eaten at *Tet* (Vietnamese New Year). Toward the top of the hill is the oath stone on which the 18th Hung king, Thuc Phan, swore to defend the country. The nearby 15th-century Top Temple is adorned with dragons and gaudily painted mural warriors stand guard outside. Smoke rises from burning incense on the three altars where the kings would pray for peace and prosperity.

Steps lead downhill from the rear right to the mausoleum of the sixth Hung king, then continue to the Well Temple, built in memory of the last princess of the Hung Dynasty, who combed her hair using the reflection in the well inside. Today, worshipers throw money in and, it is said, even drink the water.

Flat rice paddies contrast with jagged, rocky hills at Lai Chau

Streetside evidence of Mai Chau's silk-weaving tradition

The glittering altar of the Thien Tru Pagoda, part of Chua Huong

LAC

🛏 Dinner, bed and breakfast at stilt house about 50,000d; dances included in tour packages or small contribution
🚌 Mai Chau; connections from Hanoi
🚐 From Hanoi, private tours, Mon, Wed, Sat, about 315,000d

Lac is the most popular village excursion from Hanoi, so its White Thái residents are used to visitors, and many of the women sell clothing. The hope is that by "sacrificing" one village to tourism the industry's impact will be limited. Income generated by visitors has enabled many valley inhabitants to tile their roofs and buy consumer products such as TVs and motorcycles.

Lac is easily accessible from the main road in Mai Chau, along a track past the People's Committee Guesthouse. You can ask stilt-house residents if you can stay the night, and possibly borrow or rent a bicycle for a ride to nearby hamlets, where you may be offered tea made from tree bark. A dance troop performs most nights, followed by communal drinking of sweet, sticky rice wine from a large pot.

LAI CHAU

✝ 282 A2 🚌 Station several miles from town; connections south with Dien Bien Phu, north and east with Sapa
🚐 Private tours from Hanoi and Sapa

Lai Chau occupies a majestic setting in the deep, wide Da River valley, which is cloaked in dense tiers of forest. In 1993 the status of capital of Lai Chau Province was transferred from Lai Chau town to Dien Bien Phu, partly in recognition of the latter's growing importance as a hub of economic and tourist activity, and partly in deference to the side effects of the massive Son La hydroelectric power scheme being planned for the valley (due for completion in 2010).

The history of Lai Chau is entwined with that of the Black Thái seigneurial family of Deo, who achieved ascendancy by the first half of the 15th century. In 1947, the dynasty's descendant Deo Van Long (a tyrant, remembered with loathing by most older inhabitants) was installed as king of the Thái by the colonial government in return for his allegiance. The ruins of Deo Van Long's House, originally a plush colonial mansion and now overgrown with creeper and strangling figs, lie on Road 127 to Muong Te on the opposite bank of the Da River from High Hill (**Doi Cao**). Some say that before fleeing the country in 1953, Long had all his servants poisoned so they could not inform the advancing Viet Minh forces of his whereabouts. Get there by boat from below High Hill or on a 5-mile (8km) road trip, crossing one especially rickety suspension bridge. At the site beware of loose masonry and deep vaults covered in creepers.

MAI CHAU

✝ 282 C3 • 47 miles (75km) from Hoa Binh 🚌 Connections with Hoa Binh, Hanoi, Son La 🍴 Simple eating places near market 🚐 Private tours from Hanoi Mon, Wed, Sat, about 315,000d

During the first half of the journey from Hoa Binh to Mai Chau, the turtle-shaped roofs of the Muong houses predominate, but after passing Man Duc the road enters the territory of the Thái, Northwest Vietnam's most prolific ethnic minority, heralding a subtle change in the style of stilt-house architecture. While Thái are encountered in great abundance on this circuit, it is the Black Thái subethnic group who are seen most frequently. What makes the Mai Chau area interesting is that it is one of the few places en route where travelers can encounter their White Thái cousins. Some say visits here and to nearby Lac (see above) are a manicured way of encountering village lifestyle without the discomfort, and it is true that Mai Chau, an isolated farming community until 1993, has seen significant change in just a few years. Young Hanoians arrive in large groups at the weekend and appear oblivious to the impact of their presence, sometimes shattering the peace with loud portable music systems. The dignity and elegance of the Thái is all the more evident by contrast, and there is no denying that the beautiful, tranquil valley setting, engaging inhabitants and superb rice wine make this a worthwhile overnight stop.

PERFUME PAGODA

✝ 283 D3 • 37 miles (60km) southwest of Hanoi 🛏 US$7, including boat trip
🚐 Half-day private tours from Hanoi

The Perfume Pagoda (**Chua Huong** or **Chua Huong Tich**), dedicated to Quan Am, the Guardian Spirit of Mother and Child, is one of a number of shrines and towers built among limestone caves in one of Vietnam's most beautiful spots. A sampan takes visitors along the Yen River, a 2.5-mile (4km) ride through a flooded landscape, to the Mountain of the Perfume Traces. From here it is a 2-mile (3km) hike up the mountain to the cool, dark cave containing the Perfume Pagoda. The stone statue of Quan Am in the principal pagoda was carved in 1793 after Tay Son rebels had stolen and melted down its bronze predecessor to make cannon balls. This is a popular pilgrimage spot, particularly during the festival months of March and April.

PHAT DIEM CATHEDRAL

See page 96.

Sapa

Sapa has an alpine grandeur, perched high above the mountain clouds. Buffaloes wander the surrounding valleys where the Hmông minority follow a way of life unchanged for centuries.

Intricately decorated silk hangings on display in Sapa

Some examples of French colonial architecture remain

Rolling clouds keep the plantlife lush on Sapa's hillsides

SEEING SAPA

Sapa enjoys an impressive natural setting, high on a valley slope with Fansipan, Vietnam's tallest mountain at 10,312ft (3,143m), either clearly visible or brooding in the mist, and the clamor and color of ethnic minorities selling their craftwork and clothes. The town's beauty is a little compromised by the new hotels sprouting up everywhere. Certainly none of the more recent ones can compare with the lovely old French buildings—pitched roofs, window shutters and carefully nurtured gardens. While hilly, Sapa is a fairly compact town and is easy to get around on foot, but at least a basic level of fitness is required for all mountain-trekking.
Sapa enjoys warm days and cool evenings in the summer but gets very cold in winter, when snow falls on average every couple of years and settles on the surrounding peaks of the Hoang Lien Son mountains. The wettest months are May through September, with nearly 40in (1,000mm) of rain in July and August alone, the busiest months for Vietnamese visitors. December and January can be pretty miserable with mist, low clouds and low temperatures. The spring blossom is lovely, but even in March and April a fire or heater may be necessary in the evening.

HIGHLIGHTS

SATURDAY MARKET

🕐 Sat 6–6
Hmông, Dao and other minorities come to Sapa's weekly market to trade, and the Hmông, normally very reticent, have been the first to seize the commercial opportunities presented by tourism. They are engaging but persistent vendors of hand-loomed indigo shirts, trousers, skull caps and other handicrafts

Hmông minorities (opposite) congregate in the church at Sapa. Young Hmông women (left) of Sapa wearing traditional clothing

such as little brass and bamboo mouth-harps. The women, their hands stained purple by dye, sit on street corners stitching while they wait for a foreigner who might buy their clothing. Meanwhile, the girls roam in groups, bracelets, earrings and necklaces jingling as they walk, and urge their jewelry on passersby, while the little ones sing *muat mot cai di* ("buy one") to a usually responsive audience of visitors.

DRAGON'S JAW HILL

⊙ Daily 6–6 🎫 Adult 15,000d, child (5–16) 5,000d

There are outstanding views of the town and valley from the top of Dragon's Jaw Hill (**Nui Ham Rong**), immediately above Sapa town center. A path winds its way through a number of interesting limestone outcrops, miniature grottoes, an orchid garden, a peach garden and an ethnic village as it nears the summit.

Black Dao women sell their brightly patterned traditional hats and bags at the roadside

SAPA CHURCH

🕐 Daily 6pm for services, Sat 1.30pm

The slate-gray church that sits in the heart of Sapa was originally built in 1930 but was destroyed just 22 years later during hostilities with the occupying French—a troop of French artillerymen were engaged in shelling the adjacent building, in which Viet Minh troops were billeted.

In the churchyard are the tombs of two former priests, including that of Father Thinh, who was brutally murdered. In 1952, Father Thinh confronted a monk named Giao Linh, who had been discovered having an affair with a nun at the Ta Phin seminary. Giao Linh obviously took great exception to the priest's interference, for shortly after this, when Father Thinh's congregation arrived at Sapa church for Mass one foggy November morning, they discovered his decapitated body lying next to the altar.

Hilltribe girls enjoy a game of pool in Sapa

A selection of temperate fruits are laid out at Sapa's market (left)

Houses are scattered below the cloud-shrouded mountains

LAO CHAI AND TA VAN

➕ 282 B2

A guided round trip of 12 miles (20km), taking in the beautiful scenery along the way, starts by heading out past the Auberge guesthouse in a southeasterly direction. A track leads from the right side of the road down to the valley floor and then across the river by a footbridge, before continuing through the rice fields into the Black Hmông village of Lao Chai. Here you can observe a style of rural life that is led in reasonable prosperity. There is terracing here on an awesome scale, in places with more than 100 steps, the result of centuries of labor to convert the steep slopes into level fields that can be flooded to grow rice. Ta Van, a village of the Zay, is 1 mile (2km) farther on.

BACKGROUND

Originally a Black Hmông settlement, Sapa was first discovered by Europeans when a Jesuit missionary visited the area in 1918 and established an order there. By 1932 news of the quasi-European climate and beautiful scenery of the Tonkinese Alps had spread throughout French Indochina. Like Dalat farther south, Sapa was developed as a retreat for French administrators when the heat of the plains became unbearable. By the 1940s an estimated 300 French buildings—including a prison and the summer residence of the governor of French Indochina—had sprung up, and many parks and flower gardens had been cultivated. During the latter days of French rule the expatriate community steadily dwindled, and by 1953 virtually all had gone.

Immediately after the French were defeated at Dien Bien Phu in May 1954, Vietnamese forces razed a large number of Sapa's French buildings to the ground. More destruction was subsequently wrought by the Chinese, who briefly occupied the town in 1979 before being driven out again.

Since the 1990s, Sapa's population of a little more than 3,000 has been swelled by tourists, attracted by the spectacular mountain scenery, the comfortable climate and the lively weekend market. Their presence brings in much-needed revenue.

TIPS

● Weekends are peak tourist time, but during the week the few visitors who remain have the town to themselves.

● It is not possible to buy walking shoes, backpacks, coats, jackets or any mountaineering equipment in Sapa.

● Tourists wanting to trek around Sapa are no longer allowed to go it alone. Visitors must now have a touring card, sightseeing ticket and a licensed tour guide to trek five permitted routes from Sapa: round trip to Cat Cat and Sin Chai; Cat Cat, Y Linh Ho, Lao Chai and Ta Van; Lao Chai, Ta Van, Ban Ho, Thanh Phu and Nam Cang; Lao Chai, Ta Van, Su Pan and Thanh Kim; Ta Phin, Mong Sen, Takco, and climbing Mount Fansipan.

● It is possible to trek just to Cat Cat without a ticket and a guide. Homestays are permitted in six local villages: Ta Van Giay, Ban Den, Muong Bo, Ta Phin commune central area, Sa Xeng cultural village, and Sin Chai and Topas Eco Lodge. Tour guides who violate these rules will have their licenses withdrawn and tourists who do so will be disciplined, according to the People's Committee of Sapa District.

Gilded cathedral interior (above) and imposing facade (below)

PHAT DIEM CATHEDRAL

➕ 283 D3 • 15 miles (24km) south-west of Ninh Binh in the village of Kim Son ⓘ Tran Hung Dao Road, Ninh Binh, Hoa Lu District, tel 030-881958 🕐 Several services a day ▣ Private tours from Hanoi

The Red River Delta was the first part of the country to be influenced by Western missionaries: Portuguese priests were proselytizing here as early as 1627. Christian influence is still strong despite the mass exodus of Roman Catholics to the south in 1954 and decades of Communist rule. There can be up to half a dozen churches in a coastal province village, every one with packed congregations, and not only on Sundays. Phat Diem Cathedral (**Nha Tho Chanh Toa Phat Diem**) is the most spectacular of the church buildings in the area, partly for its scale but also for its remarkable Asian style. Completed in 1891, it has a belltower in the form of a pagoda, behind which the nave of the cathedral stretches for 243ft (74m), held up by 52 ironwood pillars. At the base of the belltower are two carved stone slabs, placed here so that mandarins could sit and watch the Catholic worshipers.

A suspension bridge crosses the river into Son La

SON LA

Hill villages surround the provincial capital, which is acquiring gleaming new government buildings. Town sites recall the colonial past and walks lead to natural beauty spots.

➕ 282 B2 🚌 Connections with Hanoi, Mai Chau, Hoa Binh, Dien Bien Phu, Lai Chau ✈ Na San Airport, 12 miles (20km) southeast ⓘ Near the bridge, along Tinh Doi Street ▣ Private tours from Hanoi

RATINGS	
Historic interest	●●
Photo stops	●●●
Walkability	●●●

TIPS
● Son La makes a useful stopover between Hanoi and Dien Bien Phu. ● The Son La Provincial Museum (5,000d) is on Bao Tang Tinh Son La, Youth Hill, just off Highway 6 and near the middle of town.

The road to Son La passes several particularly attractive Black Thái and Muong villages, each with a suspension footbridge and hydraulic works. Mini hydroelectric generators on the river supply houses with enough power to run a light or television, and water power is also used to husk and mill rice. Cuc Dua village, 52 miles (84km) from town, is highly photogenic, with a bridge spanning the incised river in which fish traps are set and children swim. Life is set to change for the inhabitants of the valley, which the government plans to flood by damming the Da River, displacing up to 100,000 people by 2010.

IN AND AROUND TOWN

Son La began to develop in the 18th century, and in the 19th century was part of the territory controlled by Deo Van Tri, Black Thái chieftain. In 1888 a French garrison was established here, and in response to subsequent uprisings, the French established detention units, known to the Thái as *huon mut* ("dark houses"), in the area. In 1908 a large penitentiary was built to incarcerate resistance leaders from the northwest and other regions. The Son La Provincial Museum (tel 022-852022, daily 7–11, 1.30–5.30) is, in fact, the town's old French penitentiary, constructed in 1908, damaged in 1909, bombed in 1952, and now partially rebuilt for tourists. The original dungeon and tiny cells, complete with food-serving hatches and leg irons, can be seen, as well as an exhibition relating the history of the place and the key individuals incarcerated here. The first secretary of the Vietnamese Communist Party, Le Duan, was kept here between 1931 and 1933. The Black Thái village of Ban Co and the Coong caves are nearby (▷ 194–195).

A tourist boat drifts into the darkness of Tam Coc caves

TAM COC

283 D3 • 6 miles (10km) south of Ninh Binh, west of Highway 1 Tran Hung Dao Road, Ninh Binh, Hoa Lu District, tel 030-881958 31,500d plus 23,600d for the boat ride Private tours from Hanoi

The highlight of a visit here is an enchanting boat ride up the little Ngo Dong River through the three caves, part of the beehive scenery created by limestone towers. Their exact form varies seasonally; when flooded the channel disappears and some caves may be drowned. In the dry season the shallow river meanders between fields of golden rice. Women punt pitch-and-resin tubs through the tunnels or row with their feet.

The villagers have a rowing rota and supplement their fee by selling visitors embroidery work. On a busy day the scene is like a two-way, nose-to-tail procession, so try to visit early in the day.

THAY PAGODA

283 C2 • 25 miles (40km) south-west of Hanoi in the village of Sai Son Private tours from Hanoi

Thay Pagoda (**Chua Thay**), built in the 11th century, is a tribute to herbalist Dao Hanh, who was from Sai Son village, and who was reputedly reborn as the son of Emperor Le Thanh Tong (reigned 1460–97). The complex, also known as Master's Pagoda, is divided into three: The outer part is used for ceremonies; the middle is a Buddhist temple; and the inner part is dedicated to the herbalist. There are golden-faced Buddhas with lacquered red garments and an array of demons. Water-puppet shows are staged during holidays and festivals in the middle of the pond Dao Hanh built at the front of the pagoda, which is spanned by two 17th-century bridges.

Tam Dao's hillside position attracts many visitors

TAM DAO

This relaxing hill station, developed by the French from 1902, lies high in the Tam Dao mountains north of Hanoi and is reached by a circuitous route. It is an excellent base for walks and birdwatching, and has a cooler climate than the city.

283 C2 • 53 miles (85km) north of Hanoi Tam Dao Tourism, tel 0211-824213; Mon–Fri 7–11.30, 1.30–5 50,000d levied on all visitors' vehicles at check-point on Highway 28 Several, serving local dishes Private tours from Hanoi

The resort of Tam Dao lies within a beautiful mountain range that bears the same name, a chain of three peaks that constitute a natural border between Vinh Phu and Thai Nguyen provinces. Protruding from the clouds, the three peaks are said to resemble the "three islands" of Tam Dao's name.

The former colonial hill station has a stunning location at an altitude of 3,050ft (930m) above sea level, lying in a giant rock bowl seemingly bitten out of the side of the mountain. Steep cliffs soar all around it, thickly clothed in a glorious jungle of trees entangled with lianas; the early morning mists and clouds slowly burn off as the sun rises, and the forest comes alive with the sound of bird song, animal cries and the constant humming of insects. On a good day there are clear views over the plains below. Lost in the overgrowth are colonial remains—crumbling walls, forlorn bridges, rocky balustrades and enticing gateways.

Construction of the town started in 1904. The then governor general resided in an eight-roofed mansion here—the largest villa in the whole of Indochina—and the 130-room Metropole Hotel was busy with a steady stream of expatriates coming to Tam Dao to escape the punishing summer heat of the Red River Delta. Subsequently, the town was almost completely destroyed during the First Indochina War of 1945–54, and now little remains, other than the foundations of old villas and the shell of the old church building (which has now found a new lease on life as the club-house of the Tam Dao Trades Union).

RATINGS				
Historic interest	●	●	●	
Outdoor pursuits	●	●		
Photo stops	●	●	●	●	●

TIPS

● During the summer Tam Dao is a very busy resort, particularly in July, which is high season for the Vietnamese.

● From October through March the weather can become quite cold, and the majority of hotels and restaurants shut for the winter.

CENTRAL VIETNAM

This region has two of the finest cities in Vietnam—the imperial city of Hué and the historic port of Hoi An. Its coast is garlanded with attractive seaside resorts, most notably Nha Trang, Hoi An, Long Hai and Mui Ne, and its hinterland is peppered with cool colonial hill stations.

MAJOR SIGHTS

Distinctive and delicate blooms brighten Bach Ma National Park

BACH MA NATIONAL PARK

➕ 285 E7 • Phu Loc, Thua Tien, Hué
☎ 054-871330 ⏰ Daily 🎫 Adult
10,500d, child (5–16) 5,500d, under-5s
free 🎧 Guides hired for 150,000d a
day. Private tours from Hué, Danang
and Hoi An
www.bachma.vnn.vn/home.htm

CÔNG TY ĐẦU TƯ VÀ PHÁT TRIỂN DU LỊCH THIÊN AN
KHÁCH SẠN
MORIN · BẠCH MÃ
KM 19 ĐỈNH VƯỜN QUỐC GIA BẠCH MÃ
H. PHÚ LỘC T. THỪA THIÊN HUẾ
ĐT : 871188 - FAX : 871177

Bach Ma (**Vuon Quoc Gia Bach
Ma**) was established as a hill
station in 1932, but after the
departure of the French in the
1950s its villas and hotels were
forgotten. The ruins are gradually
being uncovered, and gardens
and ponds cleared, with some of
the ruined villas now serving as
tourist accommodations. In 1991
the Vietnamese government clas-
sified the 54,440-acre
(22,031ha) granite and sandstone area a national park. Trails
lead past cascades, through rhododendron woods and up to the
4,751ft (1,448m) summit, and
wildlife includes buff-cheeked or
white-cheeked gibbon and seven
of the twelve pheasant species
recorded in Vietnam.

BA NA HILL STATION

➕ 285 E7 • 24 miles (38km) west of
Danang 🎫 10,000d per person, 5,000d
per motorcycle 🎧 Private tours from
Hué, Danang and Hoi An 🚻 🍴 🏨

Ba Na is a recently rehabilitated
hill station with cool air and
spectacular views, tucked into
the hillside 4,000ft (1,200m) up
Chua Mountain (**Nui Chua**). It
was founded in 1902 by the
French, whose villas have been
restored and rebuilt; some
accept guests, but the area is fast
being taken over by karaoke bars
and similar establishments.

Local children chill out in a hammock in Buon Tur village

BUON ME THUOT

**A good Central Highlands base for visits to ethnic minority
villages and to a national park, where elephants still
roam and elephant treks are available.**

➕ 287 E10 ℹ️ 3 Phan Chu Trinh
(within grounds of Thang Loi
Hotel), tel 050-852108; Mon–Fri
7–11.30, 1.30–5 ✈️ Pleiku, Dalat,
Nha Trang ❌ Saigon, Danang
🚌 For Buon Juin take Highway 27,
the Dalat road; turn right down a
track just before a sign advising
"Dalat 156km" 🎧 Private tours
from Nha Trang
www.daklaktourist.com

RATINGS				
Cultural interest	●	●	●	● ●
Outdoor pursuits	●	●	●	
Photo stops	●	●	●	

TIPS

● For those on tours there is
little choice as to where to
go, but independent visitors
on motorcycles have a wide
selection of villages to see.
● Do not expect English to be
spoken at any of the villages.

Buon Me Thuot, unofficial
capital of the Central
Highlands, is on the Daklak Plateau at an altitude of about 3,300ft
(1,000m), surrounded by plantations and large numbers of
Montagnards, the ethnic hilltribes. Nearby is Yok Don National
Park (▷ 126), where rare white elephants are said to roam, and
several minority villages where visitors can spend the night.
Coffee has long been the mainstay of the local economy, and the
fortunes of the area are highly dependent on the price of the bean.

The Museum of Cultural Heritage on Nguyen Du Street (daily
7.30–5), in Bao Dai's old palace, contains a limited collection of
clothes, tools and other objects of the various minority groups
that live in the area. In Buon Me Thuot Prison (daily 7.30–5) you
can see guardrooms, watchtowers and the tiny cells where revolutionaries were imprisoned from the 1930s to the 1970s. Serene
Lak Lake, about 31 miles (50km) southeast, is an attraction in its
own right, but all the more compelling for the surrounding
M'nong villages. Early morning mists hang above the calm waters
and mingle with the columns of wood smoke rising from the
longhouses. The Daklak Tourist Company can arrange overnight
stays at the M'nong village of Buon Juin; this is the only way to
watch elephants taking their evening wallow in the cool waters.
The M'nong, who are famed elephant-catchers, number about
50,000 and live in a matriarchal society.

The most interesting Ede village is Buon Tur, 9 miles (15km)
southwest of Buon Me Thuot on Highway 14. Apart from the odd
TV aerial, life is unchanged in this community of 20 stilt houses
and, despite government opposition, Ede is still taught in school.

Dalat

●

This former French hill station in the cool air of the Central Highlands served as a holiday retreat for the last emperor of Vietnam. It is now home to a quirky tree-house hotel and a prolifically artistic monk.

RATINGS	
Historic interest	● ● ●
Photo stops	● ● ● ●
Specialist shopping	● ●

Bao Dai's art deco summer palace (above)

SEEING DALAT

Dalat sits on a plateau in the Central Highlands, at an altitude of almost 5,000ft (1,500m). The town itself, once a French hill station, is centered on a lake—Xuan Huong—amid rolling countryside. To the north are the five volcanic peaks of the Lang Biang mountains, rising to 7,900ft (2,400m), and in the vicinity are forests, waterfalls, and an abundance of orchids, roses and other temperate plant life. There are numerous Honda *ôms* and taxis for getting about, but walking is by far the best way of getting the most out of a visit to the town.

🔲 287 F10

📍 35 Tran Hung Dao Street, tel
063-822317; Mon–Fri 7–11.30, 1.30–5

🚌 Ben Xe Dalat bus station, Nguyen
Thi Khai; Ben Xe Binh bus station, near
Hoa Binh Square. Buses to Saigon, Nha
Trang, Danang, Hué, Hanoi. Served by
Open Tour buses

🚲 Action Dalat, 114 3 Thang 2 Street,
tel 063-826031; Phat Tire Adventures,
73 Truong Cong Dinh Street, tel 063-
829422; An Phu, 7/2 Hai Thuong Street,
tel 063-823631,
Dalat_anphu@yahoo.com; and other
private tour operators operating out of
Dalat

🍴 Restaurants around town serving
Asian, Pacific Rim, Chinese and
Continental food

🍽 Places to eat at Dalat Central
Market, end of Nguyen Thi Minh Khai

www.vietnamtourism.com
Links lead to a short description of
Dalat; the main website is useful and
has information on booking hotels and
tours.

● Rent a motorcycle to get
around the palace and
surrounding countryside.
● Dalat produces some of the
finest handmade silk paintings
in Vietnam, sold all over town.
● The Pasteur Institute on Le
Hong Phong Street was built
to produce vaccines for the
colonial population. Though
small and modest, the yellow-
wash institute, opened in
1935, has a striking design,
made up of a series of cubes
with beveled corners; it's well
worth a visit.

*The modest sitting room (top)
in Bao Dai's Dalat palace*

HIGHLIGHTS

DINH BAO DAI

🔲 103 A2 • Le Hong Phong Street (official name Dinh 3) 🕐 Daily 7am–8pm
💰 5,000d ❓ Visitors must wear covers over their shoes to protect the
wooden floors

Vietnam's last emperor, Bao Dai, who reigned from 1925 to 1945,
had a summer palace about 1 mile (2km) west from the heart of
town. Built on a hill between 1933 and 1938, with magnificent
views on every side, it is art deco in style both inside and out, and is
altogether rather modest for a palace. The stark interior contains little
to indicate this was once the home of an emperor—almost all of Bao
Dai's personal belongings have been removed.

The impressive dining room contains an etched-glass map of
Vietnam, and in the study are Bao Dai's desk, a few personal ornaments and photographs, and a small collection of his books, which
include Shakespeare's comedies, works by Voltaire and the Brontës,
and a copy of the Bible. The emperor's bedroom and bathroom are
open to public scrutiny, and so too is the little terrace that opens out
from his bedroom, where, apparently, on a clear night he would gaze
at the stars. In the family drawing room a commentary explains who
sat on which chair.

According to US reports, by 1952 Bao Dai was receiving an
official stipend of US$4 million per year. A considerable amount of
this was ferreted away in US and Swiss bank accounts, as insurance
against the day when his reign would end. The remainder was spent
on his four private planes, which left little to lavish on his home.
Surrounding the palace are pretty and well-maintained gardens.

CENTRAL VIETNAM DALAT **101**

There is also a hunting lodge on Dinh 1, Hung Vuong, past the Lam Dong Museum (open 7–11.30, 1–4.30), which contains a collection of 1930s furniture and antique telephone switchboards. Although it is by no means sumptuous it does have a feel of authenticity. The gardens are green but somewhat lacking in intimacy. Very few visitors come here, so there's every chance you will have the place to yourself.

MORE TO SEE

DALAT CATHEDRAL

➕ 103 B2 • Tran Phu Street ⚫ Mass: Mon–Sat 5.15am, 5.15pm, Sun 5.15am, 7am, 8.30am, 2.30pm, 4pm

A single-tiered cathedral, constructed between 1931 and the 1940s, with a chicken-shaped weather vane on its turret. The stained-glass windows, with their vivid colors and use of pure, clean lines, were crafted in France by Louis Balmet, the same man who made the windows in Nha Trang and Danang cathedrals, between 1934 and 1940.

COLONIAL VILLAS

➕ 103 B2 • Tran Hung Dao Street

Many of Dalat's large colonial villas are 1930s and 1940s vintage. Some have curved walls and railings and are almost nautical in inspiration; others are more rustic. Perhaps the largest and most impressive is the former residence of the governor general on Tran Hung Dao Street, now the Hotel Dinh 2. Built in the 1930s, it has large, airy rooms and occupies a magnificent position set among mountain pines and overlooking the town.

The surreal facade of the Hang Nga Hotel (above left), and artist-monk Vien Thuc in the Lam Ty Ni Pagoda (above right)

LAM TY NI PAGODA

➕ 103 A2 • 2 Thien My, southwest of town

Lam Ty Ni Pagoda would be unremarkable were it not for the presence of its resident monk, Vien Thuc. He arrived here in 1968, and by 1987 he was finishing work on the gateway that leads up through a garden to the figure of Quan Am, Goddess of Mercy. Vien Thuc's garden was inspired by the classic Japanese garden of tranquility, and he originally called it An Lac Vien (Peace Garden). He has since decided that the name Divine Calmness Bamboo Garden has a better ring to it.

Vien Thuc is a renowned scholar, poet, artist, philosopher, mystic, divine and entrepreneur, but is best known for his paintings, of which, by his own reckoning, there are more than 100,000. This is extremely easy to believe when you wander through the labyrinth of rustic huts and shacks that are tacked on to the back of the temple, their walls lined deep with suspended sheets that bear the simple but distinctive calligraphy that spells out his philosophy: "Living in the present, how beautiful this very moment is"; "Zen painting destroys millennium sorrows"; "The mystique, silence and melody universal of love" and so on.

Vien Thuc personally shows visitors around, with both a mixture of pride in his achievement ("I work very hard") and disarming, self-deprecating modesty, cheerfully chuckling to himself as he goes. His work is widely known at international levels and he has had exhibitions in Paris, New York and the Netherlands as well as on the internet. His paintings and books of poetry are sold at prices that are creeping up all the time.

HANG NGA'S CRAZY HOUSE

➕ 103 A2 • 3 Huynh Thuc Khang Street ☎ 063-822070 ⚫ Art gallery: daily 7–7 🎟 Art gallery: 5,000d

Soviet-trained architect, arty Doctor Dang Viet Nga has, over a period of many years, built up her remarkable hotel in organic fashion. The brightly painted concrete house winds itself around trees—some rooms perch in the bough of a tree, others occupy the gardens, and all resemble scenes taken from the pages of a fairytale book. The fantasy continues within, and guests sleep inside crafted mushrooms, trees and giraffes and sip tea under giant cobwebs. There is a honeymoon room, an ant room and plenty more. Intriguing as it is, though, the hotel is not a particularly comfortable or private place to stay (▷ 242).

BACKGROUND

The city of Dalat was founded in 1897 after the site's discovery by Dr. Alexandre Yersin (▷ 31). A hill station was subsequently established to provide sick soldiers with a cooler climate in which to convalesce. The average temperature up here is around 65°F (18°C), as opposed to an average of up to 95°F (35°C) down in the Delta. By 1935 a railway line had been laid linking Dalat with Saigon, via Phan Rang, and colonials and their families took the opportunity to escape from the stultifying heat of the lowlands. The French built timber-framed houses to remind them of home, and colonial children from all over Indochina were hustled off to the distinguished French schools in Dalat, especially during the summer. In the 1940s it looked very much as if the city was destined to become the administrative capital of French Indochina, and though this never materialized, it retains its over-whelmingly French appearance.

Officially, Dalat is a city, in that it has a cathedral, a university, a research institute (nuclear physics) and a royal history (although neither a long nor a particularly proud one). But in reality it is no more than a large, albeit rather grand, market town. The modern economy of Dalat owes much to the prosperity generated by sales of vegetables and flowers to lowland Vietnam. Tourism also figures in the economy, bringing visitors who are interested in the unique culture of this fascinating place.

XUAN HUONG LAKE

✚ 103 C2

The central Xuan Huong Lake (originally the Grand Lake) was created in 1919 after a small dam was constructed on the Cam Ly River. A road runs all the way round the perimeter of the lake, providing a pleasant and easy bicycle ride.

DALAT RAIL STATION

✚ 103 C2 • Nguyen Trai Street
🕐 Daily 8am–5pm; train leaves when full 💵 78,000d per journey
Dalat's train station was opened in 1938, five years after the completion of the rack-and-pinion track from Saigon, and was closed in 1964. The station is the last in Vietnam to retain its original French art deco architecture—the stained-glass windows remain intact. Its steeply pitched roofs could handle the heaviest of alpine snowfalls, and the waiting room, formerly segregated by race, is in good condition. In 1991, a 4-mile (7km) stretch to the village of Trai Mat, home to the K'Ho ethnic minority, was reopened; a Japanese-built train travels daily here and to the Linh Phuoc Pagoda.

The many-tiered Linh Phuoc Pagoda (left)

1 Hang Nga's Crazy House
2 Da Lat Cathedral
3 Da Lat Rail Station
4 Colonial Villas

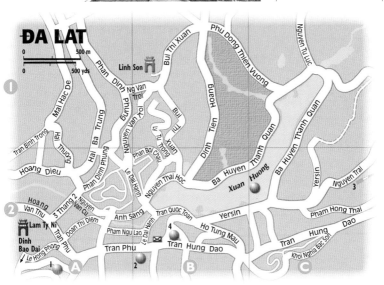

ĐA LAT

Danang

Vietnam's third-largest port has a frenetic buzz and spectacular beaches on its doorstep. Its museum houses glorious sculpture and bas-relief works of the Champa empire in an open-sided French-established institute.

The sands at China Beach (left). Danang's pretty pink and white cathedral (center). Danang, from Marble Mountain (right)

RATINGS

Cultural interest	● ● ●
Historic interest	● ● ●
Outdoor pursuits	● ● ● ●

BASICS

✚ 285 F7

🛈 Danang Tourist Office, 76 Hung Vuong Street, tel 0511-821969; Vietnamtourism, 274 Phan Chu Trinh Street, tel 0511-822990; Mon–Fri 7–11.30, 1.30–5

🚌 Dien Bien Phu Street, 3km (2 miles) from town; connections with all major cities; Hung Vuong Street, connections with Hoi An. Served by Open Tour buses

🚆 Haiphong Street, 1 mile (2km) west of town; connections with Hanoi, Saigon, Hué

✈ Airport 1.5 miles (2.5km) southwest of city

🍴 Seafood, Asian and Western restaurants; several on Bach Dang Street

☕ Cafés and bars on Bach Dang Street

🚗 Cars and guides arranged at Danang Tourist Office. An Phu Tourist Co, 9 Dong Da Street, tel 0511-818366; daily 7–6. Indochina Travel Services, 76 Le Loi Street, tel 0511-828652; daily 8–6

SEEING DANANG

Danang sits on a peninsula at the point where the Han River flows into the South China Sea. The city is ringed by huge two-lane freeways, and new roads have been driven out into the empty spaces beyond, which are quickly being fleshed out with factories, shops and houses. The most important sight in the city itself—the Museum of Champa Sculpture—sits at the southern end of Bach Dang Street, which runs along the eastern edge of the center and is lined with places to stay and eat.

HIGHLIGHTS

MUSEUM OF CHAMPA SCULPTURE

✉ Intersection of Trung Nu Vuong and Bach Dang streets 🕐 Daily 7–5
💵 20,000d 📖 Booklet 10,000d ❓ Limited labels in French and English

Close to Danang are the ruins of My Son (▷ 123), the holiest of the sites of Champa, one of the most glorious kingdoms in Southeast Asia, which reached its apogee in the 10th and 11th centuries. This museum (**Bao Tang Dieu Khac Champa Da Nang**) contains the largest display of Cham art anywhere in the world, and testifies to a lively, creative and long-lived civilization. The first Champa capital, Tra Kieu, was less than 28 miles (45km) from here, but the kingdom's territories extended far afield—other major sites included Dong Duong, Po Nagar and Thap Man and Cha Ban. Each room in the museum is dedicated to work from a different region of Champa, revealing how these parts flowered artistically at varying times from the fourth to the 14th centuries, and illustrating outside influences from Cambodia to Java. Many pieces from My Son illustrate the Hindu trinity: Brahma the Creator, Vishnu the Preserver and Siva the Destroyer. An altar is inscribed with scenes from the wedding story of Sita and Rama from the Hindu epic *Ramayana*. Ganesh, the elephant-headed son of Siva, is well represented here. At the end of the ninth century AD Dong Duong replaced My Son as the focal point of Cham art, and Buddhism became the dominant religion of court, although it never replaced Hinduism. The Dong Duong room is illustrated with scenes from the life of Buddha. From this period faces become less stylistic and bodies more graceful and flowing. The subsequent period of Cham art is known as the late Tra Kieu style. In this section there are apsaras, celestial dancing maidens whose fluid

The Cham museum has superb stone carvings (above and below)

and animated forms are exquisitely captured in stone. Thereafter Cham sculpture went into artistic decline. The Thap Man style (late 11th to early 14th century) sees mythical beasts whose range and style are unknown elsewhere in Southeast Asia. Also in this room is a pedestal encircled by 28 breast motifs, believed to represent Uroba, mythical mother of the Indrapura (My Son, Tra Kieu, Dong Duong) nation.

CHINA BEACH (MY KHE BEACH)

✉ Across Han River Bridge; right then left onto Nguyen Cong Tru Street 🍴
Once a resort celebrated in rock songs, the white sand and surf of China Beach, so popular with American soldiers, is now quiet, with souvenir and food stands. This was a military retreat for GIs during the Vietnam War, but after 1975 it was given the North Vietnamese Army code T20 Beach; locals call it My Khe. The whole area and its hotels, and indeed much of Danang, belong to the Vietnamese Army. This as yet undeveloped spot has clean water (note that at times there is a dangerous cross-current and undertow) and a glorious setting—the hills of Monkey Mountain to the north and the Marble Mountains (▷ 122) to the south.

BACKGROUND

Originally Danang was known as Cua Han (Mouth of the Han River). The French transliterated this as Tourane. In this region lie the ruins of the powerful kingdom of Champa, formed in AD192 and eradicated in 1832, but there are still about 90,000 Cham in central Vietnam. An important port in colonial days, Danang gained worldwide renown when two US Marine battalions landed in March 1965 to secure the airfield. They were the first of many to land in South Vietnam. From the 1990s Danang has seen a whirlwind period of growth, as the new River Han Bridge opens up the Son Tra peninsula for commerce. Its population of more than a million makes it the fourth-largest city in Vietnam.

● Danang is too large to explore on foot, but there are plenty of cyclos, taxis and Honda *ôms*.

● Bicycles and motorcycles are available for rent from most guesthouses and hotels.

● The border with Laos at Lao Bao is open to foreigners; daily buses leave Danang for the Lao town of Savannakhet, on the Mekong. Visas are available from the Laos consulate on Tran Qui Cap Street.

MORE TO SEE

DANANG CATHEDRAL

✉ 156 Tran Phu Street 🕐 Mass: daily 5am, 5pm
This single-spired building with a sugary-pink wash was built in 1923. Its stained-glass windows were made in Grenoble in 1927 by Louis Balmet, who also supplied the windows of Dalat Cathedral (▷ 102).

BAC MY AN BEACH

✉ 1 mile (2km) south of China Beach, 5 miles (8km) from middle of Danang
This is another clean and attractive beach with some seafood stands. Next to it is the Furama Resort (▷ 241), which has facilities for water-based and other sporting activities.

DMZ

A key 1968 Vietnam War battle took place here. The 17th parallel and the Ben Hai River divided Vietnam in two for more than 20 years.

Children pull their boat ashore in the shallows of the Ben Hai River, with Hien Luong Bridge and the (invisible) 17th parallel in the background

RATINGS	
Historic interest	●●●●●
Photo stops	●●
Walkability	●●

BASICS

✚ 284 D6

🛈 Hué Tourist Company, 18 Ly Thuong Kiet, tel 054-821626; Mon–Fri 7–11.30, 1.30–5

🚃 Khe Sanh, 2 miles (3km) from site of US base; connections with Hué (An Hoa station)

🚐 Private tours from Hué

SEEING THE DMZ

The incongruously named Demilitarized Zone (DMZ) saw some of the fiercest fighting of the Vietnam War. It covers a 3-mile (5km) strip on each side of the Ben Hai River and the 17th parallel, the one-time boundary between the Communist north and the capitalist south (see Background, ► 107). Sites are scattered around Dong Ha, north of Hué. Highway 9 branches off the main coastal Highway 1 toward the Laos border, passing Khe Sanh (now officially called Huong Hoa), one of the most evocative names associated with American involvement in Vietnam. Close to Khe Sanh are parts of the famous Ho Chi Minh Trail, along which supplies were ferried from the north to the south.

HIGHLIGHTS

TACON MILITARY BASE

✉ Along Highway 9, 2 miles (3km) from Khe Sanh village ⏰ Daily 9–5
💵 25,000d

Khe Sanh (**Huong Hoa**) is the site of one of the most famous battles of the Vietnam War. The remains of the Tacon military base, amid a coffee plantation, have been converted into a museum. In its grounds are a Chinook, an M41 tank and Viet Cong equipment. Dog tags and ID cards of US soldiers are exhibited along with pictures of the battle.

HO CHI MINH TRAIL

The labyrinth of jungle paths used by troops and porters is a popular but inevitably disappointing sight, given that its whole purpose was to be as inconspicuous as possible. Anything you see was designed to be invisible—from the air, at least. Every day up to 60 tons (54 tonnes) of supplies were carried along these lines, on foot, on ponies or on bicycles. The paths were also used to send soldiers and reinforcements, and as many as 200,000 troops made their way from Hanoi every month. The more the trail was used, the easier progress was, and by 1970 the journey from North Vietnam to Saigon, which had previously taken several months, could be completed in six weeks. Repeated American bombing of the trail failed to disrupt the flow of supplies, but disease was a serious problem, with some 10 percent of the porters falling victim to malaria and other sickness.

ROCK PILE

✉ Off Highway 9 on the road to Laos

This 755ft (230m) limestone outcrop was a US observation post in a severely contested zone, and troops, ammunition and beer all had to be helicoptered in to its apparently unassailable position. However, the sheer walls were eventually scaled by the Viet Cong.

TIPS
● Don't expect to see many sites: The area is still desolate and is mainly of historical interest only.
● Most tours of the DMZ include Khe Sanh and the Vinh Moc Tunnels.
● The Hien Luong Bridge on the 17th parallel marked the boundary between North and South Vietnam. A stone memorial at the river bridge sits in a lotus pond.

VINH MOC TUNNELS

✉ 13km (8 miles) off Highway 4 miles (6.5km) north of Ben Hai River; turn right in Ho Xa village 🎟 25,000d

Families in the heavily bombed village of Vinh Moc dug themselves shelters beneath their houses between 1965 and 1966, and eventually formed a network of interconnecting tunnels. Later the tunnels developed a more offensive role when Viet Cong soldiers fought from them, and they served a similar function to the better known Cu Chi Tunnels (▷ 149). About 5,500ft (1,700m) of the tunnels remain. Offshore is Con Co Island, an important supply depot and anti-aircraft stronghold in the war.

The Rock Pile (left), clothed in thick vegetation. The Vinh Moc Tunnels (center) can be claustrophobic. A Chinook helicopter, a relic of the war, at Khe Sanh's museum

BACKGROUND

The DMZ was the creation of the 1954 Geneva Peace Accords, marking the armistice between Ho Chi Minh's forces and the French. Although the zone divided the country into two spheres of influence, this was always intended to be a temporary measure. However, the nationwide elections that were planned for July 1956 never took place. The boundary evolved into a national border, separating the Democratic Republic of Vietnam in the north from the Republic of Vietnam in the south. The border remained in force until reunification in 1976.

On January 2 1968, a North Vietnamese regimental commander was killed while surveying the base at Khe Sanh and the American high command concluded that the North Vietnamese Army (NVA) was planning a major assault. Special forces long-range patrols were dropped into the area around the base and photo reconnaissance was increased. It subsequently became clear that between 20,000 and 40,000 NVA troops were converging on Khe Sanh. The US Marines were surrounded in a place the assistant commander of the 3rd Marine Division referred to as "not really anywhere," and there followed a heavy exchange of fire, during which B-52s carpet-bombed the surrounding area. The 77-day siege cost many thousands of lives, but the attack on Khe Sanh was merely a diversionary tactic, designed to draw US forces away from the cities. On February 1, 84,000 Communist troops simultaneously attacked 105 urban centers in the Tet Offensive, taking the US and South Vietnam completely by surprise.

Old shell cases, in plentiful supply, have more peaceful uses these days

Hoi An

●

Low-slung houses, shops and temples crowd the streets of this ancient mercantile town. At this center of the clothes trade, hundreds of tailors sew gowns, suits, bags and shoes in silks and cottons for fashion emporiums across town.

The Japanese Covered Bridge curves gracefully over the Thu Bon

RATINGS					
Cultural interest	●	●	●	●	●
Historic interest	●	●	●	●	●
Photo stops	●	●	●	●	●
Specialist shopping	●	●	●	●	●

This image of a monkey deity (below) is in a shrine at the Japanese Covered Bridge. Children sit astride a cannon (opposite) in the Hoi An museum

SEEING HOI AN

Hoi An's tranquil riverside setting, its diminutive scale (you can touch the roofs of many houses), its friendly and welcoming people and its wide array of shops and galleries have made it one of the most popular destinations for foreigners. The town is divided into five quarters, or *bangs*, each of which would traditionally have had its own pagoda and supported one Chinese clan group. Most of Hoi An's more attractive buildings and assembly halls (known as *hoi quan*) are found either on or just off Tran Phu Street. Tran Phu stretches west to east from the Japanese Covered Bridge to the market, running parallel to the Thu Bon River, where boat rides are available.

HIGHLIGHTS

JAPANESE COVERED BRIDGE

✚ 110 A1 • West end of Tran Phu Street 🖐 1 token; keep ticket to get back
Hoi An's most famous landmark is the covered bridge variously known as the Pagoda Bridge, the Faraway People's Bridge and, popularly, as the Japanese Covered Bridge (**Cau Nhat Ban**). Its popular name reflects a long-standing belief that it was built by the Japanese, although no documentary evidence exists to support this. It was built in the 16th century, perhaps even earlier. On its north side there is a pagoda, Japanese in style, for the protection of sailors. Statues represent two dogs at the west end, and two monkeys at the east; it is said that the bridge was begun in the year of the monkey and finished in the year of the dog. Scholars have pointed out that this would mean a two-year period of construction, an inordinately long time for such a small bridge, and maintain that the two animals represent points of the compass, WSW (monkey) and NW (dog). Father Benigne Vachet, a missionary who lived in Hoi An between 1673 and 1683, noted in his memoirs that the bridge was the haunt of beggars and fortune-tellers hoping to benefit from the stream of people crossing over it.

ASSEMBLY HALLS

✚ 110 A1–111 D1 • Tran Phu Street, east of Japanese Covered Bridge 🕐 Daily 7.30–6 🖐 1 assembly hall token per hall, unless free entry noted
Chinese traders in Hoi An (as elsewhere in Southeast Asia) established self-governing dialect associations, or clan houses, which owned their own schools, cemeteries, hospitals and temples. A clan house (*hoi quan*) may be dedicated to a god or an illustrious individual and may contain a temple, but is not itself a place of worship. There are five *hoi quan* in Hoi An, four for use by people of specific ethnicities—Fukien, Cantonese, Hainan, Chaozhou—and the fifth for use by any visiting Chinese sailors or merchants.
  Merchants from Guangdong would meet at the Cantonese Assembly Hall, or **Quang Dong Hoi Quan**, built in 1786 and dedicated to Quan Cong, a Han Chinese general. Fine embroidered hangings decorate the hall, which is set in a cool, tree-filled compound. Next is the All Chinese Assembly Hall (free), or **Ngu Bang Hoi Quan**, sometimes referred to as Chua Ba (Goddess Temple). Unusually for an assembly hall, this was a mutual aid society open to

any Chinese trader or seaman, regardless of dialect or region of origin. The hall helped shipwrecked and sick sailors and performed burial rites for merchants with no relatives in Hoi An. Built in 1773 as a meeting place for all five groups (the four listed above plus Hakka) and for those with no clan house of their own, it now contains a Chinese school, Truong Le Nghia, where children of the diaspora learn the language of their forebears.

The Fukien Assembly Hall, or **Phuc Kien Hoi Quan**, was founded around 1690 and served Hoi An's largest Chinese ethnic group, those from Fukien. Thien Hau, goddess of the sea and protector of sailors, is the central figure on the main altar, clothed in gilded robes; together with her assistants, she hears the cries of drowning sailors. On the right of the temple entrance is a mural depicting Thien Hau rescuing a sinking vessel. Behind the main altar a second sanctuary houses the image of Van Thien,

The splendidly renovated Fukien Assembly Hall in Hoi An

who blesses the lives of pregnant women's unborn children.

The Hainan Assembly Hall, or **Hai Nam Hoi Quan** (free), was founded in 1883 in memory of more than 100 sailors and passengers who were killed when three ships were plundered by an admiral in Emperor Tu Duc's navy. In his defense the Admiral claimed the victims were pirates, and some sources maintain he even had the ships painted black to strengthen his case. At night the building is illuminated by a man selling lanterns inside the pagoda gates.

Exquisite woodcarving is the highlight of the Chaozhou Assembly Hall, or **Trieu Chau Hoi Quen**, on Nguyen Duy Hieu Street. The altar and its panels depict images from the sea and women from the Beijing court, presumably intended to console homesick traders. Walk into the courtyard, turn around and look up at the two dragons and, below them, beautifully carved phoenix with multicolored tails and feathers.

TAN KY HOUSE

✚ 111 B2 • 101 Nguyen Thai Hoc Street
🕐 Daily 7.30–6 🎟 1 house token

This merchant house was the first to be given special recognition by the Ministry of Culture. It dates from the late 18th century and was built from jackfruit timber by the Tan Ky family. The family had originally arrived in Hoi An from China 200 years earlier, and the building reflects not only the prosperity they had acquired (by trading in silk, rice, beans, cinnamon, apple, areca nut and betel) but also the architecture of the houses of their Japanese and Vietnamese neighbors, whose styles had worked their influence on the younger family members. The interior is intact; all the furniture is mahogany and inlaid with mother-of-pearl. Seven generations have lived there; the fifth-generation member is the owner.

BASICS

✚ 285 F7
ℹ 12 Phan Chu Trinh Street, tel 0510-861276; daily 6am–7pm
🎟 75,000d; available from tourist office. Valid 1 day. Includes tokens for one museum, one old house, one assembly hall, concert, handicraft workshop, and either Japanese Covered Bridge or Quan Cong's temple. Separate ticket necessary for further sites
🚌 Hoi An Tourist, 6 Tran Hung Dao Street, tel 0510-862224, www.anphutravel.com; An Phu Tourist, 29 Phan Dinh Phung Street, tel 0510-862643, www.anphutouristhoian.com
🍴 Wide range of restaurants of a high standard, specializing in seafood; several on Bach Dang Street
🚍 0.6 mile (1km) west of town; connections with Danang
✈ Danang

www.hoianworldheritage.org
Thorough coverage of the town's sights, history, events and community, plus map and advice for tourists.

ONG HOI AN PAGODA

✚ 111 C1 • 24 Tran Phu Street

The Ong Hoi An Pagoda is in fact two interlinked pagodas built back-to-back: **Chua Quan Cong** and, behind that, **Chua Quan Am**. Their date of construction is not known, although both certainly existed in 1653. In 1824, Emperor Minh Mang made a donation of 300 *luong* (1 *luong* being equivalent to 1.5oz/42g of silver) for the maintenance of the pagodas, which are dedicated to Quan Cong, the God of War and Soldiers, and Quan Am, the Goddess of Mercy, respectively. The brightly painted crimson doors, decorated with serpentine fire-breathing dragons, are particularly striking.

TRAN FAMILY TEMPLE

✚ 111 B1 • Junction of Le Loi and Phan Chu Trinh streets ⊙ Daily 7.30–6
🔖 1 house token

Chinese and Japanese styles are fused in this building, which was built by the Chinese mandarin Tran in 1802 and has been owned by the Tran family for 15 generations. The current generation has no son, which means that the lineage has been broken. The temple is entered through a shady and luxuriant courtyard and is roofed with heavy yin-yang tiling, which requires strong roof beams; these are held up by a triple-beamed support in the Japanese style (seen in the roof of the Japanese Covered Bridge). Some beams have Chinese-inspired, ornately carved dragons. The outer doors are Japanese, the inner Chinese. On a central altar rest small wooden memorial boxes that contain the photograph or likeness of the deceased together with biographical details. Beyond, at the back of the house, is a small, raised Chinese herb, spice and flower garden with a row of bonsai trees.

As in all Hoi An's family houses, guests are received warmly and courteously and served lotus tea and dried coconut.

PHUNG HUNG HOUSE

✚ 110 A1 • 4 Nguyen Thi Minh Khai ⊙ Daily 7.30–6 🔖 1 house token

Just east of the Japanese Covered Bridge is this 200-year-old house which has been in the same family for eight generations. It presents an eclectic mix of Chinese-style balcony and Japanese-style roof, and is supported by 80 columns of ironwood, which stand on marble pedestals. During the floods of 1964, Phung Hung House became home to 160 locals who camped upstairs for three days as the water rose to a height of 8ft (2.5m).

TIPS	

● If you visit the handicraft workshop at 10am or 3pm, the music show is free.
● Hoi An itself is best explored on foot, but for venturing farther, hotels have two- and four-wheel vehicles to rent.
● On the 14th day of every lunar month, Chinese silk lanterns are hung in town and entertainment is laid on among the houses and streets.

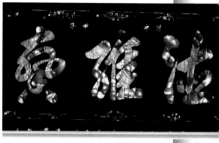

Inlay detail from an old chest in the Tan Ky House

1 Art Galleries
2 Silk Workshop
3 Handicrafts Workshop

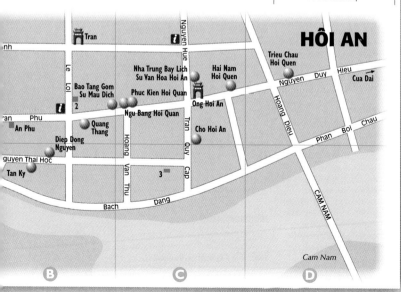

Distinctly oriental in style, the Tan Ky House (right) was built by Chinese traders. A Hoi An market trader (below) is entertained by her young son, wearing a Chinese mask

MORE TO SEE

QUANG THANG
✚ 111 B1 • 77 Tran Phu Street
🎫 1 house token
A Chinese captain built this house in the early 18th century; it was subsequently used as a shop and a residence. There are pictures of the current owner's ancestors on the walls.

FRENCH HOUSE
✉ 25 Bach Dang Street 🕐 No set hours 🎫 Tip appreciated
This example of a colonial building in the small French quarter was built in 1887 and has belonged to the same family for four generations. It has very high ceilings, mahogany French chairs and an ebony bed. The French-speaking owner is happy to discuss his family's history as well as his country's.

HOI AN MARKET
✚ 111 C1 • Between Tran Phu and Bach Dang streets 🕐 Daily
At the northern, Tran Phu Street end, Hoi An's market (**Cho Hoi An**) is covered, and sells mostly dry goods. Cloth merchants and seamstresses will produce made-to-measure shirts here in a few hours. The southern, river side is the local fish market, which comes alive from 5am to 6am as boats arrive with the night's catch.

HOI AN MUSEUM OF HISTORY AND CULTURE
✚ 111 C1 • 7 Nguyen Hue Street 🕐 Daily 8–8 🎫 1 museum token
A former pagoda houses this museum (**Nha Trung Bay Lich Su Van Hoa Hoi An**), which sets the town in its trading context, including sections on all the main cultural influences. Most interesting are the photographs of old Hoi An between the 1930s and the 1990s, and displays of ornamentation depicting watchful eyes, often incorporating the yin-yang symbol, which are believed to ward off evil spirits.

MUSEUM OF TRADE CERAMICS
✚ 111 B1 • 80 Tran Phu Street 🕐 Daily 7.30–6 🎫 1 museum token
The ceramics museum (**Bao Tang Gom Su Mau Dich**), established with financial and technical support from Japan, contains an interesting range of ancient wares, some of them removed from shipwrecks in surrounding waters. There are also detailed architectural drawings of various houses in Hoi An. Upstairs, from the front balcony, there is a superb roofscape view.

MUSEUM OF SA HUYNH CULTURE
✚ 110 A1 • 149 Tran Phu Street 🕐 Daily 7.30–6 🎫 1 museum token
Housed in an attractive colonial-era building, this museum (**Bao Tang Van Hoa Sa Huynh**) contains a modest collection, mostly of pottery, unearthed in 1989 at Sa Huynh, 75 miles (120km) south of Hoi An. The objects, dating from around 200BC, are especially significant because they have called into question the previous theory that the only cultures native to Central Vietnam were the Cham and the Viet.

CUA DAI BEACH
✚ 111 D1 • 2 miles (4km) from Hoi An, east down Tran Hung Dao Street
A few beachfront cafés line this beautiful 2-mile (3km) stretch of white sand. On a clear day the seven islands of the Cham archipelago, 8 miles (15km) offshore, are visible.

BACKGROUND
The ancient town of Hoi An (formerly Faifo) lies on the banks of the Thu Bon River. During its heyday 200 years ago, when trade with China and Japan flourished, Hoi An became a prosperous little port. Much of the merchants' wealth was spent on family

French colonial architecture in Hoi An

chapels and Chinese clan houses, which remain little altered today. Hoi An is now seeing a late but much deserved revival. The river may be too shallow for shipping but it is perfect for tourist boats; the silk merchants may not export any goods, but all they can make leaves town on the backs of satisfied customers.

The Chinese, along with some Japanese, settled here in the 16th century and controlled trade between the islands of Southeast Asia, East Asia (China and Japan) and India. Portuguese and Dutch vessels also docked at the port. During the Tay Son rebellion (1771–88; ▷ 29), the town was almost totally destroyed, although this is not apparent to the visitor. By the end of the 19th century the Thu Bon River had started to silt up and Hoi An was gradually eclipsed by Danang as the most important port of the area. Hoi An has recently emerged as one of the most popular tourist destinations in Vietnam.

A young Vietnamese boy gets a ride in an improvised boat

MORE TO SEE
DIEP DONG NGUYEN HOUSE
✚ 111 B2 • 80 Nguyen Thai Hoc Street
🕓 Daily 7.30–6 🎫 Free
This house, with two Chinese lanterns hanging outside, was once a Chinese dispensary. The owner is friendly and hospitable, and shows visitors around with pride. He has a beautifully painted doorway, decorated with Chinese characters.

Hué

For more than a century the emperors of the Nguyen Dynasty lived here in the now war-damaged Imperial City. This serene city on the beautiful Perfume River has since been given UNESCO World Heritage Site status.

RATINGS

Cultural interest	●●●●●
Historic interest	●●●●●
Photo stops	●●●●●

BASICS

✚ 285 E6

🛈 5 Ly Thuong Kiet Street, tel 054-823577; Mon–Fri 7–11.30, 1.30–5

🚂 An Cuu station, 43 Hung Vuong Street; connections with Saigon. An Hoa station, northwest corner of citadel; connections with Hanoi. Don Ba station, Tran Hung Dao; connections with local villages and Thuan An Beach. Served by Open Tour buses

🚌 Le Loi Street; connections with Saigon and Hanoi

✈ Phu Bai Airport south of city; connections with Saigon, Danang and Hanoi

🚐 There are numerous private tour operators in town

🍴 Wide range, serving Western and local food

🛍 Several on Hung Vuong Street

SEEING HUÉ

Hué straddles the Perfume River (Song Huong), 10 miles (16km) inland of the South China Sea and 62 miles (100km) south of the 17th parallel. On the western bank is the vast Imperial City, which housed generations of the country's emperors, and inside this complex is the Purple Forbidden City, the private imperial enclosure. Running along the northwestern edge of the Imperial City is the Dong Ba Canal, lined by a commercial district, and beyond the canal are the suburbs of Phu Cat and Phu Hiep, where there are several Chinese pagodas. Hué city itself spreads out from the eastern bank of the river, and to the south of it are the Imperial Tombs (▷ 118–121). Much of Hué is easily negotiated on foot.

HIGHLIGHTS

IMPERIAL CITY

✚ 117 A1 ⓞ Summer daily 6.30–5.30; winter daily 7–5 💵 55,000d 🚌 90-min tours in English, French, Japanese

Four outer walls, 23–33ft (7–10m) thick, enclose the Imperial City **(Kinh Thanh)**, surrounded by ditches and canals and pierced with towers and 10 gates. Emperor Gia Long (reigned 1802–20) began its construction in 1804, enclosing the land of eight villages and covering 2 square miles (6sq km). It took 20,000 men to construct the walls alone. Chinese custom decreed that the palace should face south, and this is the direction from which visitors approach. Massive 16ft (5m) cannon are grouped just inside the outer wall gates, four through the Hien Nhon Gate and five through the Chuong Duc Gate. These are the Nine Holy Cannon **(Cuu Vi Than Cong)**, cast in 1803 from bronzeware seized from the Tay Son revolutionaries.

To the north, over one of three bridges spanning a second ditch, is the Royal Gate, Ngo Mon (1), built in 1833 during the reign of Emperor Minh Mang (reigned 1820–40) and surmounted by a pavilion where the emperor would view palace ceremonies. Of the five entrances, this one was opened only for the emperor.

Farther north is the Golden Water Bridge (2), again reserved solely for the emperor, and set between two tanks (3) lined with laterite blocks. This bridge leads to the Great Rites Courtyard, Dai Trieu Nghi (4), on the north side of which is the Palace of Supreme Harmony (Thai Hoa Palace), used for Gia Long's coronation in 1806. Here, sitting on his golden throne, the emperor received visitors on ceremonial occasions. The 18 stone stelae in front of the palace stipulate the correct ranking of officials standing in the Great Rites Courtyard. Only royal princes were allowed to stand in the palace itself, which is perhaps the best-preserved building in the complex, with restored red and gold columns, a tiled floor and a fine ceiling.

The Purple Forbidden City, within the Imperial City (main picture). The intricately carved gateway into the Forbidden City (far left, top). Nine bronze urns, known as Cuu Dinh, which stand outside the Forbidden City (far left, bottom). Visitors admire the elaborate decoration on one of the bronze urns (above)

HUÊ IMPERIAL CITY PLAN

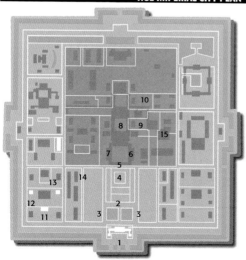

1. Royal Gate (Ngo Mon)
2. Golden Water Bridge
3. Laterite-lined Tanks
4. Great Rites Courtyard (Dai Trieu Nghi) & Palace of Supreme Harmony (Thai Hoa Palace)
5. Red Gate
6. Ta Pavilion
7. Huu Vu Pavilion
8. Central Pavilion, private apartments of the Emperor
9. Quang Minh Palace
10. Royal Reading Pavilion
11. Hien Lam Cac
12. Nine Bronze Urns
13. Thê Temple
14. Waiting Pavilion (Huu Ta Dai Lam Vien)
15. Royal (East) Theater

▮ Purple Forbidden City (Tu Cam Thanh)

CHURCH OF MOTHER OF PERPETUAL HELP

✚ 117 C3 • Nguyen Khuyen Street

🕐 Mass: Sun 8am

This three-story, octagonal steel tower is 174ft (53m) high and an attractive blend of Asian and European styles. It was completed in 1962, and marble from the Marble Mountain in Danang was used for the altar. The church lies at the junction of Nguyen Hue and Nguyen Khuyen streets.

The Thien Mu Pagoda (above). A design in the Purple Forbidden City's Royal Reading Room (inset, above). Young monks practicing martial arts (bottom)

THANH TOAN BRIDGE

✚ Off 117 C2 • 5 miles (8km) east of Hué

Thanh Toan Covered Bridge was built in the reign of King Le Hien Tong (1740–86) by Tran Thi Dao, a childless woman hoping to be blessed with a baby in return for her charity. The bridge, with its shelter for the tired and homeless, attracted the interest of several kings, who granted the village immunity from taxes. The original yin-yang tiles have been replaced with green enameled tube tiles, but the structure is still in good condition, though no longer in use.

Next comes the Purple Forbidden City (Tu Cam Thanh), surrounded by walls 1m (3ft) thick. Following its almost complete destruction during the 1968 Tet Offensive, only two mandarin palaces and the rebuilt Royal Reading Pavilion (10) still stand.

Beyond the Palace of Supreme Harmony two enormous bronze urns (Vac Dong), weighing about 3,300 lb (1,500kg) each, flank the Ta (6) and Huu Vu (7) pavilions—one converted into a souvenir shop, the other a mock throne room. At the southwest corner is the well-preserved Hien Lam Cac (11), a pavilion built in 1821, in front of which stand nine massive bronze urns (12) cast between 1835 and 1837. The central, largest and most ornate urn is dedicated to the founder of the empire, Emperor Gia Long. Next to the urns is the Temple of Generations, Thé Temple (13), built in 1821 and housing altars honoring 10 of the emperors of the Nguyen Dynasty (Duc Duc and Hiep Hoa are missing).

HUÉ MUSEUM OF ROYAL FINE ARTS

✚ 117 A1 • 3 Le Truc Street 🕐 Oct 15–Apr 13 Tue–Sun 7–5; Apr 14–Oct 14 Tue–Sun 7–5.30

💰 22,000d ❓ No cameras or camcorders; over-shoes must be worn; labeling in English

Housed in the Long An Palace (built 1845), the museum contains a collection of ceramics, furniture and bronzeware. In the front courtyard are stone mandarins, can-non, gongs and giant bells. The elegant building itself was commissioned by Emperor Thieu Tri (reigned 1841–47) in 1845, and was dis-mantled and erected on its present site in 1909. Highlights include the imperial sedan chair, covered in red and gold dragons; a beautiful, wooden divan inlaid with mother-of-pearl in a floral design; and the cloth bags used for holding betel and areca belonging to Empress Mother Doan Huy, wife of Emperor Khai Dinh. One of the ceremonial gowns on display is emblazoned with dragons rising out of a swollen sea in a riot of red, gold and green sequins.

THIEN MU PAGODA

✚ 117 A2 • North bank of Perfume River, 2.5 miles (4km) upstream of city

Hué's finest pagoda was built in 1601 by Nguyen Hoang, the governor of Hué, after an old woman appeared to him and told him of the site's supernatural significance. Five Buddhist monks and seven novices still live here. The seven-level Happiness and Grace Tower (Phuoc Duyen), built by Emperor Thieu Tri in 1844, is 69ft (21m) high, each floor housing an altar to a different Buddha. Its summit is crowned with a water pitcher to catch the rain (water represents the source of happiness). Arranged around the tower are four smaller buildings, one of which contains the Great Bell, cast in 1710 under the orders of the Nguyen Lord Nguyen Phuc Chu and weighing 4,850 lb (2,200kg). Beneath another of these surrounding pavilions is a monstrous marble turtle on which an 8.5ft-high (2.6m) stela recounts the development of Buddhism in Hué. The pagoda entrance, beyond the tower, is via a triple gateway patrolled by six carved and vividly painted guardians. The roof of the sanctuary itself is decorated with Jataka stories, which relate the previous lives of the Buddha. At the front of the sanctuary are a brass, laughing Buddha, an assortment of gilded Buddhas, and a crescent-shaped gong cast in 1677 by Jean de la Croix.

The first monk to commit self-immolation, Thich Quang Duc (▷ 35), came from this pagoda; the gray Austin car in which he drove to Saigon is kept in a garage in the temple garden.

HO QUYEN

✚ 117 A3 • South bank of Perfume River, 2.5 miles (4km) upstream of Hué, 2 miles (3km) west of rail station on Bui Thi Xuan Street; turn left up paved track

Ho Quyen is an amphitheater built in 1830 by Emperor Minh Mang as a venue for the popular staged confrontations between elephants and tigers. This royal sport had previously taken place on a river island or on the river banks, but by 1830 this was considered too risky for

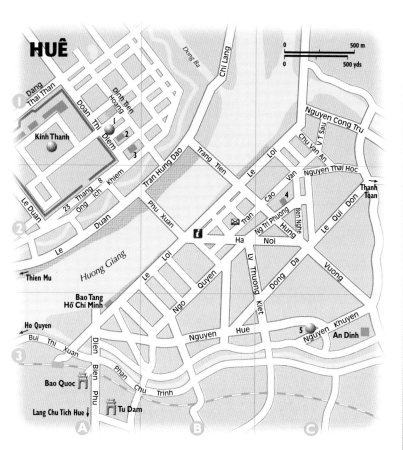

HUÊ

1	Hué Museum of Royal Fine Arts
2	Royal College
3	Military Museum
4	Vietnam Airlines
5	Church of Mother of Perpetual Help

the royal party. The amphitheater was last used in 1904 when, as was usual, the elephant emerged victorious: "The elephant rushed ahead and pressed the tiger to the wall with all the force he could gain. Then he raised his head, threw the enemy to the ground and smashed him to death," wrote Crosbie Garstin, in *The Dragon and the Lotus* (1928). Ho Quyen's walls are 16ft (5m) high and the arena is 144ft (44m) in diameter. At the south side, beneath the royal box, is a large gateway for the elephant; to the north are five smaller entrances for the tigers.

BACKGROUND

Hué was capital of Vietnam in the Nguyen Dynasty (1802–1945). To link the north and south parts of their domains—more than 930 miles (1,500km) of territory—the Nguyen emperors built the Mandarin Road (Quan Lo), interspersed with relay stations. Even in 1802, when the road was not yet complete, it took couriers just 13 days to travel between Hué and Saigon, and five days between Hué and Hanoi. If they arrived more than two days late, they were flogged. Although the Confucian bureaucracy and some of the dynasty's technical achievements were remarkable, there was continual discontent and rebellion against the Nguyen emperors. In 1885, the 13-year-old emperor, Ham Nghi, was advised to raise objections to French activities in Tonkin, and a French fleet assembled at the mouth of the Perfume River. The citizens of Hué attacked, but were devastated by the French response, which culminated in the burning and looting of the Imperial City and the signing of a treaty making Vietnam a protectorate of France. During the 1968 Tet Offensive about 3,000 Hué civilians were killed under North Vietnamese occupation, and thousands more died in the bloody battle that followed with US troops.

THE SIGHTS

Hué Mausoleums

Ornate buildings, bridges, stelae and courtyards are arranged according to predetermined rules to glorify the imperial dead. Magnificent tombs sit in peaceful locations along the course of the Perfume River.

BASICS

✚ 117 A3

🖪 5 Ly Thuong Kiet Street, tel 054-823577; Mon–Fri 7–11.30, 1.30–5

💷 Popular tombs 55,000d; others less expensive or free; camcorders 75,000d extra

🚌 An Cuu station, 43 Hung Vuong Street, Hué; connections with Saigon. An Hoa station, northwest corner of Hué citadel; connections with Hanoi. Don Ba station, Tran Hung Dao, Hué; connections with local villages and Thuan An Beach

🚆 Le Loi Street, Hué; connections with Saigon, Danang and Hanoi

✈ Phu Bai Airport, south of Hué; connections with Saigon and Hanoi

🛥 Tours available from private operators and hotels; boats to rent from outside Huong Giang Hotel, Hué or any berth on south bank, east of Trang Tien Bridge

The impressive and elaborate entrance to Emperor Khai Dinh's tomb (above). Detail on the tomb of Tu Duc (inset)

SEEING THE HUÉ MAUSOLEUMS

The tombs of seven former emperors (Lang Chu Tich Hue) and those of various other royal personages and countless courtiers and mandarins dot the countryside to the south of Hué city. Each imperial tomb follows the same stylistic formula while reflecting the tastes of the emperor in question. Every one has five design elements: a courtyard with statues of elephants, horses and military and civil mandarins; a stela pavilion with an engraved eulogy by the king's heir; a Temple of the Soul's Tablets; a pleasure pavilion; and a grave. Geomancers decreed that they should also have a stream and a mountainous screen in front.

HIGHLIGHTS

TOMB OF EMPEROR GIA LONG

✉ 10 miles (16km) south of Hué ⏰ Daily 6.30–6 🚌 Dien Bien Phu Street from Hué; right at intersection; signed along path from Ben Do 1km milestone; ferry across tributary and 0.6-mile (1km) track on opposite bank

This is the most distant and the most rarely visited mausoleum, but is well worth the effort. The tomb itself is overgrown with venerable mango trees. The only sounds are bird calls and, occasionally, the wind in the trees: otherwise a blessed silence. Devoid of tourists, touts and ticket-sellers, this is the most atmospheric of all the tombs, although, given the historical changes that were to be wrought by the dynasty Gia Long founded, it is arguably the most significant.

Being the first of the dynasty, Gia Long's mausoleum set the formula for later tombs. There is a surrounding lotus pond, and steps lead up to a courtyard with the Minh Thanh ancestral temple, splendid in red and gold. To the right of this is a double, walled and locked burial chamber, where Gia Long (reigned 1802–20) and his wife are interred. The tomb is perfectly aligned with two huge obelisks on the far side of the lake. Beyond is a courtyard with five now headless mandarins, horses and elephants on each side. Steps lead up to the stela eulogizing the Emperor's reign, a gray monolith engraved in ancient Chinese characters that have remained miraculously undisturbed during two turbulent centuries.

TOMB OF EMPEROR MINH MANG

✉ 8.5 miles (12km) south of Hué ⏰ Daily 6.30–6 🚌 As for Tomb of Gia Long, but cross Perfume River using new road bridge; on far side turn immediately left 🎧 Guides available for early visitors only, 45,000d an hour

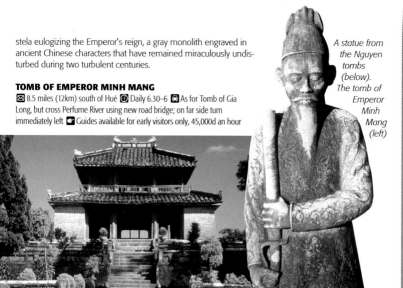

A statue from the Nguyen tombs (below). The tomb of Emperor Minh Mang (left)

The Tomb of Emperor Minh Mang (reigned 1820–40) is the finest of all the imperial tombs. Built between 1841 and 1843, it is sited among peaceful ponds, and in terms of architectural poise and balance, and richness of decoration, it has no equal in the area. The layout, along a single central sacred axis (Shendao), is unusual in its symmetry; no other tomb, with the possible exception of that of Khai Dinh, achieves the same unity of constituent parts, nor draws the eye onward so easily and pleasantly from one visual element to the next. Today, visitors pass through a side gate, but the traditional approach was through the Dai Hong Mon (15), a gate that leads into the ceremonial courtyard containing an array of statuary. Next is the restored Stela Pavilion (2), with a carved eulogy to the dead Emperor composed by his son, Thieu Tri. Continuing downward through a series of courtyards you reach, in turn, the Sung An Temple (4), dedicated to Minh Mang and his Empress; a small garden with flower beds that once formed the Chinese character for "longevity"; and two sets of stone bridges. The first consists of three spans, the central of which, Trung Dao Bridge (6), was for the sole use of the Emperor. The second, single bridge leads to a short flight of stairs, at the end of which is a locked bronze door leading to the tomb (no access).

Trung Minh

Tan Nguyet

Trung Minh

PLAN OF EMPEROR MINH MANG'S TOMB

1. Ceremonial Courtyard
2. Stela Pavilion
3. Hien Duc Gate
4. Sung An Temple
5. Hoang Trach Gate
6. Trung Dao Bridge
7. Thong Minh Chinh Truc Bridge
8. Linh Phuong Pavilion
9. Quan Lan Building
10. Truy Tu Mansion
11. Nghenh Luong Pavilion
12. Minh Lau Pavilion
13. Emperor's Tomb
14. Fishing Pavilion
15. Dai Hong Mon Gate

TOMB OF THIEU TRI

✉ 4 miles (7km) southwest of Hué in Thuy Bang village ⏰ Daily 6.30–6 🎫 Ticket required for admission beyond gatehouse, 22,000d

When building the Tomb of Thieu Tri (reigned 1841–47) in 1848, the Emperor's son Tu Duc took into account his father's wishes that it be economical and convenient. Thieu Tri, unlike his forebears, did not start planning his mausoleum the moment he ascended the throne. With no tomb to go to, on his death his body was temporarily interred in Long An Temple (now the Hué Museum of Royal Fine Arts, ▷ 116). The mausoleum is in two adjacent parts, with separate tomb and

Emperor Duc Duc's tomb (below right)

PLAN OF TU DUC'S TOMB

1. Le Khiem House
2. Khiem Cung Gate
3. Phap Khiem House
4. Hoa Khiem Palace
5. Luong Khiem Palace
6. Minh Khiem Royal Theater
7. On Khiem Mansion
8. Harem
9. Chi Khiem Temple
10. Vu Khiem Gate
11. Du Khiem Pavilion
12. Tinh Khiem Island
13. Xung Khiem Pavilion
14. Emperor Kien Phuc's Tomb
15. Chap Khiem Temple
16. Empress Le Thien Anh's Tomb
17. Emperor Tu Duc's Tomb
18. Stela Pavilion
19. Ceremonial Courtyard
20. Tien Khiem Bridge

temple areas; the layout of each follows the symmetrical axis arrangement of Minh Mang's tomb, which inspired the architectural style. The memorial temple area is to the right and reached via a long flight of steps. A gatehouse incorporates Japanese triple-beamed columns and at the back of the courtyard beyond is the temple dedicated to Thieu Tri. The stela pavilion and tomb are to the left. Thieu Tri is buried on a circular island reached by three bridges beyond the stela pavilion.

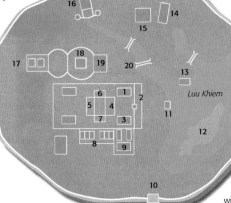

These stone figures guard the tomb of Dong Khanh

TOMB OF TU DUC

✉ 3 miles (5km) south of Hué ⊙ Daily 6.30–6
🚶 Guides available speaking German, French, English, Chinese, Japanese; negotiable rates

The tomb of Tu Duc (reigned 1847–83), built between 1864 and 1867 in a pine wood, is enclosed by a wall, within which is a lake where lotus and water hyacinth grow. On a small island in the lake the Emperor built replicas of famous temples (now rather difficult to discern). He often came here to relax, compose poetry and listen to music. The Xung Khiem Pavilion (13), built in 1865, has recently been restored with UNESCO's help and is the most attractive building here. The tomb complex follows the usual formula: ceremonial square, mourning yard with pavilion, and then the tomb itself. To the left of Tu Duc's tomb are the tombs of his Empress, Le Thien Anh (16), and adopted son, Kien Phuc (14). Many of the pavilions are crumbling and ramshackle, lending the tomb a rather tragic air. Though he had 104 wives, Tu Duc fathered no sons and had to write his own eulogy, a fact that he took as a bad omen. Shortly after his reign, France gained full control of Vietnam.

TOMB OF DUC DUC

✉ 1 mile (2km) south of Hué, on Tan Lang Street ⊙ Daily 6.30–6

Despite ruling for just three days and then dying in prison, Emperor Duc Duc (lived 1852–83) has a tomb, built in 1889 by his son, Thanh Thai, on the spot where the Emperor's body was said to have been dumped by jailers. Emperors Thanh Thai (reigned 1889–1907) and Duy Tan (reigned 1907–16) are buried in the same complex. Unlike Duc Duc, both were strongly anti-French and were, for a period, exiled in Africa. Thanh Thai later returned to Vietnam and died in Vung Tau in 1953; his son Duy Tan was killed in an air crash in central Africa in 1945. Not until 1987 was Duy Tan's body repatriated and interred alongside his father. The tomb is in three parts: the Long An Temple; Duc Duc's tomb, to the south; and Thanh Thai and Duy Tan's tombs, next to each other. The tombs are badly rundown.

TOMB OF DONG KHANH

✉ 550 yards (500m) from Tu Duc's tomb; path on other side of road from main entrance ◉ Daily 6.30–6

Built in 1889, this is the smallest of the imperial tombs, but nonetheless it is one of the most individual. Unusually, it has two separate sections. One is a walled area containing the usual series of pavilions and courtyards, plus an historically interesting collection of personal objects that belonged to the Emperor. The second, a short distance away, consists of an open series of platforms. On the lower platform is the honor guard of mandarins, horses and elephants, along with a stela pavilion; the third platform is a tiled area that would have had an awning; and the highest platform is the tomb itself. The tomb is enclosed within three open walls, the entrance protected by a dragon screen (that is supposed to prevent spirits entering).

TOMB OF KHAI DINH

✉ 6 miles (10km) south of Hué ◉ Daily 6.30–6 🚌 As for Gia Long's tomb; continue under river crossing but turn immediately left and go straight across small crossroads

The last of the Nguyen Dynasty mausoleums was built between 1920 and 1932. By the time Khai Dinh (reigned 1916–25) was contemplating the afterlife, brick had given way in popularity to concrete—which is now beginning to deteriorate.

The tomb occupies a wonderful position on the Chau Mountain, facing southwest toward a large white statue of Quan Am, which was also built by Khai Dinh. Before construction could begin, Khai Dinh had to remove the tombs of Chinese nobles who had already selected the site for its beauty and auspicious orientation. A total of 127 steep steps, lined by four dragons, lead to the honor courtyard; an octagonal pavilion in the mourning yard contains an engraved stone stela; and at the top of more stairs are the tomb and shrine of Khai Dinh, containing a bronze statue of the Emperor sitting on his throne and holding a jade scepter. The interior is richly decorated with ornate murals, floor tiles, and decorations built up with fragments of porcelain. This elaborate tomb took 11 years to build and had to be funded with additional taxes.

BACKGROUND

The Nguyen Dynasty ruled Vietnam between 1802 and 1945, and for the first time in Vietnamese history a single court controlled the land from Yunnan (southern China) to the Gulf of Siam. Gia Long, the first of the dynasty, was crowned with French support. When he died on February 3, 1820, imperial relations and mandarins were given set periods of mourning, with a minimum of three years, and astrologers chose a date for the funeral (May 27). The coffin was carried from palace to tomb on a three-day journey; at the tomb it was covered in a silk shroud, placed in an outer, resin coffin, lowered into the tomb and bricked in. Another grave next to the Emperor's was filled with items he might need for the afterlife. Ritual titles were inscribed on the tomb, animals sacrificed, and the silk thread—tied on the ancestors' altar to represent the soul—was untied and buried nearby.

TIPS

● Getting to and around the mausoleums is easiest by motorcycle or car, but all are accessible by bicycle; set out early if taking this option.
● Boat tours travel to a select number of the tombs, but still require a climb up to a road and, occasionally, motorcycle transportation to the tombs; these costs and the entrance fees are excluded from the tour price.

The elaborate tomb of Khai Dinh (top) has stone figures such as this (left)

The five peaks of the Marble Mountains offer panoramic views over Danang and the surrounding countryside

Children happily splash in the surf at Mui Ne beach

THE SIGHTS

MARBLE MOUNTAINS

⊞ 285 F7 • 7.5 miles (12km) west of Danang ◉ Daily 6–5 💵 10,000d entrance to Thuy Son 🚌 Hoi An bus from Hung Vuong Street, Danang 🚗 Private tours from Danang and Hoi An 🏛

The Marble Mountains (**Ngu Hanh Son**) were named by Emperor Minh Mang on his visit in 1825; they are, in fact, limestone crags with marble outcrops. Their five peaks are important Cham religious sites, and were used by Communist guerrillas during the Vietnam War for their view over Danang air base. Thuy Son, the most visited mountain, has several grottoes and cave pagodas, marked by steps cut into the rock. Tam Thai Pagoda was built in 1825 by Minh Mang on the site of a much older Cham place of worship, and subsequently rebuilt. Its central statue is of the Buddha Sakyamuni (the historic Buddha), flanked by the Bodhisattva Quan Am (a future Buddha and the Goddess of Mercy), and Van Thu, symbolizing wisdom. At the rear of the grotto is the Huyen Khong Cave, originally an animist and later a Buddhist site. The high ceiling is pierced by five holes through which the sun filters and, in the hour before midday, illuminates the central statue. A track leads south to Chua Quan The Am, a grotto with stalactites, stalagmites and pillars.

MUI NE

⊞ 287 F11 🚌 Services from Tran Hung Dao Street, Phan Thiet; Sinh Café bus from Saigon; served by Open Tour bus 🚗 Tours by private operators

This sandy cape east of Phan Thiet (▷ 126) has two claims to fame: its *nuoc mam* (fish sauce) and its beaches. It is dominated by sand dunes, some golden, others quite red, reflecting the underlying geology (some areas of the beach may be shifting due to natural erosion). Lining the strip of golden sand are a dozen or so resorts (▷ 246–247). The strong smell pervading the small fishing village at the end of the cape is fish sauce fermenting in wooden barrels. Labels reading *cá com* indicate that the local *nuoc mam* is made from anchovies. The fermenting process takes a year, and the end product is highly regarded—though not as highly as that from the island of Phu Quoc (▷ 152).

MY SON

See page 123.

NAM CAT TIEN NATIONAL PARK

⊞ 287 E11 • 31 miles (50km) south of Bao Loc on Highway 20; turn off at Tan Phu and follow track for 15 miles (25km) ☎ 061-856449/791226 🚗 Guided two-hour treks 45,000d; full-day and two-day treks also possible. Private tours from Saigon and Dalat

This newly created national park (**Vuon Quoc Gia Cat Tien**), about 90 miles (150km) north of Saigon on the route to Dalat, is one of the last surviving areas of natural bamboo and dipterocarp forest in southern Vietnam. It is also one of the few places in the country where populations of

large mammals can be found—tiger, elephant, bear, and the last few remaining Javan rhino. There are also 300 species of bird, smaller mammals, reptiles and butterflies. The park is managed by 20 rangers who, besides helping protect the flora and fauna, also conduct research and guide visitors. (No English spoken.)

NHA TRANG

See pages 124–125.

PLEIKU

⊞ 285 E8 🛈 Gia Lai Tourist, 215 Hung Vuong Street (in Hung Vuong Hotel), tel 059-874571 🚌 Connections with Saigon, Buon Me Thuot, Dalat ✈ Connections with Saigon, Danang 🚗 Private tours from Nha Trang and Danang

Pleiku (**Play Ku**) town, population 35,000, sits high on the Pleiku Plateau, once densely forested and still home to many ethnic minorities. The main attractions lie on the road north to Kontum—a pleasant motorcycle drive, especially early in the year when the white coffee blossom exudes a jasmine-like scent. Bien Ho, 3 miles (5km) north of Pleiku off the Quy Nhon road (Highway 19), is a large volcanic lake (access 1,000d) and Pleiku's main source of water. A platform on a promontory jutting into the water makes a good viewpoint. Northwest are several Jarai villages, the first being Plei Mrong, which gives a glimpse of Jarai life. Plei Fun, about 12 miles (20km) along the road, has Jarai graves covered by tiled or wooden roofs sheltering possessions of the deceased and guarded by carved hardwood statues. At Plei Mun, another 3 miles (5km) down the road and left 1 mile (2km) down a dirt road, there are even finer examples, as well as a traditional wooden *rong* house with a corrugated-iron roof.

This stone-carved altar illustrates the importance of the Marble Mountains as a pilgrimage site

CENTRAL VIETNAM M–P

MY SON

My Son is one of Vietnam's most ancient monuments, and a tranquil archeological treasure. More than 70 Cham buildings have survived jungle growth and years of warfare.

Weather, jungle and strife have wrought their worst on My Son, which was declared a World Heritage Site by UNESCO in 1999. Arguably, however, the jungle under which it remained hidden for so long provided its best protection—more has been destroyed since the 1960s than in the previous four centuries. More than 70 monuments, interlaced with streams and set amid coffee plantations, occupy a valley below Hon Quap mountain. The monuments are in 10 groups, each identified with a letter (A, A', B, C, D, E, F, G, H, K). Within each group, structures are named with that letter and a number.

CHAM STYLE

Much that is known of My Son was ascertained by French archeologists of the École Française d'Extrême-Orient, who rediscovered and excavated the site in 1898. It is one of the three most important of the Champa kingdom, along with Tra Kieu and Dong Duong, and was settled from the early eighth to the 15th centuries, the longest constant period of development of any monument in Southeast Asia. It fell strongly under Chinese influence, but there's also evidence of Indian culture in its graceful sculptures and buildings. Bricks are laid exactly and held together with a vegetable cement—probably the resin of the day tree. It is thought that each tower was encircled by wood and fired in what amounted to a vast outdoor kiln. Sanctuaries with fine examples of the Cham style of ornamentation through the centuries are C1, with eighth-century AD motifs, and B4, with abstract, wriggling patterns from the ninth century AD.

SITE CONDITIONS

My Son was a Viet Cong field headquarters in the Vietnam War, within one of the US "free fire" zones, and some temples were badly damaged —notably groups A, E and H; groups B and C have largely retained their temples but many statues, altars and linga (phallic symbols) have been moved to the Cham museum in Danang (▷ 104–105). The main sanctuary, A1, was reduced to rubble, after which President Nixon ordered US forces to avoid damaging Cham structures. A stone altar was restored in the 1980s, and it is possible to see some of the 10th-century brickwork. B5, also 10th-century, housed sacred books and ceremonial items used in B1, a temple dedicated to King Bhadravarman I, who started work here in the fourth century AD.

Overgrown remains of the kingdom of Champa (top and above) lie sadly scarred due to time and 20th-century hostilities

RATINGS	
Cultural interest	●●●●●
Historic interest	●●●●●
Photo stops	●●●●

BASICS

✚ 285 E7 • 40 miles (60km) south of Danang
🛈 12 Phan Chu Trinh Street, Hoi An, tel 0511-861276; Mon–Fri 7–11.30, 1.30–5
🕐 Daily 8–6
💰 75,000d
🚌 Tours from several operators in Hoi An and Danang

TIPS

● It is not clear how thoroughly the area has been cleared of mines, so it is advisable not to stray too far from the road and path.
● My Son is usually hot and dry; take a hat, sunscreen and water.
● A jeep takes you the 1 mile (2km) from the ticket office to the site; price included in entrance fee.

Nha Trang

Vietnam's only real seaside town is protected by hills and has a long, golden beach. Clear waters, blue skies, fishing boats and ancient Cham towers add to its appeal.

Bathing in the South China Sea (above). Cham remains (right)

RATINGS

Good for kids	● ● ● ○
Outdoor pursuits	● ● ● ○
Photo stops	● ● ○

BASICS

✚ 287 F10

ℹ 2 Khanh Hoa Tourism, 1 Tran Hung Dao Street, tel 058-822753

🚌 23 Thang 10 Street; connections with Saigon, Danang, Buon Me Thuot, Dalat, Hué. Served by Open Tour buses

🚆 Thai Nguyen Street; connections with Hanoi, Saigon

✈ Airport 21 miles (34 km) to north of town; connections with Hanoi, Saigon and Danang

🍴 Seafood eateries on beach road; also Italian and Indian restaurants

☕ Wide range of cafés and bars

TIPS

● Inter-province buses drop off at intersections on Highway 1, where a *xe ôm* takes passengers to the town center.

● Nha Trang airport, now used only by small aircraft, is a 5-minute drive from town. There are taxis, *xe ôms* and cyclos, but travelers with light bags could walk it.

● Breakfast in the central market (Cho Dam), at the northern end of Hoang Hoa Than Street, is amazing, with the wealth of sea and land under one roof.

SEEING NHA TRANG

There are two Nha Trangs: the sleepy, sedate seaside town, with a long, palm- and casuarina-fringed beach and one or two parallel streets, and the commercial town north of Yersin Street, a bustling place with attractive Chinese shop houses. It's the capital of Khanh Hoa Province, with a population of some 200,000 and an active fishing fleet. From Tran Phu Boulevard, parallel to the beach on the eastern shore, several roads lead into the heart of town, which is centered on Yersin and Thong Nhat streets.

HIGHLIGHTS

ISLANDS

🎫 Mama Linh's Tours, 2a Hung Vuong Street, tel 058-826693 and Hanh's Green Hat, 44 Ly Thanh Ton Street and 2A Biet Thu Street, tel 058-821309, US$7 (including lunch and pick-up from hotel), daily 7am–9pm. Boat tours from Cau Da pier, 110,000d (including lunch and snorkeling equipment), depart 9am

Several islands lie within reach of Nha Trang; tour boats anchor offshore and passengers can swim while the skipper prepares a seafood lunch. Trips take in Mieu Island and its Tri Nguyen aquarium (20,000d per person), where fish and crustacea are reared, ostensibly for scientific purposes, though there is a seafood restaurant suspiciously close by. Other nearby islands are Hon Mun, Hon Tam (5,000d per person to dock) and Hon Mot, sometimes called the Salangane Islands after the many sea swallows (*yen* in Vietnamese) that nest here. This bird produces the highly prized nest from which the famous soup is made (▷ 207). Hon Yen (Swallow Island) is strictly out of bounds and government-controlled, presumably to deter nest-collectors.

CHAM PONAGAR TEMPLE COMPLEX

✚ 125 B1 • 2km (1 mile) north of town along 2 Thang 4 Street 🕐 Daily 6–6
💵 4,000d

On a hill just outside the city is the Cham Ponagar Temple complex, known locally as Thap Ba. Originally it consisted of eight towers; four remain, and their varied styles indicate different building periods, between the seventh and 12th centuries. The largest, 75ft (23m) high, was built in AD817 and contains a fine and very large linga (phallic symbol) and a statue of Lady Thien Y-ana, also known as Ponagar and said to have re-created the world and taught the local people weaving and new agricultural techniques. The other towers are dedicated to gods: The central tower (now a fertility temple for childless couples) to Cri Cambhu; the northwest tower to Sandhaka, woodcutter and foster-father to Lady Thien Y-ana; and the south tower to Ganeca, Lady Thien Y-ana's daughter.

ALEXANDRE YERSIN MUSEUM
✚ 125 B2 • 8 Tran Phu Street ☎ 058-829540 ◷ Mon–Fri 8–11, 2–4.30, Sat 2–4.30 💰 26,000d 🈺 ❓ Labeling in French and English; no photography
This museum is within the Pasteur Institute, founded by the great scientist's protégé, Dr. Alexandre Yersin (1863–1943). Swiss-born Yersin (▶ 31) first arrived in Vietnam in 1891 and spent much of the rest of his life in Nha Trang, where he set up a laboratory to study infectious diseases affecting animals and to produce serum from horses and buffaloes. The museum contains his laboratory equipment, library and stereoscope (through which visitors can see 3-D black and white slides). The microscope with which Yersin identified the plague bacillus, *Yersinia pestis*, is also on show, as is his furniture, brought from his home—no longer standing—at Fishermen Point.

LONG SON PAGODA
✚ 125 A1 • 23 Thang 10 Street
An unusual image of the Buddha, backlit with natural light, is the focus of this sanctuary built in 1963. Murals depict the Jataka (birth of the Buddha) stories, and, to the right of the sanctuary, stairs lead to a 29ft (9m) white Buddha perched on a hilltop. The pagoda commemorates monks and nuns who died demonstrating against the Diem government (▶ 35). Behind the pagoda is an impressive 46ft (14m) reclining Buddha, commissioned in 2003.

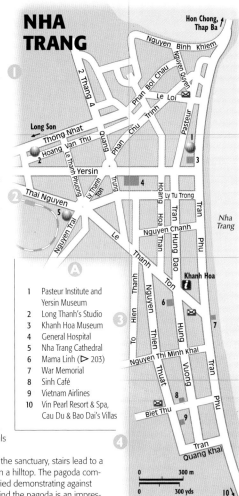

NHA TRANG

1   Pasteur Institute and Yersin Museum
2   Long Thanh's Studio
3   Khanh Hoa Museum
4   General Hospital
5   Nha Trang Cathedral
6   Mama Linh (▶ 203)
7   War Memorial
8   Sinh Café
9   Vietnam Airlines
10 Vin Pearl Resort & Spa, Cau Du & Bao Dai's Villas

BACKGROUND

Nha Trang is an important Cham settlement, which was besieged for nine months during the Tay Son rebellion in the late 18th century, before eventually falling to the rebel troops. Its fishing tradition goes back many centuries, and in 1924 a port was built to handle small coastal traders. From the 1960s its bright blue waters and offshore islands began to attract international attention, and its new-found prosperity is based firmly on tourism.

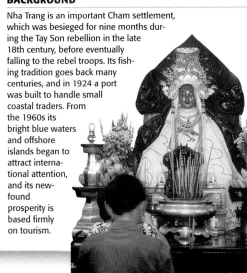

MORE TO SEE
NHA TRANG CATHEDRAL
✚ 125 A2 • Nguyen Trai Street
◷ Mass: Mon–Fri 4.45am, 5pm, Sat 5pm, Sun 5am, 7am, 9.30am, 5pm
This imposing concrete cathedral, built between 1928 and 1933, has a single, crenelated tower, a vaulted ceiling and stained glass by Louis Balmet.

LONG THANH'S STUDIO
✚ 125 A2 • 126 Hoang Van Thu Street
☎ 058-824875 ◷ Daily while Long Thanh is at work
This gallery shows the evocative work of one of Vietnam's most distinguished photographers.

A Hindu deity (left) in one of the Cham towers

125

The two Cham towers of Po
Shanu at Phan Thiet

Phong Nha Cave was known to
the Chams in the 10th century

The pink-hued ruins of the
Po Klong Garai temples

PHAN THIET

🔲 287 E11 🚹 Binh Thuan Tourist, 82
Trung Trac Street, tel 062-816821;
Mon–Fri 7–11.30, 1.30–5 🚌 Tran Hung
Dao Street; connections with Mui Ne,
Saigon. Served by Open Tour bus
🚆 Connections with Muong Man for
services to Saigon and Hanoi
www.binhthuantourist.com/eng

This little fishing town on the Ca
Ty estuary has an 18-hole golf
course designed by British golfer
Nick Faldo, regarded as one of
the best in Vietnam. Until a few
hundred years ago the Cham
and the Raglai were the region's
dominant groups, and there are
still some 50,000 Cham and
30,000 Raglai here. The best and
most accessible Cham relic is Po
Shanu, two hilltop towers dating
from the late eighth century AD,
on the Mui Ne road. Like
other towers here, they were
constructed of brick bound
together with the resin of the
day tree.

PHONG NHA CAVE

🔲 284 D5 • 31 miles (50km) from
Dong Hoi 💵 US$6, including boat ride
🚌 North on Highway 1 for 12 miles
(20km); 19 miles (30km) west to Son
River landing stage 🚤 Tours from Hué

Visitors are taken by boat only
656 yards (600m) into this
UNESCO World Heritage Site
(Dong Phong Nha), and are
dropped off to explore. The brick
foundations of a Cham temple
remain in one of the chambers.
There are stalagmites and stalactites, and powerful flashlights can
pick out ghoulish and godly
shapes in the rocks. British divers
explored 5.5 miles (9km) of the
main cave system in 1990, but
less than 0.6 mile (1km) is open
to visitors. The nearby Tien Son
cave, which was discovered in
1935 in the mountain of Ke
Bang, is also accessible up to
440 yards (400m).

PO KLONG GARAI

🔲 287 F11 • 4 miles (6km) from Phan
Rang on Highway 27 💵 5,000d
🚹 Ninh Thuan Tourist, 505 Thong
Nhat Street, Phan Rang, tel 068-822722
🚌 Local services from south side of
Phan Rang towards Dalat. Served by
Open Tour bus
www.ninhthuanpt.com.vn

Po Klong Garai is a group of
three Cham towers, perhaps the
most striking in the
country outside
My

This depiction of Siva adorns an
entrance at the Cham towers

Son (▷ 123). They were built
during the 13th century on a
cactus- and boulder-strewn hill
with commanding views over the
surrounding countryside. To the
north the remains of Thanh Son,
the former US air base, are visible. The towers are raised up on
a brick base and have been
extensively renovated, but other
than the repair work there is no
sign of mortar at all, the cohesion
of the red bricks being one of the
enduring mysteries of the Cham.
The central tower has a figure of
a dancing Siva (the Hindu god of
destruction) over the main

entrance. The door jambs are
made of what looks like polished
sandstone on which (competing
with modern graffiti) are ancient
Cham engravings. Tucked inside
the dimly lit main chamber, full
of incense smoke, is Siva's vehicle, the bull Nandi, and a number
of other statues.

YOK DON NATIONAL PARK

🔲 287 E9 • 25 miles (40km) northwest
of Buon Me Thuot, Daklak Province
☎ 050-783049 🕐 Daily 7.30–5
💵 45,000d 🍴 🥾 Guided half-day,
full-day and overnight hiking
150,000d–450,000d plus entrance fee;
elephant ride for two 255,000d an hour,
675,000d a day. Private tours from
Buon Me Thuot

The 284,000 acres
(115,000ha) that make up
this wildlife reserve (Vuon
Quoc Gia Yok Don) are home
to at least 63 species of
mammals, 17 of which are
on the worldwide endan-
gered list, and 240 species
of birds. The reserve is also
thought to be the home of several rare white elephants. Five of
the world's 25 rarest primates
survive here, as does the Asian
elephant. Within the park's
boundaries 17 different ethnic
minority groups make their
home. About 1.5 miles (3km)
beyond the Yok Don National
Park gate is Ban Don village,
which has a long tradition of tam-
ing the forest's elephants, and
beyond the third sub-hamlet is
the tomb of Khun Ju-Nop, known
as the King Elephant-Catcher,
who died in 1924. Next to his
square tomb is a taller, white
stupa commemorating his
brother, also a famous elephant-
catcher, who died in 1950. Both
were of Lao origin. Behind is the
more modern tomb of a M'nong
elephant-catcher, Y Pum B'Ya, a
son of Khun Ju-Nop.

HO CHI MINH CITY

Ho Chi Minh City is a manic, capitalistic hothouse, clogged with traffic, bursting with energy and enlivened by excellent restaurants, shops and bars. Pagodas, temples, and a bustling Chinatown are evidence of the city's vibrant past. In more recent times it was the seat of the South Vietnam government until reunification, when its official title replaced the more familiar name of Saigon.

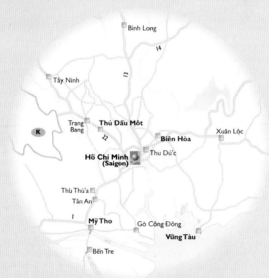

MAJOR SIGHTS

Ho Chi Minh City

✚ 286 D11 🛈 Vietnamtourism, 234 Nam Ky Khoi Nghia Street ☎ 08-9326776. Saigontourist, 49 Le Thanh Ton Street ☎ 08-8298914 🕐 Mon–Fri 7–11.30, 1.30–5

The Saigon Opera House—a classical building, fronted by a modern water feature

HOW TO GET THERE

✈ Ta Son Nhat airport northwest of the city

🚌 Mien Dong Terminal, Xo Viet Nghe Tinh Street; connections north to Dalat, Hué, Danang. Mien Tay Terminal, Hung Vuong Boulevard; connections south to Mekong Delta, Ca Mau and other destinations. Connections to Phan Thiet, Mui Ne, Nha Trang and Dalat with Open Tour buses

🚆 Nguyen Thong Street; connections with Hanoi and all points north

Schoolgirls bicycling through the city (right). Living in the shadow of capitalism (below)

SEEING HO CHI MINH CITY

Virtually the whole of Ho Chi Minh City lies to the west of the Saigon River. The city is divided administratively into 12 urban districts, or *quan*, and nine suburban districts, or *huyen*, which are further subdivided into wards. The eastern side of the river, District 2, is marshy and poor; most visitors head straight for the hotels in districts 1 and 3. Lam Son Square is the heart of Ho Chi Minh City, with key roads radiating from this point and major buildings and hotels surrounding it. Many of the city's attractions are in this District 1 (called Saigon) area, which, with a few café breaks or the odd cyclo ride, can be covered on foot. Cholon (Chinatown) is about 3 miles (5km) west of the city center, and the Port of Saigon lies downstream in districts 4 and 8. Few visitors venture here, though cruise ships berth in District 4. East of the river, over Saigon Bridge and up Highway 1, lie leafy suburbs in the walled residential compounds of Thu Duc. There is abundant transportation in the form of metered taxis, motorcycle taxis and cyclos.

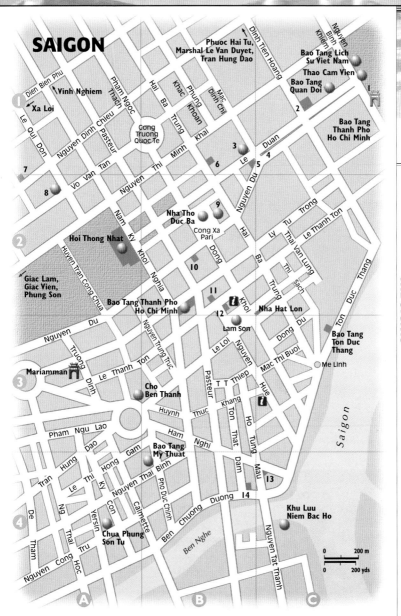

SAIGON

Phuoc Hai Tu,
Marshal Le Van Duyet,
Tran Hung Dao

Dien Bien Phu
Vinh Nghiem
Xa Loi
Pham Ngoc Thach
Le Qui Don
Nguyen Dinh Chieu
Pasteur
Hai Ba
Khac
Phung
Mac Dinh Chi
Khoan
Trung
Cong Truong Quoc Te
Khai
Minh
Thi
Vo Van Tan
Nguyen
Nam Ky
Khoi Nghia
Huyen Tran Cong Chua

Dinh Tien Hoang
Nguyen
Khiem
Binh

Bao Tang Lich Su Viet Nam
Thao Cam Vien
Bao Tang Quan Doi

Bao Tang Thanh Pho Ho Chi Minh

Le Duan

Nha Tho Duc Ba
Cong Xa Pari
Ly
Thai Van Lung
Le Thanh Ton
Tu Trong
Thi Sach
Trung
Dong

Giac Lam, Giac Vien, Phung Son

Hoi Thong Nhat

Bao Tang Thanh Pho Ho Chi Minh
Nguyen Trung Truc
Khoi
Nha Hat Lon
Lam Son
Le Loi
Nguyen
Mac Thi Buoi
Dong
Du
Bao Tang Ton Duc Thang
Me Linh

Mariamman
Truong
Dinh
Le Thanh Ton
Pasteur
T T Thiep
Khang
Ton That
Hue
Ho
Tung
Mau

Cho Ben Thanh
Huynh
Thuc

Pham Ngu Lao
Dao
Ham
Nghi
Dam

Tran
Hung
Le Thi
Ky
Hong Gam
Con
Nguyen Thai Binh
Pho Duc Chinh
Calmette
Bao Tang My Thuat
Chuong
Duong

De
Ng
Thai
Tru
Yersin
Chua Phung Son Tu
Ben
Ben Nghe

Nguyen Cong Hoc

Khu Luu Niem Bac Ho

Nguyen Tat Thanh

Saigon

0   200 m
0   200 yds

A   B   C

THE SIGHTS

KEY TO MAP

1   Memorial Temple
2   University
3   US Consulate General
4   British Consulate
5   Singapore Airlines
6   French Consulate
7   Archbishop's Palace
8   War Remnants Museum
9   General Post Office
10 Thai Airways
11 City Hall
12 Vietnam Airlines
13 Old US Embassy Building
14 Old Hong Kong and Shanghai Bank Building

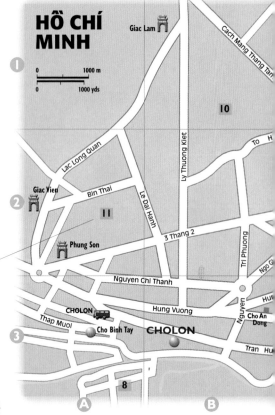

TIPS

● Cyclos charge a lot more than motos and taxis for the same distance, but the ride is more leisurely. If your cyclo driver appears to take very circuitous routes it's because some streets are out of bounds to cyclos.

● A hotel with a pool is a distinct advantage. Saigon's heat can sometimes be suffocating.

● Bars in Pham Ngu Lao, the backpacker district, stay open way beyond the normal midnight closing hours, although this isn't always advertised.

Urban District, or *Quan*

HỒ CHÍ MINH

Giac Lam

Cach Mang Thang Tan

10

Lac Long Quan

Ly Thuong Kiet

To H

Giac Vien

Bin Thai

Le Dai Hanh

3 Thang 2

Tri Phuong

Ngo Gi

Phung Son

II

Nguyen Chi Thanh

Hu

Hung Vuong

Nguyen

Cho An Dong

CHOLON

Thap Muoi

Cho Binh Tay

CHOLON

Tran Hu

8

A

B

A statue of Ho Chi Minh (below) fronts the former Hôtel de Ville

BACKGROUND

Ho Chi Minh City, Pearl of the Orient, is the largest city in Vietnam. It is also the nation's foremost commercial and industrial center. Founded as a Khmer trading and fishing port on the west bank of the Dong Nai River, it fell into Vietnamese hands in the late 17th century. Early in the 18th century the Nguyen emperors established Gia Dinh Citadel, destroyed by French naval forces in 1859. Having been rebuilt as a French colonial city, it was named Saigon (So*ai-gon*, meaning "wood of the kapok tree"). During the course of the Vietnam War, refugees spilled in and the population almost doubled, from 2.4 million in 1965 to around 4.5 million 10 years later. After reunification in 1976 the Communist authorities pursued a policy of depopulation. Today, the city is once more being rebuilt, as the wrecker's ball fells whole blocks at a time, and concrete, steel and glass monuments emerge in their place. The population now officially stands at 6 million and is rising fast.

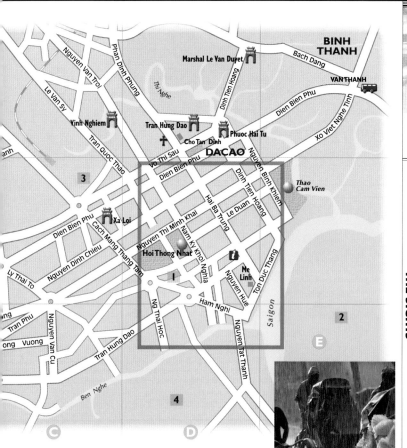

BINH
THANH

VAN THANH

DACAO

3

Thao
Cam Vien

2

E

C   D

4

DON'T MISS

REUNIFICATION HALL
This 1960s building housed the South Vietnam government until 1975 (▷ 140).

WAR REMNANTS MUSEUM
Photographs, planes, posters and propaganda in a museum that exhibits the full horror of the Vietnam War (▷ 142).

DONG KHOI STREET
Meander down this main street, crammed with shops selling silk, shoes, bags, jewelry, lacquerware, books and crafts (▷ 137).

MOTOS
If you're feeling brave, hitch a ride on the back of a *xe ôm* and cruise through the sweaty, congested streets at adrenalin-pumping speeds.

Life goes on in the city in spite of the torrential monsoon rain (above). The Reunification Hall (below), decked with flags, once housed the South Vietnam government

THE SIGHTS

Cholon

Ho Chi Minh City's "Chinatown" is a hectic area given over to bustling markets, fascinating temples and pagodas, and some wonderfully decorated Chinese assembly houses.

There's a huge variety of goods on sale in the market

RATINGS

Cultural interest	●●●●
Good for kids	●●●
Photo stops	●●●●

BASICS

✚ 130 B3 • District 5, west of downtown
ℹ Vietnamtourism, 234 Nam Ky Khoi Nghia Street, tel 08-9326776. Saigontourist, 49 Le Thanh Ton Street, tel 08-8298914; Mon–Fri 7–11.30, 1.30–5
🚉 Cholon station, serving Long An, My Thuan, Ben Luc, My Tho
🍴 Wide range of Chinese restaurants

SEEING CHOLON

Cholon (Big Market) is an area inhabited predominantly by Vietnamese of Chinese origin (Hoa). This area, southwest of downtown, is worth visiting not only for the bustle and activity, but also because the temples and assembly halls found here are the finest in Ho Chi Minh City. As in other towns in Southeast Asia with sizeable Chinese populations, early settlers established meeting rooms that offered social, cultural and spiritual support to members of dialect groups. These assembly halls *(hoi quan)* are most common in Hoi An (▷ 108–113) and Cholon. Vietnamese and Chinese gather in many of the temples, particularly elderly residents, who meet for a chat and a cup of tea. Binh Tay Market—a block away in District 6—is Cholon's main and best-known marketplace; you can also buy clothes and other goods at the multifloor An Dong Market (intersection of Tran Phu and An Duong Vuong), where the basement has a range of small restaurants. Among other Cholon highlights are Quan Am Pagoda, Tam Son Assembly Hall and the two Thien Hau temples.

HIGHLIGHTS

BINH TAY MARKET
✉ Thap Muoi Street 🕐 Daily
Along with Ben Thanh Market (▷ 135), the Binh Tay Market (**Cho Binh Tay**), sandwiched between Thap Muoi and Phan Van Khoe streets, is one of Ho Chi Minh City's largest. It is also one of the most exciting markets in the city, with a wonderful array of noises, smells and colors. Though not strictly within the area, Binh Tay has always served as the main market for Cholon; however, in 1991 a five-floor market, An Dong, opened in the district. Binh Tay sprawls over a large area and is housed in an ocher-colored building decorated with a beautiful dragon mural in blue tiles and topped by a clock tower. On a large central patio are dragon fountains, goldfish-filled ponds and a monument erected in 1930 to mark the contribution of Quach Dam of the Legion of Honor to the building of the Cholon Market.

MING DYNASTY ASSEMBLY HALL
✉ 380 Tran Hung Dao Street 🕐 Daily 5.30am–6pm
The Ming Dynasty Assembly Hall (**Dinh Minh Huong Gia Thanh**) was built by the Cantonese community, which arrived in Saigon via Hoi An in the 18th century. The hall was built in 1789 and dedicated to the Ming Dynasty, but the present building dates largely from an extensive renovation carried out in the 1960s. Among the furniture is a heavy, marble-topped table and chairs that arrived in 1850 from China. In the main hall there are three altars, which, following imperial tradition, are: the central altar, dedicated to the royal family (Ming Dynasty); the right-hand altar, dedicated to two military mandarin officers; and the left altar, dedicated to two civilian mandarin officers. The hall behind is dedicated to the memory of the Vuong family, who built the main hall and whose descendants have lived here ever since; the custodian is third generation. In a small side chapel childless women can seek divine intercession from a local deity, Ba Me Sanh.

NGHIA AN ASSEMBLY HALL

✉ 678 Nguyen Trai Street ◉ Daily 4am–6pm

A magnificent, carved, gold-painted wooden boat hangs over the entrance to the Nghia An Assembly Hall. To the left, on entering the temple, is a larger-than-life depiction of the horse and groom of Quan Cong, god of war and soldiers. At the main altar are three figures in glass cases. The central, red-faced figure with a green cloak is Quan Cong, who was a loyal military man living in China in the third century. To the left and right are his companions, the fierce-looking General Chau Xuong and the mandarin Quan Binh. On leaving, note the fine gold figures of guardians on the inside of the door panels.

QUAN AM PAGODA

✉ 12 Lao Tu Street (just off Luong Nhu Hoc Street) ◉ Daily 5.30am–6pm

The Quan Am Pagoda (**Chua Quan Am**), founded in 1816, is thought to be one of the oldest in the city. Its roof supports four sets of mosaic-encrusted figures, and inside, the main building is fronted with old gold and lacquer panels of guardian spirits. In front of the main altar, which supports a seated statue of A-Pho, the Holy Mother, is a white ceramic statue of Quan Am, the Goddess of Purity and Motherhood (Goddess of Mercy). Quan Am was thrown out by her husband for some unspecified wrongdoing, and, dressed as a monk, took refuge in a monastery. There, a woman accused her of fathering, and then abandoning, her child. Quan Am accepted the blame, taking on the sins of another, and was again turned out. Much later, when on the point of death, she returned to the monastery to confess her true identity. When the Emperor of China heard the tale, he made Quan Am the Guardian Spirit of Mother and Child, and couples without a son now pray to her. Quan Am's husband is sometimes shown as a para-keet, and the goddess usually holds her adopted son in one arm and stands on a lotus leaf (a symbol of purity). The complex also has a series of courtyards and altars dedicated to deities and spirits. Outside, hawkers sell caged birds and vast quantities of incense sticks to pilgrims.

TAM SON ASSEMBLY HALL

✉ 118 Trieu Quang Phuc Street ◉ 4.30am–6pm

Chinese immigrants from Fukien Province built this temple (**Tam Son Hoi Quan**) just off Nguyen Trai Street in the 19th century and dedi-cated it to Me Sanh, Goddess of Fertility. The bearded general Quan Cong and his red horse are represented in the courtyard; the general

Worshipers burning incense in one of the Thien Hau temples (above)

Inside the Tam Son Assembly Hall

is flanked by his military mandarin guardian, Chau Xuong, and his administrative mandarin, Quan Binh. Thien Hau is also represented here, behind the main altar, as is Ong Bon, Guardian Spirit of Happiness and Virtue. Me Sanh herself is shown surrounded by her daughters.

THIEN HAU TEMPLES

✉ 710 Nguyen Trai Street; 802 Nguyen Trai Street ◎ Daily 6am–5.30pm

Two blocks separate these temples (**Chua Pho Mieu**), both dedicated to Thien Hau, Goddess of the Sea and protector of sailors. Thien Hau was born in China and, as a girl, saved her father from drowning. Her festival is marked here on the 23rd day of the third lunar month. The temple at 710 Nguyen Trai Street, also dedicated to the Buddha, was constructed in the early 19th century, and is one of the largest in the city. An enormous incense urn and an incinerator can be seen through the main doors. Inside, the principal altar supports the gilded form of Thien Hau and

a boat. Silk paintings depict religious scenes, and a high-relief frieze shows episodes from the Legends of the Three Kingdoms. In the post-1975 era many would-be refugees prayed here for safe deliverance before casting themselves adrift on the South China Sea.

Headgear, ancient and modern (above). Binh Tay Market (right)

Some who survived sent offerings to the merciful goddess, and the temple has been well maintained since. Over the front door is a picture of a boiling sea peppered with sinking boats. A benign Thien Hau looks down mercifully from a cloud. Migrants from Fukien Province in China built the original temple at 802 Nguyen Trai Street in the 1730s (although the current building is not old). It's less busy than the first, but sometimes worshipers hurry between images of Thien Hau (shown here with a black face) praying for good fortune. Carved dragons curl around the pillars, and to the right of the altars is a frieze of a boat being swamped by a tsunami.

BACKGROUND

Eighty percent of Vietnam's ethnic Chinese live in the south of the country. Before 1975, the Hoa controlled 80 percent of industry in the south and 50 percent of banking and finance. After reunification, during a period of social, political and economic change, hundreds of thousands risked drowning or encounters with pirates in the South China Sea to flee the country, but there is still a large population of Chinese Vietnamese in Cholon. Today, they can own and operate businesses, join the Communist Party and the army, and enter university. Cholon appears to the casual visitor to be the most populated, noisiest, and in general the most vigorous part of Saigon, if not of Vietnam. It is here that entrepreneurial talent and private funds are concentrated—both resources that the Vietnamese government is keen to mobilize in its attempts to reinvigorate the economy.

TIPS

● Most of Cholon's main sights can be visited in half a day on foot.

● Despite Cholon's compact layout, the most relaxing option is to hire a cyclo for a few hours.

● Saigon's Chinatown is a bustling commercial zone. Wander the streets and visit some of the best pagodas and temples in the city.

1 Nghia An Assembly Hall

Beautiful little bonsai trees can be seen in the Botanical Gardens

The glowingly atmospheric interior of Phuoc Hai Tu

The post office has a curved ceiling designed by Gustave Eiffel

BEN THANH MARKET

➕ 129 A3 • Ben Thanh gyratory, at intersection of Le Loi, Ham Nghi and Tran Hung Dao streets, Binh Thanh District 🕐 Daily 7am–7pm

At a swirling, chaotic traffic circle, this large, covered, central market (**Cho Ben Thanh**) faces a statue of Tran Nguyen Han, a heroic 15th-century general who fought against the Ming Chinese occupiers. It is well stocked with clothes, household goods, toiletries, souvenirs, lacquerware, and embroidery, as well as food, including cold meats and fresh and dried fruits. Prices are not low, and most local people come here to browse, then buy elsewhere. But the quality is good, the selection probably without equal, and the sight of all that produce stacked high is unforgettable. Outside the north gate (**Cua Bac**), on Le Thanh Ton Street, are tempting displays of fresh fruit and cut flowers. Ben Thanh Night Market starts at dusk and is open until after midnight. As the sun sinks and the main market closes, food stands spring up on the surrounding streets, where it's possible to sit in the open and eat well and inexpensively.

BOTANICAL GARDENS

➕ 129 C1 • 2 Nguyen Binh Khiem Street ☎ 08-8293728 🕐 Daily 6am–8pm 💰 10,000d (gardens and zoo)

The Botanical Gardens (**Thao Cam Vien**) run alongside Nguyen Binh Khiem Street, at the end of Le Duan Street, where the Thi Nghe Channel flows into the Saigon River. They were established in 1864 by French botanist Jean-Batiste Louis Pierre, and by the 1970s had a collection of nearly 2,000 species, including a particularly fine display of orchids. Following the Vietnam War the gardens went into decline, a situation from

which they are still trying to recover. A small zoo in the south quarter of the gardens has live inhabitants and a life-size family of Vietnamese-speaking model dinosaurs.

CHOLON

See pages 132–134.

EMPEROR OF JADE PAGODA

➕ 131 D1 • 73 Mai Thi Luu Street, off Dien Bien Phu Street, District 3 🕐 Daily 6am–6.30pm

Behind low pink walls, just before the Thi Nghe Channel, is the Emperor of Jade Pagoda (**Phuoc Hai Tu** or **Chua Ngoc Hoan**), dedicated to the supreme god of the Taoists, though also containing other deities. These include the Archangel Michael of the Buddhists; a Sakyamuni (historic) Buddha; statues of the two generals who tamed the Green Dragon (representing the east) and the White Dragon (representing the west), to the left and right of the first altar respectively; and Quan Am, the Goddess of Mercy, Guardian Spirit of Mother and Child. The statues are, remarkably, made of papier-mâché. The Jade Emperor himself is flanked by guardians known as the Big Diamonds (Tu Dai Kim Cuong), and to his right is Phat Mau Chan De, mother of the Buddhas of north, south, east, west and center, with her two faces and 18 arms. Built by Cantonese worshipers in 1909, the pagoda is a riot of color, with gilded pictographs, woodcarvings and exquisite tilework on the roof. The Hall of Ten Hells, in the sanctuary, has reliefs showing a thousand infernal tortures. In the grounds, women sell birds that are set free to gain merit, and a pond here contains large turtles.

GENERAL POST OFFICE

➕ 129 B2 • Cong Xa Pari, District 3 ☎ 08-8292291 🕐 Daily 6am–8pm

The facade of this 1880s building has attractive cornices with French and Khmer motifs and the names of French men of letters and science. Inside, the high, vaulted ceiling and fans create a wonderfully cool atmosphere in which to scribble a postcard. Note the vast, old wall map of Cochin China.

GIAC LAM PAGODA

➕ 130 B1 • 118 Lac Long Quan Street, 1 mile (2km) northeast of Giac Vien Pagoda 🕐 Daily 6am–9pm

The city's oldest pagoda was built in 1744 and is set among fruit trees and vegetable plots. A sacred bodhi tree grows in the courtyard. Blue and white porcelain plates decorate the roof and some of the towers marking burial places of former head monks. Inside, tiers of Buddhas on the main altar are dominated by the gilded Buddha of the Past. A section behind the main temple features rows of funerary tablets, showing pictures of the deceased, and a bust of Ho Chi Minh. At the very back of the pagoda is a hall with murals picturing infernal tortures.

A Buddhist monk lights incense at the Giac Lam Pagoda, the oldest one in the city

The Ho Chi Minh Museum displays this cheerful poster

The grand entrance of the Fine Art Museum

GIAC VIEN PAGODA

➕ 130 A2 • Lac Long Quan Street, District 11

Giac Vien Pagoda (**Chua Giac Vien**) is right at the end of a narrow alley off Lac Long Quan Street (beyond No. 247). Similar in layout, content and inspiration to Giac Lam Pagoda (▷ 135), it was built in 1771 and dedicated to Emperor Gia Long (reigned 1802–20). Now restored, Giac Vien is lavishly decorated, with more than 100 carvings of divinities and spirits. Demons and gods jump out around every corner, the aromas and smoke of incense drift through the air, and rich shades gleam in the semi-darkness. Outside, a small pavilion houses urns containing the ashes of the dead.

HO CHI MINH MUSEUM

➕ 129 C4 • 1 Nguyen Tat Thanh Street, District 4 ☎ 08-9402060 🕑 Daily 7.30–11.30, 1.30–4.30 💷 15,000d 🖥 🏛 ❓ Labels in English

This building at Dragon House Wharf has been converted into a museum (**Khu Luu Niem Bac Ho**) celebrating the life and exploits of Ho Chi Minh, mostly through pictures and the occasional piece of memorabilia, including clothing. Schoolchildren are brought here to be told of their country's recent history, and visitors of all ages have their photographs taken with the portrait of Bac Ho (Uncle Ho) in the background. Around the back of the museum on an exterior wall are interesting photographs and prints, plus two carriages from early 20th-century Saigon. There's also a pleasant, breezy café on the river, and you can watch the boats from the upstairs balcony. A statue of Ho Chi Minh as a young man overlooks the river.

FINE ART MUSEUM

An eclectic mix of art and crafts ranges from ceramics and sculpture to propaganda work and modern art instalations.

➕ 129 B4 • 97A Pho Duc Chinh Street, District 1 ☎ 08-8294441 🕑 Tue–Sun 9–5 💷 15,000d 🏛 Much of the contemporary art is for sale ❓ Labeling erratic; only general descriptions in English

RATINGS	
Cultural interest	●●●
Good for kids	●
Historic interest	●●●

The Fine Art Museum (**Bao Tang My Thuat**) displays a collection of work from the classical period through to socialist realism. The museum building itself, a cream-colored art nouveau-influenced mansion, is worthy of note; it was constructed early in the 20th century by a wealthy Chinese businessman. Three floors up is a collection of ancient art that contains finds dating from the civilizations of Oc-eo through to the Cham era. More recent collections include attractive Dong Nai ceramics of the early 20th century. The museum's ground-level floor is given over to temporary displays.

HIGHLIGHTS

Among the most interesting early works is a 12th-century sculpture of Kala, a temple-guarding monster, from My Son (▷ 123) —a fanged beast with a big protuberance for a nose, bulging eyes and forest-thick eyebrows. Sandstone sculptures of Hindu gods include Laksmi, Goddess of Beauty and Good Fortune, a seventh-to eighth-century AD figure found in Soc Trang. Early 20th-century gaunt, wooden funeral statues, made by the Tay Nguyen people in the Central Highlands to represent their late relatives, line a corridor.

Go up two floors to find modern lacquered pictures such as the interior of Cu Chi by Quach Phong (1997). There's a small collection of propaganda art posters (undated), which are similar in theme but surprisingly diverse in individual style. A vast, bronze mural by Nguyen Sang (also undated) represents the nation, and there are fascinating drawings of prison riots that were produced in 1973. Some of the most interesting work here consists of montages and photography reflecting on the Vietnam War and produced by Americans.

Don't miss Sculptures and contemporary art galleries are set up in the museum's backyard.

LAM SON SQUARE

The historic and cultural heart of Saigon is a magnet for shoppers, courting couples, idlers, tourists and thousands of horn-blaring motorcyclists.

Lam Son Square (**Quang Truong Lam Son**) is at the center of Saigon in the heart of District 1. Key roads radiate from this point, and it is surrounded by important cultural and historical buildings as well as famous hotels. The Rex Hotel, once a favorite with US officers, stands at the intersection of Le Loi and Nguyen Hue boulevards. This was the scene of the daily press-briefing session during the Vietnam War that came to be known as the Five O'Clock Follies. Following many years of immobility, the crown on the sixth-floor terrace—a popular spot for a drink—has been renovated and is rotating once again.

NORTHWEST OF THE REX

Near the Rex, at the northwestern end of Nguyen Hue Boulevard, is the ornate, yellow and white French colonial City Hall, now home to the Ho Chi Minh City People's Committee. It was built in 1908 and modeled on the Hôtel de Ville in Paris. The building overlooks a statue of Uncle Ho, who offers comfort, or perhaps advice, to a child. This is a popular place for Vietnamese to have their photographs taken, especially newlyweds, who believe Ho confers his blessing on them.

NORTHEAST OF THE REX

At the end of Le Loi Boulevard is the once impressive, French-era Opera House, built in 1897 to a design by French architect Ferret Eugene and restored in 1998. It once housed the National Assembly; now it provides a schedule of theater, dance and gymnastics (▷ 183).

Facing the Opera House to the left is the Continental Hotel, built in 1880 and an integral part of the city's history. British novelist Graham Greene (1904–91) stayed here, and the hotel features in his book *The Quiet American*. Journalists, soldiers and others used to gather at the so-called Continental Shelf, a veranda, during the Vietnam War, to pick up information. There is also a lovely enclosed garden.

The Continental sits on Dong Khoi Street, formerly known as Tu Do Street and, during the French colonial era, as the rue Catinat. This road stretches from Cong Xa Pari down to the Saigon River and is lined with shops specializing in, or selling a variety of, silk clothes and accessories, jewelry, lacquerware and household goods. Facing the Continental and adjoining Dong Khoi Street is the opulent Hotel Caravelle, which houses shops selling luxury goods.

The national flag flutters over the former Hôtel de Ville (top). The gleaming facade of the Rex Hotel (above)

RATINGS	
Cultural interest	●●●○
Photo stops	●●●○
Specialist shopping	●●●●○

BASICS

✚ 129 B3 • Bordered by Nguyen Hue and Le Loi boulevards, and by Dong Khoi Street, District 1
🍴 Wide range in the area

TIPS

● The Rex Hotel is a useful landmark when exploring the central area of the city.
● On weekend evenings literally thousands of young men, women and families cruise up and down Nguyen Hue and Le Loi boulevards and Dong Khoi Street on bicycles and motorcycles in a practice known as *chay long rong* (cruising) or *song voi* (living fast).

An old Citröen outside the Museum of Ho Chi Minh City

MARIAMMAN HINDU TEMPLE

⊞ 129 A3 • 45 Truong Dinh Street
◷ Daily 7–7

The Mariamman Hindu Temple (**Chua Ba Mariamman**) houses a statue of Mariamman, Mother of the Universe, who represents power but is also specifically the Goddess of Diseases. She is flanked by her guardians, Maduraiveeran and Pechiamman. About 60 Tamil Hindus live in the city, but Chinese also hold this temple sacred, and it is not unusual to see Chinese Vietnamese worshipers clasping incense sticks and prostrating themselves in front of the Hindu deity.

This Hindu figurine is in the Sri Mariamman Temple

MUSEUM OF HO CHI MINH CITY

⊞ 129 B2 • 65 Ly Tu Trong Street, District 1 ☎ 08-8299741 ◷ Daily 8–4
🖐 15,000d 🗎 🏧

A stately, gray, neoclassic building built between 1885 and 1890 for the governor of Cochin-China now houses the fairly spartan museum of the revolution (**Bao Tang Thanh Pho Ho Chi Minh**), whose highlights are the old black and white pictures of Saigon, a 19th-century fire

A relief work from the Museum of Vietnamese History

MUSEUM OF VIETNAMESE HISTORY

A striking building houses important Dong Son artifacts and Cham sculptures, as well as other national historic relics.

⊞ 129 C1 • 2 Nguyen Binh Khiem Street, District 1 ☎ 08-8298146 ◷ Mon–Sat 8–11, 1.30–4, Sun 8.30–4 🖐 15,000d 🚫 No photography; labeling in English and French

RATINGS				
Cultural interest	●	●	●	● ●
Good for kids	●	●	●	
Historic interest	●	●	●	● ●

TIPS
● Water puppet shows are held here daily (▷ 183) for a small fee.
● A research library on the third floor up opens Mon–Sat and has a collection of books on Indochina.

The history museum (**Bao Tang Lich Su Viet Nam**) occupies an elegant 1928 building with a pagoda-based design. The collection spans a wide range of objects from the prehistoric (300,000 years ago) and the Dong Son periods (3,500BC–AD100), right through to the birth of the Vietnamese Communist Party in 1930. Particularly impressive are the Cham sculptures—the standing bronze Buddha, showing Indian stylistic influence, is probably the finest. There is also a delicately carved Devi (goddess) from the 10th century, and pieces such as the head of Siva, Hindu destroyer and creator, and Ganesh, elephant-headed son of Siva and Parvati, both from the eighth to ninth century AD. Representative pieces from the Chen-la, Funan, Khmer, Oc-eo and Han Chinese periods are also on display, along with items from the various Vietnamese dynasties and some hill-tribe objects. Other highlights include the wooden stakes planted in the Bach Dang riverbed to repel the war ships of the Mongol Yuan in the 13th century (▷ 27); a beautiful phoenix head from the Tran Dynasty (13th to 14th century), and a Hgor (big drum) of the Jorai people, made from the skin of two elephants, which once belonged to the Potauoui (King of Fire) family in Ajunpa district, Gia Lai Province. There are fine sandstone sculptures, including an incredibly smooth linga (seventh to eighth century AD) from Long An Province in the Mekong Delta. The linga represents the cult of Siva and signifies gender, energy, fertility and potency.

Don't miss The preserved body of a 60-year-old woman who died in 1869 was discovered in the city during work on apartments in 1994 and subsequently brought here.

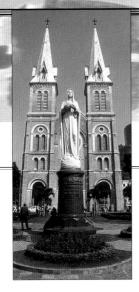

A gleeful, tree-shaded figure, outside Phung Son Tu Pagoda

Looking through a circular door at Phung Son Tu Pagoda

Notre Dame Cathedral is fronted by this graceful statue

engine and a beautiful 1921 map showing school locations and revealing the former French names of the city's streets. A mummified 19th-century man also on display was found in paddy fields in 2003; his alarming facial expression is reminiscent of the howling figure in the Edvard Munch painting *The Scream*. A few pieces of hardware (from helicopters and antiaircraft guns) are displayed in the rear compound.

NOTRE DAME CATHEDRAL

✚ 129 B2 • Cong Xa Pari, District 3
◉ Mon–Fri 8–10.30, 3–4; communion celebrated Sun 5.30am, 6.30am, 7.30am, 9.30am, 4pm, 5.15pm, 6.30pm

The twin-spired, redbrick Roman Catholic cathedral (**Nha Tho Duc Ba**) sits in the middle of Paris Square, an imposing and austere building overlooking a statue of the Virgin Mary. Built between 1877 and 1880, it is said to stand on the site of an ancient pagoda. Each of the cathedral's towers is 130ft (40m) high, and is topped with an iron spire.

PHUNG SON PAGODA

✚ 130 A2 • Set back from road at 1408 3 Thang 2 Boulevard ◉ Daily 5am–7pm

Phung Son Pagoda (**Chua Phung Son**) was built at the beginning of the 19th century on the site of an earlier structure and has been rebuilt several

times. At one time it was decided to move the pagoda, and all the temple valuables were loaded on to the back of a white elephant. The beast stumbled and the valuables tumbled out into the pond that surrounds the temple. This was taken as a sign from the gods that the pagoda was to stay where it was. The treasures were retrieved, except for a bell, which, it was said, would ring from beneath the water every full and new moon. The sanctuary houses a large, seated, gilded Buddha, surrounded by a variety of other figures from several Asian and Southeast Asian countries.

PHUNG SON TU PAGODA

✚ 129 A4 • 338 Nguyen Cong Tru Street, District 3 ◉ Daily 5am–7pm

This small temple (**Chua Phung Son Tu**) was built just after World War II by immigrants from China's Fukien province. Most notable are the wonderful painted doors with their fearsome bearded, armed warriors. Incense spirals hang in the open well of the pagoda, which is dedicated to Ong Bon, the Guardian of Happiness and Virtue; a statue of Ong Bon stands behind the main altar. Among details to look out for are little bat sculptures by the incense-seller's desk to the far right, a white monkey to the left, and a tiger to the right. Farther inside are more tigers in a savannah on the left, and a large, fire-breathing dragon on the right.

REUNIFICATION HALL

See page 140.

TOMB AND TEMPLE OF MARSHAL LE VAN DUYET

✚ 131 D1 • 126 Dinh Tien Hoang Street, Binh Thanh District ◉ Daily 7am–6pm

Le Van Duyet (1763–1831) was a Vietnamese general who put down the Tay Son peasant rebellion in the 18th century—an uprising that led to widespread reforms (▷ 29)—and was consequently promoted to marshal by Emperor Gia Long. After his death, Le Van Duyet's reputation was attacked and his tomb pillaged by Emperor Minh Mang, but under Emperor Thieu Tri's reign (1841–47) the tomb was restored, and subsequent renovation work took place in 1937. The main sanctuary contains a diverse assortment of objects, including a stuffed tiger, a miniature mountain, a baleen whale, various carved elephants, crystal goblets, spears and other weapons of war. Many of them were the marshal's personal possessions. In front of the temple (**Den Le Van Duyet**) is the tomb itself, surrounded by a low wall and flanked by two guardian lions and two lotus buds. The pagoda's attractive roof is best seen from the tomb.

This strange creature guards the Tomb of Le Van Duyet

THE SIGHTS

A military helicopter (top) sits atop the Reunification Hall. Inside the palace, many of the rooms are richly decorated (inset, above)

REUNIFICATION HALL

The former presidential palace was where South Vietnam fell to the Communists when a North Vietnamese Army tank crashed through the front gates in April 1975.

RATINGS

Good for kids	● ● ●
Historic interest	● ● ● ● ●
Photo stops	● ● ●

BASICS

✚ 129 A2 • 135 Nam Ky Khoi Nghia, District 3
☎ 08-8223652
◉ Daily 7.30–11, 1–4; hall sometimes closed for state occasions
💵 Adult 15,000d, child (5–15) 2,000d
▢ Refreshments on top floor
▣ Pamphlet 5,000d
▤ Guided tours (in English) every 10 min

TIPS

● There is a helipad and helicopter on the third level up but it costs US$1 extra to gain access.
● For US$1 you can have your photo taken sitting in the former president's chair.

Ngo Dinh Diem's presidential palace, now renamed Reunification Hall (**Hoi Thong Nhat**), dominates a large park in District 1. The French governor's residence was built here in 1868, and was later renamed the Independence, or Presidential Palace. In February 1962 planes piloted by two of the South's finest airmen took off to attack the Viet Cong, but turned back mid-flight to bomb the palace, in an attempt to assassinate President Diem, in residence since 1954. The President, who held office from 1955 to 1963, escaped with his family to the cellar, but the palace had to be demolished and replaced. (Diem was later assassinated after a military coup.) One of the pilots, Nguyen Thanh Trung, is a vice president of Vietnam Airlines and still flies.

One of the most memorable photographs taken during the Vietnam War was of a North Vietnamese Army tank crashing through the gates of the palace on April 30 1975, marking the end of South Vietnam and its government (a similar tank stands in the forecourt). The President and his cabinet were arrested here shortly afterwards.

INSIDE THE PALACE

The hall has been preserved as it was in 1975. In the Vice President's Guest Room there is a lacquered painting of the Temple of Literature in Hanoi (▷ 72–75); the Presenting of Credentials Room contains a fine, 40-piece lacquerwork showing visiting diplomats during the Le Dynasty (15th century). In the basement there are operations rooms, military maps, radios, telephones and other paraphernalia. Upstairs, foreign ambassadors met the President in the Dragon's Head Room (now the Presidential Receiving Room). Next to this is the Vice President's Room, with gold-colored furnishings. The President's living area was at the back, where he had a small cinema, a bar, a dance hall and a casino. Visitors are also shown a poorly made, but nonetheless interesting, film of the revolution.

The palace was rebuilt between 1962 and 1966 and is still filled with fabulously kitsch 1960s furnishings. It was designed according to Chinese geomancy, and even the carpet colors were chosen to calm or stimulate users of the rooms.

Don't miss A display of presidential gifts includes hollowed elephants' feet.

The former US Embassy is now the US Consulate General

An incense stick goes into the burner at Vinh Nghiem Pagoda

A gleaming Buddha statue in the Xa Loi Pagoda

TRAN HUNG DAO TEMPLE

✚ 131 D1 • 34 Vo Thi Sau Street, District 1 ⏰ Mon–Fri 6–11, 2–6

Not far from the Emperor of Jade Pagoda (▷ 135) is this small temple built in 1932 and dedicated to the worship of the victorious 13th-century General Hung Dao. A series of bas-reliefs depicts the general's successes, and the temple also contains weapons and carved dragons. Tran Hung Dao used a tried and trusted technique to defeat the Chinese in 1288, sinking wooden stakes into the Bach Dang River off the coast of northeast Vietnam. For the second time in less than 500 years the invading Chinese fleet was impaled on the poles and put out of action. In the front courtyard is a larger-than-life bronze statue of this hero of Vietnamese nationalism. A nearby park occupies the former site of the Massiges cemetery, where French military and colonial residents were laid to rest.

US CONSULATE GENERAL AND MEMORIAL

✚ 129 B1 • 4 Le Duan Street, District 3 ☎ 08-8229433 ⏰ Mon–Thu 8.30–11.30, 1.30–3.30. Closed Fri, Vietnamese and US public holidays http://hochiminh.usconsulate.gov

Running north of the cathedral is Le Duan Street, the former corridor of power ending at Ngo Dinh Diem's Palace (Reunification Hall) and lined with the former embassies of France, the US and the UK. One block from the French Consulate was the former US Embassy, a 1960s building that was quickly demolished by the Americans after diplomatic ties were resumed in 1995. The US Consulate General now stands on the site. Outside, a line of hopeful visa applicants forms every day come rain or shine. This office has the distinction of being the busiest overseas US mission for marriage visas, a title for which it vies closely with the US Embassy in Manila. A memorial outside, on the corner of Mac Dinh Chi Street, records the attack by Viet Cong special forces during the Tet Offensive of 1968 and their final victory in 1975. On the other side of the road, a little farther northeast at 25 Le Duan, is the former British Embassy, erected in the late 1950s and now the British Consulate General and British Council.

Typical Japanese pagoda architecture at the Vinh Nghiem Pagoda

VINH NGHIEM PAGODA

✚ 131 C1 • 339 Nam Ky Khoi Nghia Street, off Nguyen Van Troi Street, District 3 ⏰ Daily 7.30–11.30, 2–6

The Vinh Nghiem Pagoda (**Chua Vinh Nghiem**) was completed in 1967 and inaugurated four years later. Its Japanese style is a result of the contribution made by the Japan–Vietnam Friendship Association to the construction funds. A statue of Buddha occupies each of the tower's eight stories, and the sanctuary itself is large and airy. On either side of the entrance are two fearsome warriors, and inside is a large, Japanese-style Buddha in an attitude of meditation, flanked by two goddesses. Along the walls scrolls depict the Jataka tales.

WAR REMNANTS MUSEUM

See page 142.

XA LOI PAGODA

✚ 131 C2 • 89 Ba Huyen Thanh Quan Street, District 3 ⏰ Daily 7–11, 2–5

Food stands surround this 1956 pagoda (**Chua Xa Loi**), which contains a much-revered multistory tower housing a sacred relic of the Buddha. The main sanctuary contains a large, bronze-coated Buddha in an attitude of meditation. Around the walls paintings depict the previous lives of the Buddha (with an explanation of each life to the right of the entrance). The pagoda is historically rather than artistically important, as it became a focus of dissent against the Diem regime; it was here that several Buddhist monks committed suicide by setting themselves alight. Hundreds of monks and nuns were arrested in a raid on the pagoda in 1963, among them the leader of the Buddhist faith, then aged 80.

THE SIGHTS

Exhibits at the War Remnants Museum include complete aircraft (above). Detail of an emblem on a US airplane (left)

WAR REMNANTS MUSEUM

This sobering collection of military hardware, photographs, and other items from the Vietnam War presents a graphic account of the conflict from the nation's perspective.

RATINGS				
Cultural interest	●	●	●	● ●
Historic interest	●	●	●	● ●
Photo stops			●	● ●

BASICS
✚ 129 A2 • 28 Vo Van Tan Street, District 3
☎ 08-8295587
🕐 Daily 7.30–11.45, 1.30–5.15
🎟 16,000d
🎁 Postcards and small Vietnamese souvenirs

TIPS
● Do not underestimate the force of some of the images on display; this is not for the very young or the fainthearted.
● To help you take everything in, you need to devote a few hours to this museum.

Photographs of atrocities and military action, bombs, tanks, planes, deformed fetuses—every conceivable reminder of the horrors of modern warfare—are piled from floor to ceiling in this museum (**Boa Tang Chung Tich Chien Tranh**). In the courtyard are tanks, bombs and helicopters; inside the museum, photographs and exhibits arranged in rooms around the courtyard record man's inhumanity to man. On the whole, the war is presented exclusively from the North Vietnamese and Viet Cong view, but nevertheless this is one of the most frequently visited sites by Western, and particularly American, travelers in the city. As a denunciation of war of any kind it is certainly hard-hitting.

THE EXHIBITS
The display covers the Son My (My Lai) massacre on March 16 1968, the effects of napalm and phosphorus, and the after effects of Agent Orange defoliation (a particularly disturbing section, containing bottled malformed human fetuses). Many of the pictures are difficult to view. One of the most repellent, dated 1967, shows an American GI holding up the remaining part of the body of a Viet Cong soldier, most of whom has been blown away. One of the most interesting rooms is that dedicated to war photographers and their pictures, forming a tribute to those who died pursuing their craft. Unusually, this section depicts the war from both sides. Wall-to-wall images include shots from Robert Capa's last roll of film before the famous photographer was killed by a landmine on May 25 1954, *Life* magazine's first color coverage of the conflict, and quotes from those who perished during the war. The enduring image of war presented through the camera lens is one of mangled metal, suffocating mud and injured limbs.

The propaganda room contains records of international protests against the war in countries such as Cuba and the Congo. Other displays feature weapons—such as the experimental artillery shell full of darts—and pieces used to punish the enemy, including a guillotine used by the French and tiger cages in which Viet Cong prisoners were kept on Con Son Island (▷ 150).

THE SOUTH

Vietnam's southernmost region can be a riot of greens—palm trees, orchards and brilliant paddy fields—or a gray and hostile place, where floods devastate the plains of the Mekong Delta. The Mekong River rises between May and September, depositing the silt that formed the delta, which grows year by year. In its wake, the river leaves a web of waterways where boats chug their leisurely way through this lush and exceptionally fertile region.

MAJOR SIGHTS

Can Tho and Floating Markets

From this pleasant and breezy Mekong town you can visit the famous river markets, where fruit and vegetables swing from locals' staves as they ply the waters selling their wares.

BASICS

✚ 286 D12
🛈 Can Tho Tourist, 20 Hai Ba Trung Street, tel 071-821852; daily 7am–8pm
🚌 Nguyen Trai Street; connections with Saigon
🚤 Speedboat from Saigon and Chau Doc; speedboat operated by Victoria Can Tho Hotel (▷ 255)
✈ Airport 6 miles (10km) from town
🍴 Local seafood specialties; several along waterfront and Restaurant Alley (Nam Ky Khoi Nghia Street)
🖥 Internet cafés on Vo Van Tan Street
🚌 Tours by Victoria Can Tho and Can Tho Tourist. Private tours from Saigon

www.canthotourist.com.vn
Offers tours of Can Tho and around.

A boat laden with goods (top) at Cai Rang Floating Market. Ho Chi Minh statue (right)

SEEING CAN THO

Can Tho is a large and rapidly growing commercial city in the heart of the Mekong Delta, with strong vestiges of French influence apparent in broad, tree-lined boulevards and elegant buildings. It is also the most welcoming and agreeable of the delta towns and is easily explored on foot. Hai Ba Trung Street, alongside the river, is the heart of town, where, at dusk, families stroll in the park in their best clothes. This pleasant, leafy promenade is dominated by a giant, silver-colored statue of Ho Chi Minh. Phan Dinh Phung Street is the main commercial route, a couple of blocks west, and to its west again is Hoa Binh Boulevard, the main thoroughfare, which becomes 30 Than 4 Boulevard and runs out toward the bus station.

HIGHLIGHTS

FLOATING MARKETS

✉ Phung Hiep, 20 miles (33km) from Can Tho; Phong Dien, 9 miles (15km) downriver; Cai Rang, 4 miles (7km) south of Can Tho 🕐 Daily; busiest 6–9am
💰 Phung Hiep, Phong Dien: about 20,000d per hour for two or 30,000d per hour for four. Cai Rang: 150,000d per boat carrying one to three people; 200,000d per boat for four to six people 🚤 Sampans available to rent in Hai Ba Trung Street
The river markets near Can Tho are bustling confusions of boats, goods, vendors, customers and tourists. From their boats the market traders attach samples of their wares to bamboo poles, which they hold out to attract customers. Up to seven vegetables can be seen dangling from the staves—winter melon, pumpkin, green onions, giant parsnips, grapefruit, garlic, mangoes, onions, and Vietnamese plums—and the boats are usually piled high with one or two of the products. Housewives paddle their sampans from boat to boat, haggling over prices and gossiping. At the back of the boats, the domesticity of life on the water can be seen, down to the washing hung out to dry. Phung Hiep has a snake market (on land), and yards where fishing boats and rice barges are made.

CHUA ONG PAGODA

✉ 34 Hai Ba Trung Street
Chua Ong Pagoda, facing the riverfront park, dates from 1894 and was built by Chinese from Guangzhou. Unusually for a Chinese temple it is not free-standing but part of a row of buildings. The right side of the pagoda is dedicated to the Goddess of Fortune, and the left side belongs to the fierce and warlike General Ma Tien, whose unsmiling statue stands here. The layout is a combination of the classic pagoda style, with a small, open courtyard where the incense smoke can escape, and the meeting-house style introduced by the Chinese in Southeast Asia, complete with its own language school.

MUNIRANGSYARAM PAGODA

✉ 36 Hoa Binh Boulevard

Two monks conduct prayers twice a day (5am and 6pm) in this pagoda built in 1946 to serve the city's Khmer residents. This is a Khmer Hinayana Buddhist sanctuary, and houses a seated figure of Siddhartha Gautama (the historical Buddha), meditating under a bodhi tree.

The Cai Rang Floating Market (above) presents an enduring image of Vietnam. Calligraphy in gold surrounds the entrance to the Chinese community hall in Can Tho (inset)

BACKGROUND

A small settlement was established at Can Tho at the end of the 18th century, although the town did not prosper until the French took control of the delta a century later and rice production for export began to take off. During the Vietnam War the city was used as an important US base, and thousands of GIs made their temporary home here. Can Tho's university was founded in 1966, and a rice research institute was established here, based at O Mon, 15 miles (25km) away on Highway 91. Like the International Rice Research Institute (IRRI), its more famous counterpart at Los Banos in the Philippines (and to which it is attached), one of the Can Tho institute's key functions is developing rice hybrids that will flourish in the varied conditions of the delta. Rice-husking mills still form a substantial part of the city's industry and contribute greatly to its economy.

TIPS

● Rent a small boat to visit the floating markets; larger boats are impractical and intrusive.
● The best time to visit the floating markets is between 6am and 8am, before most of the tourist boats arrive.

Cao Dai Great Temple

●

The Holy See of the indigenous Cao Dai religion is an architectural flight of fancy, where rites of worship combine elements of the world's major religions.

Cao Dai priests (above). The Cao Dai Holy See (right) and its splendid main hall (opposite)

RATINGS

Cultural interest	● ● ● ● ●
Photo stops	● ● ● ● ●
Walkability	● ● ●

BASICS

✚ 286 D11 • 2 miles (4km) east of Tay Ninh, 60 miles (96km) northwest of Saigon
☻ Prayer ceremonies daily 6am, noon, 6pm, midnight; visitor access to balcony
🚌 Tay Ninh; connections from Mien Tay via Cu Chi
🚌 Private tour from Saigon (which includes Cu Chi)

TIPS

● Do not enter the central portion of the nave—keep to the side aisles—and do not wander in and out during services.
● Remove your shoes before going on to the balcony to watch the ceremonies.
● Do not wear sleeveless tops or shorts.

Brightly painted figure (right) at Cao Dai Temple

THE GREAT TEMPLE

Idiosyncratic Cao Dai Great Temple is the main place of worship of the Cao Dai religion (▷ 14), built in 1880 and set within a large complex of schools and administrative buildings. The twin-towered cathedral is European in inspiration but with distinct Asian features. On the facade are figures of Cao Dai saints in high relief, and at the entrance is a painting depicting French writer Victor Hugo (1802–85) flanked by the Vietnamese poet Nguyen Binh Khiem (1492–1587) and the Chinese nationalist Sun Yat Sen (1866–1925). Sun Yat Sen holds an inkstone, symbolizing the link between Confucianism and Christianity. There are nine columns and nine steps to the cathedral, representing the nine steps to heaven.

INSIDE THE GREAT TEMPLE

After removing shoes and hats, women enter through a door to the left, men to the right, and they then proceed down their respective aisles toward the altar, usually accompanied by a Cao Dai priest dressed in white with a black turban. During services the priests don red, blue and yellow robes, signifying Confucianism, Taoism and Buddhism respectively. Senior officiates wear colored robes sporting an embroidered divine eye.

Rows of pink pillars entwined with green, horned dragons line the nave, leading up to the main altar, which supports a large globe on which is painted a single staring eye—the divine, all-seeing eye. The ceiling is blue and dotted with clouds and sparkling stars, representing the heavens, and the domes are covered in a riot of dragons and vegetation in pink, orange and green. Open, lattice-work windows pierce the walls, each with a divine eye as its centerpiece. Above the altar is the Cao Dai pantheon: at the top, in the center, is Sakyamuni Buddha; next to him, on the left, is Lao Tzu, master of Taoism; and left of Lao Tzu is Quan Am, Goddess of Mercy, sitting on a lotus blossom. On the other side of the Buddha statue is Confucius. The red-faced Chinese God of war and soldiers, Quan Cong, is shown to the right. Below Sakyamuni Buddha is the poet and leader of the Chinese saints, Li Ti Pei; below him is Jesus Christ and on the next level down Jiang Zhia, master of Geniism.

At the back of the cathedral is a sculpture of Pham Com Tac, one of the religion's founders, who died in 1957. He stands on flowers, surrounded by huge, brown snakes, and is flanked by his two assistants—one the leader of spirits, the other the leader of materialism.

Don't miss During services musicians on the balcony accompany singers using a single-stringed instrument called a *dan co*, held between their feet.

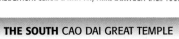

CHAU DOC AND SAM MOUNTAIN

The busy, commercial frontier town of Chau Doc straddles the giant crossroads of the Mekong. An important pilgrimage center at Sam Mountain is riddled with religious relics.

Sam Mountain makes a dramatic backdrop to Tay An Pagoda (top right). One of the pagoda's ornate bronze statues (above)

RATINGS		
Cultural interest	●●●	
Good for kids	●●	
Photo stops	●●●	

BASICS

✚ 286 C11 • An Giang Province, on border with Cambodia
💰 2,000d to enter Nui Sam area
🚌 Le Loi Street; connections with Saigon, Long Xuyen, Can Tho
🚢 Ferries from Phnom Penh, Ha Tien, Can Tho
🚗 Tours with Victoria Chau Doc (▷ 255). Private tours from Saigon

TIPS

● Sam Mountain is one of the holiest sites in southern Vietnam and is very crowded on auspicious days.
● The daily ferries along the 56-mile (90km) Vinh Te Canal to Ha Tien are a fascinating way to see village life; take plenty of water and food.

Chau Doc (formerly Chau Phu) is an attractive, bustling riverside town on the Hau or Bassac River and an important trading center for nearby agricultural communities. Until the mid-18th century this was part of Cambodia, but was given to the Nguyen Lord Nguyen Phuc Khoat after he helped quash an insurrection in the area. A large Khmer population still lives in the area, as well as the largest Cham settlement in the delta. Chau Doc District (a separate province for a while) is the seat of the Hoa Hao religion, founded in Hoa Hao village in 1939, with up to 1.5 million adherents.

The Vietnamese flock to Sam Mountain (**Nui Sam**), a barren hill honeycombed with tombs, sanctuaries and temples. Walk or drive up the hill, 3 miles (5km) southwest of town from Nguyen Van Thoai Street, for outstanding views of some of Vietnam's most fertile land.

MAIN SIGHTS

The Tay An Pagoda, facing the road at the foot of the hill, dates originally from 1847 but has been extended twice. It has an eclectic mixture of styles—Chinese, Islamic, perhaps even Italian—and inside more than 200 statues include elephants and green monsters.

Nearby, along the road to the right, is the rather featureless Chua Xu Temple, originally dating from the late 19th century but rebuilt in 1972. Revered by the Vietnamese, it honors the Holy Lady Xu, whose statue is in the new pagoda. The 23rd to 25th days of the fourth lunar month are the Holy Lady's festival, when crowds come to see the statue washed and reclothed.

On the other side of the road is the tomb of Thoai Ngoc Hau (1761–1829), a local hero of the resistance against the French, but more noted as a canal-building and swamp-draining engineer.

Hang Pagoda is a 200-year-old temple halfway up Sam Mountain (take the road to the right; entrance at street level). On the first level are vivid cartoons of the tortures of hell, while the second is at the mouth of a cave, home, during the last century, to a woman named Thich Gieu Thien. Her likeness and tomb can be seen in the first pagoda. She came here after leaving her lazy and abusive husband in Cholon and lived as an ascetic, supposedly waited on by two snakes.

Sampans take visitors from the ferry terminal near Victoria Chau Doc Hotel to Phu Hiep, a Cham village on the opposite bank of the river, which has some historic mosques.

CU CHI TUNNELS

The 124-mile (200km) complex of tunnels at Cu Chi was excavated by Viet Minh and Viet Cong fighters over 25 years of conflict.

Work began on the network of tunnels under Cu Chi town back in 1948, when the Viet Minh needed to find a way of escaping superior French weaponry and to communicate with each other in secret. Between 1960 and 1970 the network was expanded by the Viet Cong and used for storage as well as for refuge. The tunnels contained sleeping quarters, hospitals and schools, and were originally only 32in (80cm) high; some have been made bigger for larger Western visitors. The width of the tunnel entry at ground level was 9in by 12in (22cm by 30cm).

When the Americans first discovered this network they tried a variety of means to remove it. CS gas was pumped down tunnel openings, and explosives were set; river water was pumped in, and German shepherd dogs were sent to detect air holes (subsequently smothered in garlic to deter them). Craters testify to the carpet-bombing that was also employed. Some 40,000 Viet Cong were killed in the tunnels over the course of 10 years. Later, realizing the tunnels might also yield valuable intelligence, American commanders sent in volunteer "tunnel rats" to capture prisoners.

WHAT TO SEE

In Cu Chi 1, visitors are shown film footage of the tunnels during the Vietnam War before being taken underground to see some of the rooms and the booby traps that were encountered by GIs. The Viet Cong survived on cassava alone for up to three months at a time; here, and at Cu Chi 2, you will be encouraged to taste some, dipped in salt, sesame, sugar and peanuts.

In Cu Chi 2, visitors are invited to a firing range to try their hand with AK47s or a revolver for 15,000d a round. In the grounds of Cu Chi 2 is a pagoda, built in 1993 and devoted to the memory of the dead. Relatives of those who are still missing attend the pagoda, which is inscribed inside with the names of about 50,000 Vietnamese dead. Murals on the walls include imagery of the self-immolation of Buddhist monks in Saigon in 1963. The sculpture behind the temple is of a massive tear cradled in the hands of a mother.

Between the two sites is the Cu Chi military cemetery, where 10,000 soldiers are buried. There is a vast, gray, brutalist mural depicting the Vietnam War. Inside the cemetery gates is a large statue of a father weeping over the fallen body of his son.

Tiny tunnel entrance (top).
Re-created meeting room (above)

RATINGS

Good for kids	●●●●●
Historic interest	●●●●●
Photo stops	●●●

BASICS

🔲 286 D11 • 25 miles (40km) northwest of Saigon
☎ 08-7946442
🕐 Daily 7–5
💰 Ben Dinh (Cu Chi 1): 65,000d. Ben Duoc (Cu Chi 2): 65,000d
🚌 Cu Chi town; connections from Mien Tay and Ham Nghi stations, Saigon. Honda ôm or infrequent Ben Suc bus to tunnels
🍴 Snacks and ice cream
🛍 Souvenirs, flags and bottles of snake wine
🚗 Private tours from Saigon (include the Cao Dai Great Temple)

TIPS

● The Cu Chi Tunnels (Dia Dao Cu Chi) are too narrow for most Westerners, but a short section has been especially widened to allow visitors to share the experience. Tall or large people might still find it a claustrophobic squeeze.

● Cu Chi 1 (Ben Dinh) is more popular with the tourist trade; Cu Chi 2 (Ben Duoc) attracts fewer visitors and has more original tunnels.

Worshipers inside the Cao Dai Holy See

A detention center in one of the prisons

BA CHUC

✠ 286 C11 • 24 miles (38km) south of Chau Doc

On the road skirting the Cambodian border between Chau Doc and Ha Tien is an ossuary housing the bones of 1,000 Vietnamese, killed in 1978 by Cambodia's Khmer Rouge. Skulls are stacked up in a glass-sided memorial, and each section is categorized by gender and by age—from young children to grandparents.

CAN THO AND FLOATING MARKETS

See pages 144–145.

CAO DAI GREAT TEMPLE

See pages 146–147.

CHAU DOC AND SAM MOUNTAIN

See page 148.

CU CHI TUNNELS

See page 149.

HA TIEN

See page 154.

HON CHONG

✠ 286 C12 • 19 miles (30km) east of Ha Tien 🚌 From Ha Tien to Kien Luong, then *xe ôm* 🚗 🚤 Boats to the grotto and to Ngo Island (cave and statue): US$70–80 for half- or full-day trip. Hang Pagoda: adult 1,500d

Hon Chong is a popular beach with miles of clean, white sand and a string of cafés back behind the casuarina trees. Its other main claims to fame are the holy grotto and interesting limestone formations called Hon Phu Tu (Father and Son rocks), 100 yards (100m) or so offshore. Hang Pagoda (Chua Hang), inside a cave, houses a Buddha of 100 hands; a path through the temple exits right onto the beach.

CON DAO

Remote 19th-century prisons give a glimpse of a bleak past, while a spectacular national park encompasses a valuable ecological area.

✠ 286 D13 ☎ 064-830437 ✋ Prison: 1,000d. Tour: 30,000d 🚢 Passenger ships from Vung Tau weekly (overnight); tickets from shipping office, 2 Le Loi Street, Vung Tau, tel 064-580439 ✈ Flights from Saigon daily except Tue. Helicopters from Vung Tau airport Mon, Thu, Sat 8am; tickets from SSFC office, next to Tan Son Nhat airport, Saigon

RATINGS			
Cultural interest	●	●	●
Historic interest	●	●	● ●
Outdoor pursuits	●	●	● ●

TIP

● You can rent snorkeling equipment in the Con Dao National Park, and groups can share the cost of renting a speedboat.

Con Dao is a tiny archipelago of 14 islands. The biggest and only permanently settled island is Con Son, with a population of about 6,000. A trading post was set up here between 1702 and 1705 by the East Indies Trading Company; in 1773 it became home to Emperor Gia Long and mandarin families, fleeing after their defeat by the Tay Son. In 1832 Con Dao was ceded to the French by Emperor Tu Duc. The jails here were built in 1863 by Admiral Bonard to hold political prisoners—up to 12,000 of them—and the government of South Vietnam later put them to the same use.

A museum on Con Son (**Bao Tang Tong Ho Tinh**, daily 8–4) occupies the former prison governor's house and has items relating to the island's past. Three prisons are open, including one with life-size models and re-creations of the horrific conditions.

Con Dao National Park offers such activities as snorkeling, forest walks, swimming and birdwatching, and it's also the most important sea-turtle nesting site in Vietnam; several hundred female green turtles (*Chelonia mydas*) come ashore every year to lay their eggs. In the forests more than 1,000 plant species have been identified, several unique to Con Dao, and there's valuable timber and medicinal plants. This is the only place where you can see the rare pied imperial pigeon (*Ducula bicolor*), and one of few places that are home to the red-billed tropicbird (*Phaethon aethereus*). The extremely rare brown booby (*Sula leucogaster*) inhabits the most remote island, Hon Trung (*Egg Island*), a one-hour boat ride away, and there are thousands of seabirds.

Don't miss The infamous "tiger cages", where prisoners were chained and tortured, still stand at Con Son.

A riverboat trip (above) around My Tho. Vinh Trang Pagoda (right)

MY THO AND THE ISLANDS

A quiet, rural way of life survives among the fruit trees in this riverside market town, where you can watch rice-paper, rice "popcorn", coconut candy and honey in production.

My Tho sits on the banks of the Tien River, a distributary of the mighty Mekong, about 25 miles (40km) from the South China Sea. Dominating its river promenade is a statue of Nguyen Huu Huan, a resistance fighter who was captured by the French in 1875 and put to death. The town has a turbulent history, having been Khmer until the 17th century, when the advancing Vietnamese took control of the surrounding area. In the 18th century Thai forces annexed the territory, before being driven out in 1784. Finally, the French gained control in 1862.

AROUND MY THO

Vinh Trang Pagoda, at 60 Nguyen Trung Truc Street (daily 8–4) is entered through an ornate, porcelain-encrusted gate. The pagoda was built in 1849 in a mix of Chinese, Vietnamese and colonial styles, and its fairy-tale facade sits incongruously next to the encroaching forest. Not far from My Tho, the hamlet of Ap Bac was the site of the first major victory of the Communists against the Army of the Republic of Vietnam, which showed that without direct US involvement there was no prospect of the ARVN defeating the Communist forces.

THE ISLANDS

There are four islands in the Tien River between My Tho and Ben Tre—Dragon, Tortoise, Phoenix and Unicorn—which can be visited as part of a tour or by renting a boat. Dragon (**Tan Long**) Island lies immediately opposite My Tho and is a relaxing place to wander. It is especially noted for its longan crop, but there are many other fruits to sample here, as well as honey and rice whisky. Phoenix Island (**Con Phung**) is about 2 miles (3km) from My Tho. It's also known as the Island of the Coconut Monk, who established a retreat here shortly after World War II and developed a religious movement with elements of Buddhism and Christianity. He is said to have meditated for three years on a stone slab, eating nothing but coconuts. Persecuted by government and Communists, the monastery has fallen into disuse.

On Tortoise Island (**Con Qui**) there is an abundance of dragon fruit, longan, banana and papaya. Here visitors are treated to singing accompanied by a guitar and Vietnamese monochord.

RATINGS

Good for kids	●●●
Outdoor pursuits	●●●●
Walkability	●●●

BASICS

🔲 286 D12 • 44 miles (71km) southwest of Saigon

🚌 Ben Xe My Tho, Ap Bac Street; connections with Saigon, Can Tho, Chau Doc, Vinh Long, Cao Lanh

⛴ Ferry to Chau Doc from Ben Tre ferry terminal; ferry to islands from Le Thi Hong Gam Street

🍴 Good restaurants on Trung Trac Street; noodle stands at night on Le Loi Street and Le Dai Han Street intersection

▣ Island tours arranged by Mekotours (Cong Doan Tourist), based out of the Cong Doan, 61/30 Thang 4 Street, tel 073-874324; Song Tien Tourist Company, 11 Trung Trac Street, tel 073-883133; Tien Giang Tourist Company, 8/30 Thang 4 Street, tel 073-873184; private tours from Saigon

www.tiengiangtourist.com
Organizes international and local tours.

TIPS

● Prices for island tours vary according to the number of people; expect to pay about US$20 to US$25 to charter a boat for a few hours.
● Try the honey tea on one of the islands. The honey is made from the longan flower, and a splash of kumquat juice is added to balance the flavor.

PHU QUOC ISLAND

This remote, tropical island, fringed by beaches and an aquamarine sea, produces some of the best fish sauce in Vietnam.

RATINGS				
Outdoor pursuits	●	●	●	●
Photo stops	●	●	●	●
Walkability	●	●	●	

BASICS

✚ 286 B12

🚢 Daily ferry from Ha Tien; daily high-speed boat service from Rach Gia

✈ Connections with Saigon and Rach Gia

🍴 Beach and hotel restaurants; café at Phu Quoc Pearl Gallery

ℹ Discovery Tours, Tran Hung Dao Street, Duong Dong, tel 077-846050; daily 7am–8pm. Tony's Tour, tel 091-3197334, tel 077-847127, Tropicana Resort

TIPS

● There are only two asphalt roads on the island: from Duong Dong to An Thoi, and from Duong Dong to Ham Ninh.

● Motorcycles and cars with drivers can be rented from most resorts; check that the vehicle is in good working order before setting off.

Stunningly beautiful Long Beach (top) is lined by palm trees. The Phu Quoc Pearl Gallery is a popular visitor attraction (above inset)

Phu Quoc Island (**Dao Phu Quoc**), off the southwest coast, is Vietnam's largest island and remains largely undeveloped. White, sandy beaches line much of its coastline; forested hills and pepper farms are found inland. There are only a few resorts, and although new additions are planned the pace of development is slow due to the lack of power and water supplies to much of the island. Phu Quoc's northernmost tip lies just outside Cambodian territorial waters but within sight of its coast, and has in the past been disputed, claimed and reclaimed by Thai, Khmer and Viet powers. Refugees from the Khmer Rouge regime came to live at the northern town of Ganh Dau and Cambodian is still spoken here.

MAIN ATTRACTIONS

Dai Bau is a strip of white sand overlooking Turtle Island (**Hon Doi Moi**), 20 miles (32km) from Ganh Dau. The water is clear but there are no facilities. The dazzling, white sands of Sao Beach, on the southeast coast, are worth visiting by motorcycle, but poor signposting can make it hard to find. There's a restaurant at the back of the beach. Inland are wooded areas protected against clearance and development, and streams and waterfalls that lose their drama in the dry season but still provide relaxing spots to swim and walk.

Around the island, millions of fish can be seen laid out to dry—all destined to be made into fish sauce *(nuoc mam)*. Before being bottled they are fermented, and you can watch the process at the fish sauce factory in Duong Dong, where 95 massive wooden barrels act as vats, each containing fish and salt weighing 15 tons (14 tonnes) and ringing in the till at US$5,000 a barrel. If the sauce is made in concrete vats, the flavor is lost and so the sauce is less expensive.

About 6 miles (10km) south of Dong Duong is the Phu Quoc Pearl Gallery (daily 8–5.30). Just offshore, 10,000 South Sea pearls are collected each year. A video demonstrates the farming operation, and in the gallery the pearl-culturing process is illustrated and oyster meat can be tasted. Pearl necklaces are available for sale.

About 100 yards (100m) south of the pearl farm on the coastal road are two whale dedication temples (**Lang Ca Ong**, ▷ 156). In front of one is a crudely sculpted whale statue.

Don't miss Boat trips are arranged from the resorts around the An Thoi islands, off the southern coast, where you can swim and snorkel.

PLAIN OF REEDS

A rich diversity of birdlife thrives in the Mekong wetlands, where subterranean Viet Cong hiding places still survive.

The vast Plain of Reeds (**Dong Thap Muoi**) is a swamp that extends for miles north of Cao Lanh, capital of Dong Thap Province, toward Cambodia. In the rural districts Vietnamese houses are built on the highest land available, and during the wet season of a good year the floor remains inches above the rising waters. When the sky is gray the isolated plain can seem like the end of the earth, but is, in fact, an important habitat, teeming with wildlife.

BIRD SANCTUARIES

Tam Nong Bird Sanctuary (in Tram Chim National Park—**Khu Bao Ton Chim Tam Nong**) is a 20,000-acre (8,000ha) reserve, 28 miles (45km) northwest of Cao Lanh, and is home to 182 species of bird at various times of year. Its most famous resident is the red-headed crane (*Grus antigone sharpii*), rarest of the 15 known crane species, and the world's tallest flying bird. Between August and November these spectacular creatures migrate across the Cambodian border but in any month, particularly at dawn and dusk, they are a magnificent sight. Floating rice grows in the area, its leaves on the surface and its roots in the mud as much as 15ft (5m) down. So much energy is needed to grow the stalk, however, that little is left for the rice.

Storks and ibises can be seen at the White Stork Sanctuary (Vuon Co Thap Muoi), 27 miles (44km) northeast of Cao Lanh, near Thap Muoi. Again, dawn and dusk are the best times, when the sky is darkened by tens of thousands of birds flying off to feed or coming home to roost.

XEO QUYT BASE

Signs at My Long point to Xeo Quyt, a hidden Communist base (daily 8–5) 4 miles (6km) off the main road, 12 miles (20km) northwest of Cao Lanh. There was so little vegetation cover here that fast-growing eucalyptus trees were planted, but even these took three years to provide sufficient cover. The waterlogged ground prevented tunneling, so waterproof chambers sealed with plastic and resin were sunk into the mud. This base was stocked with rice, water and candles, and the Communists coordinated their resistance from here for almost 15 years of the Vietnam War. Despite frequent land and air raids the US forces never found or damaged the base. A 25-minute tour along narrow canals passes the underground shelters, offices and residences of party members. The sampans are paddled by women in Viet Cong dress, and make their way among the forest ferns and water hyacinth.

Boatwoman (top) at Xeo Quyt Base. Red-headed crane (above)

RATINGS	
Outdoor pursuits	●●●●
Photo stops	●●●
Walkability	●●●

BASICS

✚ 286 D11

🛈 Dong Thap Tourist Company, 2 Doc Binh Kieu Street, Cao Lanh, tel 067-855638; Mon–Fri 7–11.30, 1.30–5

💵 Bird sanctuary boat trips: US$20–30. Xeo Quyt trip and entrance: 6,000d

🚌 Buses from Saigon to Ly Thuong Kiet Street, Cao Lanh

🚤 Boat trips to main sites arranged by Dong Thap Tourist Company or private tours from Saigon

TIP

● During the wet season (September through November) water levels rise dramatically and all transportation around the Plain of Reeds is by boat.

Row upon row of plants at the Sa Dec flower nurseries

The US Army's pontoon bridge is still in use today

SA DEC

⊞ 286 D12 • 12 miles (20km) west of Vinh Long ⊟ Southeast of town; connections with Vinh Long, Long Xuyen ⊟ ⊟ Private tour from Saigon

A road lined with brick kilns leads to this small and friendly town, whose main avenues—Nguyen Hue, Tran Hung Dao and Hung Vuong—and attractive colonial villas reveal a lasting French influence. French novelist Margueritte Duras was born here, and parts of the film adaptation of her novel *The Lover* (1992) were filmed by the riverside on Nguyen Hue Street. Duras' childhood home is across the river and can be reached by sampan from the covered market.

Phuoc Hung Pagoda, at 75/5 Hung Vuong Street, is a splendid Chinese-style pagoda constructed in 1838 and decorated with fabulous animals assembled from pieces of porcelain rice bowls. Old turtles plod round the courtyard amid the greenery. Tu Ton Rose Garden (Vuon Hong Tu Ton), at 11/5 Vuon Hong Street (daily 6am–8pm), is west of Sa Dec and can be reached either on foot or by Honda ôm to Tan Qui Don village. This 14,800-acre (6,000ha) nursery borders the river and harbors more than 40 varieties of rose and 540 other types of plant, from medicinal herbs to exotic orchids.

SOC TRANG

⊞ 286 D12 ⊟ 101C Nguyen Chi Thanh Street; connections with Ca Mau, Can Tho, Rach Gia, Saigon ⊟ Ferry from Tra Vinh ⊟ ⊟ Private tour from Saigon

Straddling a narrow branch of the Mekong, Soc Trang is a sprawling and scruffy town with many Khmer residents. On the 4th day of the 10th lunar month (usually December) it takes on a carnival atmosphere for the

HA TIEN

This small Mekong Delta town, huddled along the river front, has several temples and tombs and gives access to beaches and Phu Quoc Island.

⊞ 286 B12 ⊟ Southeast edge of town; connections with Saigon, Rach Gia, Can Tho ⊟ Ferry to Chau Doc ⊟ ⊟ Private tour from Saigon

RATINGS			
Historic interest	●	●	●
Photo stops	●	●	●
Walkability	●	●	●

TIP

● The Cambodian border about 1 mile (2km) beyond Thach Dong Pagoda is not an authorized crossing point for foreigners.

Ha Tien lies west of a lagoon called East Lake (Dong Ho), which is bridged by a floating pontoon built by US Army engineers. Its riverside promenade, with a stilted café, is one of the most attractive in the delta. Ha Tien's history is strongly influenced by its proximity to Cambodia, to which the area belonged until the 18th century. There were Khmer incursions into the area in the late 1970s, and bitter resentments remain on both sides of the border.

Follow Phuong Thanh Street to the end to visit the Cotton Rose Hibiscus Pagoda (Chua Phu Dung) on Tomb Mountain (Nui Lang). In 1730, newly widowed Nguyen Nghi fled invaders from Laos and landed in Ha Tien with his son and 10-year-old daughter, Phu Cu, who dressed as a boy in order to be able to attend school. She subsequently became the second wife of Mac Cuu, the provincial governor, but after years of happy marriage begged her husband to let her become a nun, and in response Mac Cuu built the Cotton Rose Hibiscus Pagoda, where his wife spent the rest of her life in prayer and contemplation.

In 1708, Mac Cuu established a Vietnamese protectorate under waning Khmer rule. Den Mac Cuu is a temple built between 1898 and 1902 at the foot of Tomb Mountain, and is dedicated to him and his clan. To the left of the altar house is a map locating the tombs of clan members. Mac Cuu's own tomb lies a short distance up the hill along a path leading from the right of the temple.

Behind Tomb Mountain is Lang Mo Ba Co Nam (Tomb of Great Aunt Number Five). The honorary title was given to Mac Cuu's three-year-old daughter, who was buried alive. The tomb has become an important shrine to many Vietnamese, who seek the girl's divine intercession in times of family crisis.

Don't miss Two beautiful blue phoenix standing on turtles flank the tomb of Great Aunt Number Five.

Unmistakably the tomb of a pig, at the Matoc Pagoda, Soc Trang

Khmer *Ooc-om-bok* festival, culminating with a river boat race.

At the top end of town on Nguyen Thi Minh Khai Street is the Kleang Pagoda, a temple built in traditional Cambodian style, perched on a two-level terrace. Vivid colors adorn the windows and doors, and inside sits a fine golden Sakyamuni statue with an electric halo.

About 2 miles (3km) out of town is the Matoc Pagoda (Maha Tup in Khmer). Follow Le Hong Phong Street and fork right after the fire station. The main pagoda is on the right and is decorated with bright murals; it has been recently restored with donations from the Vietnamese and Khmer diaspora. Thousands of fruit bats roost in the trees behind the pagoda and at dusk they are an impressive sight as they fly off to find food, blackening the sky. Also behind the pagoda are the monks' living quarters and the tombs of two five-toed pigs. Living examples can be seen in the pens, lovingly cared for by the monks.

TRA VINH

➕ 286 D12 🚌 Nguyen Dan Street; connections with Vinh Long
🍴 🚌 Private tour from Saigon

This attractive capital of the province of the same name has huge trees—some well over 100ft (30m) tall—lining almost every street. It is home to a large Khmer population and has 140 Khmer temples. Hang Pagoda is about 3 miles (5km) south of town, and Giong Long Pagoda is 27 miles (43km) southeast. Neither is particularly noteworthy architecturally, but both provide the awe-inspiring sight of hundreds of storks resting in their grounds and wheeling around their pointed roofs at dawn and dusk.

Making spring rolls on An Binh Island

VINH LONG

Escape from the bustle of Vinh Long to An Binh Island and experience a tranquil way of life in the Mekong Delta. The small floating market at Cai Be will be of interest to those unable to make it to Can Tho.

➕ 286 D12 🛈 Cuu Long Tourist, 1 Thang 5 Street, tel 070-823616
🚌 1A Dinh Tien Hoang Street, 3 miles (5km) from downtown; connections with Saigon, Can Tho, My Tho, Long Xuyen, Rach Gia, Sa Dec
🚌 Range of excursions arranged by Cuu Long Tourist, 1 Thang 5 Street, tel 070-823616, or private tour from Saigon

RATINGS			
Good for kids	●	●	●
Outdoor pursuits	●	●	●
Walkability	●	●	

TIP
● Stay overnight in a homestay on An Binh Island and get up at dawn to watch the sunrise.

The capital of Vinh Long Province is a busy and somewhat ramshackle town on the banks of the Co Chien River. It was one of the focal points of the spread of Christianity in the Mekong Delta, and in addition to its interesting temples and pagodas there is a cathedral and Catholic seminary in town. There is also a Cao Dai church near the second bridge leading into town from Saigon and My Tho. River trips from Vinh Long, taking in the surrounding islands and orchards, are very enjoyable but can be expensive owing to Cuu Long Tourist's monopoly. Local boatmen risk the fine to take visitors for a much lower price. There is a small floating market and an attractive church at Cai Be, about 6 miles (10km) from Vinh Long.

An Binh Island is a 10-minute ferry ride from Phan Boi Chau Street and provides a splendid example of a typical delta landscape. The island can be explored either by boat, paddling down narrow canals, or by following the dirt tracks and teetering across monkey bridges—single bamboo poles with, if you are lucky, a flimsy handrail. Sights on the island include the ancient Tien Chau Pagoda and a *nuoc mam* (fish sauce) factory, and the welcoming residents will also show you popcorn made from rice, rice-paper production and a lovely bonsai garden. Nguyen Van Tam, also known as Mr Tiger, is the island's oldest resident, and owns a flourishing orchard with bonsai trees, which can be visited on a tour (Green Island Tour, Binh Tuan 1 Hamlet, Hoa Ninh Village, tel 070-859859).

Don't miss Paddling around the narrow channels of An Binh Island in a sampan is a great way to spend some time.

THE SIGHTS

Grand, ballustraded building in Vung Tau (top). Political posters (inset) call for support

RATINGS

Cultural interest	● ● ●
Historic interest	● ● ● ●
Outdoor pursuits	● ●

BASICS

✚ 287 E12

ℹ 207 Vo Thi Sau Street, tel 064-856445; Mon–Fri 7–11.30, 1.30–5

🚌 192 Nam Ky Khoi Nghia Street; connections with Saigon, Bien Hoa, Binh Khanh

🚢 Halong Street; hydrofoil from Ham Nghi Street Wharf, Saigon

🚁 Helicopter service from Saigon

TIPS

● There are many Honda *ôms* and taxis in town but few cyclos.

● Distances within town are quite short and can be covered comfortably on foot.

VUNG TAU

This hub of the country's oil industry and significant fishing port is also a popular coastal resort, packed with visitors every weekend.

Vung Tau sits on a rocky promontory between two hills, Nui Lon (Big Mountain) to the north and Nui Nho (Small Mountain) to the south. Vietnamese day-trippers flock here for its cooling breezes and beach-front, and the town enjoys a high level of prosperity based on oil, trade and its role as capital of Ba Ria-Vung Tau Province. As Cap Saint-Jacques, it began developing as a seaside resort at the beginning of the 20th century, but with the exception of Bai Sau (Back Beach), the beaches are narrow and have little or no sand. Bai Sau lies on the east side of town, 1 mile (2km) southeast of the center, and has a 3-mile (5km) stretch of sand, exposed to the wind and the South China Sea. The surf is usually good—sometimes ferocious.

TOWN SIGHTS

At 12 Tran Phu Street (the coast road) is Bach Dinh (daily 7–5), built in the early part of the last century as a summer residence (Villa Blanche) for French Governor-General Paul Doumer on the site of an old fort. It's now a museum for the Hon Cau, or Vung Tau, ceramics, dating from the Qing Dynasty, that were salvaged in 1990–91 from a Chinese trading junk that sank near Con Dao Island in around 1690. The find was highly significant not only for its size—48,000 pieces in all—but also because it represents some of the first pieces of stand-ing, as opposed to flat, ceramics to come from China. This collection consists of vases, goblets and small statues; some are encrusted with coral and some retain their original elegant blue and white glaze. The building is rather fine, with a mosaic frieze running around beneath the eaves. It has a glorious outlook and beautiful gardens with colorful *cay su* trees, a type of Vietnamese rhododendron.

The Whale Dedication Temple (**Lang Ca Ong**), at 77A Hoang Hoa Tham Street, is sumptuously adorned in red and gold and dedicated to the whale, the patron god of Vung Tau fisherfolk (worship of the whale was inherited from the Cham). It was built in 1911 and con-tains a number of whale skeletons in cabinets behind the main altar. The one to the right of the altar dates from 1931, while the central skeleton is believed to date from 1848. Whale and dolphin bones are brought to the temple and worshiped before being cremated: The marine mammals are credited with saving drowning sailors and fisherfolk. Photographs show the annual whale dedication ceremony.

This chapter gives information on things to do in Vietnam other than sightseeing. It is divided into five regions, which are shown on the map on the inside front cover. Within each region, towns are listed alphabetically. Entries in the Hanoi and Ho Chi Minh City sections are listed alphabetically by category.

What to Do

SHOPPING

Since the gradual liberalization of the Vietnamese economy began in 1986, shopping has become increasingly varied and enjoyable. You'll find a wide range of designer clothing, high-quality handicrafts, ceramics, lacquerware and silk goods, including tailor-made silk dresses and shirts, at relatively low prices. Some visitors even buy extra luggage to take home all their purchases! The main shopping destinations are Hanoi, Ho Chi Minh City and Hoi An. A word of warning: It is against Vietnamese law and international wildlife convention laws (CITES) to buy and trade in marine turtle products.

BASICS

The majority of shops and markets in Vietnam are open from early in the morning to late at night every day of the week. They do not close for

An array of colorful items for sale in Pho Hang Ma, Old Hanoi

lunch. Most shops now accept internationally recognized credit cards. Shops and markets accept US dollars and Vietnamese dong; at markets your change will be returned in dong. There is no sales or government tax on shop purchases. Bargaining is expected in markets and in shops except where price tags are used.

Export of wood or antiques is strictly controlled, and anything antique or antique-looking may be seized upon at customs unless you have a license. If your purchase is antique or antique-looking, you will need to get an export

license from the Customs Department (▷ 261), although this can be a time-consuming process. If you buy through a reputable shop, they can handle the paperwork for you. If you are buying a reproduction, then you need to make sure it states this on your receipt.

ANTIQUES

In Ho Chi Minh City, most antiques shops are on Dong Khoi, Mac Thi Buoi and Ngo Duc Ke streets. For the knowledgeable, there are bargains to be found, especially Chinese and Vietnamese ceramics. Also available are old watches, colonial bric-à-brac, lacquerware and carvings. To look for items off the beaten track, spend an hour or so browsing the shops in Le Cong Trieu Street, which is not marked on any maps but runs between Nam Ky Khoi Nghia and Pho Duc Chinh streets, just south of Ben Thanh Market. Here you may find interesting items of furniture, statuary and ceramics. Bargaining is expected and can deliver some pretty good deals.

Along Hang Khay and Trang Tien streets and the south edge of Hoan Kiem Lake are Hanoi's main antiques outlets. Shops sell silver ornaments, porcelain, jewelry and carvings. Much is not antique and not all is silver; bargain hard.

Remember that you need a license to take antiques out of the country (▷ "Basics").

ART AND ART GALLERIES

Contemporary art in Vietnam, as elsewhere in Southeast Asia, has benefited from an upsurge in interest from young Asian collectors with plenty of money. Exhibits in Hong Kong, New York, Paris and London have helped bring contemporary Vietnamese art to a wider public. Galleries have opened in all the major cities of Vietnam, and although much of the work displayed is purely

A stall in Dong Ba Market in Hué selling classic conical hats

commercial, artists now have the chance to show pictures that would, not long ago, have been considered subversive. Vietnam has three art colleges: one in Saigon, one in Hué and the School of Fine Arts in Hanoi, which was founded by the French in 1925.

Although most Vietnamese painting is still conservative in subject, idiom and medium, some painters of the younger generation, including Dao Hai Phong, Tran Trong Vu and Truong Tan, are experimenting with more abstract ideas; in the more liberal artistic climate of the new millennium, their work is more

expressive and less clichéd than that of 10 or 20 years ago. Even established artists such as Ly Quy Chung, Tran Luu Hau and Mai Long are taking advantage of their newly found artistic freedom to produce exciting experimental work; Trinh Cung and Tran Trong Vu are noted for their abstract paintings, and Nguyen Thanh Binh's famous but faceless schoolgirls in *ao dais* (long, flowing tunics worn over trousers) hang in drawing rooms across Asia and Europe. The popularity of this theme has been seized upon by many lesser artists. Among the most respected artists of the older generation are Professor

A craftsman displays his newly designed lacquerware boxes

Nguyen Thu, Colonel Quang Tho and Diep Minh Chau, whose work draws heavily on traditional Vietnamese themes, particularly rural landscapes, but also episodes from recent history: the battle of Dien Bien Phu, life under American occupation and pencil sketches of Ho Chi Minh. Such traditional art forms as watercolor paintings on silk and lacquerwork are still popular.

Ho Chi Minh City has acquired something of a reputation for its galleries, and a number of contemporary artists have a considerable international following. There are also countless shops that do nothing but reproduce works of art and are willing to turn their hand to anything. They will produce an oil portrait from a crumpled passport photograph, paint a stately home from a postcard, or a grand master from a photograph in a magazine. There is also a lot of lively original work inexpensively available in shops around Pham Ngu Lao and in the Dong Khoi area.

Hanoi has a few art galleries and shops. These are scattered around the Hoan Kiem Lake area. Leading Vietnamese contemporary artists are represented, and paintings are sold in US dollars. Prices are high for Vietnam but not for the Western contemporary art trade.

Many galleries sell original works of art in Hoi An. Vietnamese artists have been inspired by its old buildings, which are instantly recognizable even when distorted into a variety of shapes and hues on canvas or silk. Galleries are found everywhere, but in particular the more serious are clustered near one another on Nguyen Thi Minh Khai Street, west of the Japanese Bridge.

CERAMICS

Vietnam has a ceramics tradition going back hundreds of years. There has been a renaissance of this art since the 1990s, and shops selling new and antique (or antique-looking) ceramics abound on the main shopping streets of Dong Khoi and Le Thanh Ton in Ho Chi Minh City. Much is in traditional Chinese-style blue and white, and there is also a very attractive celadon green, often with a crackled glaze. Other styles and finishes are coming to the fore as local craftspeople brush the dust off old ideas and come up with new ones.

DEPARTMENT STORES

Ho Chi Minh City now has several good, air-conditioned department stores selling everything from electrical goods and cellular phones to clothes, jewelry, make-up and food. Prices for some of these items are equivalent to prices in the West or just a little lower. The range or quality of clothes, however, is more limited than would be expected in a Western department store, with a few exceptions where Western-brand clothes are available. Western-style supermarkets are usually found inside the department stores, selling everything from cornflakes and

Beautiful women's clothing is available to buy in old Hanoi

milk to liquor and toiletries. All supermarkets require you to leave your bags in lockers at the entrance to the stores.

FASHION

Beautiful and affordable women's clothes are now sold in designer and clothes stores in Hanoi and Saigon in particular. Vietnam has produced a number of exciting fashion designers in the past few years (▷ 24), and there is a growing number of stylish stores in the fashionable cathedral shopping area in Hanoi. These sell jackets, dresses, handbags, scarves and shoes—a phenomenon

that has appeared over a remarkably few years. The greatest concentration of shops is in the Hoan Kiem Lake area, especially on Nha Tho, Nha Chung, Hang Trong and Hang Gai streets. Imported luxury goods are sold in the Sofitel Metropole Hotel's Louis Vuitton outlet.

Tailors charge low prices and can produce skirts, shirts and jackets from patterns and photographs, but quality does vary considerably. It's worth shopping around. Demand for speedy work can create enormous strain on staff and a poorer quality end product, so if you are in town for a few days it pays to do your clothes

Bags for sale featuring vibrant colors and detailed patterns

shopping on the first day. This will also give you time to accommodate second or third fittings, which may be necessary.

Hoi An is now the main place to get clothes made. Its tailors are renowned—there are reckoned to be more than 140—and they will produce finished silk or cotton clothing in 24 hours. The quality of the stitching varies from shop to shop so see some samples first. As the range of fabrics can be limited, some people choose to bring their own. Note that Thai silk costs more than Vietnamese silk, and Hoi An silk is quite coarse.

The *ao dai* is an unforgiving garment, exquisite on a slender frame but often unsuited to larger builds. Most fabrics are synthetic, but in the bigger markets there is a lot of excellent coarse Vietnamese silk and imported cotton and wool.

Dong Khoi is the street paved with silk in Ho Chi Minh City, with many excellent clothing stores. The Russian Market (Tax Department Store) has some good men's and women's clothes, and the Saigontourist Department Store on the corner of Le Thanh Ton and Dong Khoi streets also has a wide selection. Vietnamese silk and traditional dresses are sold in the shops on Dong Khoi Street and in Ben Thanh Market. On Le Thanh Ton the shops opposite the town hall (People's Committee) are particularly good. Western-style fashions can be found in the stores lining Hai Ba Trung Street from District 1 right through District 3. However, if you are female and a UK size 12, American size 10 or European size 40 or above, or an average-sized male Westerner or larger, you'll find it difficult to buy anything that fits in these stores. There are luxury outlets such as Prada in the Hotel Caravelle and Armani, Gucci and Versace in the Sheraton.

Inexpensive T-shirts bearing the image of Ho Chi Minh or the yellow star of the Vietnamese flag are sold for a couple of dollars from stallholders in tourist hubs.

HANDICRAFTS
Handicrafts include embroidered and woven fabrics, lacquerware (▷ 161), mother-of-pearl inlaid screens and ceramics (▷ 159). There are a number of handicraft shops along Dong Khoi Street and Nguyen Hue Boulevard in Ho Chi Minh City, and in Hanoi most of the

shops selling handicrafts, including those made by ethnic minorities, are in the Old Quarter.

Ethnic minority products, fabrics, wickerware and jewelry are best bought in the uplands (where they are least expensive), but many of these items are available in Hanoi and Ho Chi Minh City. Cham fabrics, for example, are available in Saigon, while those of the Thái and Hmông minorities can be seen widely in Hanoi.

Hang Gai Street in Hanoi is well equipped for the foreign souvenir-hunter and stocks an excellent range of ethnic goods, fabrics and

A young boy selling a wood-carved junk in Ho Chi Minh City

lacquerware. Hats of all descriptions abound.

As the tourist industry has developed, so the number of handicrafts and hand-woven fabrics on sale in Hanoi has increased. You'll find a wide range of interesting pieces on sale around the popular cathedral shopping cluster of Nha Tho, Ly Quoc Su and Nha Chung streets, Hang Khay Street, on the southern shores of Hoan Kiem Lake and Hai Gai Street.

Good-quality water puppets are sold in Hanoi's water puppetry theater and inside the Temple of Literature (▷ 72–75). Masks are sold

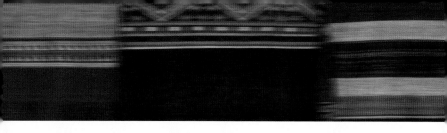

around Hoan Kiem Lake and in the Old Quarter.

In Ho Chi Minh City you can buy elaborately decorated model wooden ships in District 1, on the intersection of Hai Ba Trung and Ca Ba Quat.

HOME FURNISHINGS AND FURNITURE

This is a relatively new industry in Vietnam, but locally produced furniture and home furnishings are already having a significant impact on the global market. Craftsmanship is good, and many of the items are beautifully finished. Much of the wood is imported, as Vietnam's own resources have been severely depleted.

Intricately carved wooden sculptures of a Buddha and a tiger

Leading stores can be found in Hanoi, Ho Chi Minh City and Hoi An.

JEWELRY

This is another industry that has flourished in Vietnam in recent years. At the inexpensive end of the market, there is a cluster of gold and jewelry shops around Ben Thanh Market in Ho Chi Minh City and also in the International Trade Center on Nam Ky Khoi Nghia Street. In these stands, because skilled labor is so inexpensive, you'll rarely have to pay more than the weight of the item in silver or gold.

At the higher end of the market, there is a Bulgari outlet in the Caravelle Hotel, in District 1.

JUNK

Junk collectors will have a field day in Saigon and Hanoi. Many knickknacks were left behind by the French, Americans and Russians: old cameras, watches, cigarette lighters (most Zippos are fake), 1960s Coca-Cola signs and 1930s Pernod ashtrays. However, much is now reproduction, and to separate the authentic from the fake will require some specialist knowledge.

LACQUERWARE

The art of making *son mai* (lacquerware) is said to have been introduced into Vietnam after Emperor Le Thanh Ton (ruled 1443–59) sent an emissary to the Chinese court to investigate the process. Lacquer is a resin from the son tree (*Rhus succedanea* or *R. vernicifera*), which is then applied in numerous coats (usually 11) to wood (traditionally teak), leather, metal or porcelain. Prior to lacquering, the article must be sanded and coated with a fixative. The final coat is highly polished with coal powder. The piece may then be decorated with an incised design, painted, or inset with mother-of-pearl. If mother-of-pearl is used, appropriately shaped pieces of lacquer are chiseled out and the mother-of-pearl inset. This method is similar to that used in China, but different from those of Thailand and Burma. Designs in the north show Japanese influences, apparently because Japanese artists were employed as teachers at the École des Beaux Arts in Hanoi in the 1930s.

Lacquerware is plentiful and inexpensive, but remember that lacquer pictures are heavy to carry about and so should be bought near the end of a trip. Small lacquer trinkets, such as boxes and trays, are more portable and make ideal presents. These are ubiquitous in Hanoi, Ho Chi Minh City (on Nguyen Hue Boulevard and Dong Khoi Street in District 1) and Hoi An.

MARKETS

Every town and city in Vietnam has its markets. These bustling and fascinating affairs are the lifeblood of communities. Sellers come from far and wide, offering a vast array of the fruits of the earth and sea. Second-hand goods and household items are also sold, and it is possible to

A smiling young woman sells postcards of old Hanoi

eat well and at very little cost in most markets.

Ho Chi Minh City's Ben Thanh Market (▷ 135) sets up at sunset and has hundreds of stalls. The markets of the northwest are the most spectacular, drawing ethnic minority traders from the surrounding hills in their bright, intricately designed traditional clothing.

The Hang Be Market on Gai Ngu Street in the Old Quarter of Hanoi sells foodstuff live and dead, and functions in a swirl of cooking smells. The big Dong Xuan Market on Dong Xuan Street is a covered market selling mostly clothes and household goods.

ENTERTAINMENT 🎵

Classical Vietnamese theater (known as *hat boi—hat* means to sing and *boi* means to gesture or pose) shows close links with the classical theater of China. Emperor Tu Duc (ruled 1848–83) had a troop of 150 female artists and employed stars from China in a series of extravagant productions. Since partition in 1954, this has been replaced by what might be termed "revolutionary realist" theater.

Vietnam's repertoire of performance arts in the Western, classical tradition is limited to occasional productions at the opera houses in Hanoi and Ho Chi Minh City. There is one dedicated jazz club and a conservatory of music in Ho Chi Minh City. Some restaurants, such as the Marine Club (▷ 227), and a handful of expat bars have live music. In Hanoi, there is also one dedicated jazz club, and restaurants with live music such as Cay Cau (▷ 212). You can listen to folk music performed on traditional instruments by players in traditional dress at venues in Hoi An and Hué.

times shower audience members), and they perform with great gusto, mischief and complex choreography. On occasion in Hanoi, the shows are accompanied by fireworks—especially during battle scenes—and live music supplied by folk-opera singers and traditional instruments. Performances usually begin with the clown, Teu, taking the stage. He acts as a linking character between the various scenes.

Since the 1980s Vietnamese writers have turned their attention from revolutionary heroes

A theatrical water puppetry performance in Hanoi

WATER PUPPETRY
The most original theatrical art form in Vietnam is *mua roi nuoc* (water puppet theater). Vietnam is famous for its water puppetry and has exported this art internationally to much acclaim. You can see performances at the Water Puppetry House in Hanoi; a small show is also staged at the Museum of Vietnamese History in Ho Chi Minh City. The most famous and active troop is based in Hanoi, and in total there are about a dozen groups.

Water puppetry seems to have originated in northern Vietnam during the early years

of the last millennium, when it was associated with the harvest festival. An inscription in Nam Ha Province mentions a show staged in honor of King Ly Nhan Ton in 1121. By the time the French began to colonize Vietnam at the end of the 19th century, the art form had spread to all the major towns of the country.

As the name suggests, this form of theater uses the surface of the water as the stage. Puppeteers, concealed behind a bamboo screen symbolizing an ancient village communal house, manipulate the characters while standing in 3ft (1m) of water. The puppets—some more than 1.5ft (0.5m) tall—are carved from water-resistant sung wood, which is also very lightweight, and then painted in bright shades. Most need one puppeteer to manipulate them, but some require three or four.

Plays are based on historical and religious themes: the origins of the Viet nation, legends (for instance, the Lake of the Restored Sword, ▷ 64), village life and acts of heroism. Figures spout water when required (and some-

Distinctive, brightly colored water puppets in a Hanoi shop

to commentary on political and social issues of the day, and consequently, many plays have been censored or edited by the authorities.

TICKETING AND INFORMATION
To buy tickets in Vietnam it is best to go direct to the box office (▷ listings on pages 168–188 for opening hours). To find out about specific events, check the daily publication *Vietnam News*, which has a "What's On" section, or the monthly *The Guide*, which also covers a range of cultural events, including exhibitions.

NIGHTLIFE

Nightlife in Vietnam divides into two categories—Western and Vietnamese—though the edges are becoming increasingly blurred with time. Visitors tend to have a good meal, then head to a bar, often one with Western music, for a drink or two. Western-style bars, with cold beer, contemporary music and pool, are easy to find in the main towns but are virtually non-existent elsewhere.

The locals go for a meal and then either to a darkened café or into a karaoke bar for an hour or two. They tend to prefer nonalcoholic drinks and huge numbers of cafés exist to cater to this market.

are popular with businessmen, while in Hanoi and Ho Chi Minh City there are two Apocalypse Now venues that play Western music and have large dance floors. Some bars have areas that convert to dance floors later in the evening and during the early hours; in Saigon, these are often found in the Pham Ngu Lao area.

WESTERN BARS
Most smarter hotels catering for visitors have bars. There are numerous Western-style bars in Ho Chi Minh City,

Bia hoi *(fresh beer) for sale*   Playing a game of pool at the Café de la Poste in Dalat

VIETNAMESE BARS
A common type of Vietnamese bar is the *bia hoi*. *Bia hoi* is draft beer (fairly weak) but fresh and thirst-quenching. At around 4,000d a liter (2 US pints), it is also good value. *Bia hoi* bars are usually occupied by men and consist of a handful of tables and plastic chairs. They often sell simple food dishes—*bo luc lac* (diced steak with fries), for example. *Bia ôm* are literally translated as "cuddle" bars—another integral part of Vietnamese social fabric. In a Vietnamese *bia ôm*, the women drink beer with the men; however, they are more popular with Asian customers than Westerners.

CAFÉS
Cafés serving nonalcoholic drinks are a popular choice among Vietnamese. Young romantic couples sit in virtual darkness listening to Vietnamese love songs—often played at a deafening volume—while sipping coffee. The furniture tends to be rather small for the Western frame, but these cafés are an agreeable way of relaxing after dinner in a more typically Vietnamese setting.

CLUBBING
Clubs, as Westerners understand them, do not exist in Vietnam. The more well-heeled hotels have discos that

Hanoi and Hoi An. A smattering are found in other places where there are tourist attractions. Dalat has a handful of bars and clubs but these are mainly connected to the bigger hotels.

There are a few bars in Hué and some in Mui Ne, although the vast majority in Mui Ne are attached to the hotel resorts along the beach. Nha Trang's nightlife is focused around a few streets where the inexpensive hotels are to be found, and caters to visitors who have come for the sun, sea, sand and diving. There are more upscale bars which are attached to the more expensive hotels.

SPORTS AND ACTIVITIES

There is no shortage of sports and activities to try in Vietnam, whether you fancy trekking through the hills, windsurfing in Nha Trang or enjoying a round of golf. Other popular pursuits include birdwatching and cookery classes.

BICYCLING

Vietnam has great tracts of flat land, making bicycling a popular activity. The main hindrance is traffic on the roads; to avoid this, plan any bicycling tours off-road or on minor roads, not Highway 1. Many bicyclists prefer to bring their own all-terrain or racing bicycles, but it's also possible to rent from tour organizers. Tour operators in Ho Chi Minh

Off-road bicycling is a popular activity in Vietnam

City and Hanoi arrange a multitude of tours (▷ 202–204).

BIRDWATCHING

Vietnam may not seem like the first choice for a birdwatching trip, but for those in the know it has become one of the top "birding" destinations of the region, thanks to its 10 endemic species, the highest number of any country in mainland Southeast Asia. Around 850 species have been recorded in Vietnam, and in a three-week intensive birding trip it should be possible to tick off around 250 to 300. The best time of year is November through May.

In Nam Cat Tien National Park, in the central region, there are an estimated 230 bird species. Endangered birds include Germain's peacock-pheasant, green peafowl and the orange-necked partridge, as well as bar-bellied and blue-rumped pitta, red, black and banded broadbill, and orange-bottomed trogon. Woolly-necked stork, Siamese fireback, scaly-bottomed partridge and woodpeckers can also be seen. Close to Dalat, in the Central Highlands, is Mount Lang Bian, where it's possible to see silver pheasant, Indochinese cuckooshrike, Eurasian jay, yellow-billed nuthatch, Mugimaki flycatcher, cutia and red crossbill. The endemic collared laughing-thrush and the Vietnamese greenfinch can also be seen here. Closer to the town of Dalat, the rare and endemic grey-crowned crocias have been spotted. In Bach Ma National Park, near the coast in the central region, more than 330 bird species have been recorded, including the Annam partridge, crested argus, coral-billed ground-cuckoo, Blyth's kingfisher, ratchet-tailed treepie and sultan tit. At Tam Dao, north of Hanoi, the grey laughingthrush, chestnut bulbul, black-chinned yuhina and fork-tailed sunbird make regular appearances. Cuc Phuong National Park, south of Hanoi, has more than 300 recorded species and attracts the grey peacock-pheasant; bar-bellied, blue-rumped and eared pitta; white-winged magpie; limestone wren-babbler; Fujian niltava; and pied falconet. In the Mekong

Delta area, especially around the Plain of Reeds, there are several bird sanctuaries where it's possible to see wetland species (▷ 153).

COOKERY CLASSES

Cookery classes have not caught on in Vietnam in quite the way they have in Thailand, but the number of places offering classes and food tours is increasing, including hotels and restaurants in Hanoi, Saigon and Hoi An. Some operators run tours that include either half a day or a whole day of cooking.

Vietnam has such a wide choice of ingredients for cookery classes

GOLF

In the 1930s, Emperor Bao Dai laid a golf course in Dalat, and after a period of dormancy the game has enjoyed a resurgence. It remains chiefly an expatriate game, and the first courses to be opened in the 1990s were able to command colossal fees. There are currently 14 courses (some internationally designed and also foreign-owned), with a number of others planned or under construction, and green fees are now lower. Most are in southern Vietnam; the top two courses are in Dalat in the Central Highlands and in Phan Thiet on the coast.

GREYHOUND RACING

Dog racing is popular in Vietnam as it is the only legalized gambling available in the country. The Australian-financed greyhound stadium at Vung Tau has dog kennels and seats for 5,000. Every Saturday, 12 races are run here for a total prize pot of around US$3,000.

HORSEBACK RIDING

Horseback riding is organized by a few tour operators in

Horseback riding is becoming popular

Dalat in the central region and in Sapa in the north. Excursions, which can vary in duration from one day to several days, are accompanied by guides and, in some cases, by support vehicles (▷ 174).

KAYAKING

Kayaking in Vietnam is virtually synonymous with Halong Bay and Lan Ha Bay. Although there are a few kayaks in places like Mui Ne and Ba Be Lakes, these are locally made and designed for gentle recreational use. Anyone wishing to kayak in earnest should head straight for Halong Bay, where operators arrange special-interest tours (▷ 86–89).

SOCCER

The Vietnamese are passionate about soccer and many children long to be soccer players when they grow older. The Vietnamese league includes players and coaches from abroad.

SWIMMING

Many Vietnamese hotels have outdoor swimming pools, and those in Sapa, high in the mountains of northwestern Vietnam, have indoor pools. Pools vary in size: Beach resorts tend to have the larger pools, while those in Ho Chi Minh City's hotels are generally tight for space. Rooftop pools provide stunning views. Outside Ho Chi Minh City is a waterpark that is hugely popular with Vietnamese families (▷ 186).

TENNIS

Luxury hotels offer tennis facilities. Courts can be found in Ho Chi Minh City, Can Tho and Phu Quoc in the south; Danang, China Beach, Dalat, Hoi An, Hué, Lang Co, Phan Thiet, Nha Trang and Long Hai in the central region; and Sapa in the north.

WALKING

There are plenty of opportunities for walking and trekking. The main focus is Sapa, in the north, but some trekking is organized around Dalat. Around Sapa, the stunning scenery and way of life provide ample opportunity for trekking through the hills and staying with local people. There are walks of varying durations, demanding different fitness levels and degrees of stamina. At several national parks you can trek and stay overnight. The main national parks are Ba Be and Cuc Phuong in the north; Cat Ba, on Cat Ba Island in Halong Bay; Bach Ma, close to the coast and near Hué; Yok Don, in the Central Highlands;

and Nam Cat Tien, southwest of Dalat. Walking out of a town or city into the countryside can be a delightful experience, as you wander past paddy fields, buffalo and ducks. Trekking can be done alone or through tour operators; homestays with families from ethnic minorities must be arranged through a tour operator (▷ 202–204). Unfortunately, there are no accurate maps available for walkers in Vietnam.

WATERSPORTS

Diving takes place mainly between January and November; the height of activity is during the dry season, January through May.

Having fun riding on an aqua cycle at the Furama Resort

The biggest dive resort is Nha Trang; smaller resorts are Whale Island, Danang, Con Dao and Phu Quoc.

Windsurfing, kitesurfing and other watersports are popular in Mui Ne, which offers just about perfect conditions throughout the year. The wind is normally brisk over many days, and the combination of powerful wind and waves enables good kitesurfers to get airborne for several seconds at a time. Equipment and training are offered by a couple of outlets (▷ 178–179). Windsurfing is popular in Nha Trang, but the conditions are not quite in the same class as at Mui Ne.

HEALTH AND BEAUTY

Save some time for relaxing while you are in Vietnam—you'll find a wide range of beauty salons and pampering services. Spa treatments can be expensive, but prices are lower than those charged in major Western cities.

SPAS AND HOT SPRINGS

There are only a few authentic spas in Vietnam, but several places call themselves spas and many hotels offer spa facilities. The country's top spas are the Six Senses Spa at the Ana Mandara in Nha Trang (▷ 248) and at the Evason Hideaway at Ana Mandara on an island off Nha Trang (▷ 249). The Six Senses Spa also opened in 2006 at the Ana Mandara Villas

Dalat and Spa (▷ 242) in Dalat. The Shiseido Spa at the VinPearl Resort and Spa is on Hon Tre Island, also off Nha Trang (▷ 249). Many hotels offer massage, treatments and therapies. Ho Chi Minh City has two dedicated urban spas, one for women only (▷ 186).

At Thap Ba Hot Springs, near Nha Trang, and at Binh Chau, near Vung Tau, there are thermal baths with mud and mineral water. As a bonus, prices are very low. (Take care at Binh Chau—at some places the water is hot enough to cook an egg!)

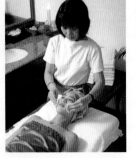

Enjoying a relaxing facial massage (left) and back massage (right)

MASSAGE PARLORS

In Ho Chi Minh City and Hanoi, central areas are full of hair salons and foot-massage parlors. Some are sleazy, but you can tell this from the outside. Generally they provide good value for money. Visitor magazines available at most hotels are bursting with advertisements, which can give you an idea of the best deals.

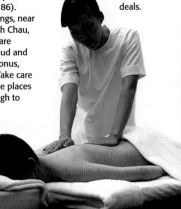

FOR CHILDREN

The Vietnamese adore children, and give them a lot of attention, hugs and pats. In the north, pinching the cheeks of babies is a sign of love and affection. Vietnam is not particularly well geared up to activities for children, and only the more expensive hotels offer specifically child-friendly facilities. Many activities, however, will appeal to both adults and children.

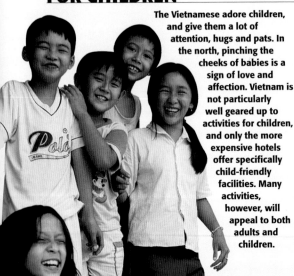

CHILDREN'S ACTIVITIES

Children in particular are likely to enjoy a water puppetry performance with its cast of attractive and lively characters, fireworks and loud music. The water park outside Ho Chi Minh City will also delight youngsters, as will boat trips along the Mekong River or some of the country's other waterways. Some attractions offer concessions for children; where this is the case, details are listed in the admission information under individual entries in this guide.

A group of laughing children at Kleang Pagoda, Soc Trang

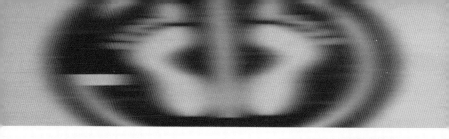

Vietnam has countless festivals celebrating ancient heroes, gods and legends with joyful or solemn ceremonies throughout the lunar calendar. Some of the country's major festivals are listed below. The following website converts the Gregorian calendar to the lunar calendar:
www.vietnamtourism.com/e_pages/tourist/festival.asp

TET

Tet is the traditional Vietnamese New Year and comes some time between late January and March. Its name is the shortened version of *tet nguyen dan* (first morning of the new period). This is the time to forgive and forget, and to pay off debts. It is also everyone's birthday—the Vietnamese tend not to celebrate their birthdays, but everyone adds one year to their age at *Tet*. Enormous quantities of food are consumed, new clothes are bought, houses are painted and repaired, and kumquat trees are brought into homes; until a government-imposed ban in 1995, firecrackers were lit to welcome in the new year. As a Vietnamese saying has it: "Hungry all year, but *Tet* three days full."

It is believed that before *Tet* the spirit of the hearth, Ong Tao, leaves on a journey to visit the palace of the Jade Emperor, where he must report on family affairs. To ensure that Ong Tao sets off in good cheer, a ceremony is held before *Tet* (*Le Tao Quan*), and during his absence a shrine is constructed (*Cay Neu*) to keep evil spirits at bay until his return. On the afternoon before *Tet* (*Tat Nien*) a sacrifice is offered at the family altar to dead relatives, who are invited back to join in the festivities.

Great attention is paid to preparations for *Tet* because the first week of the new year

is believed to dictate your fortunes for the year to come.

The first visitor to the house on New Year's morning should be an influential, lucky and happy person, so families take care to arrange a suitable caller.

Visitors to Vietnam should be aware that the entire country is on the move at *Tet* and international flights are reserved months in advance as overseas *Viet Kieu* return to Vietnam for the celebration. All domestic transportation and hotels throughout the country are reserved for days before and after *Tet*.

🔘 Movable, start of the new lunar year: Feb 7–9 2008, Jan 26–28 2009, Feb 14–16 2010, Feb 3–5 2011

THANH MINH

During the New Year of the Dead, or Feast of the Pure Light, the Vietnamese walk outdoors to evoke the spirit of the dead, and family shrines and tombs are traditionally cleaned and decorated. The festival takes place in April.

🔘 Fifth or sixth day of the third lunar month

TRUNG NGUYEN

Wandering Souls Day, in August, is one of the most important festivals in Vietnam. During this time, prayers can absolve the sins of the dead, who leave hell and return, hungry and naked, to their relatives. The Wandering Souls are those with no homes to go to. There are celebrations in Buddhist

Burning paper offerings in celebration of the Tet *festival*

temples and homes, food is placed out on tables, and ghost money is burnt.
🔘 Movable, 15th day of the seventh lunar month

TET TRUNG THU

The Mid-Autumn Festival, particularly celebrated by children, is based on various legends. One tells of a Chinese king who went to the moon and, on his return, wished to share what he had seen with the people on earth. In the evening, families prepare food, including sticky rice, fruit and chicken, to be placed on the ancestral altars. Moon cakes (egg, green bean, and lotus seed) are baked (with some variations on these ingredients, such as chocolate, offered by some of the smarter hotels), lanterns are made and painted, and children parade through towns with music and lanterns. The festival is particularly celebrated in Hanoi, where toy shops in the Old Quarter go to town decorating stores with lanterns and masks.
🔘 Movable, 15th day of the eighth lunar month: Sep 14 2008, Oct 3 2009, Sep 22 2010, Sep 12 2011

WHAT TO DO

HANOI

Hanoi is a seductive shopping destination. Its small streets are filled with boutiques selling fashion, silk and accessories, as well as antiques shops and handicraft stands. Clothes, handicrafts and home products are sold at extraordinarily low prices. These are widely available in market areas and in the Old Quarter. The streets are also one big shop themselves, where you'll find anything from *pho* stands to postcard-sellers. Street sellers also offer illegal photocopied Western books and bootleg (very poor quality) CDs and DVDs. On Le Duan Street, south of the railway station, stands sell a remarkable array of US, Soviet and Vietnamese army surplus kit.

Shops generally open all day, every day, and do not close for lunch. Late-night shopping means that after all the sights are closed, you can still make purchases. Most shops take universally accepted credit cards.

There is little by way of live entertainment in Hanoi. Traditional entertainment comes in the form of the famous and very worthwhile water puppet theater (▷ 171). Classical music concerts are staged at the principal theater/concert hall, the Opera House (▷ 170). Live, traditional music can occasionally be heard in restaurants such as Cay Cau (▷ 212), and there is a jazz bar in the Old Quarter.

Hanoi's nightlife is based around a clutch of popular Western bars catering to the expatriate and traveling community. One or two places play Western music until the early hours and have dance floors. Hanoi's bars serve the full range of alcoholic drinks and play Western music. The Bao Khanh and Hang Hanh area is packed with bars and cafés—very lively all day and evening, but like most places in Hanoi, the bars here are subject to police curfew and the majority shut around midnight. The lunar calendar year is marked by several important festivals (▷ 172), and Christmas is also celebrated here. The big events of *Tet* (New Year) and the Mid-Autumn Festival *(Tet Trung Thu)* are the main celebrations held during the year.

KEY TO SYMBOLS	
	Shopping
	Entertainment
	Nightlife
	Sports
	Activities
	Health and Beauty
	For Children

⊕ SHOPPING

ART AND ANTIQUES

ANCIENT GALLERY
11 Trang Thi Street
Tel 04-9349410
This well-known, spacious gallery, just south of Hoan Kiem Lake, is popular with visitors from overseas. It shows an eclectic mixture of styles and media, from oil paintings to lacquerwork and from painted screens to small tiles. It also displays the populist images of conical-hatted workers in fields of young rice. The larger the "paddy field painting" the more astounding the hues.
⊙ Daily 8–8

APRICOT GALLERY
40B Hang Bong Street
Tel 04-8288965
www.apricot-artvietnam.com
Prices are high at this gallery southeast of the Citadel. It is run by the owners of the Ancient Gallery (▷ 168), but the paintings it sells are more arresting and mainly on larger canvases. There are some beautiful works by Nguyen Dieu Thuy, who sometimes uses silver leaf as a highlight in her creations. The enchanting work of Le Thanh Ton captures Vietnamese life and scenes in French Impressionistic style.
🕐 Daily 8–8

HANOI GALLERY
110 Hang Bac Street
Tel 04-9261064
Hundreds of propaganda posters are for sale here, at prices ranging from US$7 to US$200. They cover various political, historical and socio-cultural themes, such as state building, communism, Ho Chi Minh, the battle at Dien Bien Phu and the Vietnam War. You'll also find old money and a few books. Poster tubes are sold as packaging for your purchase.
🕐 Daily 10–7

CLOTHES AND FASHION

CO
18 Nha Tho Street
Tel 04-8289925
This tiny clothes store has a very narrow entrance on a popular street in the Old Quarter and is a good example of a tube house, with lots of cloth and materials neatly stacked along the narrow passage entrance, which opens out at the back. In addition to being able to whip up some quality conventional items for shoppers, Co has some unusual and hugely appealing prints, quite often used for winter coats. The craftsmanship of the finished garments is superb.
🕐 Daily 8.30–9

IPA-NIMA
34 Han Thuyen Street
Tel 04-9334000
www.ipa-nima.com
Step into the glittering world of Hong Kong native Christina Yu (▷ 24), the creative force behind this increasingly successful designer label. Clothes, bags, exquisitely embroidered jewelry boxes and a limited range of sparkling shoes are available at this sought-after shop. Occasionally, the range of shoe sizes is limited. There are two more stores in Ho Chi Minh City.
🕐 Daily 9–7

Decorative weaving and lanterns for sale near Hoan Kiem Lake

KHAISILK
121 Nguyen Thai Hoc Street
Tel 04-7470583
www.khaisilkcorp.com
This is the crème de la crème of silk shops. Launched by Hoang Khai in 1980, the brand is synonymous with elegance, style and superior quality (▷ 24). All Khaisilk shops display a range of clothes for men (ties, shirts and suits) and women (scarves, *ao dai* and blouses), plus stunning handbags and other accessories. This store, west of the Vietnam Fine Arts Museum, is the main branch; there is another branch to be

found in the Old City at 96 Hang Gai Street (tel 04-8254237).
🕐 Daily 8.30–7.30

MIRRORMIRROR
37 Ly Quoc Su Street
Tel 04-9286517
www.mirror-design.com
The shop window here is not always particularly striking, but step in and browse a limited collection of designer clothes by Truong Thuy Ha. The shirts for men are particularly impressive. For women, there are some classically designed stylish dresses and some unusual interpretations of both Western and Vietnamese classic designs—for example, a pin-striped dress and bold flower prints on *ao dai*.
🕐 Daily 9–8

TAN MY
66 Hang Gai Street
Tel 04-8251579
This shop, in Hanoi's Old Quarter, is stacked full of very affordable goods over two floors. It displays the full range of silk and embroidered clothes found in many stores in this area. In addition, it sells underwear, night wear, chenille scarves, children's clothes and plain, unembroidered silk evening bags, which are surprisingly hard to come by, as the millions of bags found in the shops of Vietnam are usually decorated.
🕐 Daily 8.30–7

THINGS OF SUBSTANCE
5 Nha Tho Street
Tel 04-8286965
A stylish store, in the shadow of St. Joseph's Cathedral, selling swimwear, a small line in clothes, silk jewelry bags, attractive jewelry, leather goods and other unusual gifts. This small shop, with excellent service, offers something a little different.
🕐 Daily 9–8

WHAT TO DO

TINA SPARKLE

17 Nha Tho Street
Tel 04-9287616
tinasparkle@ipa-nima.com

A funky boutique, Tina Sparkle sells bags in a glittering array of colors and patterns—from tropical prints to sequinned flowers. The shop, on the popular cathedral street, also sells sequinned shoes by Hong Kong lawyer-turned-designer Christina Yu. Most bags retail for around US$35 and shoes for US$60, although occasional sales will leave half those amounts in your purse.
🕓 Daily 9–8

TROPICAL

65 Hang Gai Street
Tel 04-9287203

This shop on a busy main road in the Old Quarter has room for only a few customers at a time. It sells plain, flowing silk skirts (a rarity), mother-of-pearl jewelry, hair accessories, lacquerware, buffalo horns and other unusual items in its tiny premises, cluttered with gifts and clothes. The staff are particularly helpful.
🕓 Daily 9–7

HOME FURNISHINGS

CHI VANG

17 Trang Tien Street
Tel 04-9360027
chivang@fpt.vn

This shop, which occupies a beautifully restored building, sells exquisitely embroidered cloth, babies' bed linen and clothing, cushion covers, tablecloths and unusually shaped cushions. The goods are artfully arranged in a spacious interior that is fitted out with large, wooden dressers. All the items are embroidered by hand. The store is conveniently close to the Opera House and is managed by helpful staff.
🕓 Daily 8–8

INDOCHINE HOUSE

39 Hang Trong Street
Tel 04-8248071

This shop in the Old Quarter sells furniture and handicrafts made from rosewood, cassia, marble and buffalo bone. Folding screens with silk panels and dominoes, drafts and calendar sets made from black rosewood and bone make ideal presents.
🕓 Daily 9.30–7.30

MOSAIQUE

22 Nha Tho Street
Tel 04-9286181

This treasure trove, furnished in warm shades, sells embroidered table-runners, box

Water puppetry in Vietnam dates back to the 11th century

lamps and stands, beautiful silk flowers for accessorizing, silk curtains, metal ball lamps, pillow cushions and lotus flower-shaped lamps. A little more lighting would allow customers to see the sometimes subtle differences in the silk tones. The shop is in the heart of the Old Quarter.
🕓 Daily 8.30–8

NGUYEN FRÈRES

3 Phan Chu Trinh Street
Tel 04-9331699

It's a delight to wander around this artfully cluttered shop, where you'll be served jasmine tea on arrival. In addition to the usual silk items, from

cushion covers to place mats, you can buy old books inscribed with Chinese calligraphy, desks carved with Chinese iconography, porcelain, bronzes, lacquerware and small wooden statues of Christ and the Virgin Mary. The store is southwest of the Opera House.
🕓 Daily 9–8

SONG

27 Nha Tho Street
Tel 04-9288733

The Song shop, on the fashionable Nha Tho Street, is run by friendly and helpful staff. French designer Valerie Gregori-McKenzie (▷ 24) has produced some beautiful, ethereal designs in cottons, linens and silks. She also makes hats, bags, lamps, bed linen and cushion covers, which are exquisitely embroidered. Gregori-McKenzie has produced her own Vietnamese cookbook, which is sold in her shops. The other store is in Ho Chi Minh City (▷ 182), and has a larger retail space than the Hanoi outlet.
🕓 Daily 9–8

🎭 ENTERTAINMENT

CLASSICAL MUSIC, DANCE AND OPERA

OPERA HOUSE

1 Trang Tien Street
Tel 04-9330113
Fax 04-9330114
nthavinh@hn.vn.vn

A variety of Vietnamese and Western concerts, operas and plays are staged in this magnificent former French colonial palace of entertainment. Events are not held on a regular basis, so check listings in the daily publication *Vietnam News* or at the box office. Evening dress is required. Occasionally children are not allowed to attend shows. Photography is not allowed during performances.
🕓 Box office: 8–5 🎫 Ticket prices vary; around 150,000d for a performance

WATER PUPPETRY HOUSE
57 Dinh Tien Hoang Street
Tel 04-8249494
www.thanglongwaterpuppet.org
A performance at the Water Puppetry House, at the north-east corner of Hoan Kiem Lake, is unmissable. Fabulous shows are staged with exciting, live music, and the technical virtuosity of the puppeteers is astonishing. First-class tickets give seats close to the water stage, which provide good photo opportunities. In recent years the troop has performed in Japan, Australia and Europe.
🕐 Box office: 8.30–12, 3.30–8. Performances: daily 4, 5.15, 6.30, 8; additional performance on Sun at 9.30am 🎫 First-class tickets: 40,000d (child 10,000d). Second-class tickets: 20,000d (child 5,000d)

CONTEMPORARY MUSIC
MINH'S JAZZ CLUB (CAU LAC BO NHAC JAZZ)
31 Luong Van Can Street
Tel 04-8287890
Vietnamese jazz saxophonist Quyen Van Minh plays to a packed house at this Old Quarter venue. Come here to enjoy live jazz every night, table service by waiters, a well-stocked bar and a mellow, chilled-out vibe.
🕐 8.30pm–12

🍸 NIGHTLIFE
BARS AND RESTAURANTS
BOBBY CHINN
1 Ba Trieu Street
Tel 08-9348577
A super-stylish restaurant (▷ 211) with a bar. Drink at the sleek, glass-bar centerpiece and enjoy the views of Hoan Kiem Lake, or sneak to the back of the restaurant where gold drapes separate lounge areas stuffed with black sofas. Original art adorns the walls. The wine list is honored with an Award of Excellence from the *Wine Spectator* magazine, and the huge array of cocktails may entice you back for more.
🕐 Daily 11–11

FUNKY MONKEY
15B Hang Hanh Street
Tel 04-9286113
This popular, lively bar with low lighting and stylish décor is in a busy Old Quarter street that is full of restaurants and bars. There is good music, with darts, pool and bar football to keep the regulars happy. It attracts both Vietnamese and Westerners. Happy hour is from 4pm to 7pm for beer and from 7pm to 9pm for cocktails.
🕐 Daily 10am–1.30am

LEGENDS
1–5 Dinh Tien Hoang Street
Tel 04-9360345
www.legendsbeer.com

Neon lights illuminate the northern end of Hoan Kiem Lake

One of Hanoi's popular microbreweries is housed in a building that dominates the area at the tip of Hoan Kiem Lake, and offers tremendous views. The German *helles bier* (light) and particularly the *dunkels bier* (dark) are strong and tasty. The machinery and ingredients are all imported from Germany. An extensive food menu is available, and this is also a good place for snacks and ice cream.
🕐 Daily 9am–11pm

LIBRARY BAR
Press Club
59 Ly Thai To Street
Tel 04-9340888
The Library Bar is a small venue, decorated as a pastiche of an English country house, with wall-to-wall shelves stacked with old books and leather chairs with a veneer of racing green. This is a tranquil setting in which to tipple a few malts while smoking a fine Havana, and is popular with older expatriates. It is conveniently situated inside the Press Club, close to the Opera House.
🕐 Daily 6pm–11pm

MET' PUB
Sofitel Metropole
56 Ly Thai To Street
Tel 04-8266919 ext 8214
The small, wooden-furnished, bar-cum-pub at the back of the Metropole is very popular with hotel guests and older expatriates. It serves excellent pub food and a good evening buffet. Live music is played and all major sporting events are screened. Happy hour is from 5pm to 7pm.
🕐 Daily 11am–1.30am

RED BEER
97 Ma May Street
Tel 04-8260247
The former Ily Café has transformed itself into a microbrewery. The smell of hops hits you as you walk through the door and are faced with copper vats and stainless-steel vessels lining the back wall. Sit back and enjoy the outstanding Belgian brew: *bia do* (red beer) or *bia vang* (yellow beer). You can choose from a reasonable range of snacks, costing from 30,000d to 50,000d per dish. At the back of the bar, a vast traffic safety billboard, in true communist style, has been erected, adding a retro appeal. A large TV screen shows sporting events.
🕐 Daily 10am–11pm

WHAT TO DO

RELAX BAR
60 Ly Thuong Thiet Street
Tel 04-9424409
This is a cross between a thatched bar on a tropical island and an English pub. It's a popular venue for expatriates and for young, well-dressed professional Vietnamese. Funky bar tables made out of 1970s magazines and a tiny bridge over a pond at the entrance add a kitschy appeal. Western tunes, sports TV and reasonably priced cocktails keep the regulars happy. The bar is on a main road close to the Hoa Lo Prison and Hotel Guoman.
🕒 Daily 10am–1am

R & R TAVERN
47 Lo Su Street
Tel 04-9344109
www.oregoncoast.com/willy/r&r.htm
This small, popular and lively bar in the Old Quarter, not far from Hoan Kiem Lake, offers a great selection of bar food, including oysters. Eating and drinking are accompanied by live music on Thursday, Friday and Saturday evenings.
🕒 Daily 7.30am–midnight

SPOTTED COW
23C Hai Ba Trung Street
Tel 04-8241028
Spotted Friesian cows decorate this small, cheerful pub close

to Hoan Kiem Lake. Happy hour lasts until 6pm, and food is served until midnight, which is quite unusual in Hanoi and so wins some extra late-night custom. This is also the base for the running (and a bit of drinking) club Hanoi Hash House Harriers.
🕒 11.30am–3am

CLUBS
APOCALYPSE NOW
5C Hoa Ma Street
Tel 04-9712783
Like its counterpart in Ho Chi Minh City (▷ 183), Apocalypse Now is popular with a wide cross-section of club-goers. In a deep dusty pink warehouse with green shutters, it's a cavernous venue with sand sacking around the walls, billiard tables and a very large yellow and black oil painting of Marlon Brando, as the film's Colonel Kurtz, on the wall. Filled with local and visiting revelers, it plays dance music until the early hours.
🕒 Daily 8pm–2am

HO GUOM XANH
32 Le Thai To Street
Tel 04-8288806
There's a lively imagination at work at this nightclub: Few people passing by outside would envisage a wild interior with a nightly spectacle of

operatic shows. The upstairs entrance is like a submarine tube. Drinkers can hang out in this capsule before entering the main arena to be entertained by the laser and live music show nightly at 10pm. It is always packed and popular with a mainly local crowd. Drinks are fairly expensive for what is predominantly a Vietnamese venue.
🕒 Daily 6pm–midnight

🏀 SPORTS AND ACTIVITIES
COOKERY CLASSES
Sofitel Metropole
15 Ngo Quyen Street
Tel 04-8266919
The Sofitel Metropole organizes a cooking-demonstration and market tour. Participants visit the market in the early morning to buy vegetables and other produce. Returning to the hotel, they watch the chef and staff give a cooking demonstration in the kitchen, after which lunch is served with the chance to sample all the dishes made.
🕒 Tue–Sat 9am–midnight; reserve one day in advance 💰 US$50 per person

🧒 FOR CHILDREN
WATER PUPPETRY HOUSE
See page 171.

FESTIVALS AND EVENTS

JANUARY–FEBRUARY
DONG DA HILL FESTIVAL
This festival celebrates the battle of Dong Da, in which Nguyen Hue (self-appointed Emperor Quang Trung) routed 200,000 Chinese troops in 1789. A procession, which includes the carrying of the flaming Thang Long Fire Dragon of straw, accompanied by music, makes its way through Hanoi to Dong Da hill in southwestern Hanoi.
🕒 Fifth day of *Tet* (Feb 11 2008, Jan 30 2009, Feb 18 2010, Feb 7 2011)

MARCH
HAI BA TRUNG FESTIVAL
The Hai Ba Trung Festival celebrates the Trung sisters, who led a revolt against the Chinese in AD41 (▷ 27). On the third day the temple doors are opened; on the fourth, a funeral ceremony begins; on the fifth, their statues are removed for a bathing ceremony (the most important day); and on the sixth, a ritual ceremony is held.
🕒 Third to the sixth day of the second lunar month

SEPTEMBER
NATIONAL DAY
This public holiday marks the Declaration of Independence by Ho Chi Minh on September 2 1945. Parades take place in front of his mausoleum in Ba Dinh Square and boat races are held on Hoan Kiem Lake.
🕒 Sep 2

DECEMBER
Christmas is celebrated in Hanoi and is a public holiday. Midnight Mass is popular at St. Joseph's Cathedral.

THE NORTH

No other place in Vietnam has the range of ethnic shirts, baggy trousers, caps, bags and other garments that can be found in Sapa. Embroidered cloths and wall hangings are sold by vendors in the market, in the stands near the church and in shops along the main street; many of the items sold are secondhand. Note, however, that it is not possible to buy walking shoes, backpacks, coats, jackets or any mountaineering equipment in Sapa.

Mai Chau also sells ethnic minority clothing and souvenirs, and is probably the best place in the northwest for buying handicrafts. Villagers offer a range of woven goods and fabrics, and are becoming dependent on these sales for a living. There are also paintings, wicker baskets, pots and pouches, all expertly made. In Mai Chau and in Sapa ethnic minority dance troops dressed in traditional costume stage frequent displays for visitors, and act out local rites and customs. Nightlife is mainly restricted to hotel bars in the main population hubs. All good hotels have well-stocked bars, among the more popular of which are the bar at the Victoria Sapa, the Red Dragon Pub in Sapa, and the Royal Garden Harbour View in Haiphong.

Kayaking and junk cruises are popular on Halong Bay. You can rent kayaks from hotels on Cat Ba Island, and some boats taking overnight passengers also supply kayaks. Guided treks, bicycling and horseback-riding are increasingly popular, and are mainly organized out of Sapa by local and national tour operators (▷ 202–204). And when it's time to relax, the Victoria Hotel in Sapa offers a wide range of pampering treatments, in a complex with an indoor swimming pool.

KEY TO SYMBOLS	
	Shopping
	Entertainment
	Nightlife
	Sports
	Activities
	Health and Beauty
	For Children

CAT BA ISLAND

FLIGHTLESS BIRD
Seafront on Cat Ba Island
Tel 031-888517
The Flightless Bird is on the seafront on Cat Ba Island, a short distance to the left of the jetty. It is run by New Zealander Graeme Moore, and as the only real pub in town is a popular meeting point for travelers. There's also a book exchange.
Mon–Sat 5.30pm–midnight

HALONG BAY

KAYAKING AND JUNK CRUISES
Kayaking and junk cruises are now regular features in Halong Bay and Lan Ha Bay, especially in the summer. They're best joined via one of the better established tour operators in Hanoi
(▷ 202–204).

MAI CHAU

MAI CHAU ETHNIC MINORITY DANCE TROOP
Lac village
Visitors to Mai Chau are entertained by White Thái dancing, which culminates in the communal drinking of sweet, sticky rice wine through straws from a large pot. This troop, wearing traditional clothes, performs most nights in Lac in one of the large stilt houses.
🎭 Admission as part of tour or small contribution

SAPA

🏠 WILD ORCHID
Cau May Street, Sapa
Tel 020-871665
There are three outlets of this shop on Sapa's main street. They all sell attractive, well-made wall hangings with embroidered motifs, for around US$15. Cushion covers, clothes and a range of other embroidered souvenir gifts are also available.
🕐 Daily 8–8

🎭 DRAGON'S JAW HILL
At the top of Dragon's Jaw Hill there are daily performances of ethnic minority dancing with live music. A flautist and percussionists playing gongs,
drums, maracas and cymbals accompany dancing boys and girls, who act out local scenes. The performances last an hour and the admission fee includes a drink.
🕐 Dragon's Jaw Hill: daily 6–6. Performances: daily 9.15am and 3pm
🎭 Dragon's Jaw Hill: 15,000d (child 5,000d). Performances: 10,000d

🍸 TAU BAR
Tau Hotel
42 Cau May Street, Sapa
Tel 020-871322
taubar_sapa@hotmail.com
The long bar at this place beneath the Tau Hotel is made of a single tree trunk, and it's worth a beer just for that. The minimalist, subterranean venue, with white walls, bar stools, a darts board and pool table, is welcoming and relaxing.
🕐 8pm–late

⭐ HANDSPAN
8 Cau May Street, Sapa
Tel/fax 020-872110
www.handspan.com
Handspan organizes mountain bicycling tours to the villages and markets around Sapa, lasting from one to three days.
🎭 From US$19 per person (minimum two people)

⭐ TOPAS
20 Cau May Street, Sapa
Tel 022-871331
www.topas-adventure-vietnam.com
Topas offers bicycling and horseback-riding excursions. Bicycling trips range from half a day to eight days and the price includes rental of mountain bicycles, English- or French-speaking guides, water and fruit. Horseback-riding day tours are arranged to local villages in the mountains around Sapa. The cost includes saddled horses, an English- or French-speaking guide, water, fruit and transportation.
🎭 Bicycling: from US$20 per person (minimum two people). Horseback riding: from US$26 per person (minimum two people)

💟 VICTORIA BEAUTY SALON AND HEALTH CENTER
Victoria Hotel, Sapa
Tel 020-871522
www.victoriahotels-asia.com
The health center offers everything from traditional massage to reflexology. The US$37 Victoria Massage package is a combination of head, body and foot massages, plus a 10-minute massage with special natural oil.
🕐 Daily 8am–10pm

FESTIVALS AND EVENTS

FEBRUARY–MAY

THE PERFUME PAGODA FESTIVAL
Huong Son Mountain, 37 miles (60km) southwest of Hanoi
The Perfume Pagoda Festival, held at the Perfume Pagoda (▷ 91), focuses on the worship of the Goddess of Mercy. There are dragon dances and a royal barge sails on the Yen River.
🕐 Sixth day of first lunar month to end of third lunar month (Feb 12–May 4 2008, Jan 31–Apr 24 2009, Feb 19–May 13 2010, Feb 8–May 2 2011)

APRIL

THE HUNG KINGS' TEMPLES FESTIVAL
Viet Tri, Vinh Phu Province
Visitors from all over Vietnam descend on the Hung Kings' Temples on the Red River floodplain (▷ 90) for this two-week celebration, focusing on the worship of ancestors. The place bursts with vendors, food stands and fairground activities. There are swan boats, incense, drums, bamboo swings, wrestling matches, sword dances and singing.
🕐 10th day of third lunar month (Apr 15 2008, Apr 5 2009, Apr 23 2010, Apr 12 2011)

AUGUST–SEPTEMBER

DO SON BUFFALO FIGHTING FESTIVAL
Haiphong City (Do Son)
This festival, held in Haiphong and celebrating the God of the Sea, begins with an offering of a buffalo, a pig and some sticky rice. Then 12 men carrying a palanquin lead a procession of musicians, six buffalos and a further 12 men dressed in red, who wave flags to signal the start of the buffalo fight. The head of the winning buffalo is thrown into the sea.
🕐 Ninth day of eighth lunar month (Sep 8 2008, Sep 27 2009, Sep 16 2010, Sep 6 2011)

CENTRAL VIETNAM

The main shopping hub in the region is Hoi An, a great place to get clothes made or to buy handbags and attractive Chinese silk lanterns. Hoi An paintings are highly regarded, and there are a number of galleries here, as well as good lacquerwork and ceramics.

In Hué, the range of goods on sale is no longer restricted to the *non bai tho* (poem hats)—a form of the *non lá* conical hats peculiar to Hué. Poem hats are made from bamboo and have stenciled palm leaves, love poetry, songs, proverbs or simple designs, which are visible only if the hat is held up to the light and viewed from the inside. Small shops around the Huong Giang Hotel sell ceramics, silk and clothes. No Vietnamese visitors would shake the dust of Hué off their feet without having stocked up on *me xung*, a sugary peanut and toffee confection coated in sesame seeds.

Dalat has a well-deserved reputation for producing not only beautiful flowers but also some of the best handmade silk paintings in Vietnam. The potent, red Dalat wine is famous throughout the country.

Hué was the focal point of the Nguyen Dynasty for around 143 years. During this time, music of the royal court—a blend of royal and folk music—developed, and is now performed on a daily basis in the Royal (East) Theater, in the Imperial City at Hué. Royal court music often accompanies the sailing of dragonboats, river boats with large and colorful heads of dragons at their bows. Traditional folk music is performed in Hoi An, where dances are accompanied by the *dan bau*, the Vietnamese monochord or one-stringed zither.

The central region is bursting with opportunities for taking to the hills, lakes, mountains and seas. There is world-class golf at Dalat and Phan Thiet, and mountain bicycling, canyoning and kayaking in and around Dalat. Offshore, there is diving at Nha Trang, Whale Island and Danang, and boat trips around the bay of Nha Trang. Mui Ne is a major center for kitesurfing. You can also try cookery lessons in Hoi An or trips arranged by Nha Trang's famous photographer Long Thanh to local areas, including beaches and salt flats. The region also offers the greatest concentration of health and beauty clinics in Vietnam.

KEY TO SYMBOLS	
⊕	Shopping
🎭	Entertainment
▼	Nightlife
🏃	Sports
✪	Activities
♡	Health and Beauty
✿	For Children

DALAT

▼ GOLF 3 BAR AND CLUB
4 Nguyen Thi Minh Khai Street, Dalat
Tel 063-826042
The bar is in the basement opposite the nightclub and has several pool tables and a varied selection of drinks and bar food, both of which are good value for money. The club has a moderate-sized dance floor.
🕐 Daily 6pm–midnight
🎟 Admission 30,000d

HAI SON HOTEL BAR
1 Nguyen Thi Minh Khai Street, Dalat
Tel 063-822626
All the hip folk in Dalat come to the Hai Son Hotel for the number one nightclub in town. The large, modern bar gets full in the evenings with people waiting to enter the adjoining club. There's a good selection of inexpensive drinks, but the food is limited.
Daily 6pm–midnight

LARRY'S BAR
Sofitel Dalat Palace
12 Tran Phu Street, Dalat
Tel 063-825444
Larry's Bar was named after Larry Hillblom, now deceased, a Californian businessman who, in the early 1990s, spent a fortune renovating Dalat's Sofitel, Novotel and the golf course. It has live music, and a good selection of drinks and bar food.
Daily 4pm–midnight

PK'S DISCO
Novotel, 7 Tran Phu Street, Dalat
Tel 063-825777
PK's has a large dance floor and plays pop, rock and dance. The staff are friendly and the music is loud. Part of the Sofitel hotel, it has a well-stocked and expensive bar.
6pm–late

SPORTS CAFÉ
Empress Hotel
5 Nguyen Thai Hoc Street, Dalat
Tel 063-833888
The open-air bar has good views over Xuan Huong Lake. There's quite a wide selection of drinks and some reasonably priced bar food.
10am–midnight

DALAT PALACE GOLF CLUB
Phu Dong Thien Vuong Street, Dalat
Tel 063-823507
dpgc@hcm.vnn.vn
The US-owned, 18-hole golf course, rated by some as the finest in Vietnam, overlooks Xuan Huong Lake.
Daily Green fee US$85

PHAT TIRE VENTURES
73 Truong Cong Dinh Street, Dalat
Tel 063-829422
www.phattireventures.com
This company arranges exhilarating days out. There are two descents in the Datanla Falls area for canyoning, 3 miles (5km) from Dalat. You can go kayaking on Dankia Lake at the base of Lang Bian mountains, 12 miles (20km) north of Dalat. One- or two-day mountain-biking trips are organized around the countryside of Dalat. One-day rock climbing trips are also arranged.
Canyoning: moderate (three rappels) US$19; advanced (five rappels)

Martial arts at the five-star Furama Resort

US$24 (prices include equipment, vehicle, guide and lunch). Kayaking: US$30 (prices include transportation, equipment, guide and lunch). Mountain biking: from US$28 per person (prices include mountain bicycle, helmet, guide and lunch). Rock climbing: US$25 (prices include equipment, vehicle, guide and lunch)

AMUSEMENT PARK
Corner of Nguyen Thai Hoc Street and Dinh Tien Hoang Street, Dalat
There's a lot of fun at little cost at this small park, with go-carts, motorized boats (made out of old truck tires) and a few other rides.
Free entrance; pay per ride

DANANG

XQ DANANG SILK EMBROIDERY
39–41 Tran Hung Dao Street, Danang
Tel 0511-816847
www.xqhandembroidery.com
At this large embroidery store in downtown Danang, visitors can witness the creative process at work and buy a wide variety of embroidered goods.
Daily 10.30–8.30pm

CHRISTIE'S AND COOL SPOT
112 Tran Phu Street, Danang
Tel 0511-824040
This popular expatriate venue has a downstairs bar and an upstairs restaurant. Happy hour runs from 4pm to 8pm, with cocktails during normal hours costing 50,000d.
Daily 9.30am–10.30pm

FURAMA RESORT
68 Ho Xuan Huong Street
Bac My An Beach, Danang
Tel 0511-847888
www.furamavietnam.com
Between March and October, the five-star PADI diving center at the resort runs trips out to the sea off Danang. It runs a range of courses from beginners to advanced and its instructors speak four languages. The Furama also has a catamaran, a banana boat and speedboats.
Two dives: US$100. PADI Open Water Diver: US$400 (includes equipment and transportation)

FURAMA RESORT
68 Ho Xuan Huong Street
Bac My An Beach, Danang
Tel 0511-847888
www.furamavietnam.com
The health spa here has a range of body treatments and massages, as well as lessons in yoga and tai chi. The total body rejuvenation includes a neck-to-toe body wrap with light blue masque (wattle spa) or sparkling spa masque (plant and seaweed extract).
Full body rejuvenation: US$90

WHAT TO DO

HOI AN

🏬 41 LE LOI STREET
41 Le Loi Street, Hoi An
Tel 0510-862164
quanghiep@dng.vnn.vn
The whole process of silk manufacture, from the silkworm to the woven fabric, can be seen at this silk workshop run by very friendly staff. A 1940s manufacturing machine is on display downstairs. The finished fabrics are on sale.
🕐 Daily 7.45am–10pm

🏬 53A LE LOI
53a Le Loi, Hoi An
Tel 091-4097344
This small outlet is a handbag and shoe shop, where you can have your bag made (the handmade shoes are not as good) or choose from the large range on offer.
🕐 Daily 8am–10pm

🏬 DARLING DECO (LINH DECO)
16–17 Nhi Trung Street, Hoi An
Tel 0510-910717
ligiphi@dng.vnn.vn
Interior furnishings, artistic handicrafts and hand-embroidered goods are the specialties at this two-story, airy shop. There are some great beds and chairs, beautiful keepsake boxes and unusual ethnic wall hangings.
🕐 Daily 9am–9.30pm

🏬 HUNG THAI
140 Tran Phu Street, Hoi An
Tel 0510-927129
The beauty of this shop is that you can watch woodcarvers at work outside. It sells lovely decorated lacquered photo albums and other lacquerwork.
🕐 Daily 8am–9pm

🏬 LA' GAI ARTS SPACE
130 Nguyen Thai Hoc Street, Hoi An
Tel 0510-910496
www.gallerylagai.com
This gallery shows contemporary Vietnamese art, including painting, photography, video, installation and lacquerwork. It occupies an attractive old

building close to the river, and was founded by a group of artists in 2002. Coffee and tea are served in the courtyard, where there is also a conical hat display.
🕐 Daily 9am–10pm

🏬 REACHING OUT, HOA-NHAP HANDICRAFTS
103 Nguyen Thai Hoc Street, Hoi An
Tel 0510-910168
www.reachingoutvietnam.com
The arts and crafts, cards, textiles and silk sleeping bags on sale here are made by local artisans with disabilities. The shop operates a fair trade policy, and profits support people with disabilities. There

Searching for a bargain: Tourists browse through rows of CDs

is usually someone at work in the shop, and visitors are welcome to watch as they create their products.
🕐 Tue–Sun 7.30am–5.30pm

🏬 THANH HA
1A Nhi Trung Street, Hoi An
Tel 0510-864533
leco50@hotmail.com
This shop is recommended because of the speedy service, quality goods, excellent prices and the fact that, unlike many other tried and tested tailors in town, second, third or even fourth fittings are not required. Thanh Ha has an excellent line of winter coats.
🕐 Daily 8.30am–10pm

🏬 YALY
47 Nguyen Thai Hoc Street, Hoi An
Tel 0510-910474
www.yalycouture.com
Professional tailors make very good-quality Thai and Vietnamese silk outfits in this attractive old building. Prices are a little higher but you won't be disappointed with the results. Thai silk clothes are more expensive than those made with Vietnamese silk.
🕐 Daily 7am–8.30pm 🎭 Show 45,000d

🎵 CHAMPA
75 Nguyen Thai Hoc Street, Hoi An
Tel 0510-862974
Traditional arts theater performances of folk music, accompanied by the Vietnamese monochord, are staged in an upstairs room of this bar. Downstairs, hits from the 1960s and 1970s predominate.
🕐 Mon–Sat 9pm

🎵 HOI AN HANDICRAFT WORKSHOP
9 Nguyen Thai Hoc Street, Hoi An
Tel 0510-910216
www.hoianhandicraft.com
Musicians play the Vietnamese monochord at this traditional venue. At the back of the building are craftspeople, including a potter, straw mat-makers, embroiderers, conical hat-makers and woodcarvers.
🕐 Workshop: daily 7.30am–6pm. Performances: Tue–Sun 10.15am, 3.15pm

🎵 LOUNGE BAR
102 Nguyen Thai Hoc Street, Hoi An
Tel 0510-910480
Reggae sounds are played at this bar, with its big red Chinese lanterns, hanging incense cones and comfy sofas. Large tubes with taps dispense sugarcane and fermenting fruits, and there's a backgammon table for those with a competitive streak. Happy hour is between 4pm and 9pm.
🕐 Noon–midnight

TAM TAM CAFÉ
110 Nguyen Thai Hoc Street, Hoi An
Tel 0510-862212
Though mainly a café/restaurant, the Tam Tam also has a good bar. It is in an attractively renovated tea house.
Daily 9.30am–1am

TREATS
158 Tran Phu Street, Hoi An
Tel 0510-861125
A popular and well-run airy, bustling bar, with two pool tables, an attractive balcony and candy-pink walls. Sit out at roadside tables, inside or on the patio at the back. Happy hour is between 4pm and 9pm, and drinks are reasonably priced. Order coffee and you'll be in for a retro treat, as it's served in white, gold-rimmed china from an old Vietnam Airlines tea set.
Daily noon–midnight

BOAT TRIPS
Boat rides are available on the Thu Bon River, where local boatwomen will paddle you around for an hour—a tranquil way of spending the early evening.
30,000d per person per hour

HOI AN TOURIST
10 Tran Hung Dao Street, Hoi An
Tel 0510-862224
www.hoiantourist.com
Hoi An Tourist, which runs two major hotels in town, offers unusual activity tours including Chinese lantern-making classes, fishing lessons, and excursions to meet the Cham.
Prices vary

RED BRIDGE COOKING SCHOOL
Thon 4
Cam Thanh, Hoi An
Tel 0510-933222
www.visithoian.com
Visit the market to be shown local produce, then take a 20-minute boat ride to the cookery school, where you're shown the herb garden. The cooking demonstration by chefs that follows includes dishes such as warm squid salad served in half a pineapple or grilled eggplant (aubergine) stuffed with vegetables. Inside, you are able to make your own fresh spring rolls and learn Vietnamese food-carving. Then dine at the restaurant while listening to Cuban music and watching ducks swim by on the river.
Daily US$15

HUÉ

ROYAL (EAST) THEATER (DUYET THI DUONG)
Imperial City
23 Thang 8 Street, Hué
Tel 054-529219, 091-3439183

The unmistakable neon sign of the DMZ Bar in Hué

Highly enjoyable performances of traditional Vietnamese court music are held in the rebuilt Imperial City theater, accompanying elaborate dances by lavishly costumed performers.
Daily 9, 9.30, 10, 10.30, 2.30, 3, 3.30, 4 20,000d

DMZ BAR
44 Le Loi Street, Hué
Tel 054-823414
Hué's first bar is popular with younger travelers. Cold beer and spirits are served at low prices, and there's a pool table and patio.
Daily 4pm–2am

WHY NOT?
21 Vo Thi Sau Street, Hué
Tel 054-824793
Mini conical hats hang from a brick bar and fishing nets hang from the walls at this arty café-bar. It offers a reasonable selection of food and drink and has a pool table. The special cocktail—Why Not?—is a blend of Jaka, Cointreau, blue Curaçao, grenadine and fresh milk.
Daily 7.30–2am

DRAGONBOATING
Sail up the Perfume River with your own private singers and musicians. Boats are available on the stretch of riverbank between the Huong Giang Hotel and the Trang Tien Bridge, and also from the dock behind the Dong Ba Market. Tour offices and major hotels will arrange trips, including the Sinh Café (▷ 203) and Hotel Saigon Morin (▷ 245).
From 50,000d per person; night trips US$10; performance of folk songs US$40 for 90 mins, royal dance US$200 for 90 mins

MUI NE

JIBE'S BEACH CLUB
Full Moon Beach Resort, Mui Ne
Tel 062-847405
www.windsurf-vietnam.com
Jibe's has the only separate bar on the beach at Mui Ne, and drinks are less expensive here than in the resorts. There's a barbecue party every Saturday night with a happy hour. The enterprise is run and frequented by a younger crowd of vacationers.
Daily 7.30am–3am

AIRWAVES
Sailing Club, Mui Ne
www.airwaveskitesurfing.com
Airwaves rents out kite surfing, windsurfing, sailing and surfing equipment. It also has Hobie cats. Kite surfing is taught by internationally qualified instructors.
Varies, from US$9 (surfing, half-day) to US$60 (catamaran sailing, half-day)

JIBE'S BEACH CLUB

Full Moon Beach Resort, Mui Ne
Tel 062-847405
www.windsurf-vietnam.com
Jibe's is an importer of sea
kayaks, windsurfing, surfboard
and kite surfing equipment.
Watersports equipment is
available for purchase or for
rent by the hour, day or week.
Kite surfing lessons are run by
instructors certified by the
International Kite surfing
Organization, and instruction is
available in nine languages.
There's also a good range of
bathing suits for sale.
🕐 Daily 7.30am–3am 💲 Varies, from
US$5 (surf or boogie board, half-day
rental) to US$375 (kite and board,
week rental)

LOTUS DAY SPA

Sailing Club, Mui Ne
Tel 062-847442
www.sailingclubvietnam.com
Indulge yourself in the open-
sided cabins of the spa area in
the lusciously green hotel
grounds or in the privacy of
your own room. Treatments
include a rice body polish,
mineral mud wrap and
60-minute skin-purifying facial.
🕐 Daily 10–7pm; after 7pm by
appointment only 💲 Rice body
polish US$28; mud wrap US$35;
facial US$18

NHA TRANG

CRAZY KIM BAR

19 Biet Thu Street, Nha Trang
Tel 058-816072
This place serves bar food and
breakfast inside or in a small
outdoor eating area at the
front. At the back, the Wild
East Saloon, complete with
swing doors, is an added
attraction. The remaining area
focuses on the bar in the front
room and the low-slung
wicker chair area out the back.
Happy hour is from noon to
midnight, and the bar is
deservedly popular with
travelers and expatriates.
🕐 Daily 10am–1am

GUAVA

17 Biet Thu Street, Nha Trang
Tel 058-524140
A stylish cocktail bar and café
with an orange facade, a
relaxing garden and lounge
area. Sit in the large, quarry-
tiled courtyard on solid,
woodblock chairs, relaxing in
their ultra-cool, square white
cushions. Earlier in the day
Guava enjoys a Zen-like calm.
At night the palms are backlit.
Burgers, hangover breakfasts
and sandwiches are served all
day. Happy hour is between
5pm and 9pm for draft beer
and between 5pm and 10pm
for cocktails.
🕐 Daily 11am–midnight

*Parasailing: A daredevil takes a
leap of faith at Nha Trang*

ANA MANDARA RESORT

Tran Phu Street, Nha Trang
Tel 058-522222
www.sixsenses.com/evason-
anamandara
Ana Mandara is a relatively
new five-star PADI diving
resort, with a diving team
(staffed by Rainbow Divers,
▷ right) catering to every level.
🕐 Daily 7am–10pm 💲 Two dives
US$40; Open Water Diver US$275

COCO DIVE CENTER

2E Biet Thu Street, Nha Trang
Tel 058-522900
www.cocodivecenter.com
This five-star PADI instructor
center is run by the first
Vietnamese to be qualified as

a PADI master instructor. Daily
trips and courses are offered
from beginner to advanced,
and five languages are spoken
by the staff. Night dives are run
on request. Prices include all
equipment and instruction,
and there is a 10 percent
discount for those with their
own equipment.
🕐 Daily 6am–9pm 💲 Two dives
US$50; Open Water Diver US$185;
snorkeling US$15

RAINBOW DIVERS

90a Hung Vuong Street, Nha Trang
Tel 058-524351
www.divevietnam.com
A British-owned, five-star PADI
instructor development resort
that runs a full range of dives
and courses around the islands
off Nha Trang. The qualified
instructors speak a variety of
languages. There are also dives
from Whale Island Resort
(▷ 249). Price includes pickup, equipment, food and water
on the boat and fresh fruit.
🕐 Daily 6am–10pm 💲 Two dives
US$40; Open Water Diver US$275

SAILING CLUB DIVERS

Sailing Club
62 and 72 Tran Phu Street, Nha Trang
Tel 058-522788
www.sailingclubvietnam.com
This five-star PADI instructor
development resort is
managed by a Briton and
was established in 1999. Four
languages are spoken by
instructors, who offer daily dive
trips off Nha Trang. Prices
include pick-up, equipment,
lunch, soft drinks and water.
🕐 Daily 7.30am–9pm 💲 Snorkeling
US$12; Open Water Diver US$225

WAVEKILLER

La Louisiane
Tran Phu Street, Nha Trang
Tel 058-512308, 090-3572106
oceane@dng.vnn.vn
Wavekiller rents out watersports equipment, runs a few
tours and owns a bungalow
on Doc Lech Beach.
🕐 Daily 8–4 💲 From 250,000d to
800,000d; windsurfing US$10 an hour

🟢 GIOI BIEN
100A/14 Tran Phu Street, Nha Trang
Tel 058-828242
www.vnseaworld.com
Trips are run out into Nha
Trang Bay on a glass-bottomed
boat, which visits
Oceanografic, Mun Island,
Dam Bay and Tri Nguyen
Aquarium. Trippers can also
snorkel, and there is a floating
bar. Prices include the boat
ride, the oceanarium entrance
fee, a meal, fruit, water, a
mask, a kayak, a float and an
English-speaking guide.
🕐 Daily 8–3 💷 Adult 145,000d,
child (6–12) 85,0000d

⭐ LONG THANH'S GALLERY
126 Hoang Van Thu Street, Nha Trang
Tel 058-824875
Long Thanh, one of Vietnam's
most famous black and
white photographers (▷ 19),
will meet enthusiasts and
organize photographic expeditions by pre-arrangement.
💷 Negotiable with Long Thanh

💟 ANA MANDARA RESORT
Tran Phu Street, Nha Trang
Tel 058-522222
www.sixsenses.com/evason-anamandara
The wonderful Six Senses Spa
experience at the Ana Mandara
will leave you feeling
pampered and totally relaxed.
The helpful, professional staff
massage away your aches and
pains in beautiful surroundings
next to the beach. The Six
Senses Spa offers Japanese
and Vichy showers, hot tubs
and massages. The Vietnamese
Experience includes steam
and sauna with fresh herbs,
foot massage, cupping and
pressure-point activation,
scalp massage, a Vietnamese
facial using aloe vera and a
Vietnamese hair wash. The
shampoo, used by a former
empress of Vietnam, is made
from a black bean called *bo
ket*, lime and grapefruit peel.
💷 From US$45 for a 50-min massage;
Vietnamese experience US$150

🟢 QI SHISEIDO SALON AND SPA
VinPearl Resort and Spa, Hon Tre Island
Jetty: 7 Tran Phu Street
Tel 058-598188, ext 8836
www.vinpearlresort.com
Luxurious spa facilities include
a heated indoor pool and a
range of individual treatments
that make use of Shiseido
products. Packages are also
available.
💷 From US$29 (full body massage) to
US$88 (skin rejuvenation)

💟 THAP BA HOT SPRINGS
3 miles (4km) from Nha Trang,
past Ponagar Cham towers
Tel 058-835335
www.thapbahotsprings.com.vn

*Enjoying a relaxing face massage
at the Ana Mandara Resort*

Soak in mineral water or a
mud bath, in baths and pools
of differing sizes available for
individuals, couples and
groups. The water is 104°F
(40°C) and is salty and rich
in sodium silicate chloride.
The mineral mud is high in
sodium silicate carbonate,
which stimulates the
nerves under the skin. Steam
baths and massages are
also available.
💷 Mineral mud tub for two 250,000d;
for a group 50,000d per person,
25,000d per child; mineral water bath
for two 50,000d; for a group 35,000d
per person, 15,000d per child

✴ PHU DONG AMUSEMENT AND WATERPARK
Tran Phu Street, Nha Trang
Tel 058-828883
When the sea is too rough, this
small waterpark with a modest
selection of rides on the
beachfront makes an
entertaining alternative.
🕐 Tue, Thu, Sat, Sun 9–5 💷 20,000d

PHAN THIET

⛳ OCEAN DUNES GOLF CLUB
1 Ton Duc Thang Street, Phan Thiet
Tel 062-823366
odgc@hcm.vnn.vn
www.vietnamgolfresorts.com
Phan Thiet's US-owned 18-
hole golf course was designed
by Nick Faldo and is regarded
as one of the best in Vietnam.
The 6,746-yard (6,169m) par
72 course course has a fully
equipped clubhouse with bar
and restaurant.
💷 Green fee US$80, extra charges for
caddy, buggy, clubs and shoes

💟 VICTORIA PHAN THIET
Km 9, Phu Hai
Phan Thiet
Tel 062-813000
www.victoriahotels-asia.com
This hugely attractive beach
resort, close to Mui Ne, has
an on-site spa that offers Thai
massage, reflexology,
traditional Japanese shiatsu
and other face and body
massages. There is also a
sauna, Jacuzzi and beauty
salon.
💷 From US$20 (hand and reflexology)
to US$35 (full-body massage)

FESTIVAL

FULL MOON FESTIVAL
Hoi An
Hoi An has its own festival on
the 14th day of every lunar
month. The town is decorated
with fairy lights and Chinese
lanterns at night, streets are
pedestrianized and activities
are organized for visitors,
including poetry recitals,
singing and card games.
🕐 14th day of every lunar month

WHAT TO DO

HO CHI MINH CITY

Nowhere else in Vietnam is the embrace of capitalism through *doi moi* (new change) at its most evident. Hundreds of shops have mushroomed on the streets of Ho Chi Minh City, Vietnam's economic powerhouse. District 1 (Saigon) is the downtown shopping area, full of stores selling beautiful silk, cotton and linen clothing, bags, handicrafts, souvenirs, antiques and furniture. It also has a few luxury designer outlets in some of its more expensive hotels. Many stores selling larger items offer a shipping service. Shops are open early and keep on trading until late in the day without closing for lunch. Credit cards are widely accepted.

There is live entertainment for visitors in a couple of the expat bars, and there are plenty of drinking holes, privately owned or run by hotels. The greatest concentration is in District 1 (Saigon) and in the backpacker district of Pham Ngu Lao. All play Western music, and many offer pool tables, darts and TV screens for sporting events. Friday and Saturday nights are busiest, but every night of the week is a night for socializing in Saigon.

KEY TO SYMBOLS

🏬	**Shopping**
🎭	**Entertainment**
🍷	**Nightlife**
⚽	**Sports**
✦	**Activities**
♡	**Health and Beauty**
✿	**For Children**

🏬 SHOPPING

ART AND ANTIQUES

ANCIENT/APRICOT GALLERY
50–52 Mac Thi Buoi Street, District 1
Tel 08-8227962
www.apricot-artvietnam.com
This sister gallery to the one in Hanoi (▷ 168) specializes in famous artists and commands high prices.
🕙 Daily 8–8

LOTUS GALLERY
47 Dong Khoi Street and
30 Le Loi Street
District 1
Tel 08-8292695
www.lotusgallery.com
This expensive gallery show-cases works by contemporary Vietnamese painters. Many are members of the Vietnam Fine Arts Association, and have exhibited around the world.
🕙 Daily 8–8

NGA SHOP
61 Le Thanh Ton Street, District 1
Tel 08-8256289
www.vietnam-art-craft.com
Nga Shop has become one of the best known of all lacquer stores as a result of its high-quality products. Nga designs the items and oversees her craftspeople at work. There are beautiful dishes in silver and gold and small pieces of wooden furniture. Top-quality rosewood and ceramic handicrafts are also available and there is an export service.
🕙 Mon–Sat 8–8, Sun 9–6

SO CO LA
45 Ton That Thiep Street, District 1
Tel 08-8231279
Pretty shoes are in abundance here. However, the main appeal is the eclectic collection of antiques, including a His Master's Voice gramophone, window panes and old signs.
🕙 Daily 11–8

DEPARTMENT STORES

DIAMOND DEPARTMENT STORE

Diamond Plaza
34 Le Duan Street
District 1
Tel 08-8225500

Saigon's newest, wonderfully air-conditioned department store occupies a couple of floors. It sells luxury goods, clothes (including some Western brands), watches, bags and perfumes. There is also a small supermarket. A bowling alley complex and cinema dominate the store's top floor.

⏰ Mon–Fri 10–9.30, Sat, Sun and holidays 10–10

SAIGONTOURIST DEPARTMENT STORE

35 bis–45 Le Thanh Ton Street
District 1
Tel 08-8277635
deptstore@hcm.vnn.vn

Although this department store is quite small, it sells an impressive range of fashions, jewelry, perfume and make-up and also has a supermarket. The Saigontourist holding company at 102 Nguyen Hue Avenue, District 1 (tel 08-8234553) sells perfumes (Chanel and Gucci), watches (Omega and Hèrmes), ties, cigarettes, sunshades and cosmetics.

⏰ Daily 10.30–7

FASHION AND SILK

KHAISILK

107 Dong Khoi Street
District 1
Tel 08-8291146
www.khaisilkcorp.com

Khaisilk belongs to Mr. Khai's growing retail empire. He has a dozen shops around Vietnam and a second Saigon branch in the New World Hotel. Choose from a range of beautifully made, quality silks, from dresses to scarves to ties.

⏰ Daily 8–8

SAIGON IMPRESSION

125 Dong Khoi Street
District 1
Tel 08-8239271
aqhsailk@hcm.fpt.vn

There are numerous clothes shops on Dong Khoi Street, but this one stands out for its efficient service and its top-quality cotton clothes at extremely reasonable prices. Made-to-measure clothes crafted from cotton or silk can be whipped up in 24 hours, and the quality is high. Cotton skirts and dresses are well lined, a bonus as lining is not always included in Vietnam. The silk coats are stunning.

⏰ Daily 9am–10pm

Khaisilk sells a range of beautiful, quality silk products

SONG

76D Le Thanh Ton Street
District 1
Tel 08-8246986

A beautiful clothes emporium selling flowing summer dresses from French-born designer Valerie Gregori-McKenzie. There are also other stylish and unique pieces, accessories and even cookbooks based on her culinary experiences of living in Vietnam.

⏰ Daily 9–8

HOME FURNISHINGS

CELADON GREEN

51 Ton That Thiep Street
District 1
Tel 08-9144697
quasarkhanh@hcm.vnn.vn

Here you'll find beautifully designed and presented ceramics, mostly in cream and green, including complete Vietnamese tea sets, bowls, pots and dishes. This downtown shop also stocks lacquerware.

⏰ Daily 9–8

GAYA

39 Ton That Thiep Street
District 1
Tel 08-9143769
info@gayavietnam.com

A three-floor shop exhibiting exquisite items. One floor has a selection of finely embroidered tablecloths, bamboo bowls, ceramics and large home items such as screens. Another is lined with ethereal and unusual designer clothes by Romyda Keth, who is based in Cambodia (kethambre@bigpond.com.kh). If you like an item but it does not fit, the shop will take your measurements and make another, but it will take two weeks to complete it.

⏰ Daily 9–9

MOSAIQUE

98 Mac Thi Buoi Street
District 1
Tel/fax 08-8234634
mosaique@fpt.vn

Like its sister store in Hanoi, this cavernous shop is a home accessories parlor, with displays upstairs of exquisitely embroidered wall hangings and table-runners.

⏰ Daily 9–9

ORIENTAL HOME

2A Le Duan Street
District 1
Tel 08-9100194
www.madeinvietnamcollection.com

If you are taken with the Imperial style of furniture so favored in Hué, this is the

place to come. Lamp stands, ceramics and brass ornaments are also displayed in this furnishings and gift emporium. It's an environmentally conscious operation; only natural materials, such as bamboo, rattan and silk, are used in their products.

🕐 Daily 9–7.30

RED DOOR DECO
20A Thi Sach Street, District 1
Tel 08-8258672
www.reddoordeco.com
This two-story shop sells stylish, innovative and well-made furniture, fabrics and ornaments. Shoppers can pick up old French Marelli fans of various sizes, dried lotus leaves, some beautiful lamps, cushions or unusual pieces of furniture.

🕐 Daily 8–7

SAIGON KITSCH
43 Ton That Tiep Street
District 1
Tel 08-8218019
info@saigonkitsch.com
Communist kitsch items here range from big propaganda poster art to place mats and mugs. You'll also find some good examples of anti-US propaganda material for sale, plus great retro bags and funky jewelry.

🕐 Daily 9–8

🎭 ENTERTAINMENT

CONSERVATORY OF MUSIC (NHAC VIEN THANH PHO HO CHI MINH)
112 Nguyen Du Street
District 1
Tel 08-8225841
Traditional Vietnamese music and classical music concerts are performed by the young students who study music here and sometimes by local and visiting musicians.

🕐 Performances: Mon–Fri from 7pm

MUSEUM OF VIETNAMESE HISTORY
2 Nguyen Binh Khiem Street
District 1
Tel 08-8298146
There are daily 15-minute performances of water puppetry in the tiny theater in a covered outdoor part of the museum. The advantages of this performance over the Hanoi theater (▷ 171) are that you can get closer to the puppetry, and there is better light and more room for taking photos.

🕐 Museum: Mon–Sat 8–11, 1.30–4, Sun 8.30–4. Performances: daily 9, 10, 2, 3, 4; extra 1pm show on Sun
💰 Museum: 15,000d. Water puppetry: daily 15,000d

The Blue Gecko bar in Saigon is popular with Australians

OPERA HOUSE
Lam Son Square, District 1
Tel 08-8299976
Infrequent concerts are held at the Opera House. Consult the *Vietnam News* and other local publications for details of upcoming events. .

🕐 Varies depending on the performance

🌙 NIGHTLIFE

APOCALYPSE NOW
2B–2C Thi Sach Street
District 1
Tel 08-8256124
Apocalypse Now is one of the most abidingly popular bars

with the younger expatriate crowd. The ceiling is decorated with helicopter reliefs, the fans revolving as if they are the helicopter rotors. The large dance floor gets very full and hot and sticky. There is a large screen for sporting events.

🕐 Daily 7pm–midnight

BLUE GECKO
31 Ly Tu Trong Street
District 1
Tel 08-8243483
simon@hcm.vnn.vn
Saigon's Australian community has adopted this small bar, so expect cold beer (happy hour is between 5 and 7pm) and Australian flags above the pool table. Darts and a TV screen are also available.

🕐 Daily 5pm–late

CAFÉ LATIN
19–21 Dong Du Street
District 1
Tel 08-8226363
This very popular, ultramodern bar in downtown Saigon, all sleek steel lines and glass, is a favorite with working expatriates—especially Australians—and is busy every night. Sit at the bar stools or sink into the comfortable sofas that line the walls. There is a restaurant with a balcony upstairs (▷ 224).

🕐 Daily 9am–midnight

LA FENÊTRE SOLEIL
1st Floor, 135 Le Thanh Ton Street
District 1
Tel 08-8225209
It's a little difficult to find the entrance to this small café, but it is worth making the effort. In the daytime it's quiet, with large, comfortable armchairs and is a great place to enjoy a cappuccino or one of the many flavored teas. In the evening there is a different vibe and some fancy cocktails are mixed.

🕐 Daily 11.30am–midnight

HOA VIEN

28 Mac Dinh Chi Street
District 1
Tel 08-8290585
www.hoavener.com

Hoa Vien, a vast Czech *bierkeller*, houses Saigon's first microbrewery. Freshly brewed dark and light beer is available by the liter or in smaller measures, and you can tap your own beer. The bar is surrounded by copper kegs. If you want to see the brewery system, contact Ms Hanh, consul assistant, for a tour (tel 08-8290585, hoavener@hcm.vnn.vn). Food is also served (▷ 225).

🕐 Daily 9am–11pm

NUMBER FIVE BAR

5 Ly Tu Trong Street
District 1
Tel 08-8256300
Heinz@hcmc.netnam.vn

This spacious bar in an air-conditioned building has a loyal following, especially with the working male crowd. Happy hour is between 6pm and 8pm (Tiger beer only), making it a prime after-work destination. The bar staff speak English, and there is good food and a pool table. This is a popular place for watching major televized sporting events, particularly rugby and soccer, and it regularly organizes golf tournaments.

🕐 Daily 5pm–midnight

Q BAR

7 Lam Son Square
District 1
Tel 08-8233479
qbar_anh@hotmail.com

Well positioned under the Opera House, the Q Bar is the haunt of a wide cross-section of Saigon society. The interior is striking: Caravaggio murals adorn some of the walls and there are nooks and crannies for intimate seating. The restaurant of the same name is next door to the bar.

🕐 Daily 6pm–late

ROOFTOP GARDEN

Rex Hotel
141 Nguyen Hue Boulevard
District 1
Tel 08-8292185
www.rexhotelvietnam.com

Large model elephants, a motley collection of shrubbery and bonsai, and a revolving crown may give this outdoor bar and café a rather shabby air, but that doesn't detract from the hotel's fame as the venue for daily military briefings to the press during the Vietnam War. If you can peer past the leafy decoration there is a great view of Saigon.

🕐 Daily 24 hours

The rooftop terrace of the famed Rex Hotel is lit up at night

SAIGON SAIGON BAR

10th floor
Caravelle Hotel
19 Lam Son Square
District 1
Tel 08-8243999
www.caravellehotel.com

At this breezy and cool bar there is outdoor seating on a patio and on tiny balconies clinging to the edge of the skyscraper, with large chairs from which to enjoy the superb views. The Saigon Saigon signature cocktail is a mix of vodka, rum, gin, orange juice and pineapple juice, rather swamped by crème de menthe. Snacks and ice cream are available; sandwiches are served at lunchtime, and afternoon tea includes cakes on dainty, tiered dishes. All is accompanied by a 1980s pop sound track, and cigars are on sale.

🕐 Daily 11am–late

VASCO'S

16 Cao Ba Quat Street
District 1
Tel 08-8243148

On the ground level of the beautiful French villa that houses the popular and excellent Camargue restaurant (▷ 225), this bar, with several rooms and an exterior patio under the palm trees, is a huge hit with the younger expatriate community. Friday night is the most popular, and live music at weekends pulls in even more partygoers. Both the staff and the drinkers are a friendly lot.

🕐 Daily 10.30am–midnight

CLUBS

163 CYCLO BAR

163 Pham Ngu Lao Street
District 1
Tel 08-9201567
saigoncyclo@yahoo.com

This friendly venue in the heart of the backpacker district has a bar downstairs and an air-conditioned room upstairs, with live music—jazz, Latin, flamenco, country and pop—from 8pm nightly. Inexpensive drinks and light meals are served from breakfast onward by friendly and capable staff. Black-and-white photos of the fall of Saigon (in 1975) adorn the walls. Happy hour is between 9am and 6pm.

🕐 Daily 9am–midnight

BOP

8a1/d1 Thai Van Lung
District 1
Tel 08-8251901

Saigon's first jazz club, next door to the Wild Horse Saloon (► 228), is a sleekly decorated venue that has proved popular since it opened in March 2004.

WHAT TO DO

It has a Manhattan feel, with skyscraper photos lining the wall, great cocktails and good live tunes daily.

🅦 Daily 4.30pm–midnight

HEART OF DARKNESS
17B Le Thanh Ton Street
District 1
Tel 08-8231080
www.hodvn.com
The Saigon offshoot of its famous Phnom Penh parent is Khmer in style, with Cambodian carvings and interior design. Dark red curtains are hung everywhere, and there's a decorative brick wall in the window. Next to the entrance is a raised platform for seating. Every Saturday night there's a guest DJ, and every night women are served free gin between 7pm and 9pm.

🅦 Daily 5–midnight

SEVENTEEN SALOON
17 Ton Duc Thang Street
District 1
Tel 08-8227934
A large and very popular venue, Seventeen Saloon stages live music every night. There is one bar upstairs and one downstairs, each hosting different bands (usually one local and one Filipino band) that play various styles of music.

🅦 Daily 7pm–midnight

UNDERGROUND
69 Dong Khoi Street
District 1
Tel 08-8299079
This popular venue is notable for its food, but as the evening wears on, tables are packed away and the space fills with drinkers and dancers. Its extra-long bar in the basement serves up every conceivable drink. There are TV screens showing soccer, rugby, Formula 1 racing and other sporting events.

🅦 Daily 9am–midnight

🅢 SPORTS AND 🅢 ACTIVITIES

BOWLING

DIAMOND SUPERBOWL
Diamond Plaza
4th Floor, 34 Le Duan Street
District 1
Tel 08-8257778 ext 12 (lane booking)
This new complex in the heart of the city is at the top of the Diamond Plaza department store and has 24 bowling lanes. You can also rent bowling shoes here. The top floor has a fast-food outlet, video games and plenty of pool tables for those taking a break from bowling.

🅦 Mon–Sat 10am–1am, Sun 9am–1am 💷 Mon–Fri 10am–2pm

Waitresses from the popular Underground bar in Saigon

20,000d per game, 2pm–6pm 30,000d, 6pm–1am 40,000d; Sat and Sun prices slightly higher

SUPERBOWL
43A Truong Son Street
Than Binh District
Tel 08-8426405
This enormous bowling complex, just outside the Tan Son Nhat airport, has 32 lanes, video arcades and fast-food outlets. It is a great hit with the Vietnamese, especially at weekends, so reserve in advance to be sure of securing a lane.

🅦 Daily 10am–midnight 💷 40,000d per person per game, plus shoe rental

DANCING

LA CASA LATINA
11 Thai Van Lung Street
District 1
Tel 08-8223240
raphael@casalatina-vn.com
Salsa classes are run in this Mediterranean enclave on Tuesday, Wednesday and Thursday nights from 8.30pm to 9.30pm.

🅦 Tue–Thu 8.30pm–9.30pm 💷 50,000d for one lesson; 350,000d for 10 lessons

GOLF

BOCHANG DONG NAI GOLF RESORT
Dong Nai Province
Tel 061-866288
www.vietnamgolfclub.com
This 27-hole course with lakes and fairways lies in rolling countryside 31 miles (50km) north of Saigon, up Highway 1. There is also a bar, restaurant and on-site accommodations.

💷 Green fees: Mon–Fri US$55, Sat US$75, Sun US$85

GOLF VIETNAM AND COUNTRY CLUB
Long Thanh My Ward, District 9
Tel 08-7330124
hoaviet-jvc@hcm.vnn.vn
This 36-hole golfing complex with east and west courses lies just north of Ho Chi Minh City. Facilities also include tennis and badminton courts, a boating lake, a children's play area and on-site accommodations.

💷 Green fees: Mon–Fri US$73, Sat–Sun US$92

SONG BE GOLF RESORT
Lai Thieu, Thuan An District
Binh Duong Province
Tel 065-755802
www.golf-asia.com/vietnam/songbe.html
This 18-hole course lies in 247 acres (100ha), with lakes and tree-lined fairways, 14 miles (22km) from Ho Chi Minh City on Highway 13. There are also tennis courts, a gym, sauna and children's play area.

💷 Green fees: Mon–Fri US$70, Sat–Sun US$90

HORSE RACING

PHU THO RACECOURSE
2 Le Dai Hanh Street, District 11
Tel 08-9628205
Races are held Saturday and Sunday afternoons on this course, reopened with financing from a Chinese entrepreneur. Both the winner and the second horse have to be selected to collect winnings.
🎟 Tickets: 1,000d. Entrance to Turf Club: 11,000d

TENNIS

LAN ANH CLUB
291 Cach Mang Thang Tam Street
District 10
Tel 08-8627144
This pleasant tennis club, almost next door to the International Club, has courts and a swimming pool and is open to nonmembers.
🕐 Daily 6am–11pm

❤ HEALTH AND BEAUTY

BEAUTY SPAS

SAIGON SPA
172/2 Nguyen Van Huong Street
District 2
Tel 08-7442222
www.saigonspa.net
This women-only spa is in a grand, French colonial house, a few blocks from downtown. Treatments range from the herbal steam bath and herbal Jacuzzi to a papaya wrap or a Blissful Day package. A free round-trip transfer from/to districts 1 and 2 can be arranged.
🕐 Daily 9–9; reservations 8–9
🎟 Herbal steam bath and Jacuzzi US$20; 60-min papaya wrap US$35; Blissful Day package US$160

SHISEIDO
158B Dong Khoi Street, District 1
Tel 08-8291261
There's a shop and a treatment clinic at these downtown premises. Indulge in a Qi body massage or a facial, or one of the other 44 pampering options on offer.
🕐 Daily 8.30am–9pm 🎟 Qi body massage 320,000d; facial 240,000d

SPATROPIC
187B Hai Ba Trung Street, District 3
Tel 08-8228895
www.spatropic.com
A small alley next to the Tib restaurant leads to this urban spa, housed in a French villa surrounded by a pebbled, plant-filled Zen garden. Treatments range from aromatherapy facials to a sea-weed body wrap, to a half-day retreat. Men can participate in a Pampering for Him program, lasting three and a half hours.
🕐 Daily 9.30am–8pm 🎟 One-hour aromatherapy facial US$32; one-hour seaweed body wrap US$35; half-day retreat US$105; Pampering for Him US$86

The Saigon Spa offers many relaxing treatments for women

❸ FOR CHILDREN

SAIGON WATER PARK
Go Dua Bridge
Kha Van Can Street
Thu Duc District
Tel 08-8970456
swp@saigonwaterpark.com
This Western-style waterpark, 6 miles (10km) outside Ho Chi Minh City, has a variety of water slides of varying degrees of excitement and a child's pool on a 12-acre (5ha) site. It is hugely popular with the Vietnamese. Buses run here from Ben Thanh Market.
🕐 Mon–Fri 9–5, Sat 9–6, Sun 8–8
🎟 Adult 70,000d, child 30,000d, infants free

FESTIVALS

FEBRUARY

NGHIA ANH HOI QUAN PAGODA FESTIVAL
678 Nguyen Trai Street, District 5
The *Hoa* (overseas Chinese) community, together with many local *Kinh* (Vietnamese), celebrate in honor of Lord Quan Cong with unicorn, lion and dragon dances.
🕐 15th day of the first lunar month; also 24th day of the sixth lunar month (Jul)

MARCH

ONG DIA TEMPLE FESTIVAL
125 Le Loi Street, Go Vap District
A celebration of the birth of the Earth genie Phuc Doc Chinh Than.
🕐 Second day of the second lunar month

MAY

THIEN HAU PAGODA FESTIVAL
710 Nguyen Trai Street, District 5
A festival celebrating Goddess Thien Hau—the goddess of the sea and the protector of sailors (▷ 134).
🕐 23rd–24th day of the third lunar month

SEPTEMBER

NGHINH ONG FESTIVAL
Hung Thanh hamlet, Can Gio District
Traditional procession and offerings in honor of the whale cult followed by local fisherfolk.
🕐 15th–17th days of eighth lunar month

LE VAN DUYET TOMB FESTIVAL
Le Van Duyet Tomb,
Binh Thanh District
One of Ho Chi Minh City's biggest festivals. Pilgrims flock to the Temple of Marshal Le Van Duyet (▷ 139) on the 30th day of the seventh lunar month.
🕐 30th day of the seventh lunar month to the first day of the eighth lunar month

WHAT TO DO

THE SOUTH

There is little in the way of shopping in the south of Vietnam, but in the Mekong Delta it's possible to buy plenty of tropical fruits and vegetables, rice paper, rice "popcorn", fish sauce (that from Phu Quoc is most famous) and rice wines. Small outlets sell handicrafts made from coconut, especially in Ben Tre, or, in Vung Tau, wooden ornaments; Soc Trang is renowned for its gold statues. Do not buy tortoiseshell products (found especially in Ha Tien) or shell ornaments and jewels (Vung Tau); doing so is against Vietnamese law and international wildlife conventions (CITES). The region has little entertainment with the exception of Vung Tau, though many hotels have bars—these range widely in quality and standards. In Vung Tau, a popular getaway for the Saigonese, there is a cluster of bars catering to Westerners. Phu Quoc's resort hotels all have bars and are great places to unwind at sunset. Water-based activities are popular, and diving and snorkeling operations have been launched from Phu Quoc. The Mekong River provides many opportunities for boat excursions up the main thoroughfare and its small tributaries; Can Tho is the main base, although trips are also available from Chau Doc and My Tho. Both of the Victoria group hotels here offer therapies and treatments, and the thermal hot springs of Binh Thau are near Vung Tau.

KEY TO SYMBOLS

- 🛍 **Shopping**
- 🎭 **Entertainment**
- 🍷 **Nightlife**
- ⚽ **Sports**
- ✦ **Activities**
- ♥ **Health and Beauty**
- ✦ **For Children**

CAN THO

✦ TRANSMÉKONG

97/10 Ngo Quyen, P. An Cu
Can Tho
Tel 071-829540
www.transmekong.com
The company's converted wooden rice barge, *Bassac*, can sleep 12 passengers in six air-conditioned cabins with private bathrooms. Each cabin has two beds, cotton sheets, a bedside table, slippers and an elegant white ceramic bowl for the sink. Prices include dinner and breakfast, entry tickets to visited sights, a French- or English-speaking guide on board and access to a small boat.

🖐 One to two passengers US$183 per person; three or more passengers US$167 per person. Single cabin supplement additional 50 percent. Private trip (whole boat, per night) US$1,245

✦ COOKERY CLASSES

Victoria Can Tho
Cai Khe Ward
Tel 071-810111
www.victoriahotels-asia.com
Kitchen staff take you to the local market in the early morning to buy produce for these cookery courses. On returning to the hotel, the Vietnamese chef explains all the ingredients and helps you prepare a dish for lunch.

🖐 US$30 (minimum 2 people). Reservations must be made by 9pm the previous night

⭐ LADY HAU BOAT TRIP

Victoria Can Tho, Cai Khe Ward
Tel 071-810111,
www.victoriahotels-asia.com
The *Lady Hau* is a converted wooden ship that embarks on a sunrise breakfast cruise to the floating market at Cai Rang. The 3.5-hour trip involves taking a sampan up narrow creeks and visiting a noodle factory and an orchard. A romantic sunset cruise with cocktails and snacks also leaves at 5.30pm.
🍴 Sunrise cruise: US$33 per person (minimum 4 people). Sunset cruise: US$17 per person (minimum 4 people)

❤ VICTORIA CAN THO SPA

Victoria Can Tho, Cai Khe Ward
Tel 071-810111
www.victoriahotels-asia.com
The massage cabins at the Victoria Can Tho are near the river. You can hear the chug of the boats as you lie on thin mattresses covered in crisp white cotton and strewn with pink orchids, enjoying the healing treatments. These range from the 45-minute gentle Vietnamese massage or hand and foot reflexology to the Victoria massage package of reflexology, body massage, oil massage and head massage. There's also a sauna that needs an hour's notice.
🕐 Daily 10–10. Reserve in advance
🍴 From US$20 (hand and foot reflexology) to US$40 (massage package)

CHAU DOC

❤ VICTORIA CHAU DOC SPA

Victoria Chau Doc, 32 Le Loi Street
Tel 076-865010
www.victoriahotels-asia.com
Massage beds are mounted on platforms and surrounded by four-poster hangings at this Victoria hotel. Choose from a foot and hand massage, head and shoulder massage or the full Victoria massage. Every hotel guest gets a free 10-minute massage.
🕐 Daily 9–9 🍴 From US$20 (head and shoulder massage) to US$40 (full massage)

PHU QUOC

☕ AN THAI CAFÉ

3 Khu Pho, An Thoi Town
Tel 077-844307
Friendly, locally run An Thai serves excellent Vietnamese coffee, and good breakfasts, lunches and dinners. The dreamy location overlooks the small town of An Thoi and the sea. You can also enjoy cocktails and a wide selection of local and international beers.
🕐 Daily 7am–midnight

🏃 RAINBOW DIVERS

Rainbow Bar
next to Kim Hoa Resort
Tel 091-3400964 (cellphone)
www.divevietnam.com

Around Phu Quoc divers get the chance to see corals and sea life

This British-owned diving company can be contacted through any of the local hotels. The dive season runs from mid-November to early June, and divers can see excellent corals around the cluster of islands off the south coast, plus varied sea life to the north. PADI courses are available.
🍴 Two dives to the north US$75; 3 dives to the south US$100; snorkeling US$30

VUNG TAU

☕ SNAFU (AKA BB)

14 Nguyen Trai Street
Tel 064-856028
This bar is part of a strip of establishments popular with Vung Tau's expatriate community. It serves cold beer and Western snacks, and it also has a pool table.
🕐 Daily 8am–midnight

🏃 GREYHOUND RACING

Lam Son Stadium, 15 Le Loi Street
Tel 064-807309
Greyhound racing has been operating in Vietnam for several years. There are 12 races held every Saturday evening. The 437-yard (400m) track and stand for 5,000 spectators are maintained to the highest standards, and the dogs are in excellent condition.
🕐 Sat 7.15pm–10.30pm 🍴 Public area 10,000d, grandstand 20,000d, VIP stand 30,000d

❤ BINH CHAU THERMAL SPRINGS

43 miles (70km) from Vung Tau
Immerse yourself in a communal or a private pool—but be careful where you bathe; in places the sulfurous water bubbles out of the springs at 179°F (82°C). The Cu Mi Hotel, nearby, provides lodging, a restaurant and massage.
🍴 Communal pool 5,000d, private pool 30,000d–50,000d per hour

---

FESTIVALS

APRIL

BOAT FESTIVAL

Soc Trang Province
The Khmer New Year is celebrated with ritual and frantic boat racing on a tributary of the Mekong River.
🕐 Fifth–seventh days of third lunar month

SEPTEMBER

LE NGHINH ONG

Vung Tau
An annual festival that commemorates the whale starts on the beach and finishes at the Lang Ca Ong (Whale) Temple.
🕐 15th–17th days of eighth lunar month

WHAT TO DO

This chapter describes two driving tours, two walks, a tour by train and a bicycling tour that explore some of Vietnam's areas of natural beauty. The location of each walk and tour is marked on the map on page 190, where you will also find the key to the individual maps.

Out and About

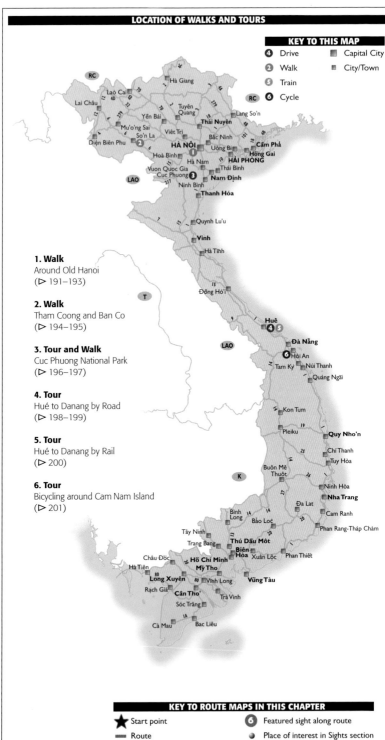

KEY TO THIS MAP

- **4** Drive
- **2** Walk
- **5** Train
- **6** Cycle
- ■ Capital City
- ■ City/Town

1. Walk
Around Old Hanoi
(▷ 191–193)

2. Walk
Tham Coong and Ban Co
(▷ 194–195)

3. Tour and Walk
Cuc Phuong National Park
(▷ 196–197)

4. Tour
Hué to Danang by Road
(▷ 198–199)

5. Tour
Hué to Danang by Rail
(▷ 200)

6. Tour
Bicycling around Cam Nam Island
(▷ 201)

OUT AND ABOUT

KEY TO ROUTE MAPS IN THIS CHAPTER

★ Start point
━ Route
▶ Route direction

6 Featured sight along route
● Place of interest in Sights section
● Other place of interest

AROUND OLD HANOI

Hanoi was founded in 1010, when it was called Thang Long, or City of the Ascending Dragon. Before its colonial transformation in the 19th century it consisted of a citadel and a number of temples surrounded by a small village of merchants. By the 15th century this had evolved into the area now called the Old City or the 36 Streets (36 Pho Phuong). Each of the streets was named after a trade or product, starting with the word *hang* (merchandise). Thus tin-makers hammered out their ware on Hang Thiec, silversmiths on Hang Bac and so on. Each of the trades built a temple, many of which still survive, including Bach Ma, or White Horse Temple, the oldest in the city.

Stunning The Huc, or Sunbeam Bridge (above), leads across Ho Hoan Kiem (Lake of the Restored Sword) to the Ngoc Son Temple

THE WALK

Distance: 1.5 miles (2.5km)
Allow: 2 hours
Start at: Ngoc Son Temple
End at: Thuy Ta Café, 1 Le Thai To

HOW TO GET THERE

Go to Hoan Kiem Lake between Old Hanoi and the newer downtown area focused on Pho Trang Thi. Ngoc Son Temple is on a small island at the northern edge of the lake, accessible by the classically beautiful Sunbeam Bridge.

★ **Ngoc Son Temple (Den Ngoc Son)**, dating from the 18th century, is one of the loveliest and best preserved in Hanoi. Like so many Vietnamese temples, it is dedicated to a national hero—in this case Tran Hung Dao, who defeated the Mongols in the 13th century (▷ 27).

From Ngoc Son Temple head over Sunbeam (or The Huc) Bridge towards the Socialist Realist-style Martyr's Monument to the southeastern edge of the 36 Streets. Turn left up Pho Hang Dau and continue for about 88 yards (80m) to the

shoe bazaar. Continue north along Pho Hang Be, passing Pho Gia Ngu fresh produce market on your left, until you reach Pho Hang Bac.

Pretty, practical boots for sale in Old Hanoi

❶ Pho Hang Bac's specialty lies in selling marble gravestones (at the eastern end of the street) and jewelry (at the western end). The marble gravestones generally have a photograph of the deceased

melded into the stone. It's a trade that isn't going to dry up, and in ancestor-conscious Vietnam a headstone from Pho Hang Bac is a necessary (and prestigious) way of honoring the deceased. Jewelry is Pho Hang Bac's other specialty. Now that the Communist-imposed prohibitions on wearing gold jewelry have been lifted, the goldsmiths' trade is once again flourishing, and nowhere more so than in this enclave.

Turn left, continuing for about 22 yards (20m), before turning right onto Pho Ma May.

❷ Pho Ma May is a tiny sidestreet that is home to the Memorial House Museum, a museum in a restored tube house that was formerly the home of a Chinese merchant. The building was lovingly restored in 1999 and now provides an excellent idea of how well-to-do traders lived in the 36 Streets in times past.

OUT AND ABOUT

Busy Pho Hang Ngang (above), in Old Hanoi, is the city's garment district

Retrace your steps from the Memorial House Museum to Pho Hang Bac. Turn right, to the west, and continue for about 110 yards (100m) to the second of two small crossroads. Turn right (north) along Pho Hang Ngang.

3 Pho Hang Ngang is devoted to the rag trade, with clothing of all kinds cluttering the pavements and entrances to narrow shops.

After about 55 yards (50m) turn left at another small crossroads along Pho Lan Ong.

4 The narrow pavement at the eastern end of Pho Lang Ong is dedicated to the sale of towels and linen, while the western end specializes in the sale of fresh herbs and spices. Vietnamese use a wide variety of fresh green leaves in their cuisine, and the stalls here also sell medicinal herbs from the traditional Sino-Vietnamese pharmacopeia.

Halfway along Pho Lang Ong, on the north (right) side, is Pho Cha Ca. Turn up this narrow street.

5 On the west side of Pho Cha Ca, about 44 yards (40m) north of the junction with Pho Lang Ong, is Cha Ca La Vong

Distinctive red lanterns (above) for sale on Pho Hang Ma

Restaurant. It serves the roasted fish for which the street was named. Just opposite is Truong Hoa Sua Bakery, an excellent French bistro serving coffee, croissants and various tempting cakes.

When you reach Pho Hang Ma running west and Pho Hang Chieu running east, turn left down Pho Hang Ma.

6 Pho Hang Ma is one of the most interesting streets in the Old City. Here there are great piles of "ghost money," together with other paper gifts for the deceased (including everything from televisions to vehicles) that can be purchased and burned as offerings.

From Pho Hang Ma, turn south (left) along Pho Thuoc Bac, continuing into Pho Hang Thiec.

7 This area is given over to the production and sale of tin and aluminum items, as well as the sale of mirrors. It is one of the noisiest sections of the 36 Streets because of the constant working of the tinsmiths.

At the junction of Pho Hang Thiec and Pho Hang Non turn left (east) along Pho Hang Quat.

8 Colorful Buddhist altars and other religious paraphernalia clutter this street, with auspicious red and gold colors predominating. Several musical instrument shops selling drums and traditional Vietnamese stringed instruments may also be found in the area, especially where Pho Hang Non meets Pho Hang Hom.

Continue east along Pho Hang Quat until you reach Luong Van Can. Turn right (south) and continue until you reach the northwestern side of Hoan Kiem Lake. Thuy Ta Café is here, at 1 Le Thai To.

9 Thuy Ta Café is a good place to enjoy an after-walk drink or ice cream. If you are in the mood for shopping, the sidestreet opposite Thuy Ta, leading west toward

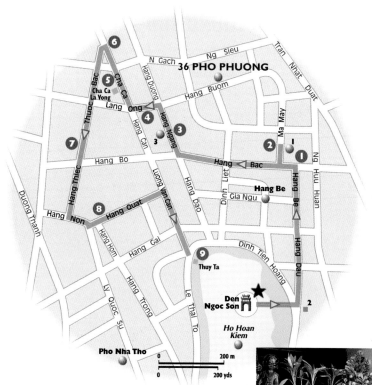

36 PHO PHUONG

1   Memorial House Museum
2   Martyr's Monument
3   Museum of Independence

St. Joseph's Cathedral (Pho Nha Tho), has art shops, souvenir stands and excellent small restaurants.

WHEN TO GO

Any time of the year except during the New Year *Tet* festivities, when most businesses will be closed as people stay home to celebrate. Commerce is at its busiest in the early morning, and the Old City is most pleasant during the warm autumn months.

WHERE TO EAT

There are numerous small restaurants and bistros scattered throughout the Old City. Try especially Cha Ca La Vong fish restaurant on Pho Cha Ca ("Roasted Fish Street"). The Thuy Ta Café, at the end of the walk on the northwestern side of Ho Hoan Kiem, serves excellent Western and Vietnamese cuisine. Nearby Pho Hang Hanh, some 22 yards (20m) to the west, is lined with restaurants and coffee shops.

PLACES TO VISIT

In addition to the trade streets devoted to specific crafts and goods, watch out for small "hole-in-the-wall" temples, narrow tube houses and busy market stands. The Old City is a good place to pick up unusual souvenirs or to sit and relax over a *bia hoi* at one of the small outdoor cafés.

Memorial House Museum
87 Pho Ma May
Tel 04-9285604/9285605
🕐 Daily 8–5.30
💴 5,000d

TOURIST INFORMATION
Vietnam Tourism
30A Ly Thuong Kiet Street
Tel 04-8264154
🕐 Mon–Fri 7–11.30, 1.30–5

Making a gravestone on Pho Hang Bac

The Cha Ca La Vong fish restaurant in Old Hanoi

THAM COONG AND BAN CO

This walk, from the former French military outpost of Son La, takes you through magnificent highland scenery, two caves and the fascinating Black Thái settlement of Ban Co.

A mountainscape near Co Noi (above). Black Thái (right) husking corn near Thuan Chau

THE WALK

Distance: 3 miles (4.7km)
Allow: 2 hours 35 minutes
Start/end at: Son La

HOW TO GET THERE

Son La is 192 miles (310km) northwest of Hanoi

TIP

● You may like to take a flashlight for your visit to the cave.

★ Son La (▷ 96) is now a provincial capital but it was a military outpost during French colonial rule.

Start the walk 2 miles (3km) north of the heart of Son La, at the turning to the caves on the main road (Hoa Ban Street). Opposite a Petrolimex fuel station there's a turning to the left (west) and a signpost marking the caves (Tham Coong). Take this path. Almost immediately, on your right, is a house with a white decoration on its roof.

❶ The curious wooden decoration on this house is shaped into multiple white blobs. This signifies that the family here has produced a lot of male children. Along the path you will see the bright red leaves of poinsettia (*Euphorbia pulcherrima*).

Continue across a metal bridge where there is a water park on the right. Just after the water park, look to the far left to see a tiled roof with a similar decoration to the previous house.

❷ This roof decoration has only one white blob, indicating that this family has one male child. To your left are glistening green rice paddies.

Take a path to the left, by a concrete post marked "BACO," a wooden, one-room house surrounded by a fence, and a gray house. The canal is to your right.

At the foot of a tall hill, there is a house on your right with domestic animals in its yard. You need to climb straight up the hill to a concrete walkway. At the walkway, turn left onto a path that leads to the wet cave (you may be allowed to peer into the wet cave but you cannot enter as it is fenced off).

To reach the dry cave, you have a further climb up a limestone face. A woman controlling the passage, at the foot of the limestone face, will point you in the right direction (you must pay 5,000d to enter). Clamber up the face for a few minutes to reach the entrance to the dry cave.

❸ The dry cave is 262ft (80m) deep and is full of stalactites; although it is fairly light, there are darker areas around the route and so you may wish to bring a flashlight. At its farthest point there is a dangling rope from which to drink water.

Return to the foot of the limestone face and enjoy the view.

4 Below are fields, ponds and streams, stilt houses, gardens and hibiscus hedgerows. Fish are bred in the ponds, which are covered with watercress *(salad soong)* and what looks like a red algae bloom, but is actually a small floating weed *(beo hoa dau)*, fed to ducks and pigs.

Retrace your steps and look out for the fish farm just before the water company offices, close to the main road. Turn right onto the main Hoa Ban Street and walk for half a mile (1km) before turning off the main road. This left turning is marked by a road sign on the right-hand side marked "250m." At this point there is a coffin-maker's workshop and a phone booth. Next to the turning is a billboard.

5 The billboard at the turning translates as: "Protect the forest, plant more to reduce deforestation."

Turn left off Hoa Ban Street toward the Black Thái (Thái Den) village of Ban Co. After 330 yards (300m) you arrive in the village.

6 Ban Co is a large, fairly typical Thái village. Thái villages *(ban)* consist of 40 to 50 houses on stilts; they are shaded by fruit trees and surrounded by verdant paddy fields. The Thái are excellent custodians of the land. Cabbage, spinach and pole beans are all grown in the fields, and you may also see people fishing.

Walk to the left for a short way and turn right up a concrete path (shortly before you reach the maroon and white government building) between a white house with Chinese symbols on the upper floor, a gray lamp post and house with a gray corrugated-iron roof (with a brick wall on the left). Return to the main street.

Walk a little farther to see the villagers at their work, and water buffaloes and horses eating. Then turn back the way you came (toward the main Hoa

Ban Street), when the road veers to the right by a big gray rock opposite a bamboo gate. Hoa Ban Street leads back into Son La.

WHEN TO GO
The best time to undertake this walk is late afternoon, when the light is at its best and villagers return to their homes.

WHERE TO EAT
There is a café and *bia hoi* to the left of the exit from the caves on the main road and a snack stall to the right. There are several *bia hoi* opposite the turn off to Ban Co.

Elegant White Thái women (right) at Thuan Chau. A rustic dwelling in Muong Village, near Moc Chau (below)

THE THÁI
The Thái number around one million and are the second-largest ethnic minority in Vietnam. There are two main sub-groups: the Black Thái (Thái Den), settled mainly in Son La, Lai Chan, Lao Cai and Yen Bai provinces, and the White Thái (Thái Trang), found predominantly in Hoa Binh, Son La, Thanh Hoa and Vính Phu provinces.

A young Hmông girl shows off her traditional dress (left), in the Ban Co vicinity

SO'N LA

CUC PHUONG NATIONAL PARK

This drive takes you to the Cuc Phuong National Park (Vuon Quoc Gia Cuc Phuong), where you can see numerous limestone caves, Vuon Thuc Vat Botanic Gardens and a mysterious tree said to change color if poison touches it.

THE TOUR

Distance:	84 miles (135km)
Allow:	8–10 hours
Start/end at:	Ninh Binh

HOW TO GET THERE

Ninh Binh is 58 miles (93km) south of Hanoi on Highway 1. It's served by regular buses from Hanoi's southern bus terminal. To drive to Cuc Phuong National Park, either rent a motorcycle or a car and driver for the day. This can be arranged through a tour agency in Hanoi, or at the Viet Hung Hotel or another tour agency in Ninh Binh.

★ Ninh Binh is a useful base for visiting other sights in the north. It is the capital of the province of Ninh Binh.

Head west from Ninh Binh along the road to Hoa Binh. After 7.5 miles (12km), at Gian Khau Bridge, turn left to Nho Quan. At Nho Quan follow the sign (in English) to Cuc Phuong National Park for a further 9.5 miles (15km) to the park's main gate. Allow about 90 minutes to reach the park.

About 330 yards (300m) before the main gate, on the right-hand side of the road, stop off at the Cuc Phuong Museum.

1 At the Cuc Phuong Museum you can look at maps of the park and pictures of the flora and fauna you'll see there. You can also learn about the ecology of the area and national park etiquette.

Continue to the Visitor Center by the main gate.

2 Buy your entry tickets here: A brochure offering an introduction to the main sights of the park, as well as a color map, is included in the price of the ticket. They can also make arrangements for lodgings and organize guided treks.

Park near the Visitor Center and walk back to visit the Endangered Primate Rescue Center, on the left-hand side of the road just before the park gate.

3 The Endangered Primate Rescue Center (▷ 84) is

Macaque (above) are protected in the national park

definitely a high point of this tour. The center cares for local animals saved from hunters or otherwise injured. It also promotes breeding and conservation programs, and tries to rehabilitate endangered primates for release into the wild. It's a good place to see animals that might otherwise be difficult to locate in the park. The center usually houses several species of langur, as well as gibbons, lorises and monkeys. There is also a 5-acre (2ha) enclosure used to prepare rescued animals for return to their natural environment.

Pass through the main park entrance and almost immediately turn left to visit the Vuon Thuc Vat Botanic Gardens.

4 The Vuon Thuc Vat Botanic Gardens showcase local flora, carefully marked with both Vietnamese and Latin names. Of almost 2,000 identified plant species, more than 400 have useful medicinal qualities, while 300 may be used as sources of human nutrition. A number of animals native to Cuc Phuong may be seen at quite close quarters here, including deer, civets, langurs and gibbons.

Continue your drive into the park along a narrow but well-surfaced road. After 1 mile (2km) on the right, pass Khu Mo Mac (Mac Lake Place), which has waterside cabin accommodations, a restaurant and a souvenir shop. Continue for a further 4 miles (7km) until you reach a signposted track on the right-hand side of the road leading to one of the largest caves, the Cave of the Prehistoric Man (Doong Nguoi Xua).

5 The Cave of the Prehistoric Man has a shop where you can rent a flashlight (5,000d) to take inside the cave. Walk along a short concrete bridge, then climb 150ft (45m) by metal ladder to reach the lower cave. Inside there are three sections. The first, where relics of prehistoric humans were discovered, is large, bright and airy. The second is dark and humid, and is inhabited by numerous bats. The third is distinguished by some beautiful stalactites. After visiting these three sections, climb up three metal ladders to the upper cave. There are thousands of yellow and red patches on the ceiling; these are patterned lichens resembling a night sky full of twinkling stars.

Return to the main road and drive a further 9.5 miles (15km) northwest until you arrive at Khu Trung Tam Park Center (which has some souvenir shops, a restaurant and an information center). On the way you will pass a signposted track to the left leading to the Cay Dang Co Thu thousand-year-old tree. About 6 miles (10km) farther on, as you approach Khu Trung Tam Park Center, another tree of venerable age, Cay Vu Huong, stands close by the road on the left-hand side.

OUT AND ABOUT

Labeling (above) identifies the trees. A beautiful orchid (right)

The surfaced road comes to an end at Khu Trung Tam, so it's time to park your vehicle and begin to walk.

6 A circular trek starts from Car Park B, where there are some small shops selling refreshments. From the rest area, look to the right where you will see a sign for Cay Cho Ngan Nam, the "Thousand Year Old Tree." The cleared track leads for 4.5 miles (7.5km) through dense jungle vegetation, past the 157ft-high (48m) tree, before winding back to Khu Trung Tam.

After refreshments and a rest at Khu Trung Tam, head back to the park entrance and retrace your way to Ninh Binh (continue 9.5 miles/15km to Nho Quan; turn right and continue east past the Gian Khau Bridge to Ninh Binh).

Or, if you are feeling energetic, take a guided trek (a guide is compulsory) for 11 miles (18km) to the northwestern limits of the park, where you can stay overnight in Kanh Muong, a Muong village.

7 The trek to Kanh Muong is pretty strenuous, and you should take plenty of liquid to drink on the way. About 5 miles (8km) into the trek, you pass Cay Sau Co Thu, another magnificent old tree, which stands to the right of the track. The Muong minority are the original inhabitants of this area and subsisted by hunting. At the village, you can see their traditional pillar houses, water wheels and brocade looms. Accommodations (which must be arranged in advance) are simple but adequate, and during the stay visitors will be entertained by displays of the traditional Muong gong festival.

In the morning, make the 11 mile (18km) return trek to Khu Trung Tam, starting early to avoid the mid-morning heat. Collect your vehicle and head back to the park entrance. Continue 9.5 miles (15km) to Nho Quan. Turn right and continue east past the Gian Khau Bridge to Ninh Binh.

WHEN TO GO

The best time to visit is winter (November through February): It is relatively dry, there are fewer insects (including mosquitoes) and the leeches are less active. In summer, there are a lot of insects, reptiles, flowers and butterflies—the latter especially in April and May.

WHERE TO EAT

There are two restaurants, one at the main gate and another 1 mile (2km) into the park at Mac Lake. There are set menus and à la carte with prices ranging from US$7 to US$12. Simple vegetarian dishes are available.

WHERE TO STAY

There are comfortable cabins at Mac Lake for 240,000–375,000d. A room in a pillar house at Kanh Muong village is 75,000d. If you bring your own tent there is a camping charge of 30,000d per night.

PLACES TO VISIT

Cuc Phuong Museum
Daily 8–5
Free

Vuon Thuc Vat Botanic Gardens
Daily 9–4.30
5,000d

CHOPSTICKS

The park is notable for the cay kim gao tree, whose wood is said to change color from pale brown to black if it comes into contact with anything poisonous. It was used to make chopsticks for Vietnamese kings and aristocrats who feared being poisoned. Chopsticks of cay kim gao wood are for sale in the park.

HUÉ TO DANANG BY ROAD

This tour takes you down the coast of the central region of Vietnam, past spectacular scenery, including the dramatic Lang Co Bay, and along a road pass that leads you through the clouds.

THE TOUR

Distance:	67.5 miles (108km)
Allow:	half a day
Start at:	Hué
End at:	Danang

HOW TO GET THERE

Rent a car and a driver from one of the many tour operators in Hué, or take an Open Tour bus from Hué to Danang—some stop at Lang Co.

TIPS

● Be prepared: The journey between Hué and Danang is precarious as it winds its way over the Hai Van Pass.
● Clouds on the Pass may obscure your view.
● A 7-mile (12km) tunnel was opened in early 2005 under the Hai Van Pass to smooth the flow of traffic along Highway 1 and reduce the number of accidents on the pass. It links Lang Co and Danang.
● To make the journey by rail, ▷ 200.

★ Hué (▷ 114–121) was the capital of Vietnam between 1802 and 1945 and is a city with a royal heritage. Key visitor attractions include the Imperial City, with its moats, canals and towers, and the Museum of Royal Fine Arts. Flowing through Hué is the "Perfume River" (the Huong Giang), which takes its name from a sweet-smelling shrub said to grow at its source.

Leave Hué and head south on Highway 1.

The road from Hué to Lang Co passes through pretty, red-tiled villages, surrounded by clumps of bamboo and fruit trees that provide shade and sustenance. Pink-flowered bougainvillea bushes create splashes of color, while windowless jalopies from the French era trundle along picking up passengers, and station wagons from the American era provide an inter-village shared taxi service.

Schoolgirls in ao dai *dress (above) on their way to school in Hué*

Continue to the village of Lang Co, about 40 miles (65km) south of Hué.

1 Lang Co is an idyllic fishing village with a number of good, inexpensive seafood restaurants. Emperor Khai Dinh apparently visited Lang Co in the first year of his reign (1916) and was so impressed that he ordered the construction of a summer palace here. This, it seems, was never carried out—even by his son Bao Dai, who was so fond of building palaces—but there is the Lang Co Beach Resort to stay in (▷ 246).

Shortly after crossing the Lang Co lagoon, dotted with coracles and fish traps, the road begins the long haul up to Hai Van Pass.

2 Hai Van Pass (Deo Hai Van)—Pass of the Ocean Clouds or, to the French, Col des Nuages—lies 1,630ft (497m) above sea-level and once marked the border between the kingdoms of Vietnam and Champa. The mountains act as an important climatic barrier, trapping the cooler, damper air masses to the north and bottling them up over Hué, which accounts for the city's shockingly wet weather. The mountains also mark a linguistic divide; the Hué dialect (the language of the royal court) to the north, is a constant source of bemusement to many southerners. The pass is peppered with

abandoned pillboxes and crowned with an old fort, originally built by the dynasty from Hué and used as a relay station for the pony express on the old Mandarin Road. Looking back to the north, stretching into the haze is the shore and lagoon of Lang Co. To the south is Danang Bay and Monkey Mountain (Hon Lao), and at your feet lies a patch of green paddies belonging to a leper colony, accessible only by boat.

The road then passes through the village of Nam O.

3 Nam O was once famous for firework manufacture. Pages of old school books were dyed pink, laid out in the sun to dry, rolled up and filled with gunpowder, but the village has suffered from the government's ban on firecrackers.

Just south of Nam O, you pass Xuan Thieu Beach.

OUT AND ABOUT

A road bridge (above) leads to the beach resort at Lang Co. An old French pillbox (right) at the summit of Hai Van Pass

Dam Thanh Lam

Huê
Hà Thanh
Phú Tuân
Vĩnh Giang
Bình Diễn
Phú Bài

| 0 | 10 km |
| 0 | 8 miles |

Lang Co
Phú Lộc
Vuon Quoc Gia
Bach Ma
Mũi Chân Mây
Đeo Hai Van
Thôn Hai
Khe Tạc
Nam Ô
Xuan Thieu
Hon Lao
My Khe
Bu Lach
An Ngãi
Đà Nẵng
LAO
Hòa Vang
Bà Nà
Ngu Hanh Son
Hôi An
Hiên
Đai Lộc
Diện Ban
Đai Lãnh
Duy Xuyen
Mỹ So'n
Quê Trung
Giǎng
Ben Giǎng

Day Truong Son

OUT AND ABOUT

④ **Xuan Thieu Beach** was dubbed "Red Beach II" by the US Marines who landed here in March 1965, marking the beginning of direct intervention by the US in the Second Indochina War. The surfaced road and military base's concrete foundations still remain.

Continue on to Danang.

⑤ **Danang** (▷ 104–105) is on a peninsula where the Han River flows into the South China Sea. It was an important port during French colonial times. The city's main attraction is the Museum of Champa Sculpture, with a collection of Cham art.

Danang's Museum of Champa Sculpture is worth a visit for both the buildings and the art

WHERE TO EAT

Stock up on food in Hué or visit one of the seafood restaurants in Lang Co.

HUÉ TO DANANG BY RAIL

The rail journey from Hué to Danang is regarded as one of the most scenic in the world—a leisurely chug around the coast on a line that clings to cliff edges like a limpet to a rock.

BY RAIL

Allow: half a day

Start at: Hué rail station *(ga xe lua)*, west end of Le Loi Street, tel 054-822175

End at: Danang rail station, 122 Haiphong Street, tel 0511-823810

TRAIN INFORMATION

Three trains a day operate in daylight hours:

• **SE1** 10.58am–1.19pm (2 hours, 21 minutes), 37,000d air-conditioned, soft seat

• **TN1** 8.16am–11am (2 hours, 46 minutes), 36,000d air-conditioned, soft seat

• **TN3** 10.42am–2.54pm (4 hours, 12 minutes), 29,000d air-conditioned, soft seat

These prices include a small meal

TIPS

• Timetables tend to change, so consult the train office or Vietnam Railways website www.vr.com.vn/English.

• The booking office is open daily 7am–10pm, but closed for sales 11am–1.30pm and 6–7pm.

• Local tour operators charge US$5 to purchase and organize the ticket.

This is an exciting journey, often passing through clouds that temporarily obscure the view. First-class cars have plenty of leg room, luggage racks and Western- and Eastern-style toilets at either end. Each car is staffed by a Vietnam Railways employee.

Between Hué and Danang a finger of the Truong Son Mountains *(Day Truong Son)* juts eastwards, extending all the way to the sea. This barrier to north–south communication has resulted in some spectacular engineering solutions. The single track, narrow gauge rail track closely follows the coastline, sometimes almost hanging over the sea.

A wonderful view of Lang Co from the Hai Van Pass (top). The Hué–Danang train route traverses beautiful scenery (above)

On foggy days the vegetation that tumbles down from the coastal heights oozes steam; on clear days you can see fishing boats drifting in the water. The magnificent spit of land on which Lang Co sits is decorated around its edge with fine, white sand pushing out into the turquoise sea. Palm trees and other vegetation jostle for position on the peninsula. This beautiful view is marred only slightly by the road bridge that crosses it.

BICYCLING AROUND CAM NAM ISLAND

This is a peaceful bicycle ride through the countryside that also passes some of the busy areas and eateries of Hoi An.

★ Make the 2-mile (4km) ride west from the Hoi An Beach resort on Cua Dai Beach to the first major left turn in Hoi An town (corner of Cua Dai and Pham Hong Thai, site of Mr Tung's office, ▷ 203).

❶ As you bicycle past paddy fields dotted with cemeteries and huts, you'll also pass the busy restaurants and food stands on the main road.

From the corner of Cua Dai and Pham Hong Thai streets, ride down as far as you can go to Phan Boi Chau Street, then turn right. Bicycle through the French district. At the corner of Phan Boi Chau and Hoang Dieu streets, ride over Cam Nam bridge.

❷ On Cam Nam bridge, look to the right to see the busy activity of Hoi An market.

Once you've crossed the bridge, take the first wide track to the left and follow it past the homes of villagers, where you'll see maize drying in courtyards. Follow the track for a few minutes until you see the main surfaced road ahead. Before this main road take the first track to the left.

❸ Ahead is one of the most ramshackle houses in Vietnam.

At the intersection, take the path to the left and continue along the riverbank. After five minutes you will reach the main road. Turn left here, then follow the main road, which bears round to the right.

❹ A makeshift hairdresser's has been set up here, and you will see cauldrons in front yards with burning incense.

The route includes quiet rural routes (above) and main roads

At the little temple with the sign "Can Dinh Nien," take the path in front of it (to your right) past tall pines. Emerge on the other side of the islet on the riverbank. Take the narrow path left.

❺ Fishing nets garland the river at this point, and there are lizards, dragonflies and butterflies along the way.

After five minutes, the path is surfaced. Bear right through a small palm and maize plantation, then turn right at a two-story green house selling drinks. Take the first right just before the plantation. Pass a cemetery on the left. Follow the path and take the first right past the pagoda. Turn left at the main road and bicycle 15 minutes back along the main road, where you'll see the bridge leading back to Hoi An.

❻ Stop for a break at the Banana Split Café or in the Brother's Café (▷ 219).

Return to Cua Dai Beach by an alternative route: Bicycle one street back from the river away from the Banana Split Café and turn right down Nguyen Duy Hieu Street, past the Chaozhou Assembly Hall, to its natural end.

❼ With a canal to the right, pass the Ancient House Resort Hotel on the right.

Bicycle for ten minutes to the end of the surfaced road, then turn

right and then left along the right side of a house. You may have to get off your bicycle because of the mud. When you see railings and a paved road, clamber up the slope in front of the railings next to a brick house. On the main road, turn right and cross a white-painted bridge. Keep on the main road through the paddy fields.

❽ Soon you pass a temple with a ceramic dragon on the front porch. Beautiful paddy fields open up, with building works on the left and, to the far right, a cemetery. You can see mountains to the far left.

After another ten minutes' bicycling, turn right to the cemetery.

❾ At the cemetery, you may be lucky enough to see water buffalo bathing in the pond.

Turn back to the main road, and turn right and then take the first left past a yellow building and billboard. After five minutes, ride under a wooden arch and over a lake before emerging on the Cua Dai road, next to a café on your right and opposite a sign reading "Hoi An café 1,500m." Turn left to the Son restaurant. If you want to bicycle on to Cua Dai Beach you must leave your bicycle (5,000d) just before the beach in a guarded parking lot.

WHEN TO GO

Start early in the morning to avoid the heat of midday.

It's easier to get around Vietnam with one of the many organized tour companies. Tours can be arranged either in the country or before you leave home. Below are a few of the vast range of excursions led by expert tour guides who can help you come to grips with Vietnam's abundant attractions and long history.

IN VIETNAM

ACTION DALAT
114 3 Thang 2 Street, Dalat
Tel 063-826031, fax 063-820532
Offers trekking, camping, boat rides, climbing and abseiling (rapelling) on Lang Bian mountain and excursions to minority villages in the region. Prices include lunch and English-speaking guides.

ANA MANDARA TRAVEL SERVICE
Ana Mandara, Tran Phu Street, Nha Trang
Tel 058-522222;
3E/14 Pho Quang Street, Tan Binh District, Ho Chi Minh City
Tel 08-9973158
anahcmc@dng.vnn.vn
www.sixsenses.com/evason-anamandara
Nationwide tours (guides speak English, French, German, Italian, Chinese, Japanese and Russian), as well as visa assistance, transportation, hotel and dinner reservations.

ANN TOURS
18 Duong Thanh Street, Hanoi
Tel 08-9231366
www.anntours.com
Knowledgeable guides offer tours across the country, as well as golf, culinary and veteran tours. Other tourist services are also available.

AN PHU TOURIST
29 Phan Dinh Phung Street, Hoi An
Tel 0510-862643;
141 Tran Phu Street, Hoi An
Tel 0510-861447;
50 Yen Phu Street, Hanoi
Tel 04-9273584;
11 Nguyen Tri Phuong Street, Hué

Tel 054-833897;
82 Dong Da Street, Danang
Tel 0511-818366;
1/24 Tran Quang Khai Street, Nha Trang
Tel 058-524471;
07 Thuong Hai Street, Dalat
Tel 063-823631;
45B Huynh Thuc Khang Street, Mui Ne
Tel 062-847830;
7 Do Quang Dau Street, District 1, Ho Chi Minh City
Tel 08-9202513
www.anphutravel.com
Offers a wide range of local and national tour services, as well as running Open Tour buses and a travel reservation system, car rental and visa extensions.

BUFFALO TOURS
13 Hang Muoi Street, Hanoi
Tel 04-8280702;
Suite 502, Jardine House, 58 Dong Khoi Street, District 1, Ho Chi Minh City
Tel 08-8279169
www.buffalotours.com
A highly regarded organization offering local and countrywide tours, as well as motorcycling, bicycling and kayaking tours. It operates the *Jewel of the Bay* boat in Halong Bay, with room for ten people. You can take kayaks out from the boat.

CAN THO TOURIST
20 Hai Ba Trung Street, Can Tho
Tel 071-821852
www.canthotourist.com.vn
Ecological and cultural tours, visiting boat workshops, creeks, orchards, mills, iron-smiths, a stork sanctuary, a fish sanctuary and a village school, plus bicycle tours.

CUU LONG TOURIST
1 Thang 5 Street, Vinh Long
Tel 070-823616
cuulongtourist1@hcm.vnn.vn
Offers one-, two- and three-day tours as well as shorter excursions and homestays around Vinh Long (▷ 155).

ET-PUMPKIN
89 Ma May Street, Hanoi
Tel 04-9260739
www.et-pumpkin.com
A professional company, with local and national tours,

particularly to the north, as well as trekking and kayaking.

EXOTISSIMO
26 Tran Nhat Duat Street, Hanoi
Tel 04-8282150;
Saigon Trade Center, 37 Ton Duc Thang Street, District 1, Ho Chi Minh City
Tel 08-8251723
www.exotissimo.com
Specializes in upscale country-wide and local tours, including bird-watching, spa, culinary, golf, bicycling and kayaking.

GREEN BAMBOO
2A Duong Thanh Street, Hanoi
Tel 04-8286504
www.greenbambootravel.com
A well-established leader in the budget market, organizing countrywide tours but also trekking, bicycling and honey-moon specialist tours.

HANDSPAN ADVENTURE TRAVEL
80 Ma May Street
Hanoi
Tel 04-9260581;
8 Cau May Street, Sapa
Tel/fax 020-872110
www.handspan.com
This well-organized company specializes in adventure tours, including trekking, kayaking, 4WD trips and mountain-biking. It has its own junk in Halong Bay and its own kayaks. The company also arranges trips out of Cat Ba and tours around Sapa, includ-ing treks, mountain-biking excursions, homestays and jeep expeditions.

HANH'S GREEN HAT
44 Ly Thanh Ton Street, Nha Trang
Tel 058-821309, fax 058-825117;
Branch office at 2A Biet Thu Street
Tel 058-824494
Arranges boat trips to islands off Nha Trang (▷ 124–125) and other local tours, plus car, motorcycle and bicycle rental.

HOI AN TOURIST COMPANY
6 Tran Hung Dao Street, Hoi An
Tel 0510-862224
hoiantravel@dng.vnn.vn
Local and nationwide tours.

INDOCHINA TRAVEL SERVICES

76 Le Loi Street, Danang
Tel 0511-828652
www.itsvietnam.com
Organizes tours into the central highlands with a special emphasis on older travelers.

KIM CAFÉ

31 Ha Tien Street, Hanoi
Tel 04-8364212
www.kimcafetravel.com
Budget tours across the country, as well as car rental, flight and Open Tour bus tickets, hotel and restaurant reservations and visa arrangement.

MAMA LINH

2A Hung Vuong Street, Nha Trang
Tel 058-826693
Boat trips to the islands and bus tickets to Hoi An, Phan Thiet, Saigon and Dalat.

MEKOTOURS (CONG DOAN TOURIST)

Hotel Cong Doan, 61 Duong 30/4, My Tho
Tel 073-874324, fax 073-878857
Trips to My Tho and Thoi Son Island, with visits to orchards, a bee farm, a fish market and a coconut-candy workshop. Homestays at Than Phu or Thoi Son Island, plus night tours (7pm–1am) with a traditional meal and folk music.

MR TUNG

21 Cua Dai Street, Hoi An
Tel 0510-914218
tungtravel@hotmail.com
This one-man company reserves bus tickets, rents out bicycles and arranges visa extensions and tours to My Son. It offers one of the lowest rates for taxis to Danang airport (US$5).

PHAT TIRE VENTURES

73 Truong Cong Dinh Street, Dalat
Tel 063-829422
www.phattireventures.homestead.com
A US-run operator offering trekking, mountain-biking, canyoning and kayaking tours with qualified instructors.

QUEEN TRAVEL

65 Hang Bac Street, Hanoi
Tel 04-8260860
queenaz@fpt.vn
www.queencafe.com.vn
A large organization handling tailor-made tours as well as nationwide and local tours for individuals and small groups. Also visa arrangements, travel reservations and car, bicycle and motorcycle rental.

SAIGON-PHU QUOC RESORT

1 Trang Hung Dao Street, Duong Dong, Phu Quoc
Tel 077-846999
www.vietnamphuquoc.com
Tours to Sao beach, Sung Hung pagoda, Khu Tuong pepper gardens and a fish factory; Mui Chu, a fishing village and pearl factory; fishing and snorkeling in the southern and northern archipelago; and squid-fishing in the western archipelago. Prices include guide, transportation, insurance, equipment, lunch and water.

SAIGONTOURIST

49 Le Thanh Ton Street, District 1, Ho Chi Minh City
Tel 08-8298914;
357 Phan Chu Trinh Street, Danang
Tel 0511-827084
www.saigontourist.net
A local state tour agency used chiefly by groups. Its specialist options include motorcycling, golf and tours to Con Dao.

SINH CAFÉ

52 Luong Ngoc Quyen Street, Hanoi
Tel 04-9261568;
246–248 De Tham Street, District 1, Ho Chi Minh City
Tel 08-8367338;
4a Bui Thi Xuan Street, Dalat
Tel 063-822663;
18b Phan Dinh Phung Street, Hoi An
Tel 0510-863948;
7 Nguyen Tri Phuong Street, Hué
Tel 054-845022;
10 Biet Thu Street, Nha Trang
Tel 058-521981;
Mui Ne Resort, Mui Ne
Tel 062-847542
www.sinhcafevn.com
One of the largest budget operations in the country. Organizes off-the-peg local and nationwide tours, car rental, hotel and flight reservations, visa arrangement and Open Tour bus services.

TIENGIANG TOURIST TRAVEL SERVICE

08-30/4 Street, My Tho
Tel 073-873184
www.tiengiangtourist.com
Offers trips to Unicorn Island, close to My Tho, with visits to fruit gardens, orchards, coconut-candy workshops, traditional houses and music performances.

TONY'S TOUR

Tel 091-3197334 (cell phone)
Tel 077-847127 (Phu Quoc)
Tel 08-8206481 (Saigon)
galaxy-pms@hcm.vnn.vn
tonyphuquoc@yahoo.com
Tony (Huynh van Anh) knows Phu Quoc extremely well and speaks fluent English. He provides island tours, snorkeling and deep-sea fishing excursions, car and motorcycle rental, as well as hotel and transportation reservations.

TOPAS

24 Muong Hoa Street, Hanoi
Tel 04-9283637;
20 Cau May Street, Sapa
Tel 020-871331/091-2397473 (cell)
www.topas-adventure-vietnam.com
A Danish-Vietnamese operator offering treks, bicycling tours, horseback-riding and family tours in and around Sapa. National and local tours, including Halong Bay kayaking trips, can be organized by the Hanoi office.

VICTORIA CAN THO CAI KHE WARD

Can Tho
Tel 071-810111
www.victoriahotels-asia.com
Trips up the Mekong and visits to communities making rice vermicelli, rice "popcorn" and bricks. Trips to a fish farm, orchards and Soc Trang can also be arranged.

VICTORIA CHAU DOC

32 Le Loi Street, Chau Doc
Tel 076-865010
victoriachaudoc@hcm.vnn.vn
The hotel organizes river tours and a trip to Sam Mountain, a forest tour and cultural, historical and spiritual tours, from a few hours to all day.

The Hanoi tourist office can arrange a variety of trips for you

VIDOTOUR

145 Nam Ky Khoi Nghia Street,
District 3, Ho Chi Minh City
Tel 08-9330457
www.vidotourtravel.com
A very efficient group travel
organizer offering general
tours, as well as bird-watching,
golfing, cooking, trekking,
kayaking and bicycling tours.

IN THE US

ADVENTURE CENTER

1311 63rd Street, Suite 200,
Emeryville, CA
Tel 800/227-8747, fax 510/654-4200
www.adventurecenter.com
Tours from Hanoi to Saigon
and to northern hill-tribe areas.

GLOBAL SPECTRUM

3907 Laro Court, Fairfax, VA 22031
Tel 800/419-4446
www.asianpassages.com
Well-informed outfit running
tours with a cultural twist,
sometimes away from the
usual routes, plus veterans
tours, all lasting 8 to 30 days.
Volunteer work attachments
can be arranged after trips.

MILITARY HISTORICAL TOURS

4600 Duke Street, Suite 420
Alexandria, VA 22304
Tel 703/212-0695
www.miltours.com
Tours for veterans to coincide
with specific anniversaries.
Costs average around
US$3,000 per person.

MYTHS & MOUNTAINS

976 Tree Court, Incline Village, NV 89451
Tel 775/832-5454, fax 775/832-4454
www.mythsandmountains.com
Cultural and adventure tours of
one to five weeks include
motorcycling the Ho Chi Minh
Trail and an art tour.

NINE DRAGONS TRAVEL AND TOURS

1476 Orange Grove Road,
Charleston, SC 29407
Tel 317/281-3895, fax 317/536-3163
www.nine-dragons.com
This US company has offices
in Saigon, Danang and
Hanoi, and offers guided
and customized tours.

TOURS OF PEACE

Vietnam Veterans, 8000 S. Kolb Road,
Suite 43, Tucson, AZ 85706
Tel 520/326-0901
www.topvietnamveterans.org
A not-for-profit organization
that runs two-week tours for
veterans, including transportation, guides and hotels.

VIETNAMGOLFTOURS.COM

PO Box 16768, Seattle, WA 98116
Tel 206/755-2377
tom@vietnamgolftours.com
www.vietnamgolftours.com
Golfing trips run by Tom
Kramer.

IN THE UK

ADVENTURE COMPANY

15 Turk Street, Alton, Hampshire
GU34 1AG
Tel 0870 794 1009, fax 01420 541 022
www.adventurecompany.co.uk
Two- to three-week tours and
family adventures (children
must be aged over five years).
The average price includes
flights.

AUDLEY TRAVEL

6 Willows Gate, Stratton, Audley,
Oxfordshire OX27 9AU
Tel 01869 276330
www.audleytravel.com
Tailor-made tours with private
guides and vehicles to suit all
budgets. Specialist tours can
also be organized.

DISCOVER ADVENTURE

Throope Down House,
Blandford Road, Coombe Bissett,
Salisbury, Wiltshire SP5 4LN
Tel 01722 718444
www.discoveradventure.com
An adventure specialist
running two-week group
bicycling tours.

GUERBA ADVENTURE AND DISCOVERY HOLIDAYS

Wessex House, 40 Station Road,
Westbury, Wiltshire BA13 3JN
Tel 01373 826611
www.guerba.co.uk
Small group adventure and
discovery holidays, ranging
from one to five weeks, with
experienced local guides and
locally owned hotels.

REGENT HOLIDAYS

15 John Street, Bristol BS1 2HR
Tel 0870 499 0911
www.regent-holidays.co.uk
Tailor-made holidays and
specialist tours, including birdwatching, bicycling, kayaking
and trekking.

SILK STEPS

Compass House, Rowdens Road, Wells
Somerset BA5 1TU
Tel 01749 685162
www.silksteps.co.uk
Historical and cultural tailor-
made tours of 14–21 days.

SYMBIOSIS EXPEDITION PLANNING

3B Wilmot Place, London NW1 9JS
Tel 0845 123 2844, fax 0845 123 2845
www.symbiosis-travel.com
Organizes environmental and
cultural bicycling tours and
charity fund-raising challenges,
as well as tailor-made tours.

TRANS INDUS

75 St. Mary's Road and the Old Fire
Station, Ealing,
London W5 5RH
Tel 0208 566 2729, fax 0208 840 5327
www.transindus.co.uk
Tailor-made tours, usually of
two weeks' duration.

VISIT VIETNAM (TENNYSON TRAVEL)

30–32 Fulham High Street, London
SW6 3LQ
Tel 020 7736 4347
www.visitvietnam.co.uk
Small group tours and tailor-
made tours, plus independent
packages. Trips usually last
between one and three weeks.

This chapter lists places to eat and stay, broken down by region, then alphabetically by town. Entries in the Hanoi and Ho Chi Minh City sections are listed alphabetically.

Eating and Staying

EATING IN VIETNAM

Vietnam's food is a major part of its appeal. This unique cuisine has developed over many centuries, absorbing a variety of national influences, such as Chinese and French, and adding them to local ingredients like _nuoc mam_ (fish sauce), green leaves and chilies, with a dash of innovative flair. The result is some of the most exciting, original and tasty food available anywhere between Paris and Beijing.

Western influence: pasta dishes, familiar brands of food, and eating take-out food in the street

In Vietnam you will find a wide selection of eating places, ranging from smart local, French and international restaurants to humble food stands, which offer exceptional meals. The accent is on local, seasonal, fresh produce, and rich pickings from the sea along Vietnam's 1,250-mile (2,000km) coastline area, which are available far inland. Hearty stews are the tradition in the more remote north; along the coast, the tendency is toward salad dishes. Restaurants generally offer a variety of regional cuisines, though some specialize in certain areas.

MEALS AND MEALTIMES
Breakfast is usually eaten between 6am and 7am and traditionally consists of a bowl of _pho_ (▷ What to Eat, opposite). Hotels tend to serve breakfast up until about 10am; here you may be offered a cooked breakfast (eggs, bacon, tomatoes), or a simpler meal of bread or croissant with preserves. Lunch is eaten at about 11am and is the most substantial meal of the day; restaurants catering to visitors carry on serving until 2pm. Dinner is a smaller meal for the Vietnamese, but restaurants serve evening meals between 5pm and 11pm, except in remote areas, where dinner may be served only until about 9.30.

All Vietnamese food is dipped, whether in fish sauce, soya sauce, chili sauce, peanut sauce or the particularly pungent prawn sauce _mam tom_. Each new course is served with a new set of dips. Your waiter can advise you on picking the right dip for your dish. Many restaurants provide fish sauce, chili sauce and rice as part of the price of the meal. More expensive establishments charge extra for rice.

Dessert choices in Vietnamese restaurants are usually limited to fruit, ice cream, _banh flan_ (crème caramel) or _che_ (beans and dried fruit in a sweet or savory syrup).

WHERE TO EAT
It is possible to eat out at very little cost in Vietnam, especially outside Hanoi and Saigon. Peripherals such as furniture, service and ambience are regarded as distractions from the main task of plowing through plates, crocks, casseroles and tureens of piping-hot meats, vegetables and soups. Smarter restaurants, particularly those serving foreign cuisine, can prove quite expensive, especially if wine is served. Some restaurants add 5 percent service charge and the government tax of 10 percent to the bill. But with judicious shopping around it is not hard to find excellent value for money, particularly in small, family restaurants.

For day trips, an early morning visit to the markets will produce a picnic fit for a king. Hard-boiled quails' eggs, thinly sliced garlic sausage and salami, pickled vegetables, beefsteak tomatoes, cucumber, pâté, cheese, warm baguettes and fresh fruit will feed four for around a dollar a head.

There are vegetarian restaurants in Vietnam, most serving tofu dressed to look like meat rather than specifically concocted vegetarian dishes. In other restaurants be wary when ordering apparently vegetarian dishes, as vegetables are often cooked with pork, beef or prawns.

CHILDREN
Given the large proportion of the population aged 16 and under, it isn't surprising that, in the main, Vietnamese restaurants have no problem catering to children. Indeed, any restaurant frequented by Vietnamese families is likely to

have children running around everywhere. Lively and exuberant behavior is generally tolerated and taken as a matter of course. In most places the waitstaff will make a big fuss of Western children, especially those with fair hair. In the smarter establishments, such as those in hotels, unruly children may not be as popular.

If your children do not develop a taste for Vietnamese food, try eating at restaurants with a mixed or exclusively international menu, where children are more likely to be satisfied with the standard fare of pizzas, pastas, burgers and sausages in abundance.

lunch. In many cities they are abandoning their tiny plastic stools in favor of tables and chairs. The steamed, broken rice is eaten with fried chicken, fish, pork and vegetables; soup is normally included in the price of the dish.

● The most common type of spring roll is deep-fried (*cha gio* in the south, *nem ranh* in the north), but there are also delicious fresh or roll-it-yourself versions, such as *bi cuon* or *bo bia*. Essentially, these are salads with prawns or grilled meats wrapped in rice paper. Customers can roll their own, but it's not easy, and you can end up with sagging versions that collapse into your lap.

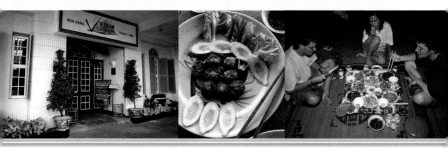

Vietnam House restaurant (left); Vietnamese delicacies (middle and right), served in traditional surroundings

ETIQUETTE
Dinner table etiquette is pretty informal: Meals are generally a family occasion, and an opportunity for conversation. It's impolite to start before everyone has been served rice, and to take too much of one dish for yourself. Dishes are set in the middle of the table for all to dip into with their chopsticks: Take one or two pieces at a time. Spoon soup into your bowl and eat it with your spoon or put your bowl to your lips. It's perfectly acceptable to hold your rice bowl up to your mouth and shovel the rice in with your chopsticks.

Nose-blowing is seen as unhygienic: If you must, turn away from the table. It's considered bad manners to use one of the readily available toothpicks without covering your mouth.

The practice of tipping varies widely. The locals do not normally tip if eating in small family restaurants but may tip extravagantly in expensive bars. Foreigners normally leave small change, which is quite acceptable and is appreciated by the waitstaff.

WHAT TO EAT
● *Pho* is a noodle soup made from stock flavored with star anise, ginger and other spices and herbs; individual recipes often remain a closely guarded secret. *Pho* is served with chicken or beef and is eaten in the morning and often in the evening, but rarely at lunchtime. *Pho* restaurants offer plates of fresh green leaves—mint, cinnamon, basil, spiky *ngo gai*—and extras such as bean sprouts, chopped red chilies, barbecue sauce and sliced lemons, so that patrons can make their own versions.

● *Com tam* (broken rice) is served in street stands, which do a brisk trade at breakfast and

● There is a bewildering variety of seafood on offer. One particularly tasty dish is crab in tamarind sauce, combining a fusion of flavors such as sour tamarind, garlic and scallion (spring onion); to eat it you must be willing to crack, crunch, poke and suck the meat from the farthest recesses of the crab's claws and legs.

● The tiny nests of the brown-rumped swift (*Collocalia esculenta*), also known as the edible-nest swiftlet or sea swallow, are collected for bird's-nest soup throughout Southeast Asia. The semi-oval nests are made of silk-like strands of saliva secreted by the birds, which when cooked in broth soften and become a little like noodles. The nests are believed to have aphrodisiac qualities, and the Vietnamese Emperor Minh Mang (reigned 1820–40) is said to have owed his extraordinary vitality to his inordinate consumption of bird's-nest soup. Red nests are the most highly valued. Collecting the nests is a profitable but extremely precarious business that involves climbing rickety ladders to cave roofs, sometimes in almost total darkness save for a candle strapped to the head.

FRUITS OF VIETNAM
● The custard apple, or sugar apple (*Annona squamos*), has a scaly green skin that you squeeze to reveal the flesh inside. This is then scooped out with a spoon.

● Durian (*Durio zibethinus*) is a large, prickly fruit with yellow flesh, infamous for its pungent smell; in fact, it is banned from many hotel rooms. Nevertheless, if you can overcome the smell the durian has an alluring taste, and durian-flavored chewing gum, ice cream and jams are available.

● Jackfruit (*Artocarpus heteropyllus*) is similar in appearance to durian, but its yellow flesh is

EATING

smoother. The fruit tastes slightly like custard.

● Mango (*Mangifera indica*) comes in hundreds of different varieties with subtle variations in flavor, and is delicious with sticky rice and a sweet sauce.

● Mangosteen (*Garcinia mangostana*) is a small fruit in a hard, purple shell. Cut or squeeze the shell to reach its sweet, white flesh.

● Papaya (*Carica papaya*), introduced into Southeast Asia in the 16th century, is large, round

where patrons sit on plastic stools. Most of these *bia hoi* cafés also serve simple and inexpensive food, and almost all their customers are men. As the beer is fresh it has to be consumed within a short period of brewing. As a result, most towns, even quite small ones, have their own breweries, and each community imparts to its beer its own local flavor.

Unfortunately, bars and restaurants do not sell *bia hoi* as its low price—just 1,500–2,000d per pint (half liter)—offers them little benefit.

Durian fruit (top); a makeshift griddle (above left); fresh fruit and vegetables (middle); rice paper (right)

or oval, and yellow- or green-skinned, with bright, orange flesh and a mass of round, black seeds in the middle.

● Pomelo (*Citrus grandis*) is a large, round fruit with dense, green skin, thick pith, and flesh not unlike that of the grapefruit, but less acidic.

● Rambutan (*Nephelium lappaceum*) is bright red and hairy—*rambut* is the Malay word for "hair"—and has slightly rubbery but sweet flesh.

● Salak (*Salacca edulis*) is a small, pear-shaped fruit with a rough, brown, scaly skin and yellow-white, crisp flesh. It is related to the sago and rattan trees.

● Tamarind (*Tamarindus indicus*) comes as brown seed pods with dry, brittle skins, or a brown, tart-sweet fruit whose flesh has a high tartaric acid content and is used to flavor curries, jams, jellies and chutneys, as well as for cleaning brass and copper.

DOG MEAT

Westerners may be taken aback by some of the dishes on offer in northern restaurants. One establishment advertises its specialty with the question: "Who can resist a steaming bowl of broth with a pair of dog's paws?" Dog meat (*thit chó* or *thit cay*) is an esteemed delicacy in the north of Vietnam, but is usually served only in specialist outlets at certain times of the month. These tend to be shacks on the edge of a town, and you are unlikely to order dog meat inadvertently in a standard restaurant.

BEER

Locally produced fresh beer is called *bia hoi*. It is cold and refreshing, and weak and inexpensive enough to drink in quite large volumes. As a rule, beer is consumed in small pavement cafés,

Hence bar customers have a choice of Tiger, Heineken, Carlsberg, San Miguel, 333, Saigon Beer or Huda. All are brewed in Vietnam, but many visitors prefer to try and stick to the local beers (333, Saigon and Huda), which are the most inexpensive brands and which many consider to have more distinctive flavors than the mass-produced international brands. This is not always possible, however, as many bars and restaurants stock only the more expensive beers produced by big international brewers.

WINE

Rice and fruit wines are produced and consumed in large quantities in upland areas, particularly in the north of Vietnam, though rice wines are fairly widely available throughout the country. There are two types of rice wine: *ruou nep* and *ruou de*. Ruou nep is a viscous wine made from sticky rice. It comes in different colors—purple and white—which are as a result of the different types of rice used to make it. Among Vietnam's ethnic minorities, who are recognized as masters of rice wine, *ruou nep* is drunk from a ceramic jar through a straw. This communal drinking is an integral part of the way of life of the Montagnards, and no doubt contributes substantially to the strengthening of clan ties. A word of warning: It is possible to become very drunk on *ruou nep* without realizing it. Ruou de is a rice spirit and is very strong.

There is a very wide range of different fruit wines but unless you make a real effort it can be quite hard to find them. Wines are made from just about all upland fruits, including plum, strawberry, apple and, of course, grapes—but grape wine in Vietnam is generally disappointing. Most restaurants offer New and Old World wines

EATING

and some offer the local Dalat wine, which is not very highly rated by wine experts, but has the advantage of being inexpensive. The other fruit wines on offer are fiery and warm, strong and, by the bottle, cost very little.

Snake wines are another variant enjoyed in Vietnam. Chinese tradition holds that snake wines increase virility, and as a result they are normally found in areas with large Chinese populations. In fact snake wine is, strictly speaking, a spirit, rather than a wine. Other wines are made using the bodies and parts of sea horses, geckos, silkworms and honey bees.

SOFT DRINKS

Soft drinks and bottled still and sparkling mineral water are widely available. It is probably not wise to drink tap water (▷ 267).

Tea and coffee are sold everywhere, but if you are used to American or European beverages the local versions can be an acquired taste. The Vietnamese tend to drink coffee black, but restaurants catering to the tourist trade are always happy to provide milk. There are also some unusual coffee flavors that take some courage to sample—for example, coffee that has passed through the innards of a weasel!

Local produce at Dalat's market (left); goat soup (middle); snake liquor (right)

MENU READER

Ordering Vietnamese food can be a daunting prospect, but knowledge of a few key words will help you work out what's available on the menu, order what you want and avoid any embarrassing blunders. This menu reader will help you translate some common words, dishes, and ingredients.

MEAT (THIT)
bò kho stewed beef
bò nhúng dam beef dipped in vinegar
bò nuong lá lot/mo chài grilled beef wrapped in vegetable leaf/pork fat
bò tung xeo sliced grilled beef
bún mang vit duck with bamboo-shoot noodles
bún thit nuong grilled pork and noodles
cánh gà chiên nuoc mam fried chicken wings in fish sauce
càri gà chicken curry
cha giò thit/tom pork/shrimp spring rolls
chân gà rút xuong boneless chicken-feet salad
dua dau heo pickled pork
ech frog
ech chiên bo frog fried in butter
ech lan bôt deep-fried frog
gà chicken
gà nuong grilled chicken
gà quay roasted chicken

goi gà/gà xé phay chicken salad
heo sua quay roasted young pork
lap xuong Chinese sausage
nem chua pickled pork wrapped in vegetable leaf
nem nuong grilled pork rolls
oc snails
oc hap gung snails steamed with ginger
oc len xào dua snails with coconut milk
oc nhoi pork-stuffed snails
thit bò beef
thit dê goat
thit gà chicken
thit heo pork
thit vit duck

vit duck
vit lap dry duck
vit quay roasted duck

FISH/SEAFOOD (CÁ/HAI SAN)
cá com chiên dòn deep-fried anchovy
cá hap steamed fish
cá lóc nuong dat sét grilled trout wrapped in clay
cá lóc nuong lá chuoi grilled trout wrapped in banana leaf
cá lóc nuong trui trout grilled in straw
cá tai tuong chiên xù deep-fried fish
cá trê chiên cham mam gung fried catfish with ginger sauce
com hen mussel rice
cua crab
cua hap bia crab steamed in beer
cua hap gung crab steamed with ginger

Heo sua quay, *or roasted pork, is traditionally served during* Tet

EATING

cua rang me tamarind crab
goi hen xào dhe mussel salad with star fruit
goi tôm ngó sen lotus stem and shrimp salad
hào song raw oyster
khô muc trôn buoi dried squid mixed with grapefruit
lau cá fish hot pot
lúón eel
muc squid
muc tuoi lan bot chiên deep-fried squid

hu tíu pork noodles
mì quang Quang Nam noodles
mì vit tiem Chinese duck noodles
mì xào giòn crispy fried noodles

RICE/VEGETABLES (COM/RAU CAI)
bap/ngô corn
bông bí xào fried pumpkin flower

mien vermicelli
nuoc tuong soya sauce
trung egg

DRINKS
cà phê dá iced coffee
cà phê den black coffee
cà phê sua dá iced coffee with milk
cam vat orange juice
mot chai bia bottle of beer
mot chai nuoc suoi bottle of mineral water

Local dishes from Hoi An (left); fruit and vegetables on sale in Hanoi's Old Quarter (middle)

Dried goods on sale in Ho Chi Minh City's Ben Thanh Market

muc xào stir-fried squid
nghêu nuong grilled clam
nuoc nam fish sauce
sò shellfish
sò nuong/hap grilled/steamed shellfish
tôm shrimp
tôm càng nuong grilled lobster
tôm hap bia shrimp steamed in beer
tôm hùm lobster
tôm nuong grilled prawn
tôm sú hap nuoc dua tiger prawns steamed in coconut

SOUP (CANH/XÚP)
canh chua cá sour fish soup
canh rau vegetable soup
cháo gà chicken rice soup
cháo hen mussel rice soup
cháo trang hot vit muoi rice soup with salted duck eggs
cháo vit duck rice soup
hoành thành wonton soup
pho soup with flat, white, rice noodles
xú bong bóng cá fish soup
xúp cua crab soup
xúp mang cua crab and asparagus soup

NOODLES (MÌ)
bánh canh fat round rice noodles
bún bò hué Hué beef noodles

bông cai cauliflower
bông cai xào fried cauliflower
cà chua tomato
cà rot carrot
cai bó xôi xào toi spinach fried with garlic
com chiên Duong Chau Cantonese fried rice
com niêu rice in clay pot
dau beans
dau hu tofu
dua chua pickled vegetable
dua leo cucumber
giá bean sprouts
hành tây onion
khoai tây potato
mang bamboo shoot
nâm mushroom
oi Da Lat green pepper
rau muong spinach
rau muong xào toi morning glory fried with garlic
rau sà lách lettuce

OTHER BASICS
bánh mì bread
cha giò spring rolls

mot lon bia can of beer
nuoc chanh lemon juice
nuoc dua coconut
ruou de rice wine
sinh to thom pineapple shake
trà/chè (N) tea
noc huan sparkling water

FRUIT/OTHER DISHES (TRÁI CÂY/CÁC MÓN KHÁC)
bánh khoái Hué sizzling cake
bánh xèo sizzling cake
trái/qua bó avocado
trái/qua buoi grapefruit
trái/qua cam orange
trái/qua chanh lemon
trái/qua choi banana
trái/qua chôm rambutan
trái/qua dào peach
trái/qua du dû papaya
trái/qua dua hau watermelon
trái/qua mân/roi plum
trái/qua nhan longan
trái/qua quyt mandarin
trái/qua thóm/dua pineapple
trái/qua vai lychee

COOKING METHODS
chiên/rán fried
hap steamed
luoc boiled
nuong grilled
quay roasted

EATING

HANOI

Hanoi is famous for its food, and many Hanoi dishes have been adopted throughout the country, often with regional variations. By far the most famous dish is the noodle soup known as *pho*. Strictly speaking, *pho* is made with beef, but chicken *pho* is also common. Star anise, ginger and the rich stock of marrow bones are used as flavorings, and the dish is served with a variety of green leaves (such as mint and basil), fresh lemon and chili in special *pho* restaurants. Hanoi is also famous for *cha ca* Hanoi—fresh fish cooked in butter on a charcoal burner at the table, and flavored with dill. *Cha ca* Hanoi is eaten with *bun*, a type of white noodle, which is a staple of Hanoi cuisine. The relative wealth of Hanoi in recent years means that for visitors, eating out is now a pleasure rather than a necessary ordeal. There are some excellent restaurants in the city, offering a very wide range of cuisine.

PRICES AND SYMBOLS

The restaurants are listed alphabetically (excluding Le, La, Il and The). The prices given are for a two-course lunch (L) and a three-course dinner (D) for one person, without drinks. The wine price is for the least expensive bottle.

For a key to the symbols, ▷ 2.

69 RESTAURANT BAR

69 Ma May Street
Tel 04-9261720
69@hn.vnn.vn

Climb a steep flight of stairs to reach the dining room of this old quarter restaurant, and try to get one of the two tables squeezed on to the balcony. There are plenty of Vietnamese and seafood dishes—the Hong Kong duck (chargrilled and stuffed with five spices, ginger, onion and garlic) is good, as is the sunburnt beef: beef strips deep-fried in five-spice butter. Honey grilled beef in satay sauce with five spice and steamed rice is divine. Mulled wine is offered on cold nights, as are traditional variants such as violet sticky rice wine.
Ⓞ Daily 7am–11pm
Ⓦ L 50,000d, D 60,000d, Wine from 160,000d

AL FRESCO'S

23L Hai Ba Trung Street
Tel 04-8267782
It's only a short walk from Hoan Kiem Lake to this popular Australian grill bar serving ribs, steak, pasta, pizza and fantastic salads. Giant portions and a lively atmosphere make it a memorable experience. Mouthwatering tangerine chicken kebabs followed by jumbo ribs and apple crumble and ice cream will leave you more than full. Special lunch menus at 90,000d are good value for two courses, including endless refills of tea or coffee. On Tuesdays there's a two-for-one pizza offer. The restaurant delivers food between 11am and 10pm, and is the only place in Hanoi delivering ice cream.
Ⓞ Daily 11–10
Ⓦ L 100,000d, D 120,000d, Wine from 225,000d

AU LAC

57 Ly Thai To Street
Tel 04-8257807
Aulaccafe@hn.vnn.vn
This café-cum-bar serves light meals and good coffee on wrought-iron furniture in the patio garden of a French villa behind the Sofitel Metropole. Breakfasts, sandwiches, pizzas, soups and pastas are available. The green papaya salad with grilled beef and sesame seeds is recommended, as are the sautéed oysters with turmeric and lemon grass. Popular with local expats and Vietnamese businessmen. Happy hour is between 5pm and 8pm, and beers are fairly priced.
Ⓞ Daily 7am–11pm
Ⓦ L 40,000d, D 60,000d, Wine from 189,000d

SPECIAL

BOBBY CHINN

1 Ba Trieu Street
Tel 04-9348577

One of the most stylish restaurants in Vietnam, with an excellent wine list. Rosebuds hang suspended like droplets from the ceiling, gold drapes abound and a glass facade ensures views of Hoan Kiem Lake. The Asian fusion food is good value, with set menus from 320,000d. Dine, at tables strewn with rose petals, on foie gras wrapped in rice paper with ginger sauce, pan-roasted salmon on wasabi mashed potatoes, grilled vegetables and ginger demi-glaze, or filet mignon mashed potato with mushroom ragout in a red wine sauce. To round off, sample the warm chocolate pudding.
Ⓞ Daily 11am–11pm
Ⓦ L 135,000d, D 175,000d, Wine from 250,000d

EATING

LE BEAULIEU

Sofitel Metropole Hotel
15 Ngo Quyen Street
Tel 04-8266919 ext 8206
www.sofitel.com

A good French and international restaurant whose Sunday brunch buffet is regarded as one of the best in Asia. Take your pick from a great selection of French seafood, oysters, prawns, cold and roast meats, and cheese, all piled high on platters. This great lunch includes free-flowing champagne.

🕒 Daily 6.30–10.30, 11.30–2, 6.30–11
🍴 L 200,000d, D 250,000d, Wine from 225,000d

BISTROT

34 Tran Hung Dao Street
Tel 04-8266136

Erratic service, paper napkins and an unpriced menu are all part of this French restaurant's eccentricity, which is worth braving for the highly rated food. Steak Roquefort and duck are always good choices, as is the charcuterie and duck and cognac pâté served with hot bread. The rabbit "Chasseur la Rochefoucauld" is beautifully tender.

🕒 Daily 10–2, 6–10.30
🍴 L 50,000d, D 60,000d, Wine from 250,000d

LA BRIQUE

6 Nha Tho Street
Tel 04-9285638

Cool, bare brickwork provides an austere setting for the most deliciously succulent *cha ca* Hanoi, served to the sounds of singer Manu Chao. Dinner is by candlelight, and the specialty is cooked on charcoal at your table and served with herbs and white noodles. Seafood is also a strong feature on the menu, with such dishes as crab soup with corn, stuffed squid and squid satay. The restaurant is on the Old City shopping street of Nha Tho.

🕒 Daily 10am–10.30pm
🍴 L 50,000d, D 55,000d, Wine from 180,000d

BROTHERS

26 Nguyen Thai Hoc Street
Tel 04-7333866
www.elephantguide.com/brothers-hn

Part of the pleasure of dining here is the sumptuous surroundings. Brothers is set in a beautifully restored villa close

to the Fine Arts Museum, and its leafy patio with umbrella-shaded tables is a haven of peace, filled with stands offering tempting dishes. The buffet lunch, with a range of starters, main courses and desserts, is one of the best-value meals in the country. Dinners are nightly barbecue buffets.

🕒 Mon–Sat 11–2, 6.30–10, Sun 6.30–10
🍴 L 50,000d, D 100,000d, Wine from 260,000d

CAFÉ THYME

18 Lo Su Street
Tel 04-8267929

The Canadian owner of this small, cozy restaurant tucked into an Old City street has worked in Hanoi for many years and keeps the menu in step with the seasons. Tantalizing dishes include onion tart with red cabbage quenelles, roast clams with crispy shallots, succulent crab cakes with orange and thyme mayonnaise, and lamb shank braised in sweet capsicum, citrus and espresso. The number of fine choices leaves you no option but to return—especially if you could not manage the fresh Dalat strawberries with Chantilly cream or frozen mango and Grand Marnier soufflé.

🕒 Daily 9am–11pm
🍴 L 80,000d, D 100,000d, Wine from 300,000d

CAY CAU RESTAURANT

De Syloia Hotel
17A Tran Hung Dao Street
Tel 04-8245346
www.desyloia.com

Popular with well-to-do Vietnamese, this small restaurant offers excellent set-price meals from 130,000d (eight courses) and a huge range of delicious food. After an appetizer of eel and mushroom

CLUB OPERA

59 Ly Thai To Street
Tel 04-8246950

An extensive Vietnamese menu is on offer in this small and intimate restaurant in the attractive setting of a restored French villa, close to the Opera House. Tables are beautifully laid, and the food is appealingly presented with exquisitely carved vegetables. The seaweed salad with shrimp and dried shredded squid is delicious. Beef, chicken and fish (fried grouper fillet with ginger sauce, for example) complete the repertoire. The dessert menu is decidedly uninspired, however, considering the varied savory menu on offer. The backroom bar is reminiscent of an English village pub.

🕒 Daily 11–2, 5.30–10.30
🍴 L 90,000d, D 115,000d, Wine from 400,000d

soup or beef and bindweed salad, try the full crab menu—fried, soft-shell crab with butter—or simmered pigeon with garlic in a clay pot. Tofu dishes figure prominently on the menu. If room remains, death by chocolate or blueberry cheesecake are tempting. Eat outdoors or inside under a decorated wooden ceiling. There is live music from 7.30pm to 9.30pm daily.

🕒 Daily 11–2, 6–10
🍴 L 40,000d, D 55,000d, Wine from 300,000d

COM CHAY NANG TAM

79A Tran Hung Dao Street
Tel 04-9424140

This popular little vegetarian restaurant is down an alley off

EATING

Tran Hung Dao Street, near the Ambassadors' Pagoda. It serves excellent and inexpensive dishes in a small, family-style dining room. The set meals range in price from 20,000d to 150,000d. Dishes incorporate a wide range of ingredients: sweetcorn cakes, beef salad with banana flower, star fruit and pineapple, and snowballs (light potato and mushroom croquettes). To accompany the 59 vegetarian options there are lots of freshly squeezed juices (wine is not served). Keep some room for the delicious banana and chocolate crêpes.

🕐 Daily 11–1.30, 5–10
🍽 L 15,000d, D 25,000d

LES COMPTOIRS
The Press Club
59A Ly Thai To Street
Tel 04-9340888
www.hanoi-pressclub.com

This central European-style café is on the ground level of the Press Club, and is convenient for a sandwich or a cup of tea after a visit to the nearby museums. Pastries, salads, pizzas, cookies and Illy coffee are on hand to ensure a revitalizing break. English-language newspapers, magazines and books are available for browsing.

🕐 Daily 7am–10pm
🍽 L 70,000d, D 100,000d, Wine from 130,000d

CYCLO BAR, RESTAURANT & GARDEN
38 Duong Thanh Street
Tel 04-8286844
Cyclo's is a fun place with a garden bar and children's play area. Guests are seated in red-cushioned cyclos backed by beer barrels and can enjoy a set meal from 50,000d or choose from the à la carte menu. Appetizing starters

range from onion soup with red wine and cheese croutons to terrine of eggplant (aubergine), feta cheese and black olives, and might be followed by duck breast served in kumquat sauce or duck liver in cognac and grapes. The large dessert menu, which includes chocolate mousse in Armagnac and *poire belle Hélène*, completes this culinary adventure.

🕐 Daily 9am–11pm
🍽 L 65,000d, D 90,000d, Wine from 200,000d

DAKSHIN
94 Hang Trong Street
Tel 04-9286872
www.elephantguide.com/dakshin
Southern Indian *dosas*—pancakes served with different sauces—are the specialties in this popular Indian vegetarian restaurant. The menu provides a useful glossary of the many unusual dishes served in the dining room, which is elegantly laid out with rattan furniture. There are nearly 100 dishes, such as cauliflower fritters, *dosas* and curries, all served on stainless-steel platters lined with a banana leaf. Prices are reasonable; set meals with five options are available for 50,000d. Desserts include Gulab *jamun*, *khoya* balls immersed in cardamom- and saffron-flavored syrup. Wine is not served.

🕐 Daily 10–2.30, 6–10.30
🍽 L 40,000d, D 50,000d

THE DELI
The Press Club
59A Ly Thai To Street
Tel 04-8255337
www.hanoi-pressclub.com
Keep The Deli delivery menu by the telephone for pizza, pasta, healthy salads and sandwiches, especially during the rainy season or if you fancy a quick lunch on the move. There is free delivery within a 6-mile (10km) radius. Edible goodies include the flame-grilled Greek lamb kebab sandwich and the colossal double chocolate brownie.

🕐 Daily 7am–10pm
🍽 Take-out meal: 90,000d

IL GRILLO
116 Ba Trieu Street
Tel 04-8227720
Despite stiff competition from newer places, this long-

established Italian restaurant remains popular. Two giant liquor bottles sit on its big, dark bar; the floor is tiled and the tables laid with checked tablecloths. Classic dishes, served to the sound of opera, include Parma ham with melon and *carpaccio di vitello*, followed by homemade pastas, veal, chicken, dumpling filled with roasted beef, pork, and ham served with a light ham and cream sauce.

🕐 Mon–Sat 10–2, 5.15–11, Sun 5.15–11
🍽 L 140,000d, D 180,000d, Wine from 170,000d

HANOI GOURMET
1B Pho Ham Long Street
Tel 04-9431009
For lovers of fine wine, cheese and cold cuts, this delicatessen (no dinner price) south of Hoan Kiem Lake, with a couple of tables at the back, is a great discovery. Find a free afternoon, go short on breakfast, then come here for a long, leisurely lunch. Stocks are replaced from France every few weeks. The counter displays an array of salads, baguettes and other breads, smoked salmon, cheeses and assorted terrines.

🕐 Daily 8.30am–9pm
🍽 L and D 80,000d, Wine from 100,000d

HIGHWAY 4
5 Hang Tre Street
Tel 04-9260639
www.highway4.com

Enter this restaurant through red swing doors to enjoy ethnic minority dishes from the north. Highway 4 is the most northerly road in Vietnam, running along the Chinese border, and is much used by owners of Minsk motorcycles. The restaurant itself is a visual and culinary treat. Superb fruit and rice wines are sold, the latter displayed in large medicinal bottles stuffed with preserved cobra, silkworm and gecko. You may need some rice wine for courage to face the exciting and rather alarming menu. Items include ostrich sautéed with cashew, mushrooms and onion, fried scorpions with chili and lemon grass, sauerkraut sautéed with pigs' intestines, and the pièce de résistance: bull's penis steamed with Chinese herbs.

🕐 Daily 10am–1am
🍷 L 60,000d, D 75,000d, Wine 36,000d

HOA SUA
28A Ha Hoi Street
Tel 04-9424448
www.hoasuaschool.com
A French training restaurant south of Hoan Kiem Lake for disadvantaged youngsters, where visitors can eat superbly prepared French and Vietnamese cuisine in an attractive and secluded courtyard setting. It is popular, reasonably inexpensive and offers a children's menu. The roasted duckling fillet with apple and Calvados sauce is delicious, and the preserved pigeon shepherd's pie is recommended. Traditional daily specials are also available.
🕐 Daily 11–10
🍷 L 50,000d, D 60,000d, Wine from 165,000d

JASPAS
4th floor, Hanoi Towers
49 Hai Ba Trung Street
Tel 04-9348325
Expatriates, children and older, professional Vietnamese customers form much of the clientele of this noisy restaurant serving Western food. The pita bread sandwiches are tasty, or for something more substantial try the Caribbean chicken, glazed spring duck breast or vegetarian burgers.

A set lunch for US$9 for four courses is good value. The chocolate mud pudding or Mars bar cheesecake will delight young ones. For the adults, there's a big TV screen for sporting events. The one drawback is air-conditioning that is usually too cold.
🕐 Daily 6am–11pm
🍷 L 100,000d, D 120,000d, Wine from 230,000d

KOTO
61 Van Mieu Street
Tel 04-7470337
kotohanoi@koto.netnam.vn
www.koto.com.au
A training restaurant next to the Temple of Literature for underprivileged young people. The vegetarian menu includes risotto with zucchini (courgettes) and tomato and eggplant (aubergine) salad with tahini, yogurt dressing and pita bread. Non-vegetarians may choose from lemon grassskewered chicken kebabs served on wok-tossed vegetables with steamed rice, *bun bo mai bo* (southern-style marinaded beef with noodles, herbs and peanuts served with a sweet sauce) or beerbattered fish and chips with tartar sauce. Desserts are mainly fruit based, with dishes such as tropical fruit in ginger and lime syrup served with sorbet. Sandwiches are also sold.
🕐 Mon–Thu 6.30–4.30, Fri–Sun 6.30–4.30, 6–9.30
🍷 L 50,000d, D 60,000d

LITTLE HANOI
21–23 Hang Gai Street
Tel 04-8288333
An all-day restaurant/café perfectly positioned on a busy corner of the Old City. The sandwiches are particularly outstanding for 45,000d; so too are the cappuccinos, the homemade yogurt with honey and the apple pie. Shop till you drop and then dive in here for an Earl Grey tea and a glance at the English-language newspapers and magazines, relaxing amid the wooden floors, rattan furniture and wooden ceiling fans. Healthy and not-so-healthy breakfasts are also served.
🕐 Daily 7.30am–11pm
🍷 L 50,000d, D 65,000d, Wine from 220,000d

THE RESTAURANT
The Press Club
59A Ly Thai To Street
Tel 04-9340888
www.hanoi-pressclub.com

The Restaurant has consistently remained one of the most popular dining experiences in Hanoi. Set in a smart complex close to the Opera House, it is luxuriously furnished, with polished, dark wood floors and print-lined walls. The menu is expensive: Start with crisp veal sweetbreads with langoustine and artichoke-heart purée on lobster essence. Then move on to the gimmicky deconstructed Vietnamese *pho* with lobster, foie gras and truffle, or chargrilled squab with wild forest mushroom tossed pasta. Chocolate pavlova with passionfruit ice cream is a highlight of the chocolate-heavy dessert menu. Alfresco dining is also possible.
🕐 Mon–Fri 11–3, 6–11, Sat, Sun 6–11
🍷 L 270,000d, D 320,000d, Wine from 350,000d

MOCA CAFÉ
14–16 Nha Tho Street
Tel 04-8256334
moca@netnam.vn
With its exposed, dark, redbrick wall and chrome flue, Moca Café would look more at home in Chicago or Manchester than in Hanoi. Its high open space, big windows, wafting fans and marbletopped tables are very inviting. Cinnamon-flavored cappuccino, smoked salmon and Bengali specials are all served on pretty, floral crockery. Service can be slack at times.
🕐 Daily 7am–midnight
🍷 L 60,000d, D 100,000d, Wine from 120,000d

EATING

NO NOODLES

20 Nha Chung Street
Tel 04-9285969

This is Hanoi's original sandwich bar. Delicious and inexpensive sandwiches are made so big here that they barely fit into the average mouth. This is a perfect place for a quick lunch on the move—try mouthwatering Camembert and bacon, smoked beef, salami with avocado, or a range of fruit juices and salads.

🕐 Daily 9am–9pm
🍴 Take-out meal: 30,000d

RESTAURANT 202

202A Hue Street
Tel 04-9760487

This restaurant on several floors in a nondescript building serves superb Vietnamese and French food, and is excellent value. The extensive menu covers dishes from eel soup to roast rabbit, pigeon, turtle steamed with Chinese medicinal herbs and Dong Co duck stewed with mushroom. There is a set meal of eight courses for 80,000d for lunch and dinner.

🕐 Daily 10am–10pm
🍴 L 30,000d, D 40,000d, Wine from 180,000d

LA SALSA

25 Nha Tho Street
Tel 04-8289052
www.lasalsa.com

La Salsa is a Spanish enclave in the middle of Hanoi, with perfect views of the cathedral and a pleasing menu. The chorizo and warm goat's cheese salad, with olive oil and thyme toast, is divine. Overall the food is a broad European mix, with the likes of beef tenderloin, French sausage and white beans, duck leg confit and paella on the menu, and is enhanced by a full range of tapas.

🕐 Daily 8am–11pm
🍴 L 95,000d, D 115,000d, Wine from 250,000d

SAN HO

58 Ly Thuong Kiet Street
Tel 04-9349184
ando@hn.vnn.vn

Hanoi's most popular seafood restaurant offers a series of set meals from 250,000d with nine or ten courses, or an à la carte selection. The fruits of the sea dish includes winkles

SEASONS OF HANOI

95B Quan Thanh Street
Tel 04-8435444

Seasons of Hanoi is housed in a finely restored and authentically furnished colonial villa with a small patio fringed by a hedge and fairy lights. The food is fresh and delicious, but service can be slack. Dine on stewed eel with red wine, fish kebabs with satay sauce and stewed duck in tofu sauce. The dessert list is hugely disappointing after the extensive mains and appetizers menu, with only the coconut ice cream just about proving a temptation. Reservations are recommended.

🕐 Daily 11–2, 6–10
🍴 L 80,000d, D 100,000d, Wine from 200,000d

with garlic-butter sauce, oyster porridge, raw oysters served with wasabi sauce and ginger in vinegar, as well as winkles, cockles, clams and scallops. For dessert, try the sweetened bird's-nest delicacy with gingko nut. This is a pleasant, airy restaurant, with live piano music between 7pm and 9pm.

🕐 Daily 10–2, 5–10
🍴 L 120,000d, D 140,000d, Wine from 240,000d

TANDOOR

24 Hang Be Street
Tel 04-8245359

Exceptional Indian food is freshly prepared at this small but long-standing restaurant. Authentic curries, tandooris and breads are served by the same family who run Dakshin (▷ 213). Tuck into onion *pakora*, chili potato *bhaji*, chicken *irani* (marinated in a rich mixture of yogurt, cream, lime juice, cashew paste and green chilies), kebabs, masalas and curries. Set lunches are available for 55,000d (45,000d for vegetarians), and Halal food is also served. No wine.

🕐 Daily 11–2.30, 6–10.30
🍴 L 50,000d, D 60,000d
🚭 Section

TASSILI

78 Ma May Street
Tel 04-8280774
www.elephantguide.com/tassili

With its cheerful yellow hues, this is a dazzling addition to

Hanoi's culinary scene, named after an Algerian desert. The food in Tassili is strongly Mediterranean in style, with lots of lamb; items include New Zealand lamb stew with green olive and pita bread, couscous, Greek-style octopus, hummus, kebabs, homemade pastas, Spanish cold cuts and more. The Italian chef places the highest emphasis on the quality of the food and ingredients, and everything is served piping hot. The royal couscous with a steaming lamb stew is perfect for a grim Hanoi winter's day.

🕐 Daily 10–2, 4–10
🍴 L 120,000d, D 160,000d, Wine from 350,000d

EATING

THE NORTH

Each region of Vietnam has its own culinary tradition, reflecting the influence of the climate and geography, as well as the wealth or poverty of the population. Northern Vietnam is mountainous, temperate and poor, and in general food here is plain, with little diversity in the way it is cooked. Most popular is boiled food such as chicken, pork and vegetables. Rice is a staple and is used to accompany nearly all meals, as well as being a vital ingredient of rice wine. Drinking rice wine is a communal event in this part of Vietnam, and should not be missed, if only for the experience rather than the taste! In Sapa, the only northern town that is really equipped for the tourist trade, you will find a handful of places serving excellent Asian and international cuisine.

PRICES AND SYMBOLS

The restaurants are listed alphabetically (excluding Le, La, Il and The). The prices given are for a two-course lunch (L) and a three-course dinner (D) for one person, without drinks. The wine price is for the least expensive bottle.

For a key to the symbols, ▷ 2.

SAPA

BAGUETTE & CHOCOLAT

Thac Bac Street
Sapa
Tel/fax 020-871766

The Baguette & Chocolat is an appealing place with a pleasant

DIEN BIEN PHU

LIEN TUOI

27 Muong Thanh 8 Street
Dien Bien Phu
Tel 023-824919

MUONG THANH HOTEL

25 Him Lam-TP
Dien Bien Phu
Tel 023-810043

The best available restaurant in town is housed in a massive, bamboo barn, where the tables are set out in long rows, medieval style. The building is open-sided and well ventilated by numerous fans. Dishes are varied and should satisfy all tastes, with several omelettes for breakfast, Dien Bien Phu spring rolls (mushrooms, meat, onion, carrot and mayonnaise) for starters, spaghetti and other types of pasta, chicken, grilled duck with honey, boar, pork, frog and curry as main dishes, as well as a selection of tofu dishes and seafood, which is recommended.

This local restaurant is the only real alternative eatery to the Muong Thanh Hotel (▷ right and 239), and is next to Hill A1 (▷ 82). Dishes are served in a vast, impersonal dining room, and cover a wide range, from banana salad to venison and turtle stews. There are no fewer than 14 fish dishes, which include steamed fish with beer, steamed cuttlefish, and steamed sweet-and-sour shrimp. To accompany your meal you can take your pick of soft drinks, a selection of beer and rice wines.

🕐 Daily 7am–10pm
🍴 L 30,000d, D 35,000d, Rice wine from 10,000d

🕐 Daily 6am–10pm
🍴 L 25,000d, D 35,000d, Wine from 150,000d

seating area. In addition to the delicious pastries, breakfasts, sandwiches, pasta, pizzas and dishes such as sautéed venison with lemon grass and sautéed Chinese noodles with shrimp are served. Caramelized apple with honey and cinnamon or a selection from the full cake cabinet will complete your

meal. You can also buy picnic kits from 35,000d. Profits from the sale of the cakes and pastries go toward the Hoa Sua School, which trains local, ethnic minority young women to work in hotels and restaurants in Vietnam.

🕐 Mon–Sat 7am–9.30pm, Sun 7–2
🍴 L 25,000d, D 40,000d, Wine from 127,000d

EATING

BAMBOO BAR AND RESTAURANT

Cau May Street
Sapa
Tel 020-871075

This spacious hotel restaurant has great views of Mount Fansipan. The extensive menu includes some great breakfast possibilities; the delightfully thin pancakes with chocolate sauce are a must. For dinner, try the special set meals, which offer as many as 5 courses. Song and dance performances are given by local Hmông groups on weekend evenings.

🕒 Daily 6.30am–11pm
🍴 L 40,000d, D 64,000d, Wine from 140,000d

BON APPETIT

25 Xuan Vien Street
Sapa
Tel 020-872927

This friendly, central place serves a good mix of Western breakfasts, burgers, French baguette sandwiches, stews and a variety of Vietnamese dishes. The food is certainly aimed at a tourist clientele, so don't expect to find any unusal local dishes on the menu. Try their excellent spring rolls accompanied by a huge pile of edible leaves including mint, lettuce and cilantro (coriander). A small selection of desserts and cakes are on offer changing on a daily basis.

🕒 Daily 7.30am–10.30pm
🍴 L 100,000d, D 150,000d, Wine from 150,000d

CAMELLIA

Cat Cat Street
Sapa
Tel 020-871455

Reached through the main market, Camellia is a great place from which to watch the local shoppers going about their business. The long menu has a full range of Vietnamese fare, which includes some twists on conventional themes. The beef steak is rather dry, but the grilled deer is good and the spicy Camellia salad is excellent. Warm and strong apple wine makes an ideal accompaniment.
Recommended dishes include fried beef with garlic, ginger and celery, and stuffed squid with sausage in sauce; apple cake with honey is one of the best desserts. In winter the rice

TA VAN

Victoria Sapa Hotel
Sapa
Tel 020-871522
www.victoriahotels-asia.com

Sitting high above Sapa is this first-class restaurant with three walls that have been replaced by glass doors, so that you can enjoy the views while you eat. A large, central, raised fireplace dominates this restaurant and warms the dining room on cold days. The set dinners for 200,000d are excellent value and provide a vast range of delicious options; a choice of 12 appetizers followed by 14 main course options such as seafood ragout with saffron sauce and grilled spare ribs Latino style with BBQ sauce. The eight dessert options include Brazilian coconut tarte and chocolate mousse. The à la carte menu is no less inviting with grilled shrimp and T-bone steaks.

🕒 Daily 6.30am–10pm
🍴 L 150,000d, D 200,000d, Wine from 350,000d

bowls are warmed. There is also a selection of Western food, including pizzas, hamburgers and healthy breakfasts.

🕒 Daily 6.30am–11pm
🍴 L 40,000d, D 50,000d, Wine from 149,000d

DELTA

33 Cau May Street
Sapa
Tel 020-871799

Sapa's popular Italian restaurant serves good portions of pasta, pizzas and warming soups, as well as tasty seafood options such as calamari in *bianco*—squid, anchovies, capers and white wine. If you crave a hearty, meaty meal, order the Australian ribeye steak. There is a particularly good wine list. Photographs hang on the restaurant walls, and the tables are decorated with green and burgundy tablecloths. Delta is on the main road and offers good people-watching vantage points near the windows.

🕒 Daily 7.30am–10pm
🍴 L 95,000d, D120,000d, Wine from 135,000d

MIMOSA

22 Cau May Street
Sapa
Tel 020-871377

A path leads off the main road to this small, slightly chaotic, family-run restaurant serving delicious local specialties and occupying an old house. Seating is cozy and comfortable indoors or fresh and airy on the small terrace. A long menu of good Western and Asian dishes should satisfy all palates. Mimosa is very popular; as a result, service can be excrutiatingly slow during busy periods. The menu lists pizzas, pastas and burgers, as well as dishes containing boar, deer, rabbit, frog, eel, chicken, beef and pork. To finish, try the homemade brownies or *crêpes*. There is a reasonably varied vegetarian menu.

🕒 Daily 7am–11pm, until midnight during high season
🍴 L 30,000d, D 35,000d, Wine from 130,000d

THE RED DRAGON PUB

21 Muong Hoa Street
Sapa
Tel 020-872085
reddragonpub@hn.vnn.vn

The Red Dragon is furnished like an English tearoom, complete with faux-Tudor beams and checked tablecloths. The friendly owners serve food that will appeal to homesick Brits, including a variety of teas, full English cooked breakfasts, baked potatoes and shepherd's pie. In the pub upstairs, which has a small balcony, you can sup beer or strawberry wine and admire the outstanding valley views. Christmas lunch here is a must.

🕒 Daily 8am–11pm (bar from 11am, food until 9.30pm)
🍴 L 45,000d, D 65,000d, Wine from 160,000d

CENTRAL VIETNAM

Food is much spicier in central Vietnam and, since no part of this region is very far from the coast, seafood is inevitably a specialty. It is particlarly good in Hoi An, where fish wrapped in banana leaf is a perennial favorite, and in Nha Trang and Danang. The royal court exerted an influence on Hué cuisine that is still evident to this day. Meals tend to consist of several light dishes, delicately flavored and requiring painstaking preparation—in short, dishes fit for a king. Hué food is known for its refined but often fiery taste. Shrimp and rice cakes *(banh beo)* and rice paper figure promimently, and much emphasis is placed on presentation and appearance. One Hué specialty is *bun bo Hué*, a beef soup made with rather slippery, round noodles laced with chili oil of exquisite piquancy. Another is the famous sizzling pancake *banh khoai* stuffed with soya shoots and shrimp, and eaten either by itself or rolled in rice paper with fresh, green leaves, sliced star fruit and thinly sliced green banana. In addition to its fish, Hoi An is known for the Chinese and Japanese influences on its food. *Cao lau*, a wonton noodle soup unique to the city, is made with slices of pork and croutons and water drawn from one well. In Nha Trang, the local speciality is *nem nuong*, grilled pork wrapped in rice paper with salad leaves and *bun*, fresh rice noodles. The French bread in Nha Trang is also excellent.

BAC MY AN BEACH

CAFÉ INDOCHINE

Furama Resort
68 Ho Xuan Huong Street
Bac My An
Tel 0511-847888
www.furamavietnam.com

This resort restaurant, decorated with pink Chinese lanterns, rattan furniture, banana trees and old colonial photographs, enjoys open-sided views over the infinity pool and onto the beach, and has a predominantly Asian menu of Vietnamese, Indian, Japanese and fusion dishes. Try the oyster mushroom soup and the martini shrimp—jumbo shrimp flamed with martini and finished with tomato, and served in a filo basket. The ice creams and sherbets are hugely popular.
🕐 Daily 6.30am–11pm
🍴 L 165,000d, D 195,000d, Wine from 320,000d

BUON ME THUOT

BUON JUIN

Thang Loi Hotel
1 Phan Chu Trinh Street
Buon Me Thuot
Tel 050-857615

Buon Juin is the best restaurant in town, set on the ground level of the hotel, overlooking Liberty Square. The menu offers a good selection of Vietnamese and international cuisine (the fries are particularly good). Their prices are reasonable, and the service is friendly and efficient. Fans help to make the restaurant pleasantly cool.
🕐 Daily 7am–10pm
🍴 L 30,000d, D 35,000d, Wine 180,000d

DALAT

LONG HOA

6, 3 Thang 2
Dalat
Tel 063-822934

In the best traditions of French family restaurants, this place serves delicious food and superb breakfasts, and is fairly priced. It is popular with Dalat's few expatriates and visitors alike. The chicken soup and steak are particularly good. Sample the homemade strawberry wine, which can be bought by the bottle for around 100,000d. Service is erratic; don't be surprised if your main course comes at the same time as your starter. It's best to arrive early.
🕐 Daily 10.30am–9.30pm
🍴 L 50,000d, D 65,000d, Wine 210,000d

LE RABELAIS

Sofitel Dalat Palace
12 Tran Phu Street
Dalat
Tel 063-825444
www.sofitel.com

Eating in the sumptuous dining room of Le Rabelais, with its elegant furnishings, terrace and views down to the lake, is one of the highlights of a visit to Dalat. The restaurant specializes in French cuisine, and there is an excellent wine list. Staff are attentive and knowledgeable. Note that smart dress is required. After dinner retire to the Le Rabelais Piano Bar for live music until 10pm.
🕐 Daily 6am–10am, 6pm–10pm
🍴 L 300,000d, D 350,000d, Wine from 400,000d

STOP AND GO CAFÉ

2A Ly Tu Trong Street
Dalat
Tel 063-828458

This bohemian café, serving coffee, cakes and snacks, is

EATING

also an art gallery run by the locally distinguished poet Mr Duy Viet, who was born in the house. Sit inside, enjoying the early morning sunlight that fills the house, or on the terrace as he bustles around rustling up breakfast and pulling out volumes of visitors' books and his own collected works. The garden is an attractively overrun wilderness where tall fir trees sigh in the breeze.

🕐 Daily 7.30am–8.30pm
🍴 L 32,000d, D 48,000d, Wine 80,000d

DANANG

CHRISTIE'S AND COOL SPOT
112 Tran Phu Street
Danang
Tel 0511-824040

Christie's old premises were demolished during the construction of the River Han Bridge; its new location is one block in from the river, where it has merged with the Cool Spot bar. Frequented by expatriates from Danang and outlying provinces, it has a small bar downstairs, and a restaurant above serving cold beer and Western and Japanese food, plus a magnificent all-day breakfast. Its homemade pizzas are tasty, as is its homemade lemon pie. Happy hour runs from 4pm to 8pm, with cocktails during normal hours ringing in at 50,000d.

🕐 Daily 9.30am–10.30pm
🍴 L 50,000d, D 60,000d, Wine from 180,000d

HOI AN

CAFÉ 111/HAI'S SCOUT CAFÉ
111 Tran Phu Street/
98 Nguyen Thai Hoc Street
Hoi An
Tel 0510-863210

The central area of these back-to-back cafés has an exhibition of the World Wildlife Fund's work in the threatened environment around Hoi An (www.wwfindochina.org). Between them the two cafés offer good food in a relaxing courtyard, with bamboo trees and garden furniture, or in the attractive interior setting. Barbecues are held nightly between 6pm and 9pm, and good-value carryout baguettes and set meals are offered.

🕐 Daily 7.30am–11pm
🍴 L 32,000d, D 45,000d, Wine from 80,000d

CAFÉ DES AMIS
52 Bach Dang Street
Hoi An
Tel 0510-861616

Customers come back again and again to this hugely popular restaurant facing the river, despite the limited range of dishes on offer. The daily set meal consists of five very tasty fish, seafood or vegetarian dishes, concocted by the owner, Mr Nguyen Manh Kim, who spends several months a year cooking in Europe.

🕐 Daily 8.30am–10pm
🍴 L and D 65,000d

THE CARGO CLUB RESTAURANT AND HOI AN PATISSERIE
107–109 Nguyen Thai Hoc Street
Hoi An
Tel 0510-910489
www.elephantguide.com/cargoclub

Riverside and streetside vantage points add to the appeal of The Cargo Club, as does its attractive interior. Housed in a pair of beautiful old shop houses overlooking the tranquil waters of the Son River, the restaurant serves breakfasts, brunches and sandwiches, homemade ice cream and an array of cakes and desserts from its huge patisserie counter. Among items on the mainly international restaurant menu are goat's cheese and spinach lasagne and a delectable passion mousse with chocolate. A morning and afternoon tea or coffee plus two cakes will set you back 48,000d.

🕐 Daily 8am–11pm
🍴 L 40,000d, D 45,000d, Wine from 190,000d

NHU Y (AKA MERMAID)
2 Tran Phu Street
Hoi An
Tel 0510-861527

The candy-pink walls of this little restaurant are framed by

BROTHER'S CAFÉ
27 Phan Boi Chau Street
Hoi An
Tel 0510-914150

These cloistered French houses have been renovated

with exquisite taste by Khaisilk (▷ 24). The garden leads down to the river, and dining alfresco is a delight. The menu has good Vietnamese specialties, and at 256,000d the daily set meal still offers good value in lovely surroundings with white umbrellas and white-clothed tables. Interior dining, roadside, is also possible. Hoi An spring rolls are beautifully presented, and the Brother's-style steamed shrimp comes bathed in coconut juice inside the coconut. The set daily meals rules exclude single diners.

🕐 Daily 9am–10pm
🍴 L 100,000d, D 125,000d, Wine from 280,000d

a beautiful, purple creeper flower (hoa cat dang). At night its charm is enhanced by the illuminated red Chinese lanterns strung up outside. Miss Vy turns out all the local specialties, as well as some of her own; the five-course set dinner is particularly recommended. Diners are aided by pictures on the menu. One particularly good choice is the white rose and grilled tuna with turmeric accompanied by stir-fried green beans. There is a streetside cake cabinet for passing visitors.

🕐 Daily 10–10
🍴 L 36,000d, D 42,000d, Wine from 190,000d

EATING

TAM TAM CAFÉ

110 Nguyen Thai Hoc Street
Hoi An
Tel 0510-862212

This is a great little café in a renovated tea house with an attached restaurant serving French and Italian cuisine. Tam Tam is a relaxing place for a drink, an espresso or a meal. Upstairs, in the dining room with white ceiling fans and low-hung lamps (using small fish baskets as shades), customers are offered a series of set meals for 75,000d which could include a large hunk of garlic bread, pasta with a choice of sauces and *crêpes* or ice cream. You'll taste some of the best pesto in Vietnam here—made from freshly plucked Vietnamese basil.

🕒 Daily 9.30am–1am
🍽 L 42,000d, D 55,000d, Wine from 237,000d

THANH

76 Bach Dang Street
Hoi An
Tel 0510-861366

This lovely little Chinese restaurant is in an open-sided old house overlooking the river: It is recognizable by its Chinese style and by the *hoa cat dang*, a purple creeper

draped over its walls. Excellent shrimp is served here—try the shrimp fried in ginger. You can also order the Hoi An

specialties *cao lau* and white rose (rice-flour dumplings with shrimp-meat filling).

🕒 Daily 7am–11pm
🍽 L 25,000d, D 35,000d, Wine from 158,000d

YELLOW STAR CAFÉ

73 Nguyen Thai Hoc Street
Hoi An
Tel 0510-910430

People and carts mill around the corner of Le Loi and Nguyen Thai Hoc streets, where this open-fronted, balconied restaurant is set, making it a good place for people-watching. Views are particularly good between 3.30pm and 4.30pm, when the setting sun illuminates the buildings on Le Loi Street. The views, friendly service, and an eclectic menu that includes full cooked breakfasts, chicken balti, good sausage and mashed potatoes and a coconut fruit crumble combine to make this a very popular choice.

🕒 Daily 8am–11pm
🍽 L 38,000d, D 48,000d, Wine from 158,000d

HUÉ

DONG TAM

66/7 (7 Kiet 66), Le Loi Street
Hué
Tel 054-828403.

Tucked away in the little *hem* (alley) opposite Century Riverside (▷ 245) is Hué's vegetarian restaurant. Sit in a pleasant and quiet little yard surrounded by hanging orchids and topiary, while choosing from the reasonably priced menu, which has fairly simple tofu dishes. The restaurant is a popular choice with the city's resident monks.

🕒 Daily 10–10
🍽 L and D 20,000d

HOTEL SAIGON MORIN RESTAURANT

30 Le Loi Street
Hué
Tel 054-823526
www.morinhotel.com.vn

The nightly buffet in the Morin's candlelit courtyard, accompanied by traditional music, is a vast spread of beef, squid, fish, pork, shrimp pancakes, rice cakes and apple fritters. Diners sit in the courtyard, centered on a fountain, while the musicians sit under an arch of illuminated, hanging Hué conical hats,

elegantly attired in headdresses and costumes of deep

sapphire-blue and scarlet.

🕒 Daily 7.30pm–9.30pm
🍽 D 160,000d, Wine from 400,000d

LAC THIEN

6 Dinh Tien Hoang Street
Hué
Tel 054-857348

Lac Thien and its neighbor Lac Thanh are arguably Hué's most famous restaurants and are run, with fierce rivalry, from adjacent buildings by two branches of the same family. Lac Thien serves excellent dishes from a diverse and inexpensive menu; its Huda beers are long and cold, and the family is riotous and entertaining. Similar reports are given about Lac Thanh, next door. For hungry diners, Lac Thien serves a filling *banh khoai*, Hué's specialty pancake—shrimp, meat and eggs served with green salad, figs, green bananas and peanut sauce. The restaurant is designed as a cafeteria, its mint-green walls plastered with red graffiti testifying to the success of the food.

🕒 Daily 7am–10pm
🍽 L 20,000d, D 25,000d

THE TROPICAL GARDEN RESTAURANT

27 Chu Van An Street
Hué
Tel 054-847143

Dine alfresco in a leafy garden under a gazebo-like structure in this restaurant, just a short walk from the Perfume River. The staff are attentive and serve dishes such as beef soup with star fruit, mackerel baked in pineapple and an aromatic banana dessert flambéed with wine.

🕒 Daily 8.30am–10pm
🍽 L 40,000d, D 50,000d, Wine from 124,000d

EATING

LA CARAMBOLE
19 Pham Ngu Lao Street
Hué
Tel 054-810491

Hué's most popular restaurant is attractively decorated, with beautiful kites and multicolored feathers adorning its ceiling. Its specialty is a range of Hué imperial-style set meals, starting from as little as 64,000d for nine courses, including soup, rice cakes, steamed fish with five-spice sauce, fried vegetable with squid and *banh khoai*. Á la carte items include a meaty duck *à l'orange*, pizzas and croque-monsieur for children.
📷 Daily 7am–11pm
🍴 L 40,000d, D 50,000d, Wine 210,000d

MUI NE

BAMBOO VILLAGE BEACH RESORT RESTAURANT
Km 11.8, Ham Tien
Mui Ne
Tel 062-847007

This resort restaurant, with views over the sea, offers international and Vietnamese choices and some excellent seafood. The carpetbag steak (steak stuffed with clams) and the Thai-style sautéed prawn with garlic, served with rice, are highly recommended.
📷 Daily 7am–11pm
🍴 L 75,000d, D 85,000d, Wine from 262,000d

COCO BEACH RESORT
58 Nguyen Ninh Chiau
Mui Ne
Tel 062-847111

A French chef has worked his magic on a great menu in this roadside restaurant in the grounds of the resort. Start with salmon marinated with

hazelnut oil, followed by barracuda escalope with mushroom purée and tomato butter or roasted duck breast with honey apples and Chinese

vermicelli. A perfect fruit sherbet and red fruit pastries could be saved for a second visit.
📷 Tue–Sun 3pm–11pm
🍴 L 160,000d, D 200,000d, Wine 380,000d

L'OCEANE RESTAURANT
Victoria Phan Thiet Resort
Km 9, Phu Hai
Phan Thiet
Tel 062-847171

Sea views are magnificent from this resort restaurant; the premier position is at a table on the elevated terrace dining area. Guests have plenty of choices from a menu that focuses on Malaysian, Indonesian and Japanese food.
📷 Daily 6.30am–10.30pm
🍴 L 96,000d, D 112,000d, Wine from 288,000d

NHA TRANG

ANA PAVILION RESTAURANT
Ana Mandara
Tran Phu Street
Nha Trang
Tel 058-522222

Vietnamese and fusion dishes are offered by Jim Tawa, the New Zealand chef here. Buffet breakfasts are a feast, seafood lunch buffets are available in

LUNA D'AUTONNO
Mui Ne
Tel 062-847591

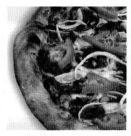

One of the best Italian restaurants in the country occupies a bamboo-roofed rustic building surrounded by plants, close to the Sailing Club (▷ 247). Portions are huge, the menu is inspired, and there is a full wine list. Diners are spoilt for choice with daily fish specials, pasta dishes that include *penne in carrozza* (mozzarella, anchovies, cream, tomato and feta cheese) and ravioli, veal, squid, beef and wood-fired pizzas. Barbecues are hosted on Friday and Saturday nights, and there is salsa music on Saturday nights.
📷 Daily 10.30am–10.30pm
🍴 L 75,000d, D 95,000d, Wine 220,000d

the restaurant as well as à la carte for lunch and dinner, and a buffet dinner is also available at the nearby Beach Restaurant (daily 6am–11pm).
📷 Daily 24 hours
🍴 L 160,000d, D 200,000d, Wine from 192,000d

CYCLO CAFÉ
5A Tran Quang Khai Street
Nha Trang
Tel 058-524208

Italian and Vietnamese dishes are served at this outstanding little restaurant with tables spilling onto the sidewalk. There is real attention to detail in the bamboo furniture and in the cooking. The vodka penne and steamed fish with ginger are popular. There are also vegetarian dishes. Happy hour is between 7pm and 8pm.
📷 Daily 7am–10pm
🍴 L 35,000d, D 45,000d, Wine 60,000d

EATING

LAC CANH

44 Nguyen Binh Khiem Street
Nha Trang
Tel 058-821391

This very popular restaurant specializes in beef and beautifully succulent squid, which customers barbecue at their table and dip in a selection of sauces. Fish is also excellent, as is eel mixed with vermicelli. The restaurant itself is smoky and minimally furnished, but the atmosphere is great fun. It can be hard to get a table as it's often packed with locals, so arrive early. Customers who linger too late are hustled out at closing time.

◯ Daily 9am–9.30pm
🍴 L 32,000d, D 40,000d

GOOD MORNING VIETNAM

19B Biet Thu Street
Nha Trang
Tel 058-815071

This popular Italian restaurant in the budget district of Nha Trang is part of a small chain of five. Among the offerings are hot sandwiches, risotto Gorgonzola and heaps of pasta dishes, as well as braised mackerel in a caramelized pepper sauce. Vegetarians have a choice of tofu options. Desserts include tiramisu and a great crêpe suzette—a thin pancake in orange sauce and flamed in liqueur, served with ice cream.

◯ Daily 10am–11pm
🍴 L 60,000d, D 80,000d, Wine 210,000d

LA LOUISIANE

Tran Phu Street
Nha Trang
Tel 058-812948
louisiane@hotmail.com

Opposite the turning for the former airport, this large, blue resort complex with canary-yellow and blue iron chairs and small mosaic tables is centered around a small swimming pool right on the beach, and is a popular, laidback hangout. It serves a range of homemade Western snacks and Vietnamese meals, as well as homemade ice cream, and houses a French patisserie. There are cocktails, beers and nonalcoholic drinks. Happy hour is from 8pm to 10pm.

◯ Daily 7.30am–midnight
🍴 L 36,000d, D 50,000d, Wine from 120,000d

SAILING CLUB

72–74 Tran Phu Street
Nha Trang
Tel 058-826528
Fax 058-816906

The busy Sailing Club restaurant, an attractive place on the beachfront, serves Vietnamese, Japanese, Italian and Indian food. The restaurant enjoys the best position in the complex, a beautifully designed space overlooking the beach and ocean beyond. The Vietnamese and Japanese menu here offers good grilled salmon with teriyaki sauce, fish curry with eggplant (aubergine) and *tenzaru soba* (cold buckwheat noodles

topped with seaweed). The bar area spills onto the beach and is decorated with an unusual burgundy and gold mosaic mural flecked with fish. Happy hour is between 6.30pm and 10pm.

◯ Daily 7am–11pm; bar noon–4am
🍴 L 60,000d, D 70,000d, Wine 280,000d

TRUC LINH

21 Biet Thu Street
Nha Trang
Tel 058-821259

Fresh seafood is displayed on large platters on the sidewalk to entice customers to this lovely, open-sided, thatched-roof restaurant next to the Truc Linh Villa Resort. The full culinary spectrum of tasty Asian and Western delicacies can be enjoyed here, from breakfast to dinner. Treats include Earl Grey tea, pork and herbs with peanut dip as an appetizer, and stuffed crab or minced frogs in lemon grass for the main course. Only the excessively loud music detracts from the friendly and welcoming atmosphere.

◯ Daily 7am–11pm
🍴 L 36,000d, D 42,000d, Wine 150,000d

WHITE HOUSE

30B Nguyen Thien Thuat Street
Nha Trang
Tel 058-524438

Rows of tables are set out in this large, open-sided restaurant, where the columns are fake trees and a countryside mural covers one wall. This is a a great favorite for clients with demanding tastes. A mix of cuisines produces gnocchi in imported Italian blue cheese sauce, sautéed sea cucumber with leg of duck, jellyfish and fillet steak in pepper sauce. Crustacea and other seafood are also available.

◯ Daily 9am–11pm
🍴 L 48,000d, D 60,000d, Wine 120,000d

HO CHI MINH CITY

In this cosmopolitan city everything is available, from the best of Hanoi food to the rarest of southern food, and every conceivable international cuisine. As a consequence of its relative youth and the fact that this prosperous port city has always been open to outside influence, there is no specifically local tradition, though the large Chinese population makes this the best place to try a variety of different kinds of noodles. District 5 is Chinatown and many restaurants here and in the city center offer a wide range of specialties. Other Asian food abounds in Saigon, including Japanese, Korean and Indian, a reflection of patterns of trade past and present. Thai influence is prevalent in *tom yam* (spicy soup). European dishes are well provided with vegetables from temperate Dalat throughout the year; the French baguette is ubiquitous, ice cream is popular and there is a thriving café society. Sizzling steak and fries is a common dish in the local hostelries. To make life easier for the chopstick-wielder, beef is sometimes diced before cooking to produce *bo luc lac*. Pham Ngu Lao, the backpacker area, is bursting with low-cost restaurants, many of which are just as good as the more expensive places elsewhere. Streetside stands are also well worth investigating; their staples are *pho* (rice-noodle soup), *bánh xeo* (savory pancakes), *cha giò* (spring rolls) and *banh mi pate* (baguettes stuffed with pâté and salad). The Ben Thanh night market on the side streets around Ben Thanh is a major draw for Vietnamese and overseas visitors. A good range of food stands set up at dusk here and motor traffic is forbidden.

PRICES AND SYMBOLS

The restaurants are listed alphabetically (excluding Le, La, Il and The). The prices given are for a two-course lunch (L) and a three-course dinner (D) for one person, without drinks. The wine price is for the least expensive bottle.

For a key to the symbols, ▷ 2.

ASHOKA

17/10 Le Thanh Ton Street, District 1
Tel 08-8231372

This beacon of Indian cuisine has an extensive menu of delicious food. Its set lunch (65,000d for vegetarians, 85,000d for meat eaters) lists 11 options, with another extraordinary 19 curry dishes. Highlights in the low-lit, comfortably air-conditioned restaurant are mutton shami kebab, prawn vindaloo and *kadhai* fish—barbecued chunks of fresh fish cooked in a *kadhai* (a traditional Indian-style wok) with Peshwari

SPECIAL

AN VIEN

178A Hai Ba Trung Street, District 3
Tel 08-8243877

Go down an alley to this intimate three-floor restaurant, which serves the most fragrant rice in Vietnam. Each room is small and furnished in Vietnamese style. The food is excellent, the service attentive and the interior rich with carpets, tasseled lampshades, silk-embroidered cushions and menus, bowls of lilies and pink napkins arranged in lotus-leaf style. The *banh xeo*, crispy fried squid, combination *"mam"* special (pickled fish, pork and duck eggs) and steamed eel in claypot with coconut milk are recommended. A durian- and bean-sweetened porridge and a very good coconut caramel are on the dessert menu.
🕐 Daily 11–11
🍴 L 80,000d, D 95,000d, Wine from 250,000d

ground spices, and sautéed with onion and tomatoes. Try the Coke with ice cream float for dessert.
🕐 Daily 11.30–2.15, 5–10.30
🍴 L 45,000d, D 65,000d, Wine from 280,000d

AU LAC DO BRAZIL

238 Pasteur Street, District 3
Tel 08-8207157

A top Brazilian steak restaurant in an attractive, colonial-style

building where the food is delivered direct from the skewer to your plate in a nightly all-you-can-eat *Rodizio*. Flash a small token if you don't want your plate to be piled high; otherwise your protests are ignored. As the night wears on and more alcohol is consumed, the whole experience becomes more confusing and entertaining. Downstairs, try the national Brazilian cocktail, *caipirinha*, served up by the most welcoming staff.
🕐 Daily 9am–11pm
🍴 L 80,000d, D 240,000d, Wine from 172,000d

AU PARC

23 Han Tuyen Street, District 1
Tel 08-8292772

Facing onto the park in front of the old Presidential Palace, this attractive, European-style café serves light meals on mosaic-covered tables over two floors. Its strawberry crumble and ice cream should not be resisted. Other temptations include green mango salad with tomatoes, onions, basil, squid and shrimp, and falafel with tahini sauce. There are 27 sandwich options, from the basic BLT to baked brie with caramelized onions and green apple, and there is a children's menu. A good Sunday brunch is served between 11am and 3.30pm for 150,000d per person.
🕐 Mon–Sat 7am–9.30pm, Sun 8–3.30
🍴 L 90,000d, D 180,000d, Wine from 172,000

AU MANOIR DE KHAI

251 Dien Bien Phu Street, District 3
Tel 08-9303394
Fax 08-9330583

The eponymous Mr Khai, known for his silk empire (▷ 24), has added this French restaurant to his substantial business portfolio. It is set in an elegantly restored villa and garden on which no expense has been spared. Dine among art-works, gilded mirrors and flowers, or alfresco by candle-light, and take your pick from a sublime menu that includes fish soup lightly perfumed with saffron, gratinated baby scallop and crabs with herb cream, lamb's sweetbread salad with duck's liver, salmon steak roasted with tarragon and white cham-pagne butter sauce and nougatine ice cream and raspberry sauce.

Ⓒ Daily 11–1.30, 6–9.30
Ⓦ L 400,000d, D 560,000d, Wine from 315,000d

AUGUSTIN

10 Nguyen Thiep Street, District 1
Tel 08-8292941

Prices are reasonable at this small and central restaurant for some of the best and most straightforward French cooking in Saigon. Tables are quite closely packed together, and there is a congenial atmos-phere. Try the excellent gratinée onion soup, baked clams, vibrant hot goat's cheese salad and rack of lamb roasted with garlic butter. Melting Armagnac chocolate cake served with crème anglaise makes a magnificent conclusion.

Ⓒ Mon–Sat 11.30–2, 6–10.30
Ⓦ L 100,000d, D 140,000d, Wine from 250,000d

BI BI

8A/8D Thai Van Lung Street, District 1
Tel 08-8295783

A relaxed, brightly decorated and informal restaurant, popu-lar with diplomats and bankers and serving excellent French food. Highly recommended are the incomparable Chateaubriand (400,000d for two) and the tiger shrimp with parsley and cognac. The set lunch of three courses plus coffee at 140,000d is good value. Daily specials are listed in French; the owner also speaks English.

Ⓒ Daily 11.30–2, 5.30–10
Ⓦ L 150,000d, D 180,000d, Wine from 260,000d

BLUE GINGER

Saigon Times Club
37 Nam Ky Khoi Nghia Street, District 1
Tel 08-8298676

Expect a feast at this stylish, welcoming and comfortable restaurant, which has more than 100 dishes on its menu. This romp through the versatile Vietnamese diet includes deep-fried calamari and plum sauce, grilled whole blue crab, grilled blood clam, and classic Hanoi fish with fresh dill and turmeric (*cha ca thang long*). Dine indoors in the cellar-like restaurant or outdoors in a small courtyard, served with courtesy by the helpful staff.

Ⓒ Daily 7–2, 5–10
Ⓦ L 60,000d, D 70,000d, Wine from 320,000d

LE BORDEAUX

F7–F8 D2 Street
Cu Xa Van Thanh Bac
Binh Thanh District
Tel 08-8999831

Unfortunately, Le Bordeaux is in rather an awkward location, but if you can find it you are in for a real treat. This restaurant has a stylish look, a warm atmosphere and a welcoming owner. It receives the highest accolades for its French dishes, which cover a wonderful range of traditional cooking and use seasonal ingredients to delight any connoisseur.

Ⓒ Tue–Sat 11.45–1.30, 6.45–9.30
Ⓦ L 220,000d, D 260,000d, Wine from 320,000d

BRODARD

131 Dong Khoi Street, District 1
Tel 08-8223966

This long-standing interna-tional restaurant with a conventional menu is in the heart of town and operates as a bar, café and restaurant. Its wood-paneled interior, large windows and beautiful potted palms create a relaxed and airy feel that attracts an expa-triate and Vietnamese clientele. Both local and international tastes are accom-modated with salads, pasta, pizzas, ribs and seafood (sole rolls—sautéed fillet of sole stuffed with salmon).

Ⓒ Daily 6.30am–11pm
Ⓦ L 128,000d, D 144,000d, Wine from 240,000d

CAFÉ LATIN

19–21 Dong Du Street, District 1
Tel 08-8226363

There's an international feel to the menu of this second-story restaurant, which offers daily specials, sandwiches, bagels and main meals. From its galaxy of intriguing dishes try beer-battered barramundi and tartar sauce, roasted pumpkin, roasted capsicum, feta, endive, olive tapenade, Parmesan toasted wrap, tapenade-crusted lamb cutlets or warm eggplant (aubergine) salad and hot feta dressing. All this delicious food can be rounded off with a selection of desserts such as miniature lime curd tart, mango, coconut praline and vanilla ice cream, or sticky date pudding with toffee sauce and ice cream.

Ⓒ Daily 9am–midnight
Ⓦ L 80,000d, D 110,000d, Wine from 210,000d

LA CASA LATINA

11 Thai Van Lung Street, District 1
Tel 08-8223240

The lively atmosphere of this mixture of restaurant and bar makes it a fun place to relax and enjoy delicious, good-value Mediterranean flavors. There is a wide range of tasty fish dishes and an impressive dessert list that includes cardamom chocolate cream with pistachio sauce and lemon sorbet and vodka. With its Latino sounds, cocktails, happy hour between 7pm and 8pm and Cuban cigars, this is a prime central venue.

Ⓒ Daily 10–3, 5–12
Ⓦ L 75,000d, D 100,000d, Wine from 230,000d

CAMARGUE

16 Cao Ba Quat Street, District 1
Tel 08-8243148
Fax 08-8232828

Camargue is one of Saigon's longest standing restaurants and has remained one of the most successful places in town. Housed in a large French villa with an upstairs open-air terrace and stylishly decorated tables, it serves consistently excellent food from an international menu with a strong French influence. Professional waitstaff provide diners with appetizers that verge on the unusual—green lentil cappuccino served with crunchy duck and pistachio dumplings, or gently sautéed scallops with a rum butter sauce. The grilled and sliced duck breast, *pommes sarladaises* and béarnaise sauce perfumed with raspberry vinegar, followed by white chocolate parfait with fresh raspberries and an almond pastry, are recommended.
Ⓒ Daily 9–4, 6–11
Ⓦ L 175,000d, D 210,000d, Wine from 300,000d

CAY BO DE

175/6 Pham Ngu Lao Street, District 1
Tel 08-8371910
This is Saigon's most popular vegetarian eatery. Set in the heart of backpacker land, it serves very good food at amazing prices. The Mexican pancake, vegetable curry, rice in coconut and braised mushrooms are classics. There's also a wide choice of soups and stir-fried vegetable dishes. It is a struggle to spend 30,000d per head.
Ⓒ Daily 7am–11pm
Ⓦ L 16,000d, D 24,000d

CHAO THAI

16 Thai Van Lung Street
District 1
Tel 08-8241457
Chao Thai is widely regarded as the best Thai restaurant in town. The interior design is classic Thai, fully complementing the food. The dining area is small but attractive, and service is efficient. Among the delights are shrimp cakes with plum sauce, deep-fried mullet with mango salad topping and roasted duck curry. A delivery service is available.
Ⓒ Daily 11–2, 6–10.30
Ⓦ L 80,000d, D 95,000d, Wine from 316,000d

CIAO CAFÉ

72 Nguyen Hue Street, District 1
Tel 08-8251203
This boldly designed, diner-style café is hard to miss, with its exterior painted in large, brown polka dots, and, not surprisingly, it is a popular choice as a rendezvous spot. Inside, the eclectic decoration bombards the eye. Stained-glass fruit designs adorn the windows, and a small fish tank sits on the counter. The café is usually busy with customers seeking its sandwiches, tasty burgers, spaghetti and pizzas. Coffee and ice cream are available in abundance, and there is also a children's menu.
Ⓒ Daily 7am–11.30pm
Ⓦ L 35,000d, D 45,000d

COM NIEU SAIGON

6C Tu Xuong Street, District 3
Tel 08-9326388
The theatrics that accompany the serving of the specialty baked rice have earned this informal restaurant something of a reputation. One waiter smashes the earthenware pot before tossing the contents across the room to his nimble-fingered colleague standing by the table. The staff are well trained in this startling skill, and will safely deliver to your table a good selection of soups and salads. Steamed clams with onion and ginger and the kidney are recommended. Deep-fried cow's womb and duck's feet are more challenging additions to a vast menu.
Ⓒ Daily 9am–10pm
Ⓦ L 25,000d, D 30,000d

GREEN LEAF CAFÉ

Bong Sen Hotel
117–123 Dong Khoi Street, District 1
Tel 08-8291516, ext 8029
Beautiful heliconia plants and plantation-style chairs in deep forest-green and cream furnish this air-conditioned café. Breakfast, soups, sandwiches, baguettes and cakes are served for customers on the run. Those with more time should try the coconut shrimp—shrimp dipped in beer, battered and rolled in coconut and then deep-fried and served with orange marmalade sauce and french fries. Pasta, sausage and mashed potatoes, and Mexican burritos also form part of the eclectic menu.
Ⓒ Daily 7am–11pm
Ⓦ L 45,000d, D 60,000d, Wine from 220,000d

HOANG YEN

7 Ngo Duc Ke Street, District 1
Tel 08-8231101
The friendly staff at this plain and unfussy restaurant serve absolutely fabulous Vietnamese dishes, as the throngs of local lunchtime customers testify. Soups and chicken dishes are ravishing. For the more daring visitors there is sautéed cow's womb with green chili or buttered frogs' legs. Your meal is accompanied by loud Vietnamese music. No wine.
Ⓒ Daily 10am–10pm
Ⓦ L 30,000d, D 45,000d

HOA VIEN

28 bis Mac Dinh Chi Street, District 1
Tel 08-8290585
Fax 08-8226043
Saigon's first microbrewery has set up shop in an amazing, vast Czech *bierkeller*. The food here has improved dramatically in recent years and is very useful for soaking up the alcohol. Sitting among the huge, glistening, copper tanks, you can tuck into smoked chicken drumsticks, beer garden sausages, grilled salmon with bacon, Czech-style fried cheese, steamed goat's ribs with beer, Australian steak with young pepper or fried squid with tempura.
Ⓒ Daily 9am–11pm
Ⓦ L 75,000d, D 90,000d, Wine from 180,000d

LA FOURCHETTE
9 Ngo Duc Ke Street, District 1
Tel 08-8298143

French posters and prints decorate this excellent and authentic little French bistro, where there's a warm welcome and a range of well-prepared dishes in generous portions at fair prices. The glorious selection of meals includes clams with butter, garlic and parsley, beef tenderloin from Australia, local beef with a myriad of sauce options (the local steak is as tender as any import) and fried squid with cognac.

Daily 11.30–2.30, 6.30–10
L 100,000d, D 120,000d, Wine from 220,000d

HOI AN
11 Le Thanh Ton Street, District 1
Tel 08-8237694

Hoi An is housed in a beautiful replica of a traditional Hoi An house—a theme repeated in the interior decoration and in the staff uniforms. This is a sister (and almost neighboring) restaurant of Mandarin (▷ 227) and meets the same exacting standards. The menu has a wide and varied selection of dishes, such as tiny rice custards with crumbled shrimp, delicious sautéed lobster in tamarind sauce, grilled beef with lemon grass and roasted duck with pepper sauce. The Discovery menu includes six courses for 320,000d.

Daily 5.30–11pm
D 140,000d, Wine from 360,000d

HUONG LAI
38 Ly Tu Trong Street, District 1
Tel 08-8226814

Former street children operate this interesting little restaurant behind the City Hall, and well-executed dishes are served here. Visitors sit in a small, upstairs, terra-cotta-tiled room surrounded by exposed brick work, Chinese textile paintings and batik wall hangings. The chef's repertoire encompasses lotus stem and shrimp salad, mouthwatering sautéed shrimp with coconut sauce, braised spare ribs and a host of other tantalizing items. The set lunch meal of six

dishes for two at 160,000d is good value.

Daily 11.50–2.10, 6–9.15
L 45,000d, D 60,000d, Wine from 89,000d

INDIAN CURRY-RICE RESTAURANT
66 Dong Du Street, District 1
Tel 08-8232159

Enter the compound of the green and white downtown mosque and walk to the right and around the back to reach this small, cafeteria-like restaurant. The aroma will greet you before you see the superb spread of vegetarian and meat curries and stuffed bread—pots, pans and stoves are all on public view. A curry extravaganza of chicken, fish, goat, beef, squid, shrimp and crab served with yellow rice by the very friendly staff provides a filling meal.

Daily 10–8
L and D 30,000d

INDOCHINE
32 Pham Ngoc Thach Street, District 3
Tel 08-8239256

An unabashedly long menu covering just about all Vietnamese specialties is found at this themed restaurant with staff dressed in costume and menus in the shape of conical hats. Enjoy house specialties of baby clams in white wine and grilled duck breast with orange or pepper sauce. Well-chosen salads such as chicken and banana-flower salad and grapefruit salad with shrimp and pork can be followed by steamed and fried crustacea and fish; the squid is especially succulent. Staff are attentive and service is efficient.

Daily 11.30–2, 5.30–10
L 110,000d, D 120,000d, Wine from 272,000d

LE JARDIN
31 Thai Van Lung Street, District 1
Tel 08-8258465

European visitors flock to this excellent little French restaurant, which is part of the French Cultural Institute, with a small, shaded garden and fairly priced food. Particularly good options include the beef skewers with cumin seeds and the apple crumble and ice cream. On your second visit opt for the red mullet with aniseed

sauce or moussaka followed by profiteroles.

Daily 11–2, 5–9.30
L 55,000d, D 75,000d, Wine from 192,000d

JAVA
38–42 Dong Du Street, District 1
Tel 08-8230187

Rich smoothies such as the Fountain of Youth (a strawberry and cherry concoction), Watermelon Wavelength and Big Bold Banana are mixed for around 36,000d each in the inviting environment of this glass-fronted café. Rattan furniture, sofas and low-hung camouflage-print lamps make this a popular spot for expatriates. Java is a useful stop for breakfast or brunch, serving snacks such as bagels with cream cheese and smoked salmon and muffins.

Daily 7.30am–11.30pm
L40,000d, D 64,000d

LEMONGRASS
4 Nguyen Thiep Street, District 1
Tel 08-8220496

Enjoy the full gastronomic experience at this pleasantly decorated, downtown restaurant, which is a hit with visitors owing to its convenient central location. Attractively served food includes dishes such as deep-fried calamari served with plum sauce and baked seafood with glass noodles in a clay pot. Several vegetarian options are available (braised tofu, black mushrooms and snow peas), but choose carefully: The tofu dishes can be a bit bland.

Daily 11–2, 5–10
L 55,000d, D 70,000d, Wine from 180,000d

LUONG SON (BO TUNG XEO)
31 Ly Tu Trong Street, District 1
Tel 08-8251330

Noisy, smoky, chaotic and usually packed, this large restaurant serves some of the tastiest food in Vietnam. Its specialty is *bo tung xeo* (sliced beef barbecued at the table and served with mustard sauce), whose flavors and aromas are unforgettable. Beef, barbecued squid and other delicacies are superb. There's also the opportunity to sample unusual dishes such as deep fried scorpion, porcupine, fried cricket, steamed chicken with sea-leech, grilled raw oyster with cheese, coconut worm and cockerel's testicles.

◎ Daily 9am–10pm
🍷 L 45,000d, D 55,000d, Wine from 120,000d

MA MO BBQ
19 Le Thanh Ton Street, District 1
Tel 09-3955889 (cellphone)
This very informal, all-expense-spared Korean barbecue restaurant opens onto the sidewalk on the corner with Thai Van Lung Street. Tables are made of old oil drums—as they were in Korea in the 1950s and 1960s—and the dining area is brightly lit. Beef soup is served at lunchtime, and in the evening (from 5pm) barbecued pork is grilled at the table (160,000d per kg). Excellent *kimchi* (pickled vegetables) and Korean rice wine are also served.

◎ Daily 7am–10pm
🍷 L 32,000d, D 56,000d

MANDARIN
11A Ngo Van Nam Street, District 1
Tel 08-8229783
One of the finest Vietnamese restaurants in Saigon serves up a mix of exquisite flavors from across the country in an elegant setting enhanced by richly colored silk tablecloths. The delicious deep-fried crab spring rolls are served on a bed of artfully carved carrot flowers. To follow, the mullet fish in a clay pot is especially good. Set meals give good value: Business lunches are 180,000d for three courses, and a healthy set lunch is 250,000d. Service is slightly intrusive, but fortunately the anodyne background music is only just audible.

◎ Daily 11.30–2, 5.30–10
🍷 L 136,000d, D 172,000d, Wine from 336,000d

MARINE CLUB
17A4 Le Thanh Ton Street, District 1
Tel 08-8292249
This nautical-themed restaurant is a long-standing feature of the HCMC culinary scene and retains its popularity thanks to its attentive staff and owner. The menu is mostly French but also includes pizzas from the wood oven—probably the best in Saigon (a delivery service is

NAM PHAN
64 Le Thanh Ton Street, District 1
Tel 08-8292757
nam-phan@hcm.vnn.vn
Mr Khai of Khaisilk fame (▷ 24) certainly knows how to bring out the best in old buildings. Here, again, he has worked his magic and created a stunning setting. Dine indoors in unadulterated luxury—white orchids creatively arranged, food served on silver lacquer trays, grey suede chairs, imitation bas-reliefs of Champa art—or outside, where white, wrought-iron furniture is set under umbrellas in the plant-filled garden. Described by the owners as "high-end," the individual dishes are delicious, though the menu is oddly put together and makes it rather difficult to construct a full meal. The mix includes young pork rib with fermented galangal, stuffed squid with ground meat and tomato soup, trademark triangle spring rolls and banana cake with coconut cream.

◎ Daily 11–3, 5–11
🍷 L 240,000d, D 290,000d, Wine from 410,000d

also available). Piano music and sizzling cocktails add to the atmosphere and make this a popular place with young expatriates. Jazz musicians play once a month.

◎ Mon–Sat 11–2, 6–11, Sun 6–11
🍷 L 155,000d, D 245,000d, Wine from 315,000d

NINETEEN
Caravelle Hotel
19 Lam Son Square, District 1
Tel 08-8234999
This lavish incarnation of what was formerly the acclaimed

Port Orient restaurant is furnished with ostrich-leather seating and imported Cararra marble. It serves what is regarded by many locals as the best buffet in town. There's sushi, Chinese *dim sum,* plenty of cheeses and an array of delicious puddings. Wine, which is included in the price, flows freely.

◎ Daily 7am–10pm
🍷 L 352,000d, D 416,000d

PACIFIC
15 Le Thanh Ton Street, District 1
Tel 08-8256802
This central and excellent *bia hoi*, which is packed with locals and visitors every night, deserves special mention for its unusual service and prices. Beer, which comes in pint glasses and costs next to nothing (8,000d a pint), is set on the table just as you sit down. A reasonable range of simple, inexpensive dishes—deer, beef, squid and french fries, barbecued goat and stew with snakehead fish—is served by the amiable and welcoming waiters.

◎ Daily 9am–10pm
🍷 L 36,000d, D 48,000d

PHO
37 Dong Khoi Street, District 1
Tel 08-8296415
Eating in this Japanese-run *pho* shop in the heart of a shopping street is not unlike eating in a household dining room. It is attractively and eccentrically furnished with heavy wooden tables and chairs and has an interesting personal collection of pictures and ornaments on display. Each bowl of *pho* is carefully served with all the requisite accompaniments to this energizing meal—mint, lemon, bean sprouts, chilies and chopped chives. Variations on a theme come in the form of shrimp and chicken. The Latin jazz sounds are a little incongruous.

◎ Daily 7am–midnight
🍷 L 18,000d, D 18,000–30,000d

PHO HOA PASTEUR
260C Pasteur Street, District 3
Tel 08-8297943
Pho Hoa Pasteur is probably the best known of all *pho* restaurants, and is packed with customers and dizzying

EATING

aromas. The *pho* is good but costs more than average; it comes in 10 options and is served inside the small restaurant, where tables are tightly arranged. Chinese bread and wedding cake *(banh xu xe)* provide the only alternatives in this specialist restaurant.

🕐 Daily 6am–midnight

🍴 L 20,000d, D 22,000d

QUCINA

7 Lam Son Square, District 1
Tel 08-8246325

Unusual, lacquered art by New York artist Sylvia Hommert adorns this smart and chic Italian restaurant in the basement of the Opera House. Its cool white lines, slate floor tiles, tiny alcoves for romantic dining and classical music all exude stylishness. Some highlights on the menu are *carpaccio e ruccola*, thinly sliced raw tenderloin, shaved Parmesan, arugula (rocket) and olive oil; *tonno al burro nero*, grilled tuna in black butter; and *tronchetto* and rolled chocolate cake with vanilla cream.

🕐 Mon–Sat 6–11

🍴 L 150,000d, D 180,000d, Wine from 350,000d

RESTAURANT 13

13 Ngo Duc Ke Street, District 1
Tel 08-8239314

Locals, expatriates and travelers rate this very informal restaurant a hit. It serves fresh, well-cooked Vietnamese dishes such as chicken in lemon grass (no skin, no bone)—a great favorite—and beef *(bo luc lac)* that melts in the mouth. If you have a strong stomach, other dishes from the vast menu, which does not list prices, are steamed fallopian tube with onion, dough-wrapped crayfish, and sautéed heart and liver with garlic. Vegetarians, soup-lovers and squid-eaters have their own options too. Wine is not served.

🕐 Daily 6am–11pm

🍴 L 50,000d, D 60,000d

SANTA LUCIA

14 Nguyen Hue Boulevard, District 1
Tel 08-8226562

This popular downtown Italian restaurant is in a convenient, spot on the main boulevard. Dishes include pancakes filled with ricotta and spinach and

TEMPLE CLUB

29–31 Ton That Thiep Street, District 1
Tel 08-8299244

You can catch an intriguing and evocative glimpse of colonial living in this beautifully furnished club and restaurant, open to non-members. Laid out in French colonial style, it exudes understated chic, with carved doorways, exposed brickwork, purple silk lanterns in the bar area and stunning wooden screens. The food is superb: Examples are Hué-style spring rolls, deep-fried soft-shell crab, grilled tiger shrimp and simmered crab in coconut juice. Bizarrely, you can also order fish and chips. The chocolate whiskey mousse is sinful. It's advisable to reserve a table in advance.

🕐 Daily 11am–midnight (L 11–2, D 5.30–10.30)

🍴 L 100,000d, D 125,000d, Wine from 240,000d

baked in béchamel sauce, and *carpaccio de vitello*—thin slices of raw veal served with olive oil, garlic and Parmesan cheese. Most pasta-based meals are served in large portions, but the tasty ravioli dishes are not too big. Piped opera music completes the effect.

🕐 Daily 9.30am–11pm

🍴 L 80,000d, D 95,000d, Wine from 370,000d

TIB

187 Hai Ba Trung Street, District 3
Tel 08-8297242

Tib is a little pocket of Hué in Saigon, furnished in the dark wood so favored by that city. The extensive menu has a good selection of Hué specialties, including such standout dishes as crumbled shrimp wrapped with fresh rice paper and stir-fried vermicelli with crab. The atmosphere is convivial and the restaurant, which is down an alley off the main road, is popular with Vietnamese families. The incredible wine stock is a bonus.

🕐 Daily 11–10

🍴 L 50,000d, D 60,000d, Wine from 190,000d

UNDERGROUND

69 Dong Khoi Street, District 1
Tel 08-8299079
www.elephantguide.com/underground
The symbol employed by London's underground system is displayed by this bar, which, steeped in Stygian gloom, seems an unlikely place to find some of Saigon's best food. The bar is popular with expatriates and vistors to the city, and the menu spans the full Mediterranean–Mexican spectrum and is superb. Portions are gigantic and prices very reasonable for a flavorsome pizza or Mexican burger with chili con carne, guacamole and sour cream. Lunchtime specials are excellent value (house specialties are sausage and mashed potatoes and lamb kebab), and there is a vast array of cocktails. Eat inside the cavernous bar or outdoors at the entrance under umbrellas.

🕐 Daily 9am–midnight

🍴 L 80,000d, D 112,000d, Wine from 180,000d

WILD HORSE SALOON

8A1/2D1 Thai Van Lung Street, District 1
Tel 08-8251901
www.elephantguide.com/wildhorse
Unmissable with its monumental beer-barrel facade, this Tex-Mex restaurant is a popular spot for a Sunday roast dinner. Dine at solid wood tables on pasta, burgers, Mexican meatballs, crab cakes or Texas-style rack of lamb. The Sunday roast of pork, chicken, beef or lamb is served with boiled vegetables, roast potatoes, gravy, stuffing, crackling and applesauce. A separate bar area, entered through a massive, cut-out beer barrel, shows sports on TV. There is also live music.

🕐 Daily 10.15–2, 4.30–12

🍴 L80,000d, D 96,000d, Wine from 240,000d

EATING

THE SOUTH

Food in the south is more diverse and much more abundant than in the north, with a greater variety in cooking styles and sweeter flavors. The most commonly used ingredient in southern dishes is fish, and in the Mekong Delta coconut milk imparts a distinctive taste to many dishes—such as mild Vietnamese curry, normally eaten with bread in this region, rather than with rice. Some southern specialties are *banh xeo* (a delicious sizzling pancake; the southern equivalent of *banh khoai* in Hué), *canh chua* (sour soup with a tomato and fish base), *ca kho to* (braised fish in a clay pot) and *hu tiu*, another type of noodle. The famous Vietnamese spring rolls may be served one of two ways. "Fresh" *(bi cuon)* spring rolls consist of cooked pork or shrimp wrapped with lettuce and other leaves in rice paper and eaten cold. The more common *cha gio* are small, deep-fried spring rolls preferably eaten piping-hot. As the rice basket of Vietnam, the Mekong Delta uses rice as its staple, rather than noodles. The quality of the crop has improved, and Vietnam now produces types of fragrant rice previously available only from Thailand. A popular southern variant is *com tam*—broken rice—which is inexpensive and often served freshly steamed with roast pork *(heo quay)* for lunch or even breakfast. The south is also where most tropical fruits are grown, and almost all meals here are rounded off with pineapple, mango, papaya, mangosteen or banana.

SPECIAL IN CAN THO

NAM BO
50 Hai Ba Trung Street
Can Tho
Tel 071-823908
Custard-yellow and brown awnings identify this delightful French house on a street corner, which provides the best (and most popular with visitors) setting for eating in Can Tho town. The balcony seating area overlooks the market clutter and riverside promenade, and the dishes are a mixture of Vietnamese and French cooking. Among the best items are pumpkin-flower soup, a tasty fried calamari in tamarind sauce, sautéed frogs' legs with mushrooms and shrimp with mango sauce. The Can Tho fried spring rolls are a must, and are served with a beautifully carved carrot and tomato decoration. Snake meat, Western dishes for children and vegetarian options are all available.

🕐 Daily 6am–11pm
🍴 L 36,000d, D 48,000d, Wine from 100,000d

PRICES AND SYMBOLS

The restaurants are listed alphabetically (excluding Le, La, Il and The). The prices given are for a two-course lunch (L) and a three-course dinner (D) for one person, without drinks. The wine price is for the least expensive bottle.

For a key to the symbols, ▷ 2.

CAN THO

BELLEVUE RESTAURANT
Golf Can Tho Hotel
2 Hai Ba Trung Street
Can Tho
Tel 071-812210
Set on the hotel's 11th story, the tiny Bellevue is more attractive and has a more appetizing menu than its sister, The Golf (▷ below). There are excellent views from a small, external balcony along a large stretch of the river. The French menu includes pumpkin soup with cream among the starters, main courses such as stuffed duck's leg with pineapple, and a choice of desserts such as orange cream.
🕐 Daily 7am–10pm
🍴 L 88,000d, D 104,000d, Wine from 160,000d

THE GOLF RESTAURANT
Golf Can Tho Hotel
2 Hai Ba Trung Street
Can Tho
Tel 071-812210
This large and rather anonymous but friendly restaurant with high ceilings serves a mainly conventional Vietnamese menu of fried squid salad, steamed pigeon with lotus beans and steamed duck with sautéed orange, as well as spaghetti and other pasta dishes and expensive house sandwiches.
🕐 Daily 6am–11pm
🍴 L 60,000d, D70,000d, Wine from 160,000d

RESTAURANT HOANG CUNG
Saigon Can Tho
55 Phan Dinh Phung Street
Can Tho
Tel 071-825831
Though large and a little impersonal, the Hoang Cung provides good-value meals. The menu combines straight-forward dishes, such as baked onion soup and breaded pork chops with mashed potatoes, with the more unusual—shark's fin and crab-meat soup, fish bladder and crab-meat soup and deep-fried eel. The dessert menu is limited to fruit.
🕐 Daily 6am–11pm
🍴 L 40,000d, D 50,000d, Wine from 285,000d

SPICES RESTAURANT
Victoria Can Tho
Cai Khe Ward
Can Tho
Tel 071-810111
www.victoriahotels-asia.com
A sampan stuffed with flowers and jars of goodies is the focal point of this restaurant, whose Vietnamese and French menus include a market salad with fresh herbs and raspberry dressing, duck filet mignon lacquered with soya caramel and a light homemade shrimp

ravioli with a dash of basil and a sprinkling of secret spices. The double menu can be topped off with pumpkin tarte tatin with pistachio sauce and cashew-nut ice cream, or hot chocolate cake and coconut ice cream. Terrace dining is also possible.

🕒 Daily 6am–10pm (B 6–10, L 12–2, D 7–9.30)
🍴 Vietnamese menu L 96,000d, D 136,000d; French menu L 150,000d, D 196,000d; Wine from 288,000d

HA TIEN
HAI VAN
4 Tran Hau Street
Ha Tien
Tel 077-850344
Open-fronted, bright and airy, this popular café on the main riverfront road serves a reasonable selection of Chinese, Vietnamese and international cuisine. All the traditional Vietnamese dishes are available here, with additions such as fried eel with chili and lemon grass and sweet and sour lobster ribs with rice. Those who prefer Western fare can order omelettes with bread and butter.
🕒 Daily 6am–11pm
🍴 L 30,000d, D 45,000d

TRUNG NGUYEN CAFÉ
Nguyen Van Hai Street
Ha Tien
You can sit at this small, stilted wooden café overlooking the river and the pontoon bridge, surrounded by pink bougainvillea, and watch the world go by, refreshed by a light river breeze. If you're not afraid of experimenting with new tastes, try the weasel coffee. Beer is also sold here.
🕒 Daily 7am–9pm
🍴 L 16,000d, D 24,000d

SPECIAL IN CHAU DOC
LA BASSAC
Victoria Chau Doc
32 Le Loi Street
Chau Doc
Tel 076-865010
www.victoriahotels-asia.com

The extravagant French and Vietnamese menus at this riverside restaurant outstrip the setting, which has the air of a conservatory and is pervaded by cheesy instrumental love tunes. Ignoring this, tuck into a delicious meal of duck liver parfait with Cumberland sauce and melba toast, followed by rack of lamb coated in Mekong herbs, sweet-potato purée and pork wine reduction, or spaghetti with flambéed shrimp in vodka paprika sauce. Leave room for the sublime frozen strawberry yogurt in meringue on an orange Grand Marnier sauce. Alternatively, try the shrimp paste on sugar-cane, or the eel and banana-blossom fondue. The menu includes low-fat and low-calorie options, indicated by a heart symbol.

🕒 Daily 6am–10pm 🍴 French menu L 120,000d, D 150,000d; Vietnamese menu L 85,000d, D 105,000d; Wine from 300,000d

HON CHONG PENINSULA
TAN PHAT RESTAURANT
Binh An
This restaurant on the waterfront of Hon Chong Peninsula's main town serves excellent seafood dishes, including succulent squid cooked in ginger. It's a real treat to sit out under the moonlight next to the dock, where fishing boats are moored, and to eat while listening to water lapping against wet wood, chattering families on board and the tinny sounds of fishing accessories and boats knocking each other in the evening tide.
🕒 Daily 7am–9pm
🍴 L 25,000d, D 35,000d

MY THO
QUAN THU 46
15 Trung Trac Street
My Tho
Tel 073-874696
A small, local restaurant on the main riverfront street, around the corner from the Chuong Duong hotel. The Quan Thu 46 specializes in *banh xeo*, divine savory pancakes filled with bean sprouts, mushrooms and prawns. It also serves crab claws fried with rice flour. Look out for the local specialty, *hu tieu my tho*—a spicy soup of vermicelli, sliced pork, dried shrimps and fresh herbs.
🕒 Daily 6am–9pm
🍴 L 15,000d, D 30,000d

PHU QUOC
THANG LOI RESTAURANT
Ong Lang Beach
Phu Quoc
Tel 077-985002
www.phu-quoc.de
You can sit among jack fruit and mango trees at this breezy, seaside restaurant (part of the Thang Loi Resort), and dine on German or Vietnamese food or choose from a huge range of vegetarian dishes. The menu includes Wiener schnitzel—a rarity in Vietnam—as well as delicious seafood options such as squid in coconut milk sauce. Bananas fried in lemon rum is the perfect end to a tropical island meal.
🕒 Daily 7am–9pm
🍴 L 50,000d, D 60,000d, Wine from 80,000d

EATING

TROPICANA RESORT RESTAURANT

Duong Dong
Phu Quoc
Tel 077-847127
Fax 077-847128
www.tropicanaphuquoc.com

One of the island's best restaurants with a sunny terrace and well-stocked, semi-enclosed bar, allowing relaxed alfresco dining overlooking the sea. From the list of Vietnamese and European favorites, enjoy succulent stir-fried squid, braised shrimps in coconut milk, Italian spaghetti dishes or a range of other alternatives from the set menus. The restaurant, which is next to the pool, also offers covered dining.

🕐 Daily 6.30am–10pm
🍽 L 35,000d, D 45,000d, Wine from 30,000–250,000d

VUNG TAU

CAY BANG

69 Tran Phu Street
Bai Dau Beach
Tel 064-838522

Vung Tau's most celebrated seafood restaurant is well worth the detour of 2 miles (3km) northwest from Bai Truoc and the middle of town. People travel for many miles to eat here, and it is packed on Sundays and busy the rest of the week. Crab, squid and fish specialties are served in a rough and ready setting overlooking the sea.

🕐 Daily 10am–9pm
🍽 L40,000d, D50,000d, no wine

TOM'S

148/2 Quang Phu Street
Tel 064-895798

Run by an Australian called Paul, Tom's serves outstanding food with attentive service and outdoor dining under the shade of trees overlooking the South China Sea. Particularly recommended is the lamb shank and prawns in beer. The bar also serves excellent burgers and beef sandwiches. Tom's also has a book-share service with shelves of good books for swapping.

🕐 Daily 7am–10.30pm
🍽 L 60,000d, D 75,000d, Wine from 100,000d

WHISPERS

15 Nguyen Trai Street
Tel 064-856028
Fax 064-854298

Large portions from an extensive Western menu, including imported beef, are served at this restaurant on the busy central road close to Bai Truoc (Back Beach). The Sunday roast is especially recommended and, with huge portions that are served piping-hot, it is fantastic value for money at just 160,000d.

🕐 Daily 8am–10pm
🍽 L 96,000d, D 120,000d, Wine from 40,000d

Blackened Barramundi at Bobby Chinn's in Hanoi (above); Western visitors enjoy a taste of Vietnam (above left); a dust café in Hanoi (bottom left); cha ca Hanoi, a dish of fish, herbs and spring onions (below)

STAYING IN VIETNAM

Accommodation options in Vietnam range from luxury suites in five-star hotels and spa resorts to small, family hotels (mini-hotels) and homestays with local people. The types of places to stay are limited in range, partly due to the country's as yet underdeveloped tourism industry; but it is possible for accommodations to offer a real insight into Vietnamese life, and to provide an invaluable part of the whole Vietnam experience.

Typical M'nong house; a rural tourist chalet; the Sunflower Hotel, Cat Ba Island; beach huts at Cat Na

RESERVATIONS
Nearly all hotels nowadays have a website or an e-mail address that can be used to make reservations and to check current offers. It's always worth reserving in advance, especially if you plan to tour the country, and it's advisable to follow up an e-mail with a phone call, as e-mail can be unreliable in Vietnam. Reservations are essential during peak times, especially December through March, during busy festivals such as *Tet* (Vietnamese New Year), Christmas, December 31 and Easter.

HOTELS
A star classification is awarded to hotels by the Vietnam National Administration of Tourism (VNAT), and while this may not tally with the requirements expected in other countries, modern hotels in Vietnam are comfortable and well run and, by international standards, offer good value for money. Most staff speak English in the top establishments, but not in less expensive or more remote hotels—although most places employ someone with a smattering of a foreign language.
● If you pay more than US$20 for a room, facilities should include private bathroom (though not necessarily with a bathtub), air-conditioning, minibar, television, telephone and usually a safe.
● Between US$10 and US$20, you can expect the same facilities. Occasionally there may be no minibar, but the room should have a private bathroom, possibly with only a plastic shower-head and with or without a bath/shower cubicle.
● Below US$10 there may be air-conditioning, but you are more likely to have a fan. The room may have a private bathroom, but the shower will not have a shower curtain or shower stall.

● Rooms up to about US$4 a night may have a shower in the washroom—literally a shower attachment on the wall, placed very close to the lavatory and not in its own separate cubicle.
● Sheets, towels and mosquito nets (where necessary) are always provided. Many hotels also have ceiling fans as well as air-conditioning; expensive hotels will have a stand-alone fan. In some inexpensive hotels pillows are made from foam rubber.
● Vietnam is a tropical country. In the listings that follow, swimming pools are outdoors unless otherwise stated.

Hotels at the lower end of the price range usually offer quite good value for money. In particular, private mini-hotels are worth seeking out. These are family-run, and the owners often take a close interest in their guests and are willing to advise on local sightseeing. Staying in mini-hotels is a good way to get to know Vietnamese people. Mid-range and tourist hotels may provide good breakfasts, which are often included in the price. However, many luxury and top-range hotels charge extra for breakfast, and also add value-added tax (VAT) and a service charge. The majority of hotels (apart from private mini-hotels) have restaurants, where standards vary widely. Most hotels have a laundry service; the more expensive the hotel, the greater the charge, and VAT and a service charge will also be added.

BEACH RESORTS
There are luxurious five-star beach resorts in Nha Trang, Mui Ne, Hoi An and Danang, some with spa facilities of very high standards, where you can enjoy excellent service and food in beautiful surroundings. Many resorts have private beaches

or at least a beachfront area, and the vast majority have swimming pools.

BOATS
It's possible to spend a night on a boat in Halong Bay or on the Mekong Delta. Standards on the boats range from fairly luxurious to basic. Most guests reserve their stays through tour operators, but you can make arrangements in Halong City or Cat Ba Island for Halong Bay (▷ 86–89), and through hotels and tour operators in Can Tho for a Mekong River trip (▷ 144–145).

cheaper than hotels for long stays. Some hotels in Ho Chi Minh City rent out their own serviced apartments, many for fairly short periods (a few days), although the shorter the rental period, the higher the price per night. Apartment sizes vary from a cramped single bedroom to a more spacious four bedrooms, and prices generally vary with the facilities available.

CHECKING IN AND OUT
● It is perfectly acceptable to ask to see a room before taking it. This is especially recommended in the event of any confusion over the provision

Sofitel Metropole Hotel, Hanoi; Rex Hotel name plate detail; smart hotel bedroom; Riverside Hotel, Saigon

GUESTHOUSES
Guesthouses differ slightly from hotels and mini-hotels in that guests are made to feel like members of the family. It's quite common for guests to be invited to eat with the owners. For long-staying visitors, the guesthouse is usually a very economical option.

HOMESTAYS
In places such as Sapa and Mai Chau, in the northern uplands, you can stay in an ethnic minority stilt house. In general, this type of accommodation is quite strictly controlled by the Vietnamese authorities, and minority houses are out of bounds in most of the Central Highlands. Don't expect luxuries; the host families have precious few themselves. You are likely to sleep on a rush mat with a hard pillow; bathrooms are basic and consist of a cold shower and a hole-in-the-ground lavatory. Make your reservation through a tour operator or through the local tourist office—do not simply turn up in a village, as you will not be welcome. In the Mekong Delta, you can stay on farms and in orchards. This is an interesting way to see an attractive part of rural Vietnam, and here guests sleep on camp beds and share a Western-style bathroom with hot and cold water.

NATIONAL PARKS
National parks offer a wide range of accommodations, from air-conditioned bungalows to shared dormitory rooms or campgrounds where, sometimes, it is possible to rent a tent.

SERVICED APARTMENTS
Large towns have serviced apartments, which are ideal for people staying in one place for a considerable period of time, as they are generally

of "twin" (two-bed) rooms or "double occupancy" rooms, where two guests may share one bed for no extra charge.
● You will be asked to leave your passport at the reception desk for the duration of your stay. You can reclaim it temporarily in order to go to the bank or to buy an air ticket.
● Check-out time varies from hotel to hotel.
● Hotels are generally willing to store your luggage for you until the end of your check-out day.

PRICING
● Until recently there was a dual charging system in Vietnam, under which foreigners were charged much higher sums for rooms (in US dollars) than locals (who paid in dong). This practice still exists in some remote places, but if you stand your ground you can sometimes get the dong price.
● Many hotels do not charge anything for the cost of local telephone calls, and some offer daily, complimentary bottled water.
● Larger and more expensive hotels add 10 percent VAT and a 5 percent service charge to the price. Smaller hotels quote inclusive prices.
● Credit cards are widely accepted, but there is often a 2 to 4 percent fee for paying this way.
● Although room rates are still sometimes quoted in US dollars, all places accept Vietnamese dong. Tipping is not expected in hotels.

ONLINE RESERVATIONS
www.asiatravel.com/vietnam.html
www.circleofasia.com/bookings/vietnam-hotels.asp
www.discovermekong.com
www.precisionreservations.com/default.aspx
www.traveltovietnam.com
www.vietnam-hotel-reservations.4t.com
www.vietnam-hotels-discount.com

STAYING

HANOI

Hanoi is well served with hotels, ranging from the best and most luxurious in the country to inexpensive mini-hotels. They are clustered mainly around the Old City and well placed for restaurants and cafés. One disadvantage of staying in the Old City is the tendency for rooms to be cramped and noisy; some rooms don't even have windows. Rooms in this area do, however, represent the best value in Hanoi. Some of the most expensive hotels are outside the center, in more residential areas or in the diplomatic and government suburb (Ba Dinh District). In summer, air-conditioning is essential, but in winter, while the weather is still warm, air-conditioning and fans are not needed and some hotels use heaters. Many hotels provide internet access, which is often (but not always) free for guests, and is usually in the reception area. Guests with laptops may be able to plug in via the room telephone socket. An internet access card can be bought for a few US dollars at a post office or internet shop. Generally, there is no shortage of accommodations in Hanoi, and most places can be viewed on the internet and reserved by e-mail.

PRICES AND SYMBOLS

Prices are for a double room for one night. All the hotels listed accept credit cards unless otherwise stated. Note that rates vary widely throughout the year.

For a key to the symbols, ▷ 2.

ANH DAO

37 Ma May Street
Tel 04-8267151
www.camellia-hotels.com
This popular hotel in the northern part of the Old City area (▷ 68–71) has a variety of rooms. The large rooms have big double beds, wooden floors and balconies, but bathrooms are basic. Choose a superior or deluxe room if you can; although the standard rooms have the same facilities, some do not have windows, and bathrooms are small. The unflustered, English-speaking staff are most welcoming and can arrange free transportation to the train station.
US$15–30, including breakfast and taxes
33

DAN CHU

29 Trang Tien Street
Tel 04-8254937
www.danchuhotel.com
A pleasant, friendly, state-run hotel with clean, spacious rooms that are good value for this prime location between the Opera House (▷ 67) and Hoan Kiem Lake (▷ 64–65). The older rooms, overlooking Trang Tien Street, are least expensive; rooms in a new building set well back from the street cost US$15 more, as they are bigger, brighter and quieter,

and some overlook a small courtyard. There is a bar and restaurant, a beauty salon and a massage and sauna room.
US$40–90, including breakfast and taxes
56

DE SYLOIA

17A Tran Hung Dao Street
Tel 04-8245346
www.desyloia.com
This attractive, friendly small hotel is south of Hoan Kiem Lake but within walking distance of the Opera House and the Vietnam History Museum. Facilities include a restaurant (▷ 212), baby-sitting service, satellite and cable TV and in-house movies, minibars, use of a rattan bicycle and a laundry service. The daily set lunch is excellent value. Guests are welcomed with roses and complimentary fruit.
US$80–145, including breakfast and taxes
33 (16 non-smoking)

EDEN

78 Tho Nhuom Street
Tel 04-9423273
eden@hn.vnn.vn
This popular mini-hotel is in a very busy street close to some good restaurants and the Hoa Lo Prison (▷ 63), and has its own restaurant. The less expensive rooms are small and lack light, but discounts offered can halve the price of the room. Some rooms have wedge-shaped baths, and satellite TV; phones and minibars are standard. There is also an internet and e-mail service.
US$30–45, including breakfast and taxes
35

GALAXY

1 Phan Dinh Phung Street
Tel 04-8282888
www.tctgroup.com.vn
The only recommended hotel north of the Old City is this well-run, three-star business hotel built in 1918, facing Hanoi's squat water tower and only a few minutes' walk from the middle of town. Suites are comfortably carpeted and fully equipped, and they have satellite TV and minibars. The bathrooms come with shower and bathtub, and bedside reading lights are provided—a luxury neglected by many expensive hotels.
US$50–60, including breakfast and taxes
60

GUOMAN

83A Ly Thuong Kiet Street
Tel 04-8222800
www.guomanhotels.com
Friendly and efficient staff run this popular business hotel, which occupies an attractive building very close to the Hoa Lo Prison and handy for the train station. Rooms are comfortable and have satellite TV, safe-deposit boxes, minibars and tea- and coffee-making equipment. The fitness gym includes sauna and massage facilities, a health center and a Jacuzzi, and diners can choose from four restaurants. The hotel charges an additional US$10 for a twin room.
US$70–100, including breakfast, excluding taxes
152 (32 non-smoking)

HANOI DAEWOO

360 Kim Ma Street
Tel 04-8315000
www.hanoi-daewoohotel.com

The Hanoi Daewoo is one of Vietnam's most luxurious hotels, a giant of a building with an adjoining apartment complex and office tower. Rooms are plushly decorated and have private bathrooms with marble bathtubs and showers, plus satellite TV, safe-deposit boxes, minibars and internet. Guests can swim in the large pool, browse in the shops and dine in one of four restaurants: the Café Promenade, serving international food; La Paix, which has an Italian menu; Silk Road, for excellent Chinese food; and the Edo, serving some of the finest Japanese food in town. Alternatively, there's the delicatessen, Le Gourmet, serving pastries and cakes, and two bars, Palm Court Lobby Lounge and Lake View Rooftop Lounge—the lake in question being Lu Lake, in Ba Dinh District, the diplomatic and government quarter. The hotel has a large collection of Vietnamese modern art.

US$135–300, excluding breakfast and taxes
411

HILTON HANOI OPERA

1 Le Thanh Tong Street
Tel 04-9330500
www.hanoi.hilton.com

Built adjacent to, and architecturally sympathetic with, the Opera House, the Hilton Hanoi Opera is a lofty edifice providing the highest levels of service and hospitality. Its foyer is in art deco style, with marbled flooring, enormous decorated columns and an elegantly curved balcony. Rooms—which have views of the Opera House or the city—are furnished in traditional Vietnamese style and have coffee-makers, mini-refrigerators, TVs, broadband internet access, minibars and bathrooms with tubs and showers. Two rooms are specially adapted for guests with disabilities. There is a set lunch available at the Chez Manon restaurant at 85,000d for six courses, and the hotel also has a Chinese restaurant, a bakery and a sports bar. Other amenities include a florist, a gift shop, an airline desk and a laundry and valet service.

US$110–245, including breakfast, excluding taxes
269 (non-smoking on one floor)

HANOI HORISON

40 Cat Linh Street
Tel 04-7330808
www.swiss-belhotel.com

A tall chimney stack stands in front of the Hanoi Horison—a relic of the brickworks that once stood on this site. The busy, popular hotel is conveniently placed for the Temple of Literature (▷ 72–75), and has very comfortably furnished

---

rooms with satellite TVs, mini-bars, music systems, coffee- and tea-making equipment, and private bathrooms with both a bathtub and a shower. The circular swimming pool is in rather an exposed position. There are several restaurants, a lobby bar, a casino, high-speed internet access and an ATM.

US$95–125, including breakfast, excluding taxes
250

HOA LINH

35 Hang Bo Street
Tel 04-8243887
hoalinhhotel@hn.vnn.vn
www.hotels-in-vietnam.com

This hotel, in the Old City, has lovely bedrooms decked out in the dark wood of Hué imperial style—headboards are ornately carved with dragons, while screens and bedside tables are inlaid with mother-of-pearl. The larger, more expensive rooms have both a double and a single bed, plus a balcony. It is worth paying the extra cost for a view of the decoration on the crumbling buildings opposite. Rooms have satellite TV, tea- and coffee-making equipment and minibars. Bathrooms are basic, with plastic showers and no shower curtains. Free internet use.

US$15–30, including breakfast and taxes
17 rooms

HO GUOM

76 Hang Trong Street
Tel 04-8243565
hoguomtjc@hn.vnn.vn

Despite its proximity to the popular Hoan Kiem Lake area, the Ho Guom is a peaceful place, set back from the road in a quiet courtyard, which is overlooked by the green-shuttered windows of some rooms. All rooms, which are furnished in Hué imperial style, have satellite TVs, minibars and bathrooms with tubs; a 300-seat restaurant serves Western, Asian and Vietnamese food, and staff are friendly and most helpful.

US$25–45, including breakfast and taxes
34 rooms

HONG NGOC 1

34 Hang Manh Street

Tel 04-8285053

www.hongngochotel.com

This small, family-run hotel, one of a trinity in the Old City (see below), is spotlessly clean throughout, with cheerful and helpful staff. The largest rooms, whose balconies have street views, are huge, so the heavy imperial-style furniture is not too oppressive; the 14 rooms at the back of the hotel are smaller and do not have balconies. All rooms have minibars, satellite TVs and private bathrooms with tubs.

US$50–95, including breakfast and VAT; service tax not charged

26

HONG NGOC 2

14 Luong Van Can Street

Tel 04-8267566

www.hongngochotel.com

This small and quiet hotel has amenities similar to those of its sister, Hong Ngoc 1 (see above), and sits in a prime location in the heart of the 36 Streets, on the connecting road to Hoan Kiem Lake. In addition to the standard facilities, Hong Ngoc 2 has an elevator and offers baby-sitting services. Pets are allowed.

US$30–50, including breakfast and VAT; service tax not charged

26 rooms (10 non-smoking)

HONG NGOC 3

39 Hang Bac Street

Tel 04-9260322

www.hongngochotel.com

The third member of the Hong Ngoc group is also in the heart of the Old City. Rooms are small, but not cramped, and some come with both a double and single bed. All are furnished with Hué imperial-style beds and chairs inlaid with mother-of-pearl, and have minibars, satellite TV and private bathrooms with tubs. The seven rooms at the back of the hotel are quieter, and the top room has a good view over the older rooftops of the city. There is an internet and e-mail service. The restaurant serves Asian, European and Vietnamese food.

US$28–45, including breakfast and taxes

25 (all non-smoking)

HOTEL CAMELLIA 2

13 Luong Ngoc Quyen Street

Tel 04-8283583

www.camellia-hotels.com

The sister hotel of the nearby Anh Dao (▷ 234) has a convenient location in the middle of the Old City and has been refurbished with fairly large rooms. The top-range rooms have balconies and writing desks; all rooms have phones, satellite TV and minibars, and bathrooms with tubs. Competent, English-speaking staff run all five hotels in this group, and Camellia has an official travel desk in the foyer. There is free internet access for guests.

US$14–37, including breakfast and taxes

28

NIKKO HANOI

84 Tran Nhan Tong Street

Tel 04-8223535

www.hotelnikkohanoi.com.vn

Despite its rather forbidding exterior, this hotel has a tranquil air inside, with a cool, marble lobby. It overlooks Lenin Park and Bay Mau Lake, in the south of the city, and is popular with Japanese guests, who appreciate the excellent Japanese restaurant, Benkay. Also here are a Chinese restaurant, Tao-Li, and a brasserie, plus a cake shop and the Portraits bar. Spa, sauna and massage facilities are available. Rooms are large and brightly furnished and have satellite TV, internet access, safe-deposit boxes and in-room fitness equipment. Some rooms are equipped for guests with disabilities.

US$220–260, including breakfast, excluding taxes

255 (non-smoking on request)

MOON RIVER RETREAT

Bac Cau

Ngoc Thuy Village

Gia Lam District

Tel 04-9438896

wildrice@fpt.vn

Snugly placed in a bend of the Red River, a 15-minute drive from the city and well signposted 2 miles (3km) from Chuong Duong Bridge, this is an appealing place in which to wind down, eat and sleep. Four exceptionally and sumptuously designed rooms, with terra-cotta floor tiles, red-lacquer furnishings and carved beds, are available in old Hanoi-style houses. The bathrooms have sunken baths, marble sinks, pebbles on the floor and slate walls, all oozing cool chic. The dining room is like a temple, and the gardens are designed with style and peace in mind. A restaurant serves Vietnamese food and has tables on the shaded courtyard, and there are special events such as pottery and cooking classes and organized sports. Future plans include a spa and more guest rooms.

US$85–150, including breakfast, excluding taxes

4

PRINCE

34 Hang Tre Street

Tel 04-9349063

ngoxuanthang@hn.vnn.vn

This extremely friendly hotel on the fringes of the Old City is good value and can offer help with tours and bicycle rental, as well as services such as laundry and dry-cleaning and baby-sitting. The comfortable, double-glazed rooms have simple, dark wood furniture and private bathrooms with showers and/or tubs, plus coffee- and tea-making equipment and satellite TV. All rooms have city views; larger rooms have balconies.

US$14–25, including breakfast and taxes

9

STAYING

QUEEN TRAVEL HOTEL

65 Hang Bac Street
Tel 04-8260860
www.azqueentravel.com
This travel café in the heart of the Old City underwent a major transformation in 2006. Old dormitories have been replaced by beautifully furnished, bright and airy private rooms, all equipped with satellite TV, air-conditioning and a shower. Vietnamese handicrafts decorate the attractive lobby. The travel desk offers a good range of tours, including trekking, mountain-biking and kayaking. There is free internet use.
US$55–95, including breakfast
9

SHERATON HOTEL

11 Xuan Dieu Road
Ho Tay District
Tel 04-7199000
www.sheraton.com/hanoi
The Hanoi Sheraton is some distance out of town on a scenic spot overlooking the West Lake. It is opulent and luxurious, as might be expected from the Sheraton group. Rooms have satellite TV, coffee-makers, refrigerators and broadband internet access, and the private bathrooms, furnished in marble, have separate tubs and showers. Other services available to guests include baby-sitting and laundry, and there is a whirlpool, a hot tub, a sauna and an illuminated outdoor tennis court. The swimming pool is in a courtyard that opens up onto a lawn leading down to the lakeshore. At the Nutz eatery, which serves light snacks, you can sit on a terrace overlooking the West Lake; there are also two other restaurants—the Oven D'Or, serving international food, and Hemispheres, serving fine Southeast Asian cuisine—and a lobby bar.
US130–200, including breakfast, excluding taxes
229 (non-smoking on request)

SOFITEL PLAZA HANOI

1 Thanh Nien Street
Tel 04-8238888
www.sofitel.com
This vast, 20-floor hotel overlooks the West Lake and

SOFITEL METROPOLE

15 Ngo Quyen Street
Tel 04-8266919
www.sofitel.com

At this elegant and renowned French colonial hotel in the heart of central Hanoi there is a long tradition of catering to the rich and famous. Charlie Chaplin, Graham Greene, Catherine Deneuve and Michael Caine have all been guests at this prestigious hotel, which is, not surprisingly, often fully booked. Staff speak English, French, Japanese and Russian. Le Beaulieu serves French dishes, and Hanoi specialties are on the menu of the Spices Garden; there are also three bars, including the Met Pub, which hosts live music, and the poolside Bamboo Bar. Among other amenities are a business center, a fitness center, a bookstore, a beauty salon, a hairdresser, a car rental desk, and dry-cleaning and baby-sitting services. Rooms are simply but attractively designed and have satellite and cable TV, safe-deposit boxes, minibars and private marble bathrooms. One room is equipped for guests with disabilities.
US$150–280, excluding breakfast and taxes
265 (163 non-smoking)

is a 40-minute drive from the airport. Rooms are generously furnished in pleasing, neutral tones and have writing desks, minibars, safe-deposit boxes and satellite and cable TV. All rooms are reached by glass-walled elevators and have floor-to-ceiling windows

affording splendid panoramic views. Ten are equipped for guests with disabilities. The large, all-weather swimming pool has a retractable roof and is bordered by the Pool Garden Café, a gym and a spa. Chinese and Vietnamese food is served at the Ming Palace restaurant, and a brasserie provides Western and Asian buffets. There are three bars and a nightclub.
US$135–190, excluding breakfast and taxes
322 rooms (85 non-smoking)

SUNWAY HOTEL

19 Pham Dinh Ho Street
Tel 04-9713888
www.sunway-hotel.com
An extremely comfortable, quiet and friendly hotel south

of Hoan Kiem Lake and close to Hanoi Gourmet, which is an attraction in itself (▷ 213). Breakfast is good and varied at the Sunway, and there is a restaurant for dinner and a lobby bar. All rooms have satellite TV, telephones, mini-bars, tea- and coffee-making equipment, safe-deposit boxes, plus a very useful control panel by the bed that operates all the room's lighting. There is drinking water in the private bathrooms, and triple-glazed windows give good soundproofing. One room is suitable for guests with disabilities. The restaurant, Allante, serves a good mix of Vietnamese and international dishes, and there is a lobby bar and a business center with high-speed internet access.
US$90–135, including breakfast, excluding taxes
145 (38 non-smoking)

STAYING

THE NORTH

If you plan to stay in the northern part of Vietnam, bear in mind that there are few smart hotels or Western-style creature comforts outside the main tourist sites. This is a poor and underdeveloped region where, even in the bitter cold of winter, there may be no access to hot water, and where, outside towns such as Sapa, English is rarely spoken. Sapa is the main center of accommodations in the northwest; here it's possible to find both luxurious and inexpensive places to stay, and it makes a good base for exploration of the region. However, distances are great, mountain roads are circuitous, and it is quite likely that you will have to stay overnight elsewhere. Nowhere else matches the standard or quantity of Sapa's hotels, but there is some choice in Dien Bien Phu and Son La. On the Mai Chau–Dien Bien Phu–Sapa circuit it is possible to stay in ethnic minority houses in certain villages; this is best arranged in places like Sapa or Mai Chau, where the practice is well established and lack of a common language may not be such a hindrance, or as part of a trip organized by tour operators in Hanoi. Accommodations are communal, and guests sleep either on wooden beds or, in a bamboo home, on the floor. Mattresses, pillows, sheets and mosquito nets are provided. Clean, cold-water showers and outdoor natural toilets are available in all homestays. Groups of two to three people can usually arrange homestays for about US$126 per person, including transportation, food, an English-speaking guide and transfers.

PRICES AND SYMBOLS

Prices are for a double room for one night. All the hotels listed accept credit cards unless otherwise stated. Note that rates vary widely throughout the year.

For a key to the symbols, ▷ 2.

CAT BA ISLAND

NOBLE HOUSE
Cat Ba Town, Cat Ba Island
Tel 031-888363

Overlooking the pier on the main waterfront road, this hotel has stylish and well-equipped rooms. There are good views and rooms have minibars and satellite and cable TV; the more expensive rooms include breakfast in the price. There's a popular bar, and the restaurant serves modestly priced Vietnamese and Western dishes.
US$20–30, including breakfast and taxes
5

PRINCES
Nui Ngoc Road, Cat Ba Island
Tel 031-888892
www.princeshotel-catba.com
Princes, opposite the hydrofoil ticket office, is currently the most comfortable and best-equipped hotel in Cat Ba. The airy, well-furnished rooms have satellite TV, bathrooms and hot water. The hotel has a laundry service, a lobby lounge and bar, internet and e-mail access, and there is a pleasant open courtyard at the back.

US$22–30, including breakfast and taxes
80 rooms

CUC PHUONG NATIONAL PARK

NATIONAL PARK ACCOMMODATIONS
Nho Quan District
Ninh Binh Province
Tel 030-848006
Cuc Phuong National Park has several types of accommodations—at the main gate (headquarters), half a mile (1km) from the gate, and at the park center, 12 miles (20km) from the gate. The

headquarters' concrete cabins have twin beds, air-conditioning and private bathrooms; less expensive bungalows are available with shared bathrooms and ceiling fans. There are more cabins with private bathrooms and air-conditioning in the center, at a slightly higher rate, as well as wooden stilt houses with no facilities. In addition, you can arrange to camp at the headquarters and in the center, or organize homestays with ethnic minorities in the park.
US$16–40
6 bungalows

DIEN BIEN PHU

KHACH SAN CONG TY BIA (BEER HOTEL)
Hoang Van Thai Street, Dien Bien Phu
Tel 023-824635
Fax 023-825576

If rolling out of bed and drinking beer first thing in the morning appeals to you, this curious little place may be a good choice. The Beer Hotel is next door to a home brewery and close to the Victory Monument (▷ 83), which can

STAYING

be seen from the third floor. The smell of hops hangs in the air but is not overwhelming, and a bottle of the *bia hoi* (fresh beer) fills four glasses for 7,000d. Rooms are basic, with no minibar, but they do have a TV and a basic shower, which has hot water but no stall. Credit cards are not accepted.

🍴 160,000d–240,000d, including breakfast
🛏 10
🅢

MUONG THANH HOTEL
25 Him Lam-TP, Dien Bien Phu
Tel 023-810043

Dien Bien Phu's best hotel is on the main thoroughfare, some distance from the major sights. All rooms are simply but adequately equipped and ranged around a large courtyard. At one side is the pool, incongruously surrounded by giant African animal sculptures and open to nonresidents for 10,000d. Other facilities include one of the few Western restaurants in town (which also serves Vietnamese food, ▷ 216), internet access, a souvenir shop, bicycle rental, karaoke, a steam bath and fitness center, and Thai massage. Guests are given free transfers to the airport.
🍴 US$18–23, including breakfast and taxes
🛏 70
🏊 📺 🅢

HAIPHONG
HARBOUR VIEW
4 Tran Phu Street, Haiphong
Tel 031-827827
www.harbourviewvietnam.com
Haiphong's largest and most luxurious hotel occupies an elegant French colonial building, slightly out of the center but near the river. Rooms are comfortably and neutrally

furnished and have coffee- and tea-making equipment, minibars, safe-deposit boxes, phones, in-house movies and cable TV. The hotel's two restaurants serve Vietnamese and international cuisine, with a daily buffet lunch starting at US$7, and laundry and baby-sitting services are also available.
🍴 US$65–92, including breakfast and taxes
🛏 127
📺 🅢

HALONG
HA LONG 1
Halong Road, Bai Chay
Halong City
Tel 033-846320
A shuttered, white French villa set among frangipani along the bay road out of town has been converted to a hotel. Rooms, some with a sea view, have TVs and minibars, and huge private bathrooms with tubs and bidets. The hotel has several restaurants serving Vietnamese and international food, shops, a travel agency and tennis courts.
🍴 US$55–65, including breakfast and taxes
🛏 23
🏊 🅢

HALONG PLAZA
8 Halong Road, Bai Chay
Halong City
Tel 033-845810
www.halongplaza.com
This joint Thai-Vietnamese venture has produced an excellent hotel with wonderful sea views, especially from upper floors. The 20-floor building is centrally placed, near the Bai Chay ferry station, and has a bar, a café and three highly rated restaurants serving international and Asian food. There are massage and sauna facilities, and laundry and valeting services, and you can reserve a seat on the 300-passenger boat service here. Rooms are luxuriously designed and have vast private bathrooms, minibars, satellite TV and in-house movies, safe-deposit boxes and complimentary fresh fruit, tea and coffee.
🍴 US$75–150, including breakfast and taxes
🛏 200
🏊 📺 🅢

LAI CHAU
LAN ANH HOTEL
Lai Chau
Tel 023-852682
Fax 023-852298
www.lananhhotel.com
The Lan Anh Hotel brings welcome respite in the hottest valley in northwest Vietnam. It has clean and comfortable rooms in stilt houses set around a courtyard. The staff can organize hotel, bus and airline reservations, as well as jeep, car, moto and bicycle tours; boat trips along local rivers; and treks to Ban Cho, a White Thái village, and to White and Blue Hmông villages. The restaurant has a limited menu and is open from 6am to 9pm. The friendly manager, Thang, speaks English and French.
🍴 US$12–30, including breakfast
🛏 50 rooms
🅢

SAPA
AUBERGE DANG TRUNG
7 Muong Hoa Street, Sapa
Tel 020-871243
auberge@sapadiscovery.com

The biggest attraction at this hillside hotel is its flourishing garden, tended with pride by Mr Dang Trung, the French-speaking owner. Sweet peas, honeysuckle, snapdragons and roses grow alongside subalpine flora and a collection of orchids. Rooms are simply furnished, but clean and bright, and have bathtubs, satellite TV and log fires in winter; those higher up are more expensive and have great views. Tours, flight reservations and vehicle rental can be arranged here. There is a laundry service and a restaurant.
🍴 US$10–35, excluding breakfast, including taxes
🛏 30 rooms
🅢

BAGUETTE & CHOCOLAT

Thac Bac Street, Sapa
Tel 020-871766
This small hotel, restaurant and café (▷ 216), in a quiet part of downtown Sapa, is run as a training hotel offering placements in hotels and restaurants throughout Vietnam for local ethnic minority women. There are only two twin and two double rooms, each with a private shower unit, and the whole operation is well run and extremely clean and comfortable. Gas heaters are provided in winter. Downstairs there's a stylish restaurant and café, with a small boulangerie attached.

💰 US$14–35, including breakfast and taxes
🛏 4

CAT CAT

Cat Cat Street, Sapa
Tel 020-871946
www.catcathotel.com
Friendly owner Le Loan runs this tall complex of buildings perched on a hill with views of the Sapa valley and Mount Fansipan. Rooms are large and plain, with wooden floors and fireplaces, two double beds, bathtubs and very hot water. TVs are available on request. Rooms 209 and 309 have 240-degree mountain views. Guests can relax in swing chairs, have a massage and eat in the vegetarian restaurant. Half an hour's free internet access is provided.

💰 US$10–20, including breakfast and taxes
🛏 32

DARLING

Thac Bac Street, Sapa
Tel 020-871961
Fax 020-871963
The top bedroom of the Darling, with its curios—wooden bathtub and large,

VICTORIA SAPA

Sapa
Tel 020-871522
www.victoriahotels-asia.com

This wooden villa, on a small hill overlooking the town and built in mountain chalet style, is the best hotel in Sapa. The exquisitely decorated, wooden-floored rooms have balconies or terraces at garden level, to take advantage of the spectacular views of Mount Fansipan, satellite TVs, in-house movies, safe boxes and minibars. In winter there are open fires in the bar and dining rooms. Guests have access to mountain bicycles, an indoor pool, sauna, massage, billiards, petanque and a floodlit tennis court. The hotel has private sleeper carriages on the train from Hanoi to Lao Cai (▷ 50). Special weekend packages are available on the web.

💰 US$135–250, excluding breakfast and taxes
🛏 77
🏊 Indoor

orange, layered bedside lamps—and vast terrace, enjoys the best view in all of town. A short walk from central Sapa, the hotel has cozy rooms with ethnic curtains, small balconies, private bathrooms with tubs, fireplaces, free tea, in-house movies, minibars and safe-deposit boxes. Car and motorcycle rental and internet access are available. The slightly out-of-center location ensures that it is not usually as busy as other hotels.

💰 US$6–35, including taxes, excluding breakfast
🛏 45
🏊 Indoor

TOPAS ECO LODGE

Office: 24 Muong Hoa Street, Sapa
Tel 020-872404
Fax 020-872405
www.topas-eco-lodge.com
Adventure tour operator Topas has created an eco lodge perched on a plateau overlooking the Hoang Vien Valley, 11 miles (18km) from Sapa. Solar-powered, palm-thatched cabins, each with its own bathroom and porch, enjoy fantastic views over the valley, home to Red Dao and Tày minorities. Trekking, horseback-riding, mountain-biking and handicraft workshops are organized daily for guests and are included in the price.

💰 US$105–169, including all meals, taxes and transportation to and from Sapa. Each additional night is discounted.
🛏 25

SON LA

HOA BAN 2

Group 6
Chieng Le Ward, Son La
Tel 022-852395
A stuffed tiger welcomes you to the foyer of this small hotel, where the facilities are basic but comfortable. Rooms have two large beds (one king and one queen), TVs, phones and hot water. Only two rooms have bathtubs. There is no restaurant, but the hotel is on the main road and close to local eateries.

💰 120,000d–150,000d
🛏 16
🔧

NHA KHACH UY BAN NHAN DAN TINH SON LA (PEOPLE'S COMMITTEE GUESTHOUSE)

Highway 6, Son La
Tel 022-852102
This large hotel in a secluded position, signed Nha Khach, just off Highway 6, has been extended and upgraded, and now has 70 rooms, all with air-conditioning and fans, TVs and minibars. The restaurant serves Vietnamese and Western food. Reservations by phone are necessary.

💰 US$15–30, including breakfast and taxes
🛏 70
🔧

STAYING

CENTRAL VIETNAM

The central region covers a huge swathe of the country and a wide range of environments. For most visitors, however, this region means coastal resorts, and there is no shortage of reasonably priced accommodations by the sea. Several resorts have been built right on the beach or on offshore islands, and some are of outstanding quality. Among the best beach resorts are those on the Mui Ne peninsula, near Phan Thiet. Nha Trang has good hotels, though these are mainly town establishments rather than beach resorts. But the fresh sea breeze, brilliant sunshine and (in some instances) views of the sea make this a relaxing place to stay. Other popular bases in the central region are Hué, whose range is limited; Hoi An, which offers everything from downtown luxury to beach resorts and local homes; and Danang, with its first-class beach resort. Away from the coast, in the Central Highlands, the contrast is marked. Here, the weather is cloudier, cooler and wetter, and many hotels are state-run, though the number of private hotels is increasing. Dalat, the largest town in the interior, has a choice of accommodations, from the luxurious to the basic. Staying in ethnic minority stilt houses is a restricted option and, in many parts of the region, impossible. Other than in a few places outside Buon MeThuot, foreign visitors are no longer permitted to stay with ethnic minority families.

PRICES AND SYMBOLS

Prices are for a double room for one night. All the hotels listed accept credit cards unless otherwise stated. Note that rates vary widely throughout the year.

For a key to the symbols, ▷ 2.

BACH MA NATIONAL PARK

NATIONAL PARK ACCOMMODATIONS
2 miles (3km) from Cau Hai, off National Route 1
Tel 054-871330
www.bachma.vnn.vn
There are six guesthouses in the park's 54,000 acres (22,000ha). Two are near the park gate and have five simply but attractively designed rooms, with air-conditioning; some share bathrooms. Four guesthouses are near the highest point, 4,100ft (1,250m) up, where there are several trails taking less than a day; these have private bathrooms and fireplaces. The biggest rooms accommodate six people. There are also campgrounds near the summit of Bach Ma. Credit cards are not accepted.
🛏 100,000d–200,000d, excluding breakfast and entrance fee, including taxes
🛌 36
🅢

BUON ME THUOT

CAO NGUYEN
65 Phan Chu Trinh Street, Buon Me Thuot
Tel 050-851913
caonguyenhotel@daklaktourist.com.vn
Daklak Tourist runs this modern hotel with a moderate range of facilities, 490 yards (450m) from the Daklak visitor office in the central part of town. Rooms have minibars, TVs and private bathrooms (which may have no shower curtains); it's worth paying US$10 extra for one of the six large suites. The staff are friendly and helpful and speak some English, and the restaurant, though not large, has a reasonable selection of food.
🛏 US$35–45, including breakfast and taxes
🛌 35
🅢

THANG LOI
1 Phan Chu Trinh Street, Buon Me Thuot
Tel 050-857615
thangloihotel@daklaktourist.com.vn
This modern hotel has a prime location, next to the main post office, the telephone office (which has a 24-hour ATM) and the four main streets of Buon Me Thuot. Rooms are all large, if rather drab, and have private bathrooms; those on the third floor are more spacious and have bigger bathrooms, with separate shower cubicles. All have satellite TVs and phones. The staff speak good English, and the food in the 200-seat restaurant is fresh, well presented and plentiful. The Daklak Tourist office is based in the hotel grounds and can arrange homestays in the M'nong village of Buon Juin (US$5 per person, excluding breakfast).
🛏 US$35–$50, including breakfast and taxes
🛌 40
🅢

SPECIAL IN BAC MY AN

FURAMA RESORT
68 Ho Xuan Huong Street
(5 miles/8km from Danang)
Tel 0511-847888
www.furamavietnam.com

This 5-star beach resort is beautifully designed and furnished, and has a fabulously opulent foyer and two swimming pools. All rooms have balconies or terraces and overlook the ocean, the tropical garden or the freshwater lagoon, and all have satellite TV with in-house movies, private marble bathrooms, minibars, safe-deposit boxes and tea- and coffee-making facilities. Two rooms are equipped for guests with disabilities, and there are a large number of office services. There are two restaurants, and light snacks are available at the poolside Lagoon Bar. Fitness fans can enjoy watersports, mountain biking, and beach volleyball. There is a free shuttle to Danang, Marble Mountains and Hoi An.
🛏 From US$160–500, excluding breakfast and taxes
🛌 198
🎿🎽🅢

WHITE HORSE HOTEL
9–11 Nguyen Duc Canh Street,
Buon Me Thuot
Tel 050-815656
Fax 050-815588
The Thang Loi's main rival is an independently run hotel in a contemporary building, with rooms that are spacious and attractively decorated (with satellite TV). The staff are friendly and helpful, and have a good understanding of English. The rooftop restaurant specializes in seafood and there are European options on the menu. Cars and motorcycles can be rented at the hotel.
US$20–40, including breakfast and taxes
22

DALAT
ANA MANDARA VILLAS DALAT AND SPA
Le Lai Street, Dalat
Tel 063-520558 (Nha Trang Resort)
www.six-senses.com
In late 2006 the doors opened in this complex of restored French villas on a hillside 10 minutes' drive from downtown Dalat. Each villa has three to five bedrooms with private bathrooms (tubs and showers), phones, safe-deposit boxes, minibars, coffee- and tea-making equipment and satellite TV. Every villa here has a small backyard, a conservatory, a communal sitting room and a terrace for private dining. All living rooms and some bedrooms have fireplaces. A number of pools scattered about the hotel complex ensures each guest has easy access to one of them. The central villa has a French bistro and a wine bar, and another houses the Six Senses Spa, which has outdoor pools and hot tubs with river and mountain views.
US$155–400, excluding breakfast and taxes
50 in 13 villas

EMPRESS HOTEL
5 Nguyen Thai Hoc Street,
Dalat
Tel 063-833888
empress@hcm.vnn.vn
This particularly attractive hotel—arguably the best in Dalat—has a fine position overlooking Xuan Huong Lake.

All rooms are arranged around a small sunny courtyard that is a great place for breakfast. Rooms are large, and although the furnishings are dated, the beds are comfortable; the private bathrooms have either tubs or showers, as well as toilets. All rooms have satellite TV, in-house movies, minibars, refrigerators, safe-deposit boxes and phones. Laundry and dry-cleaning services are available. Staff are attentive and courteous, and the restaurant serves Vietnamese and Italian food.
US$60–110, including breakfast, excluding taxes
27

GOLF 1
11 Dinh Tien Hoang Street,
Dalat
Tel 063-824082
www.golfhotel.vnn.vn
This large, white hotel facing the golf course, half a mile (1km) from downtown Dalat, has recovered its popularity after being briefly overshadowed by Golf 2 and Golf 3 (see below). Staff are friendly and helpful, and rooms have satellite TVs, tea- and coffee-making facilities and phones, and private bathrooms with tubs. There's a doctor and nurse on call and a same-day laundry service, and the restaurant serves Asian, European and international dishes, plus some Vietnamese specialties.
US$27–50, including breakfast and taxes
36

GOLF 3
4 Nguyen Thi Minh Khai Street,
Dalat
Tel 063-824082
www.golfhotel.vnn.vn
Rooms are comfortable in this central hotel next to Dalat market. Every room has a private bathroom—with a tub in all but the least expensive rooms—as well as a phone, safe-deposit box, minibar, satellite and cable TV, video and CD player and tea- and coffee-making equipment. Hotel amenities include a bar with karaoke, a disco and nightclub, a restaurant serving international food, a beauty salon and a shopping arcade.

The only drawback is that rooms facing the street are noisy because of the proximity of the market.
US$42–80, including breakfast, excluding taxes
78

HANG NGA'S CRAZY HOUSE
3 Huynh Thuc Khang Street,
Dalat
Tel 063-822070
Fax 063-831480

If you fancy a fantasy night in a mushroom, a tree or a giraffe, then this is the place for you—an architectural meander through curves, twists and bizarre ornamentation. The guesthouse was designed by Hang Nga, whose father, Truong Chinh, was one of the triumvirate who took power after the death of Ho Chi Minh. Trees are entwined among the concrete structure, and there is an art gallery in the grounds (▷ 102). Rooms have satellite TV, minibars and phones, and the furniture is sturdy, if not particularly comfortable. There's a coffee house and bar and a rooftop barbecue restaurant, and laundry and dry cleaning services are also available.
US$30–45, including breakfast and taxes
9

NOVOTEL DALAT
7 Tran Phu Street,
Dalat
Tel 063-825777
www.accorhotels.com
Formerly the Du Parc Hotel, the Novotel faces the post office and is near the Sofitel (▷ 243), with which it shares

STAYING

its management and many facilities, including golf, tennis and the restaurants and bars. Its restored rooms are comfortably furnished and have satellite TVs, in-house movies, phones, minibars and safe-deposit boxes. There is a lobby restaurant, and breakfast is available; the landmark Café de la Poste is just over the road.

🏨 US$60–170, including breakfast, excluding taxes
ℹ️ 144 (20 non-smoking)
🔁

SOFITEL DALAT PALACE
12 Tran Phu Street,
Dalat
Tel 063-825444
www.sofitel.com
This rambling old building was built in 1922, and in 1995 was

restored to its former glory, with new curtains, furniture, statues, gilt mirrors and chandeliers in every room. The view over Xuan Huong Lake to the hills beyond is superb, and the extensive hotel grounds are beautifully laid out. Rooms have private bathrooms with tubs, minibars, satellite and cable TVs and safe-deposit boxes. Baby-sitting services are available, and there are indoor and outdoor playgrounds. Guests can get a discount on green fees at the nearby golf course and play on the hotel tennis courts. The restaurant and brasserie serve local and international food, and there's a bar and a piano bar.
🏨 US$200–350, excluding breakfast and taxes
ℹ️ 43 (5 non-smoking)
🔁

DANANG

BAMBOO GREEN CENTRAL
158 Phan Chu Trinh Street,
Danang
Tel 0511-822996
In the heart of town, within reach of the Museum of Champa Sculpture (▷ 104–105), this tower-block hotel has a restaurant, a nightclub, tour-arranging and laundry services, and a fitness center offering massage, sauna and steam room. Guest rooms are plain but pleasant and have phones, TVs and minibars.
🏨 US$45–70, including breakfast and taxes
ℹ️ 46
🔁

BAMBOO GREEN RIVERSIDE
68 Bach Dang Street,
Danang
Tel 0511-832591
riversidets@dng.vnn.vn
There are pleasant river views from this efficiently run hotel near the Han River bridge, which leads to My Khe beach. The two-bedded rooms have phones, minibars, satellite TVs and private bathrooms with tubs. General services include internet access, air reservations and car rental, laundry and airport transfer. The restaurant serves Vietnamese, European and Asian food, and there's a karaoke bar and a massage room, as well as a 24-hour ATM outside the hotel's main

door. Another hotel in the Bamboo group, with similar amenities, is the Bamboo Green Harbourside, close to the cathedral (177 Tran Phu Street, tel 0511-822722, fax 0511-824165).
🏨 US$40–60, including breakfast and taxes
ℹ️ 40
🔁

HOI AN

SPECIAL IN HOI AN
ANCIENT HOUSE RESORT
61 Cua Dai Street,
Hoi An
Tel 0510-923377
www.ancienthouseresort.com
This very beautiful resort hotel is built in the style of Hoi An's ancient houses, with a clay-tile roof and Chinese lanterns, and is set around a small garden with a series of landscaped ponds. All the

rooms are decorated in white, with Marelli fans and bronze lamps, and have minibars, phones, cable TVs and private showers or baths. Behind the hotel, in the grounds, is a traditional wooden house divided into three: an area for living, another for worship, and a warehouse. Next to it is a building where *pho* noodles are made to supply the town's restaurants. The resort includes a nightclub, beauty salon, billiards room, sauna and spa and a restaurant and coffee bar. There is a free shuttle to the town and beach, and free bicycle rental.
🏨 US$60–90, including breakfast, excluding taxes
ℹ️ 42 (non-smoking on request)
🛏️ 📺 🔁

STAYING

HA AN HOTEL

6–8 Phan Boi Chau Street, Hoi An
Tel 0510-863126
tohuong@fpt.vn

In the heart of the French quarter, the Ha An is a family-run boutique hotel with a white balustraded balcony and pleasant gardens. The rooms are attractively decorated in scarlet and white and have ethnic minority drapes on the walls; rooms around the front yard, opposite an open-air café, are a little larger. All have private bathrooms and phones, and complimentary bottled water and fruit are provided. There is a communal seating area with TV, internet and e-mail access, a laundry service, a restaurant and bar and a beauty salon.

US$20–45, including breakfast and taxes
25

HOI AN BEACH RESORT

Cua Dai Beach, Hoi An
Tel 0510-927011
www.hoiantourist.com

Choose between Vietnamese-style houses and villa rooms in this quiet, attractively designed resort with its own stretch of private beach between the De Vong River and Cua Dai Beach. The spacious rooms are simply designed, with large, private bathrooms; some have small terraces or balconies overlooking the river. All have satellite and cable TV, phones, safe-deposit boxes, minibars, tea- and coffee-making equipment, and there are extra touches such as free bottled water, umbrellas and slippers. The large restaurant overlooks the river and there are two pools, a beauty salon, volleyball and badminton courts, a Jacuzzi, a sauna and steam bath, laundry and baby-sitting services.

Activities include parasailing and jet- and water-skiing, and there is a speedboat to take guests to Cham Island. A free shuttle travels between the hotel and the frenetic streets of Hoi An.

US$100–120, including breakfast and taxes
110

HOI AN HOTEL

10 Tran Hung Dao Street, Hoi An
Tel 0510-861728
www.hoiantourist.com

The Hoi An is in a three-floor colonial building set well back from the road in spacious grounds, with comfortable rooms arranged around a beautiful pool. Some rooms are fairly small and some are more stylish than others, but all have phones, private bathrooms with tubs and showers, minibars, satellite TV. The hotel is popular with European tour groups, and has a range of leisure options, including a pool table, tennis and badminton courts, a Jacuzzi, spa, sauna, steam bath, barber, beauty salon and art gallery. There's a children's playground, laundry service, internet services, airport pickup, tour desk, and car, motorcycle and bicycle rental. Choose from two restaurants, the café-bar or pool bar.

US$70–150, including breakfast and taxes
160

HOI AN RIVERSIDE RESORT

175 Cua Dai Road, Hoi An
Tel 0510-864800
www.hoianriverresort.com

This resort, just a five-minute bicycle ride from the beach, faces the Thu Bon River, enjoying wonderful views. The dark, slate-lined swimming pool is surrounded by white umbrellas, white mattressed seats and hammocks, all set in landscaped gardens. Standard rooms have balconies, wooden floors and ethnic-minority drapes, and all have private showers, satellite TV, phones, minibars, internet access and safe-deposit boxes. The resort is owned by Khaisilk (▷ 24) and has a store selling the company's products. There's a badminton court, billiards

SPECIAL IN HOI AN

VICTORIA HOI AN BEACH RESORT

Cam An Beach, near Cua Dai Beach
Tel 0510-927040
www.victoriahotels-asia.com

This appealing resort is laid out like a traditional fishermen's village, with clay-tiled

houses, streets and ponds on the white-sand beach between the sea and the river delta. All rooms, some with balconies, have sea or river views, and are decorated with Japanese, French or Vietnamese themes. Standard rooms have private showers; the most expensive rooms have four-poster beds and private bathtubs. Phones, satellite TVs, minibars, safe-deposit boxes and coffee- and tea-makers are provided in every room. The swimming pool is large but slightly exposed. The hotel has restaurants, a library, laundry, tour-arranging services and a free shuttle between the hotel and town. There are children's activities and tennis courts, and a pet elephant, Darling, ambles up and down the beach giving rides.

US$130–240, excluding breakfast and taxes
105

room, spa and fitness center, and you can take Vietnamese cooking lessons, sometimes visiting the market with the chef to buy ingredients. Vietnamese and international dishes are served at the Song Do restaurant, which has river views, and there are two bars, one by the pool.

US$129–189, including breakfast and taxes
60

STAYING

MINH A

2 Nguyen Thai Hoc Street, Hoi An
Tel 0510-861368

The Minh A is a welcome alternative to the area's top-of-the-range resorts. It is a 200-year-old family house, next to the busy market, where guests are really made to feel part of the family. Each of the four rooms, which is separated from its neighbor by panels, is individually laid out and has a fan. The bathrooms have four separate showers and toilets and are communal. The family room has a view of the market and the bougainvillea-covered house opposite; another room houses a shrine to Quan Cong, the god of war, and has a tiny balcony overlooking the orchid-filled courtyard and furnished with a miniscule table and two chairs. Credit cards are not accepted.

💶 US$12–20, excluding breakfast, including taxes
🛏 4

VINH HUNG 1

143 Tran Phu Street, Hoi An
Tel 0510-861621
www.vinhhunghotel.com

An attractive, 250-year-old building with a splendidly ornate reception room, decorated with dark wood in Chinese style, this popular hotel has a range of rooms. Some are large and traditionally furnished, with private bathrooms and small tubs; others (in the downstairs area) are rather small and lack a window, with showers only. All have phones, minibars, and satellite and cable TV; there's a laundry service and a restaurant serving Asian and European food.

💶 US$20–50, including breakfast and taxes
🛏 12
🚤 🔵

HUÉ

CENTURY RIVERSIDE

49 Le Loi Street,
Hué
Tel 054-823390
www.centuryriversidehue.com

White steps lead up to the entrance of this imposing hotel, whose foyer is decorated with chandeliers and sturdy columns. The more expensive rooms have fabulous river views, and all have bathrooms with tubs, complimentary fruit and bottled water, satellite TV, minibars, refrigerators and phones. Vietnamese and Western dishes are served at the three restaurants; there are also two bars, tennis courts, bicycle and motorcycle rental, a tour desk, a beauty salon, massage and a laundry service.

💶 US$75–165, including breakfast, excluding taxes
🛏 158
🚤 📺 🔵

DONG LOI

119 Pham Ngu Lao Street,
Hué
Tel 054-822296
interser@dng.vnn.vn

This inexpensive family-run hotel is surrounded by internet cafés, shops and restaurants. All rooms have small private bathrooms, phones and cable TV; the most expensive have bathtubs. Some rooms are darker than others, but all are individually decorated, spotlessly clean and comfortable. Breakfast is served at the delightful La Carambole Restaurant (▷ 221) next door. The hotel can arrange tours, as well as bicycle, car and motorcycle rental. It provides internet access and a laundry service.

💶 US$15–35, including breakfast and taxes
🛏 65
🔵

HOTEL SAIGON MORIN

30 Le Loi Street,
Hué
Tel 054-823526
www.morinhotel.com.vn

The Morin, which faces the Perfume River, is the oldest, grandest and most famous hotel in Hué. It was built in 1901 by the eponymous Mr. Morin, a French businessman. It is set around a large courtyard filled with wrought-iron furniture; this is where diners

sit for the hotel's buffet nights (▷ 220). All rooms are large, comfortable and carpeted, and have three single beds, two of which are pushed together to make a larger bed. All have private bathrooms, plus extensive minibars and snack bars, tea- and coffee-making equipment, high-speed internet access, safe-deposit boxes, phones and satellite TV. The hotel also provides complimentary fruit baskets and bottled water. Services include airport pickup, car rental, a 24-hour ATM, baby-sitting, same-day laundry

service, an arts and crafts shop, a beauty salon, massage and sauna, billiards and pool. The in-house tour service can arrange a variety of trips, including a boat journey with traditional Hué folk music. Asian, Vietnamese, European and Hué specialties are served in the two restaurants, while the Garden Bar offers snacks and drinks, as well as the nightly barbecue.

💶 US$120–160, including breakfast, excluding taxes
🛏 146
🚤 📺 🔵

HUONG GIANG (PERFUME RIVER HOTEL)

51 Le Loi Street,
Hué
Tel 054-822122
www.huonggiangtourist.com

This hotel has a superb position on the river, and its rooms are comfortable, despite the heavy wooden, lacquered imperial-style furniture. The more expensive rooms overlook the river and are decorated with mother-of-pearl; the less expensive rooms are designed in bamboo. All rooms have private bathrooms, albeit rather spartan ones, plus satellite TV, minibars, phones and safe-deposit boxes. The Royal Restaurant is decked out with heavy red furniture and decorated columns; it specializes in Hué dishes. The Hoa Mai has a menu of Vietnamese, Asian and European food, as well as local specialties and the riverfront terrace bar has great views. Other facilities include sauna and massage, tennis courts, a post office, filmprocessing, laundry and dry cleaning, a tour desk and a hairdressing and beauty salon.

🎖️ US$79–230, including breakfast, excluding taxes
🛈 150
🛏️📶🅂

LA RÉSIDENCE HÔTEL AND SPA
5 Le Loi Street
Hué
Tel 054-837475
www.la-residence-hue.com
Opened in 2005 and already set to become a classic hotel, this beautiful colonial villa prides itself on its first-class service, excellent cuisine and an environmentally conscious spa. La Résidence, once the home of the French governor of Hué, overlooks the Perfume River, providing some stunning views. Nearly all rooms have a large balcony and a river view. There are a number of suites each of which is themed: Suite d'Ornithologue, as the name suggests, gives the occupant the feeling of a bird sanctuary, while Voyage en Chine takes you on a journey through ancient China. Relax in the hotel's comfortable bar, Le Gouverneur, and admire the fresco created by Roland Renauc, a locally based French artist.

🎖️ US$100–200, including breakfast, excluding taxes
🛈 122 (7 suites, all non-smoking)
🛏️🅂

THUAN HOA
7 Nguyen Tri Phuong Street
Hué
Tel 054-822523
Near the heart of the former French Quarter and in the vicinity of the bus station, this hotel lacks the colonial charm of some of Hue's other hotels, but it is comfortable, spacious and friendly. Rooms have all the standard amenities, and additional services include a travel agency, sauna, massage, tennis court, vehicle and bicycle rental.

🎖️ US$23–50, excluding breakfast and taxes
🛈 71
🅂

KONTUM
DAKBLA 1 HOTEL
2 Phan Dinh Phung Street, Kontum
Tel 060-863333
Fax 060-863336
Set in attractive grounds, this hotel has a small restaurant and a jetty on the riverbank. The friendly, helpful staff have a basic understanding of English and French. Rooms, although drably decorated, are large, and have private bathrooms, minibars, phones and satellite TVs. The restaurant on the first floor serves good, reasonably priced Vietnamese and international food, and the hotel provides a taxi service, tennis courts, karaoke and dancing. The hotel is the first building on the right as you cross the bridge into Kontum.

🎖️ US$15–20, including breakfast and taxes
🛈 42
🅂

LANG CO
LANG CO BEACH RESORT
National Route 1A, 22 miles (35km) from Danang Airport
Tel 054-873555
langco@dng.vnn.vn
www.huonggiangtourist.com
The green-roofed villas of the resort are set back from the beach on the Lap An lagoon, on the beautiful Lang Co peninsula. The hotel has a large outdoor pool, a bar and a 300-seater restaurant, which serves French, Vietnamese, Chinese and Hué royal court dishes (▷ 218). Rooms are based on traditional Hué design, and are equipped with satellite TVs, phones (with bathroom extensions) and safe-deposit boxes. Tennis courts, a beauty and hairdressing salon, health and fitness club, sauna and laundry services are available, and there are facilities for guests with disabilities.

🎖️ US$30–145, including breakfast, excluding taxes
🛈 76
🛏️📶🅂

THANH TAM RESORT AND HOTEL
Central Lang Co Beach
Tel 054-874456
This comfortable collection of bungalow accommodations north of Lang Co village overlooks the sea. Amenities are limited, but they do have a good seafood restaurant. Sports facilities include windsurfing, volleyball and badminton. The helpful tour desk will reserve onward tickets to most destinations.

🎖️ US$10–30, excluding breakfast and taxes
🛈 25
🅂

MUI NE
BAMBOO VILLAGE BEACH RESORT
Km 11.8, Ham Tien, Phan Thiet, Mui Ne
Tel 062-847007
www.bamboovillageresortvn.com
Attractive, simple bamboo huts are scattered around a lovely shady spot at the top of the beach. The most expensive cabins have two beds, small bathrooms and private balconies that look out on to the beach. Rooms are rustic but comfortable, and have satellite TVs and phones. There are also 14 "lodges," which are in fact rooms, but these are not as inviting. Transportation can be arranged here to Ho Chi Minh City or to the airport. On site there is an excellent restaurant, two swimming pools (one with Jacuzzi), a children's play area,

table tennis and pool, a library, internet access and sports such as windsurfing and paddlesurfing. Comfortable and self-contained, this is a good place for families.

🎖️ US$80–190, including breakfast and taxes
🛈 65
🛏️🅂 In top-rate rooms only

COCO BEACH RESORT

58 Nguyen Ninh Chiau,
Phung Haum Tian
Phan Thiet, Mui Ne
Tel 062-847111
www.cocobeach.net

FULL MOON BEACH

84 Nguyen Dinh Chieu
Phan Thiet, Mui Ne
Tel 062-847008
fullmoon@windsurf-vietnam.com
www.windsurf-vietnam.com

SAILING CLUB

24 Nguyen Dinh Chieu, Ham Tien
ward, Phan Thiet
Tel 062-847440
www.sailingclubvietnam.com

Thatched wooden cabins and three two-bedroom villas face the beach in a tranquil setting, with a swimming pool, a children's wading pool and a play area. Coco Beach is well run by German owners and was the first resort on Mui Ne; competition has since stepped up, but it remains among the best. Rooms can be dark, but have private terraces. Villa bathrooms have tubs; cabin bathrooms have enclosed shower stalls. All rooms provide mosquito nets, minibars, hot water and phones. There are two restaurants: Champa, a French restaurant, open afternoons and evenings, and the Paradise Beach Club restaurant, whose yellow-and-white striped chairs are right on the beach, and which is open all day. The resort shop sells souvenirs and crafts, and a library has books in English, French and German. Also available are a flight reservation desk and internet and e-mail access. The resort is very child-friendly and provides baby-sitting and bottle-cleaning and sterilization, plus games and videos for older children.

🛏 US$75–180, including breakfast and taxes
🛈 34
🖥 🚭

Accommodations at Full Moon Beach are in a variety of brick and bamboo rooms; the most attractive rooms have a sea view and constant breeze. Bamboo suites are a little dark, but have two double bedrooms each, plus pleasant bathrooms with mosaic floors. The brick rooms are more comfortable, with low-slung, Japanese-style beds and low ceilings. Only the four-person villas have air-conditioning. There's internet access and a swimming pool, and the resort is next to Jibe's restaurant and bar and the windsurfing and kiteboarding center.

🛏 US$50–80, including breakfast and taxes
🛈 25 (including cabins)
🖥 🚭

NOVOTEL CORALIA OCEAN DUNES & GOLF RESORT

1 Ton Duc Thang Street
Phan Thiet, Mui Ne
Tel 062-822393
www.accorhotels-asia.com
Strictly speaking, this resort is not really on Mui Ne, but it does have a beach setting and its own private stretch of sand. Rooms are comfortable and plushly furnished, with private bathrooms with bathtubs, tea- and coffee-making equipment, safe-deposit boxes, minibars, TVs, slippers and bathrobes, and private balconies. The hotel provides a laundry service, and there are two swimming pools, several restaurants, a bar, tennis courts and a gym. It's also possible to dine by candlelight right on the beach. Guests are given a

Opened in 2002, this Australian-owned resort has been designed in a most attractive style, with simple and cool cabins and rooms surrounded by dense and glorious vegetation. There's a small pool close to the beach and a good restaurant and bar. The costlier cabins have mosquito nets and ethnic minority cloths artfully draped on the walls; upper floors have air-conditioning, the lower floors fans only. Bathrooms have walk-in hot showers (except for the top-range bungalows, which have tubs). Cable TV and phones are supplied. The Restaurant @ Sailing Club serves fusion dishes and specializes in seafood, and there's a bar with a beachfront terrace. Home furnishings and ornaments are sold in the shop, and there's a spa, internet and fax services and watersports and tours. Bicycles and motorcycles are available to rent. You can have a massage in the beach pavilion or in your room.

🛏 US$60–115, including breakfast and taxes
🛈 30
🖥 🚭

20 percent discount on green fees at the adjacent Ocean Dunes Golf Club.

🛏 US$60–90, including breakfast, excluding taxes
🛈 122 (11 non-smoking)
🖥 🚭

MY KHE (CHINA BEACH)

TOURANE

My Khe Beach, Phuoc My Ward, Son Tra
District, 1 mile (2km) from Danang
Tel 0511-932666

touranehotel@dng.vnn.vn

Simple red-roofed chalet
houses sit one road back from
the famous China Beach, with
rooms designed in French
colonial style. All rooms have
satellite TVs, phones and
private bathrooms. There are
garden views from 20 rooms,
sea views and balconies from
the more expensive rooms
and five suites. The restaurant
serves Asian and European
food, and there are tennis and
badminton courts, tour and
laundry services, massages, a
sauna and a steam bath.

🛏 US$23–35, including breakfast
and taxes
🛈 29 in 5 chalets
🔄

MY KHE BEACH HOTEL

241 Nguyen Van Thoai Street, My Khe
Tel 0511-836125

This hotel faces the beach and
is set back a little on the other
side of the quiet beach road.
Rooms are in blocks, among
the sea pines. The suites have
sea views, sitting rooms and
double and single beds; 27
less expensive rooms have
garden views. All have phones,
satellite TVs and private bathrooms. Conroy's Bar, one of
three eating outlets here,
offers sandwiches, hamburgers
and cold beer, as well as
seafood. There are tennis and
badminton courts, a steam
bath, sauna and massages.

🛏 US$20–39, including breakfast and
taxes
🛈 52 in 5 villas
🔄

NAM CAT TIEN NATIONAL PARK

NATIONAL PARK ACCOMMODATIONS

Tan Phu District
Tel/fax 061-791228

These guesthouses offer basic
accommodations in bunga-
lows, with four beds per room,
a fan and/or air-conditioning
and mosquito nets. There is an
outside toilet-block with a sink
and cold shower. A small
restaurant nearby serves food,
snacks and beers.

🛏 US$11 per room
🛈 5

NHA TRANG

BAO DAI'S VILLAS

Tran Phu Street, Nha Trang
(approach to Cau Da village)
Tel 058-522222

www.vngold.com/nt/baodai

These French colonial villas, on
a small promontory, were built
in 1923 for Emperor Bao Dai
and his wife, Queen Nam
Phuong. They now form a
guest resort with magnificent
views over the harbor and
islands. The large villa rooms
are essentially big studios with
bedrooms, sitting rooms and
dining areas in an open-plan
space. The furniture is heavy
and the bedspreads are gold-
colored. All rooms have
minibars, phones, satellite TVs
and private bathrooms with
tubs. A restaurant overlooking
the bay serves seafood, or you
can eat barbequed food at an
open-air beachside eatery.
Motorcycle and bicycle rental,
internet, tennis courts and fishing tours are all available, and
there's a laundry service.

🛏 US$25–80, including breakfast and
taxes
🛈 48
🔄

BLUE HOUSE

12/8 Hung Vuong Street, Nha Trang
Tel 058-824505

Down a quiet alley, this small,
neat, blue building is run by a
welcoming family (with little
English) and is excellent value
for money. Rooms are large
and clean, and come with
minibar and TV; those with air-
conditioning are more expensive. Breakfast is taken in a
pleasant terrace area.

🛏 US$5–12, excluding breakfast
🛈 14
🔄 Some rooms

LA SUISSE HOTEL

34 Tran Quang Khai Street, Nha Trang
Tel 058-524353

lasuissehotelnt@dng.vnn.vn

This friendly, well-run hotel on
five floors sits close to the liveliest part of Nha Trang. The best
rooms (VIP) are large and have
balconies with sea views. All
rooms have bathrooms with
tubs. Plants are crowded onto
the suite balconies. The top-
floor restaurant and open-air
bar have fantastic sea views.
There is free internet access.

🛏 US$15–45, including breakfast, taxes
🛈 24 🔄

ANA MANDARA

Tran Phu Street, Nha Trang
Tel 058-829829

www.six-senses.com

In Nha Trang's finest beach
resort guests are pampered
from head to toe. Bungalows
designed in native wood and
rattan are set amid extensive
tropical foliage on the beach
off Nha Trang's main boulevard. The 17 villas have 35
garden-view rooms, 11 sea-
view rooms, and more
expensive deluxe rooms and
suites. All rooms have a private terrace, king-size or twin
beds, bathtubs, phones, safe-
deposit boxes, satellite TVs,
minibars, and coffee- and
tea-makers. There are two
pools, one with a Jacuzzi, a
tennis court, and several
places to eat. The Pavilion
restaurant, with veranda
tables overlooking the
gardens and Nha Trang Bay,
serves Vietnamese and international food; the poolside
Beach restaurant and bar
specializes in seafood, which
can be cooked to guests'
liking or presented the chef's
way. Private meals can also
be provided on the villa terrace. The Six Senses Spa has
a sauna, steam baths and
treatment rooms where a
whole range of therapies is
on offer, plus activities such
as t'ai chi and aikido
(▷ 180). Among guest
services are fax, translation
and internet access, laundry
and dry cleaning, an air-conditioned library, a craft shop
and travel and tour information. Airport transfer can be
arranged at 24 hours' notice,
for US$10 per person.

🛏 US$205–446, excluding breakfast
and taxes
🛈 74
🔄 🔄

STAYING

NHA TRANG LODGE

42 Tran Phu Street, Nha Trang
Tel 058-521900
www.nhatranglodge
Most rooms in this 14-floor building dominating the main road in Nha Trang overlook the beach, and some have extraordinary sea views. Rooms are comfortable, if rather small, with phones, satellite TV, minibars and private bathrooms. Service is efficient, and guests have the use of a pool, tennis courts, a disco, casino, billiards room and car rental, plus massage, sauna, steam bath, business amenities and an ATM in the foyer.

US$50–145, including breakfast, excluding taxes

121

QUE THAO
(PERFUME GRASS INN)

4A Biet Thu Street, Nha Trang
Tel 058-524286
www.perfume-grass.com
huanaz@dng.vnn.vn
Rooms are basic, but stylish and clean, in this great, quiet little hotel in the budget district of Nha Trang, near all the bars and restaurants. It's efficiently run by the family owners and has a range of accommodations whose prices depend on whether you would like air-conditioning, bathtubs and breakfast. All rooms have private toilets and hot showers. There is an internet service in the reception area. Advance reservation is recommended.

US$10–25, excluding breakfast, including taxes

21

Some rooms

VINPEARL RESORT AND SPA

Hon Tre Island (Reception and jetty: 7 Tran Phu Street, Nha Trang)
Tel 058-598188
www.sofitel.com
There has been investment and development on Hon Tre on a colossal scale and the sight of another sprawling resort on this tropical island may not appeal to everyone. For those who welcome it, there's a bewildering range of facilities, including a spa, the largest pool in Southeast Asia, restaurants, a children's playground and a casino. Opulent rooms are beautifully finished in dark woods, rattan and

marble. All have balconies, some with sea views; those described as "hill view" rooms actually face a blank quarry wall. Phones, minibars, safe-deposit boxes, tea- and coffee-making equipment, radios, satellite TVs and kimonos are all provided. There are rooms equipped for guests with disabilities.

From US$160, excluding breakfast and taxes

230

WHALE ISLAND RESORT

Boat from Dam Mon pier
Tel 058-840501
www.whaleislandresort.com
A 2.5-hour journey north of Nha Trang brings you to this relaxing resort, among the aquamarine waters of the South China Sea. Bamboo cabins are scattered around the area, and have mosquito nets, fans, shower rooms, sinks and toilets. All sorts of water sports are available, including diving, catamarans, windsurfing and canoeing. Between April and July, you may see whale sharks offshore. Rates are all-inclusive; the longer the duration of the stay, the lower the rates. Prices include transportation from Nha Trang and boat transfer to Whale Island, plus meals at the seafood restaurant.

US$120–165

23

YOK DON NATIONAL PARK

NATIONAL PARK ACCOMMODATIONS

Buon Don District
Dak Lak Province
Tel 050-783056
parcyd@dng.vnn.vn
Each basic national park guesthouse room includes two beds, a TV, hot shower and fan.

EVASON HIDEAWAY AT ANA MANDARA

Ninh Van Bay, accessible by speed boat from Nha Trang (20 minutes)
Tel 058-522222
www.sixsenses.com

Opened in November 2004, the stylishly discreet Evason Hideaway makes the most of Ninh Van Bay's setting, tucking itself between the rocks and mountains and overlooking the coral reef and white-sand beach. The scattered villas have large, stand-alone wooden bathtubs, wine cellars, plunge pools, and verandas or floating terraces and sundecks. CDs and in-house video movies are available on request, and standard amenities are minibar, safe-deposit box, tea- and coffee-making equipment, phone and satellite TV. The restaurant serves fusion meals and is open to the fresh air (with retractable screens in case of bad weather). The Six Senses Spa blends into the rocks beside a waterfall, providing every conceivable treatment, and tennis courts, water sports, dive facilities and trekking are available. Transfers can be arranged from the airport at 24 hours' notice, for US$10 per person.

US$650–2,000 excluding breakfast and taxes

52

Three of the rooms have air-conditioning. There is also a campground with tents for rent at US$5.

US$8 per person, US$3 per person for campground

4

Some rooms

HO CHI MINH CITY

Ho Chi Minh City has a huge range of accommodations, including some of the country's finest hotels, many newly built, and some interesting historical hotels, which tend to belong to and be run by the state tourist agency Saigontourist. Expect efficient and friendly service at the best hotels and high standards of facilities. Most of the better, mid-range hotels are concentrated in the middle of town, Districts 1 and 3, and near the airport. Increasingly, however, good hotels can be found throughout the city, particularly privately run mini-hotels. Saigon plays host to many long-stay business visitors, and there are a number of apartment developments where they may feel more comfortable. Although the most high-profile apartment buildings are rather expensive, there are less costly versions, and even relatively small hotels sometimes have top-floor apartments. Most visitors on a tight budget head straight for the Pham Ngu Lao area, which has the greatest concentration of budget hotels and guesthouses. This area is also full of low-cost eateries and travel agencies.

PRICES AND SYMBOLS

Prices are for a double room for one night. All the hotels listed accept credit cards unless otherwise stated. Note that rates vary widely throughout the year.

For a key to the symbols, ▷ 2.

ARC EN CIEL

52–56 Tan Da Street, District 5
Tel 08-8554435
www.arcenciel-hotel.com

This is the best hotel in Cholon (▷ 132–134), and is within walking distance of all the major Chinatown pagodas. Run by Saigontourist, it has four restaurants and a rooftop bar with fine views. Standard rooms have TVs, minibars and firm mattresses, but not much of a view; the bathrooms are small. Some rooms have bathtubs. Superior rooms, with bigger bathrooms, cost an extra US$5. Reception has the only safe-deposit box.

US$30–60, including breakfast and taxes
86

BONG SEN

117–123 Dong Khoi Street, District 1
Tel 08-8291516
www.hotelbongsen.com

The standard rooms at this well-run Saigontourist hotel in the shopping district are small —though bigger than in its sister hotel, the Annex. They have TVs, minibars, phones and showers. Superior rooms (only slightly more expensive) are larger and have bathtubs in the bathrooms. Only the most expensive rooms have city views. Eat in the restaurant and the Green Leaf Café (▷ 225).

SPECIAL

CARAVELLE

19 Lam Son Square, District 1
Tel 08-8234999

One of the city's top hotels sits in the heart of downtown. It incorporates the old Air France Caravelle hotel, onto which extra floors have been added (there are 24 floors in total). All rooms have tea- and coffee-making equipment, a phone, minibar and cable TV. The deluxe room has a DVD player, magazines and a fax. The hotel's restaurant, Nineteen, serves an excellent buffet lunch and dinner (▷ 227), and Saigon Saigon, the rooftop bar, draws the crowds until the early hours. Boutiques, a pool, a health center and treatments give this luxurious hotel added appeal. One room is equipped for guests with disabilities.

US$321–$980, excluding breakfast and taxes
335 (100 non-smoking)

A laundry, airport transfers, massages and a steam room are available.

US$40–120, including breakfast, excluding taxes
127

BONG SEN HOTEL ANNEX

61–63 Hai Ba Trung Street, District 1
Tel 08-8235818
www.hotelbongsen.com

Rooms in this well-managed, central hotel are very small and decorated with attractive photographs. Bathrooms are adequately sized, and the complimentary drinking water is a bonus for a hotel in this class. Rooms with city views cost an extra US$15. All rooms have a TV, minibar and phone, and there's a laundry service, car rental and airport transfer. The restaurant, the Co Noi, is on the eighth floor.

US$50–$150, including breakfast, excluding taxes
57

CONTINENTAL

132–134 Dong Khoi Street, District 1
Tel 08-8299252
www.continentalvietnam.com

Built in 1880 and renovated in 1989, the Continental is an integral part of the city's history (▷ 137), facing the

Opera House in central Saigon. The whole place has an air of faded colonial splendor. Its large but dated rooms are in need of an upgrade, but the hotel's character shines through. The restaurant, the Venezia, is claimed by the

hotel as the city's first Italian eatery, and is run jointly by a Vietnamese and an Italian. Other hotel facilities include a business center, fitness room and pool, car rental, airport transfer and a baby-sitting service. All rooms have a phone, cable TV, minibar and private bathroom, and—probably to stamp out the theft of souvenirs—every item in the room is for sale. Some rooms have a garden view.

🅦 US$70–150, including breakfast, excluding taxes

ℹ 83

EQUATORIAL

242 Tran Binh Trong Street, District 5
Tel 08-8397777
www.equatorial.com

A free shuttle takes you to this rather out-of-the-way hotel between Cholon and downtown Saigon. When you arrive, you'll find a marble-cool oasis of calm and a team of friendly staff. Rooms are large and airy, with high ceilings, terraces and views of the hotel garden, and all have a phone, cable TV, tea- and coffee-making equipment, minibar and voice mail. The Equatorial has the biggest ballroom in the city; exhibits and conferences are regularly held here. The large swimming pool has a sunken bar, and there's a well-equipped gym and massage service, and Japanese, Chinese and Western restaurants.

🅦 US$170–800, excluding breakfast and taxes

ℹ 333 (non-smoking on request)

GRAND

8 Dong Khoi Street, District 1
Tel 08-8230163
www.grandsaigon.com

This 1930s building in the heart of the shopping district has been extensively renovated; happily, the stained glass and marble staircase have largely survived the process. The attractive pool (try to get a poolside room) is surrounded by a plant-filled patio. Rooms all have cable TV, in-house movies, a minibar, phone and safe-deposit box. The hotel can arrange car rental and a laundry service. There is a 12th-floor restaurant, the Belle Vue, with panoramic views, a coffee

DUXTON

63 Nguyen Hue Boulevard, District 1
Tel 08-8222999

This stylish boutique hotel in the middle of Saigon is run by Vietnam Tourism and was formerly known as the Saigon Prince. Beds are beautifully made-up with cushions and silk bedspreads, and top-of-the-range rooms come with large desks, complimentary fruit and attractive black-marble bathrooms hung with flower prints. All rooms have tea- and coffee-making equipment, cable TV and in-house movies, a safe-deposit box and minibar, and in the health center—with its waterfall shower—there's a sauna, Jacuzzi, steam room and spa (with different opening hours for men and women). There's also a nightclub, and the Western/Vietnamese restaurant and Japanese restaurant are open 24 hours.

🅦 US$75–270, excluding taxes. Breakfast included for executive rooms and suites only

ℹ 192 rooms (28 non-smoking)

shop and patisserie, a beauty salon, a sauna, a steam bath and Jacuzzi and massage. Nonresidents can use the swimming pool for US$3.

🅦 US$100–200, including breakfast and taxes

ℹ 128 (1 floor non-smoking)

HONG HOA

185/28 Pham Ngu Lao Street, District 1
Tel 08-8361915
www.honghoavn.com

There are three types of room in this airy, well-run family hotel in the heart of the backpackers' district. The least expensive is small and has no refrigerator or TV; the mid-priced rooms have a bathtub; and the most expensive are the largest, with a balcony and satellite TV, but a shower only. Downstairs is a supermarket and banks of computers with email connection.

🅦 US$13–18, excluding breakfast, including taxes

ℹ 9

LEGEND

2A–4A Ton Duc Thang Street, District 1
Tel 08-8233333
www.legendsaigon.com

The Legend overlooks the river and has Saigon's most ostentatious foyer, with large bronze horse statues dominating the entrance and two golden phoenixes guarding the lobby bar. Business clients, particularly from Japan, favor this hotel, which has extensive business facilities. The Legend's three restaurants serve a mix of Asian food. Other facilities include a massage and fitness center, a staffed children's play area and a jazz bar with live music from Tuesday to Sunday. The Sunday lunch buffet in the Atrium Café is very good, and barbecued food is cooked by the outdoor pool, at the poolside bar. Rooms have tea- and coffee-making equipment, cable TV with in-house movies, a minibar, phone and voice mail, and there are baby-sitting and laundry services. Two rooms are equipped for guests with disabilities.

🅦 US$180–850, excluding breakfast and taxes

ℹ 283 (42 non-smoking)

LINH

40/10 Bui Vien Street, District 1
Tel/fax 08-8369641
linh.hb@hcm.vnn.vn

This is a well-priced, small and very friendly, family-run hotel in the middle of the Pham Ngu Lao budget area. All rooms have two beds and a small private bathroom with a shower. There is free internet access for guests and an amazing range of amenities, given the price, including cable TV, air conditioning, hot water, phone and refrigerator.

🅦 US$7–20, excluding breakfast, including taxes

ℹ 5

STAYING

MAJESTIC

1 Dong Khoi Street, District 1
Tel 08-8295517
www.majesticsaigon.com

Built in 1925, this riverside hotel has been tastefully restored. The top-of-the-range rooms have wooden floors, queen-size beds and beige and black marble bathrooms, plus fantastic river views from their balconies. Other rooms are smaller and a little cramped. All have minibars, phones, safe-deposit boxes and cable TV. From the ninth-floor Bellevue bar (4pm–midnight) there are magnificent views of the river and the docks beyond. Facilities include an airport transfer, baby-sitting, laundry services, sauna and massages.
US$120–300, excluding breakfast, including taxes
176

MOGAMBO

20 bis Thi Sach Street, District 1
Tel 08-8251311
www.elephantguide.com/mogambo
The Mogambo is perfect for budget-conscious visitors. The small hotel is above a bar-diner and surrounded by some of the city's best restaurants. The large rooms, five with king-size beds and five with two beds, have writing desks, bathrooms with tubs, minibars, satellite TV and phones, and complimentary bottled drinking water. The hotel can arrange car rental, tour guides, flight bookings and laundry, and the restaurant serves an international menu.
US$24–40, excluding breakfast, including taxes
10

NEW WORLD

76 Le Lai Street, District 1
Tel 08-8228888

Business travelers make up a large quota of the guests at this hotel on the edge of District 1 and close to Ben Thanh Market. Staff are efficient, friendly and speak English. The striking lobby is surrounded by glass, and has dusted gold and beige columns and a domed atrium; this lavishness of style is matched in the bedrooms, which have marble private bathrooms and writing desks, as well as standard amenities such as safe-deposit boxes, cable TV with in-house movies, phones and minibars. Eating options include a restaurant serving a choice of Chinese and Western food, a patisserie and a bakery, and there's a dry-cleaning service, an ATM, a nightclub, a gym, floodlit tennis courts, a jogging track and a health center. The Executive Floor is excellent value with breakfast, afternoon tea and refreshments available all day.
US$120–200, excluding breakfast and taxes
552 (4 floors non-smoking)

RENAISSANCE RIVERSIDE

8–15 Ton Duc Thang Street, District 1
Tel 08-8220033
www.renaissancehotels.com/sgnbr
This popular, well-run riverfront hotel has Vietnam's highest atrium. While the hotel is large, in both style and feel it is almost a boutique hotel. Rooms are comfortable and have cable TV, voicemail, a minibar and a safe-deposit box. Those with a river view cost extra. The rooftop pool, which is open to nonresidents for US$10, has fabulous views, and there are sauna and massage and

health club rooms. The restaurant serves Western and Eastern food, and you can take afternoon tea (daily 3.30–6) at the lobby café, served on tiered chrome cake stands for US$8, or wine and cheese between 5pm and midnight. Hotel services include baby-sitting and laundry. Two rooms are equipped for guests with disabilities.

US$95–750, excluding breakfast and taxes
336 (208 non-smoking)

REX

141 Nguyen Hue Boulevard, District 1
Tel 08-8292185
www.rexhotelvietnam.com

The historically important Rex hotel (▷ 137) in the heart of Ho Chi Minh City has unusual interior design. The large lobby is decorated entirely in wood, furnished with numerous wicker chairs, and dominated by the ceiling, a vast replica of a Dong Son drum. Superior rooms have small bathtubs and face an internal courtyard; deluxe rooms are double the size, but those on the main road are noisy. Interior deluxe rooms are similar, but some have private balconies. All have phones, cable TV and minibars, and the hotel can provide airport transfer and a laundry service. The Mimosa Club has an open-air pool, a rooftop tennis court, a fitness center with massage, sauna and steam rooms, and a beauty salon. Four rooms are equipped for guests with disabilities. In addition to its restaurants and cafés, guests can also visit the Bingo Club, a gaming center with slot machines, gaming tables and video games: Remember to bring your passport, as the Bingo Club is open only to foreign visitors.

US$120–600, including breakfast and taxes
227

SHERATON

88 Dong Khoi Street,
District 1
Tel 08-8272828
www.sheraton.com/saigon

Saigon's newest smart hotel is sandwiched into a downtown street and has proved popular since it opened in late 2003. The Saigon Café serves very good lunches and dinners, and Level 23 is a must for an evening drink, not least for the wonderful views across Saigon. There's also a restaurant, nightclub and bars, and there is live entertainment in The Lounge. The hotel also has shops, a pool, a spa, and squash and tennis courts. Baby-sitting and laundry services are available. Modern, stylish rooms are equipped with coffee- and tea-makers, minibars and cable TV, and all have private bathrooms with both tubs and showers. Some rooms are equipped for guests with disabilities.

US$150–850, excluding breakfast and taxes
380 (non-smoking on request)

SPRING

44–46 Le Thanh Ton Street,
District 1
Tel 08-8297362

In a central position near several excellent restaurants, the Spring hotel is comfortable and well run by friendly and helpful staff. Top-of-the-range rooms have king-size beds; standard rooms are only slightly smaller, but the bathrooms are much smaller and space is tight. Other in-room amenities include TVs and in-house movies, minibars, refrigerators, safe-deposit boxes and phones. Hotel guests have free internet use, and local phone calls. There's a restaurant and bar, a laundry service and car rental, and tours can be arranged here.

US$34–75, including breakfast, excluding taxes
45

SOFITEL PLAZA SAIGON

17 Le Duan Street,
District 1
Tel 08-8241555
www.accorhotels-asia.com

This smart, fashionable and comfortable hotel surpasses many other large hotels in the city because of its superb design—from the sculptures in the lobby to the attractive rooftop pool (open to non-residents for US$10). The more expensive rooms have balconies, and all have mini-bars, phones and cable TV. The Provençal restaurant often hosts cooking classes, and there's a free shuttle to downtown Saigon. Laundry and baby-sitting services, massage, a sauna and steam room are all available.

US$120–1,500, excluding breakfast and taxes
322 (35 non-smoking)

There are various hotel options in Ho Chi Minh City, from the budget to the high profile

STAYING

THE SOUTH

South of Saigon lies the Mekong Delta, a rural area with few great places to stay. With the notable exception of Phu Quoc island, the long and muddy coastline has little to offer in the way of attractive beach or sea bases. The Hon Chong peninsula, however, is rated as the best beachfront in the Mekong. The small towns of the Mekong Delta are normally monopolized by the provincial tourist board, but Can Tho has passed responsibility for much of its visitor trade into private hands; here, and at Chau Doc, hotel standards are high. An interesting change from standard hotels are the occasional homestays that can be arranged on farms and in the many orchards of the Mekong region. Private agencies in Ho Chi Minh City can reserve places (▷ 202–204), or once you are in the Mekong Delta, go to the local tourist office to make arrangements. Southeast of Ho Chi Minh City are Vung Tau and Long Hai, the former with a huge number of competitively priced hotels and guesthouses. These are primarily intended for the domestic tourist market or for overseas businesspeople, but they do provide a good standard of accommodations for vacationers too. A few attractive seaside hotels and resorts line the Long Hai–Ho Coc stretch of coast, including simple and inexpensive A-frame huts and beach cabins. The island of Phu Quoc is also home to a growing selection of seaside resorts; most of these are run by Saigontourist, but there are also privately run businesses in operation.

STAYING

CAN THO

GOLF CAN THO HOTEL

2 Hai Ba Trung Street, Can Tho
Tel 071-812210
www.golfhotel.vnn.vn

Although the Golf Can Tho Hotel is the tallest in town, lacks for nothing in facilities and is excellent value, it

possesses little charm. Rooms are large, plainly decorated and well equipped with minibars, safe-deposit boxes, phones, cable TVs and balconies overlooking the river. The restaurants, on the ninth, tenth and eleventh floors, provide fine dining, and the views from the Windy Restaurant on the ninth floor are superb. Other facilities include a massage center with sauna and steam bath, a karaoke bar, nightclub, beauty parlor and car rental and laundry services.

🅑 US$60–200, including breakfast and taxes
🛏 101
📺 🍴 ♿

HOA BINH HOTEL

5 Hoa Binh Avenue
Can Tho
Tel 071-820536
www.hoabinhhotel.com

This is a perfectly comfortable, quiet, budget hotel, just 10 minutes' walk from the riverside promenade, next to a bank with an ATM machine and around the corner from an excellent bakery. Rooms are simply furnished and could do with some updating, but at this price represent good value as they all have air-conditioning, stand-alone fans, spacious bathrooms with piping-hot water and limited satellite TV.

🅑 US$25–50, including basic breakfast and taxes
🛏 56
🍴

SAIGON CAN THO

55 Phan Dinh Phung Street,
Can Tho
Tel 071-825831
www.saigoncantho.com.vn

In this comfortable, central business hotel run by Saigontourist, standard rooms have balconies, and larger rooms have desks; all have cable TV with in-house movies, a minibar and phone, and guests receive complimentary fruit and a welcome drink on arrival, and free mineral water every day. The restaurant is open 24 hours. A small sauna, massage and steam-bath area is laid out in small cabins; massages are discounted by 10 percent for hotel residents.

🅑 US$40–55, including breakfast and taxes
🛏 46
♿

CHAU DOC

MEKONG GUESTHOUSE

Duong Len Tao Ngo, Nui Sam
Tel 076-861870
mekongguesthouse@yahoo.com

Walkers in the area might appreciate this small, basic guesthouse on the lower slopes of Nui Sam mountain. Free transportation leaves from Chau Doc's Mekong Café, 5–6 Nguyen Huu Canh Street; otherwise a xe ôm will take you here for 8,000d. All rooms have fans, mosquito nets, blankets and cold-water showers, except the dormitory, which has a shared bathroom. Food is served all day—there is a lunch and dinner menu—and breakfast is less than a US dollar. There is plenty of seating, and hammocks swing

VICTORIA CAN THO

Cai Khe Ward, Can Tho
Tel 071-810111

One of the most beautiful hotels in Vietnam has a riverside garden location, a breezy, open reception area, and an emphasis on comfort. The focal point is the floodlit pool, flanked by the lobby bar and restaurant. Elegant rooms are equipped with coffee- and tea-makers, a minibar, safe-deposit box, phone and cable TV. Guests staying in suites receive rice, rice wine, pineapple and dragonfruit jam and incense sticks. Other facilities include a tennis court and massages, plus baby-sitting and laundry services. Packages are available, offering one night (US$92), including taxes, per person for a two/king-bed room, breakfast, dinner, a boat cruise to Cai Rang, a 10-minute hand or foot massage, a welcome drink and fruit basket, a homemade gift, and use of the tennis court, sauna and gym. A shuttle usually takes guests from the Ninh Kieu jetty on Hai Ba Trung Street in town to the little peninsula on the banks of the Hau River; when this is out of operation, the *Victoria Hotel* speedboat connects with Saigon (5 hours) and Chau Doc (3 hours).

US$108–245, excluding breakfast and taxes

92

VICTORIA CHAU DOC

32 Le Loi Street,
Chau Doc
Tel 076-865010
resa.chaudoc@victoriahotels-asia.com

This old, cream building with its riverfront pool is the perfect place in which to relax and look out over the busy, three-way Mekong intersection on which the hotel sits. The best room is the junior suite, whose balcony faces the tributary heading to Phnom Penh. Solid-wood lampstands, desks, gold-colored curtains and champagne in the minibars are added extras; cable TV and in-house movies are standard. Superior rooms are just as attractive as the suites but smaller; some rooms have showers but no bathtubs. Oscar, the white-faced gibbon rescued from a Saigon animal market, plays with guests in the grounds, and the hotel offers baby-sitting, laundry, sauna and massage services. The Victoria Group runs a speedboat from

Saigon to Can Tho, from Can Tho to Chau Doc and on to Phnom Penh.

US$100–220, excluding breakfast and taxes

92

CON DAO

SAIGON CONDAO HOTEL

18 Ton Duc Thang Street,
Con Dao
Tel 064-830155/830567
www.saigoncondao.com

The Saigon Condao Hotel is a Saigontourist property in converted French buildings on the waterfront. There are seven villas with a total of 36 rooms overlooking the sea in tropical, landscaped gardens. Facilities include sauna, massage, tennis courts and karaoke. All rooms have satellite TV, in-house movies, a minibar and phone, and the hotel provides same-day laundry, car rental, and a tour and travel desk. The restaurant serves international, Asian and seafood specialties.

US$40–60, including breakfast and taxes

36

HA TIEN

DONG HO

2 Tran Hau Street,
Ha Tien
Tel/fax 077-852141

This blue-shuttered building on the quiet riverside is Ha Tien's main draw. Rooms are brighter and a little smarter than at the nearby To Chau (▷ 256), but are basic. Those with a balcony overlooking the river and pontoon bridge are the best options. All the rooms have two beds and a private bathroom, and air-conditioning is available. Bottled water is sold in the foyer. No credit cards are accepted.

160,000d, including breakfast and taxes

17

Some rooms

under thatched-roof areas. Extra services include DVDs to rent, a book exchange, internet access and bicycle rental.

Dormitories US$2, doubles US$6

10

US$2 extra

TO CHAU
56 Dong Ho Street,
Ha Tien
Tel 077-852148
Fax 077-852141

The views are the main attraction of this small hotel on the riverfront. Rooms are very large but very spartan, though all come equipped with air-conditioning, TV, minibar and private bathroom with hot water. The best rooms are those with a view of the To Chau River, as these have balconies. The owner and his family are friendly and speak a little English.

💵 160,000d–192,000d, including breakfast and taxes
🛏 11
🛗 Available for 30,000d extra

HON CHONG PENINSULA

GREEN HILL GUESTHOUSE
905 Hon Chong,
Binh An
Tel 077-854369

Just above Duong Beach, perched on a hill, this all-white guesthouse is the friendliest, most pleasant place to stay on the peninsula. Run by the welcoming, English-speaking owner, Tuyen, the building is enhanced by flourishing bougainvillea. All rooms have a private bathroom with tub and hot water. Some of the top-of-the-range rooms have balconies, and all enjoy panoramic views of the bay. Three deluxe rooms can accommodate up to four people. Vietnamese meals are cooked by Tuyen's wife in the restaurant (open 6am–midnight), and he serves great milky coffee.

💵 From 200,000d, excluding breakfast; no taxes
🛏 9 rooms
🛗

MY LAN
Opposite Duong Beach,
Hon Chong
Tel 077-759044
Fax 077-759040

The large, clean rooms in this secure, gated hotel on the beach road are excellent value for money. Housed in smart, new cabins, they have ultra-clean, white-tiled floors, TVs and ceiling fans, as well as air-conditioning, shower units and suitcase holders. The

open-fronted 24-hour restaurant serves a good breakfast; its menu is in Vietnamese only, but some staff speak basic English. Dinner options include fried squid, fried rice with shrimp and crab soup.

💵 US$15–20, including breakfast and taxes
🛏 24
🛗

LONG HAI

ANOASIS BEACH RESORT
2 miles (3km) east of Long Hai
Tel 064-868227
www.anoasisresort.com.vn

Anoasis is run by Anoa, a Frenchwoman of Vietnamese origin who, in 1992, flew her helicopter and husband from Paris to Hanoi. Scenically, this is one of the most appealing of all Vietnam's resorts, set in 32 acres (13ha) of tropical trees and unspoiled vegetation, with views of the mountains and the ocean. It belonged to the last emperor of Vietnam. Cabins are scattered through a parkland setting with wide views over the sea. Rooms are attractively finished, and everything is on a generous scale, with baths big enough for two, and comfortable and attractive furnishings. Phones, cable TV, minibars and balconies or decks are standard. There's a good restaurant with a French chef, a gigantic pool, a private beach,

tennis courts, massage and a jetty, and the resort provides airport transfers and a laundry service. To reach Anoasis, take a *xe ôm* from Ba Ria or the Vung Tau hydrofoil and then taxi or motorcycle.

💵 US$112–158, including breakfast, excluding taxes
🛏 15 cottage cabins, 12 family cabins, 17 pavilion rooms, 2 ocean villas
🏊 🛗

MY THO

CHUONG DUONG
10 30 Thang 4 Street,
My Tho
Tel 073-870875
Fax 073-874250

By far the best hotel in town, the Chuong Duong is a large, new hotel occupying a prime riverside location in front of the erstwhile hydrofoil ferry. All rooms overlook the river and are inoffensively decorated in beige and diluted orange, and all have a private bathroom, satellite TV and minibar. The in-house restaurant has a long menu including Mekong specialties such as stir-fried sea cucumber with Chinese mushrooms, plus a range of Euro-Asian, Chinese and Vietnamese dishes; some of its tables overlook the river.

💵 US$20–40, including breakfast and taxes
🛏 27
🛗

PHU QUOC

KIM HOA RESORT
Khu Pho I,
Duong Dong
Tel 077-848969

This small resort has wooden bungalows on a clean strip of sand, each with one double and one single bed. The bathrooms have showers without units. There are also more basic rooms that are not on the beach, but which have small bathrooms. Standard in-room amenities are refrigerators, satellite TV and phones. The resort has a restaurant specializing in seafood dishes, and can arrange fishing, snorkeling and sightseeing trips, as well as car and motorcycle rental. Free pickup is available from the airport.

💵 US$26–40, including breakfast and taxes
🛏 56
🛗 Some rooms

MANGO BAY

On Lang Beach
Phu Quoc
Tel 0903-382207
www.mangobayphuquoc.com

This welcoming, Australian-owned resort has a number of different bungalows and rooms, a beachfront restaurant serving fresh seafood and Vietnamese and Western dishes, and a beach bar. There are eight rammed-earth bungalows with fans, tiled floors and bamboo furniture, and three traditional Phu Quoc fishermen's bungalows. The five rooms have a wonderful, large communal veranda. Some rooms have outdoor bathrooms in bamboo-enclosed patios. The resort can arrange night squid-fishing, a free small boat, swimming and snorkeling equipment, fishing trips, car and motorcycle rental, and pays 50 percent of the taxi fare from the airport, or the full fare for a moto taxi.

🍴 Veranda rooms US$25, rammed earth bungalows US$50, fishermen's bungalows US$45. Prices excluding breakfast ☎ 16 rooms

SAIGON-PHU QUOC RESORT

1 Trang Hung Dao Street,
Duong Dong,
Phu Quoc
Tel 077-846999
www.sgphuquocresort.com.vn

Overlooking the sea on a hillside garden, cabins and villas surround an attractive

swimming pool in this pleasant resort. All rooms have satellite TV, phone, minibar, private bathroom with tub or shower and safe-deposit box. The costlier President Suite has two TVs, a computer, a kitchenette and a Jacuzzi; the VIP is less expensive, brighter and better, with a sea view and bathtub. An enviable list of facilities includes a reasonably priced restaurant serving international food, internet access, play equipment, a beauty salon, motorcycle rental, fishing, tennis, massage, snorkeling, horseback riding and bicycling. Baby-sitting and laundry services are available, and a shop in the lobby sells clothes and crafts. Airport transfers are included in the price. One cabin is equipped for guests with disabilities.

🍴 US$76–320, including breakfast and taxes
☎ 90
🏖️ ♿

THANG LOI

Ong Lang Beach
Phu Quoc
Tel 077-985002
www.phu-quoc.de

For complete peace and quiet, this German-owned rustic place is a good bet, with wooden cabins set in a remote coconut plantation on Ong Lang Beach. Cabins are furnished basically with bamboo furniture, fans and mosquito nets, but with extra touches, including shelves and hooks; some have hot water. There's a good bar and restaurant, a library and CDs, and a newly built jetty juts out into the sea, a short walk from the cabins. There is no air-conditioning.

🍴 US$10–30, excluding breakfast, including taxes
☎ 15

TROPICANA RESORT

Duong Dong,
Phu Quoc
Tel 077-847127
www.tropicanaphuquoc.com

Here you'll find high-quality wooden cabins and rooms in a tropical garden next to the beach. There is a pool and a good restaurant. Cabins have terraces with seating, large glass doors, rustic wooden fittings, mosquito nets and good hot showers. No boat tours are offered, but one-day motorcycle rental is available at 100,000d; for 400,000d you can rent a four-wheel drive with driver. Two-way airport transfer is available free; travel from the port is 200,000d.

🍴 US$20–75, including breakfast and taxes
☎ 35
🏖️ ♿

VINH LONG

CUU LONG

1 1 Thang 5 Street
Vinh Long
Tel 070-823656

Set back from the river with a huge, green, glass-fronted facade, the Cuu Long is well maintained and its comfortable, carpeted rooms all have private bathrooms with tubs. There is a restaurant, internet connections and a travel service (Cuu Long Tourist), and massage and tennis courts are available. The hotel is in a convenient spot, opposite the wharf where boats leave for An Binh Island.

🍴 US$30–75, including breakfast and taxes
☎ 54
♿

MEKONG HOMESTAYS

Cuu Long Tourist,
1 Thang 5 Street,
Vinh Long
Tel 070-823616
cuulongtourist1@ hcm.vnn.vn

Facing Vinh Long town in the Co Chien River, a tributary of the Mekong, is a large island that is further sliced into smaller islands by ribbons of narrow canals. Two of these smaller islands are An Binh Island and Binh Hoa Phuoc. Cuu Long Tourist runs 12 homestays on these islands—a wonderful way to immerse yourself in local life. The accommodations are basic, with camp beds, shared bathrooms and mosquito nets, and include a home-cooked dinner made from the fruits of the delta (elephant-ear fish with abundant greens, including mint, spring rolls, and beef cooked in coconut). Evening drinks are taken on the patio or terrace or on the riverfront, chatting with the owner. Travel is by sampan or on foot down the winding paths that link the communities. A stay includes tea and fruit at a traditional house,
visits to see rice cakes and popcorn being made, and a trip to a brick factory to see the pyramid kilns and watch terra-cotta pots being created. The boat trip, transfers, dinner and local guide are all included in the price.

US$67, including one breakfast
11 homestays

VUNG TAU

GRAND

2 Nguyen Du Street,
Vung Tau
Tel 064-856888
www.grand.oscvn.com

An excellent restoration project has brought this hotel, in a great position overlooking the sea, back to its former glory. Rooms are comfortable and clean, and all have satellite TV, safe-deposit box, phone, minibar, tea- and coffee-maker, internet access and private bathroom. The more expensive rooms have extras such as complimentary fruit, flowers and mineral water, and free use of the swimming pool and fitness center. The restaurant serves Asian and European dishes, or you can relax over a drink in the bar or on the terrace. Other hotel services include tennis courts, a steam bath, massages, laundry, dry cleaning services and car rental.

US$60–120, including breakfast and taxes
59

PALACE

11 Nguyen Trai Street,
Vung Tau
Tel 064-856411
palacevt@hcm.vnn.vn

This renovated and expanded hotel, just a few minutes' walk from Bai Truoc (Front Beach) and close to popular bars and restaurants, offers comfortable rooms and efficient service. Rooms have a minibar, phone and cable TV, and there is an attractive swimming pool under the shade of a tamarind tree. A gym, massage facilities and a tennis court are available, and the restaurant serves European and Asian dishes and seafood.

US$40–80, including breakfast and taxes
120

PETRO HOUSE

63 Tran Hung Dao Street,
Vung Tau
Tel 064-852014
petro.htl@hcm.vnn.vn

Central, comfortable and decorated in colonial style, this boutique hotel has full amenities, including a swimming pool, a business center and Ma Maison, a good French restaurant. Rooms have cable TV and phones. Though not on the beach, this is one of the most popular choices in town.

US$80–150, including breakfast and taxes
75

ROYAL HOTEL

36 Quang Trung Street,
Vung Tau
Tel 064-859852
rht@hcm.vnn.vn

This hotel occupies a prime seafront site facing Bai Truoc (Front Beach), and some of its rooms have spectacular views. The decoration is slightly old-fashioned, but all rooms have a private bathroom with tub, minibar, safe-deposit box, phone, satellite TV and in-house movies. The pool is shared with the adjoining Rex Hotel, and there is a seafood restaurant, a Japanese restaurant, car rental and airline reservation desk. The hotel can arrange tours of Vung Tau.

US$50–80, including breakfast and taxes
53

SAMMY

157 Thuy Van Street,
Bai Sau (Back Beach),
Vung Tau
Tel 064-854755
sammyhotel@hcm.vnn.vn

Easily the best hotel along the Back Beach, Sammy is a large and very comfortable place, somewhat glitzy and known for its efficient service, good views, business facilities and its highly recommended Chinese restaurant. Rooms have a minibar, safe-deposit box and cable TV, and there's a beauty salon, nightclub, massages and sauna, and a laundry service. Customers also have use of the Ocean Park swimming pool opposite, at reduced prices.

US$35–80, excluding breakfast, including taxes
119 (non-smoking on request)

Planning

BEFORE YOU GO

CLIMATE

● Vietnam stretches more than 1,118 miles (1,800km) from north to south, and the weather in the two principal cities, Hanoi in the north and Saigon in the south, is very different. Average temperatures tend to rise the farther south you venture. The exceptions to this rule are the interior highland areas, where the altitude makes it much colder.

● In the north, winter stretches from November through April, with temperatures averaging 61°F (16°C), and little rainfall. The summer begins in May and lasts until October. During these months it can be very hot, with an average temperature of 86°F (30°C), along with heavy rainfall and the occasional typhoon.

● Central Vietnam has a transitional climate, midway between that in the south and that in the north. Hué has a reputation for particularly poor weather; it is often overcast, and an umbrella is needed whatever the month—even during the short "dry" season between February and April.

● In the south, temperatures are fairly constant through the year—77°F (25°C) to 86°F (30°C)—and the seasons are determined by the rains. The dry season runs from November through April (when there is virtually no rain whatsoever) and the wet season from May through October. The hottest months are March and April, before the rains have broken. Typhoons are common in coastal areas between July and November.

TIME ZONES

Vietnam is 7 hours ahead of Greenwich Mean Time, 12 hours ahead of New York and 15 hours ahead of Los Angeles.

CITY	TIME DIFFERENCE	TIME AT 12 NOON VIETNAM
Amsterdam	-6	6am
Auckland	+3	3pm
Bangkok	0	12 noon
Berlin	-6	6am
Brussels	-6	6am
Chicago	-13	11pm*
Dublin	-7	5am
Johannesburg	-5	7am
London	-7	5am
Madrid	-6	6am
Montréal	-12	12 midnight*
New York	-12	12 midnight*
Paris	-6	6am
Perth, Australia	+1	1pm
Rome	-6	6am
San Francisco	-15	9pm*
Sydney	+3	3pm
Tokyo	+2	2pm

* = the previous day

● In the hill resorts of Dalat, Buon Me Thuot and Sapa, nights are cool throughout the year, and in the "winter" months, between

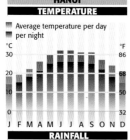

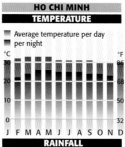

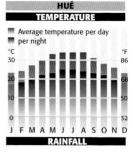

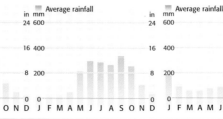

WEATHER WEBSITES

ORGANIZATION	NOTES	WEBSITE
Rain or Shine	A simple but effective weather site with five-day forecasts for 800 cities worldwide.	www.rainorshine.com
Weather Report	Key in Ho Chi Minh City or Hanoi for a five-day forecast.	www.weather.com
	Note the heat index—although the temperature may be 92°F (33°C), it might actually feel much hotter.	

October and March, it can be distinctly chilly, with temperatures falling to 39°F (4°C). Even in the hottest months of March and April, the temperature rarely exceeds 79°F (26°C).

WHEN TO GO

● Climatically, the best time to visit Vietnam is from December through March, when it should be dry and not too hot. In the south, days are warm and the evenings are cool. The north and highlands are chilly, but should be dry, with clear blue skies.

● The visitor industry's busiest season is November through May, when hotel prices rise and reserving flights can be a problem.

● Travel in the south and the Mekong Delta can be difficult at the height of the monsoon season (particularly September, October and November).

● The central regions and north sometimes suffer typhoons and tropical storms from May through

If you come in monsoon season, bring the right clothes

November. Hué is at its wettest from September to January.

CUSTOMS AND DUTY-FREE

● Visitors can bring unlimited amounts of foreign currency with them but it must be declared on their customs forms.

● The duty-free allowance is 200 cigarettes, 50 cigars or 5oz (150g) of tobacco, 50fl oz (1.5 liters) of spirits, perfume and jewelry for personal use, and personal gifts for friends and relations.

● All luggage entering (and leaving) Vietnam is X-rayed.

● You may not import weapons, illicit drugs, pornographic material, anti-government literature, photographs or movies, or culturally unsuitable children's toys.

● Export of wood products or antiques (anything that appears to be more than 20 years old) is forbidden. If the product you have bought is antique, or looks antique, it may require an export permit from customs (General Department of Customs, 51 Nguyen Van Cu Street, tel 04-8265260).

VISAS

● Valid passports with visas issued by a Vietnamese embassy are required by all visitors, irrespective

EMBASSIES IN VIETNAM		
COUNTRY	**ADDRESS**	**TELEPHONE AND FAX**
Australia	8 Dao Tan Street, Hanoi	tel 04-8317755, fax 04-8317711
	Landmark Building, 5B Ton Duc Thang Street, Ho Chi Minh City	tel 08-8296035, fax 08-8296031
Canada	31 Hung Vuong Street, Hanoi	tel 04-7345000, fax 04-7345049
	The Metropolitan, 235 Dong Khoi Street, Ho Chi Minh City	tel 08-8279899, fax 08-8279935
France	57 Tran Hung Dao Street, Hanoi	tel 04-9445700, fax 04-9445717
	27 Nguyen Thi Minh Khai Street, Ho Chi Minh City	tel 08-8297235, fax 08-8291675
New Zealand	63 Ly Thai To Street, Hanoi	tel 04-8241481, fax 04-8241480
United Kingdom	Central Building, 31 Hai Ba Trung Street, Hanoi	tel 04-8252510, www.uk-vietnam.org
United States	7 Lang Ha Street, Hanoi	tel 04-7721500, 04-7721510

VIETNAM EMBASSIES AND CONSULATES ABROAD		
COUNTRY	**ADDRESS**	**WEBSITE**
Australia	6 Timbarra Crescent, O'Malley, Canberra, ACT 2606, tel 0061 2 6286 6059/6290 1549, fax 0061 2 6286 4534	www.au.vnembassy.org
	Vietnam General Consulate, 489 New South Head Road, Double Bay, Sydney, NSW 2008, tel 0061 2 9327 2539/ 0061 2 9327 1912, fax 032 81653	vnconsul@ihug.com.au
Canada	226 Maclaren Street, Ottawa, Ontario, K2P OL6, tel 001 613/236-0772/613/232-1957, fax 001 613/236-2704	vietnam@lstar.ca
France	62–66 rue Boileau, 75016 Paris, tel 0033 1 44 14 64 47/44 14 64 00, fax 0033 1 44 14 64 24	vnparis@imaginet.tr
Hong Kong	15/F Great Smart Tower, 230 Wan Chai Road, Wan Chai, tel 00852 5914517/5914510, fax 00852 5914524/5914539	vnconsul@netvigator.com
South Africa	87 Brooks Street, Brooklyn, PO Box 13692, Hatfield 0028, Pretoria, tel 0027 12 3628119/3628118, fax 0027 12 3628115	embassy@vietnam.co.za
United Kingdom	12–14 Victoria Road, London W8 5RD, tel 0044 20 7937 1912, fax 0044 20 7937 6108	www.vietnamembassy.org.uk
United States	1233 20th Street, NW Suite 400, Washington, DC 20036, tel 001 202/861-0737, fax 001 202/861-0917	www.vietnamembassy-usa.org/
	Consulate General of Vietnam, 1700 California Street, Suite 475, San Francisco, CA 94109, tel 001 415/922-1707; fax 001 415/922-1848	info@vietnamconsulate-sf.org

PLANNING

of citizenship. Citizens of Thailand, Philippines, Malaysia, Singapore and Indonesia receive a free 30-day visa upon arrival. Japanese passport holders receive a free 15-day visa upon arrival. Time needed to process a visa varies from country to country and according to the type of visa required.

● Visa regulations are ever changing, so check well before you are due to travel. Usually it is possible to extend visas within Vietnam but not during Party Congresses. Check your visa carefully: Any incorrect details will be noticed by the famously eagle-eyed immigration officers.

● Tourist visas (US$30) generally take five to seven days. Travel agencies will probably add their own mark-up, but you may find it worth paying to avoid one or two journeys to an embassy.

● Visas are also available on arrival in Vietnam (US$45), providing authorization has been obtained from a Vietnamese embassy overseas or the immigration police in Vietnam. Your travel agent will contact the Vietnamese agent, who will require your passport details, exact flight schedule and a fax number. An authorization letter will be faxed to your travel agency; you need to show this when boarding the plane to Vietnam. Head for the landing visa desk before joining the normal immigration line.

● If you plan to stay for a while, or make a trip to Laos or Cambodia and then return to Vietnam, a multiple-entry visa will make life much simpler.

● Visas are normally valid only for arrival by air, at Noi Bai (Hanoi airport), Tan Son Nhat (Saigon airport) and Danang International Airport.

● The standard tourist visa is valid for one month for one entry (mot lan) only. You can extend it for one month at tour operators (▷ 202–204) for US$15–30. Your hotel may also do it for you for a small extra charge. Some agencies say it takes one to three days; others say it takes a week.

● A visa valid for one month can usually be extended only for one month. A further one-month extension may be possible.

● Those wishing to enter or leave Vietnam by land must specify the border crossing when applying. It is possible to alter the

point of departure at immigration offices in Hanoi and Saigon.

● Business visas are valid for three months (US$60) or six months (US$110) and usually enable multiple entry (nhieu lan). It costs US$85 for a three-month multiple-entry visa extension and US$140 for a six-month extension.

WORKING IN VIETNAM

● Officially, anyone working in Vietnam should have a business visa and a work permit. In practice, authorities take a fairly relaxed view of foreigners working in Vietnam for short periods. Those with specific skills, notably computer skills and English-language teaching, will not find it hard to get work. In Hanoi and Saigon there are countless language schools keen to engage native speakers. The best ones pay quite well—but you need relevant qualifications.

● If you plan to work in Vietnam, contact your embassy, who will be able to provide the most up-to-date information.

● www.uktradeinvest.gov.uk is a British government agency dealing with developing business in different countries. It provides free up-to-date information.

● www.business-in-asia.com has excellent information about working in Vietnam or investing in businesses there.

● Voluntary work is best organized in advance through volunteer agencies such as Voluntary Service Overseas, www.vso.org.uk. People with specific skills, and those available for four months or more, are of greatest use.

● The first port of call for further information should be the NGO Resource Centre, La Thanh Hotel, 218 Doi Can, Hanoi, tel 04-8328570, fax 04-8328611, www.ngocentre.org.vn

TRAVEL INSURANCE

● Insurance is crucial. A good insurance policy should cover you in case of theft, loss of possessions or money (often including cash), the cost of any medical and dental treatment, cancelation of flights, delays in travel arrangements, accidents, missed departures, lost baggage, lost passport, personal liability and legal expenses.

● Check the small print; some policies exclude "dangerous

activities" such as scuba diving, horseback riding or even trekking.

● Not all policies cover ambulance, helicopter rescue or emergency flights home.

● Find out whether your policy pays medical expenses direct to the hospital or doctor, or whether you have to pay and then claim the money back later. If the latter applies, keep all records.

● If you have something stolen, make sure you get a copy of the police report, as you will need this to substantiate your claim.

WHAT TO TAKE

● Items such as light shirts and shorts can be bought cheaply in Vietnam, but good-quality underwear and socks cannot. Inexpensive shoes are also available, as are bags for carrying home extra purchases.

● Take long-sleeved shirts for cool evenings, severely air-conditioned restaurants and to prevent sunburn.

● Long trousers and socks help keep mosquitoes from biting in the evening.

● Warm clothing is necessary for upland areas in winter.

● Women may consider wearing dresses rather than jeans when traveling, for easier access to squat toilets.

● Bring a good pair of walking boots, especially if traveling to the Central Highlands and northern Vietnam.

● Bring any prescription drugs needed. Sanitary products are not available everywhere, so bring your own supply.

● Earplugs are useful to combat the high noise levels in the cities.

● Other useful items include passport photographs, a small first-aid kit, a flashlight, insect repellent, photocopies of your passport and visa, a strong padlock to lock bags in hotel rooms, and a money belt.

WHAT NOT TO TAKE

● Bottled water is widely available. There is no need to bring water filters unless trekking in remote areas.

● Most hotels provide mosquito nets, but check in advance.

● Slide film is available in Saigon and Hanoi but rarely elsewhere; print film is more widely sold.

● Maps are available in Saigon and Hanoi.

● Dictionaries are available inexpensively in most towns.

PRACTICALITIES

ELECTRICITY
● Voltage is generally 220V (frequency 50Hz), but in some places 110V is still in use. Always ask before plugging anything in.
● Plugs are usually for two small round pins; some are for two flat pins. A number of top hotels now use three-square-pin sockets. Bring a universal adaptor.

LAUNDRY
● All hotels and guesthouses offer a laundry service. The more expensive the hotel, the more expensive the laundry, with a 10 percent VAT (IVA) and 5 percent service charge added in the more expensive places.

MEASUREMENTS
Most clothes marketed to Westerners are made for export and come in US, UK and European sizes; otherwise sizes are small, medium, large and extra large. In US terms, women's small is size 6, medium is size 8, large is size 10 and extra large is 12–14 (in UK terms, that's 8, 10 and 14–16 respectively).

PUBLIC TOILETS
● Toilets in hotels, guesthouses and restaurants are Western-style, and the majority are clean, though there are exceptions.
● In some small Vietnamese restaurants there are squat toilets, and you will need to bring your own toilet paper.
● In hotels and restaurants there is plenty of toilet paper, soap and individual hand towels. Women's bathrooms are often prettily decorated with frangipani buds floating in bowls.

SMOKING REGULATIONS
● Smoking is permitted throughout Vietnam.
● Some hotels offer non-smoking rooms and floors.
● A few restaurants have non-smoking sections.

CHILDREN
● Diapers are available in supermarkets in large towns. In more remote regions, such as the north, the Central Highlands and smaller towns, take them with you.
● Vietnam is a tropical country, so children should wear hats,

CLOTHING SIZES
Use the clothing sizes chart below to convert the size you use at home.

UK	Metric	USA	
36	46	36	SUITS
38	48	38	
40	50	40	
42	52	42	
44	54	44	
46	56	46	
48	58	48	
7	41	8	SHOES
7.5	42	8.5	
8.5	43	9.5	
9.5	44	10.5	
10.5	45	11.5	
11	46	12	
14.5	37	14.5	SHIRTS
15	38	15	
15.5	39/40	15.5	
16	41	16	
16.5	42	16.5	
17	43	17	
8	36	6	DRESSES
10	38	8	
12	40	10	
14	42	12	
16	44	14	
18	46	16	
20	46	18	
4.5	37.5	6	SHOES
5	38	6.5	
5.5	38.5	7	
6	39	7.5	
6.5	40	8	
7	41	8.5	

CONVERSION CHART
FROM	TO	MULTIPLY BY
Inches	Centimeters	2.54
Centimeters	Inches	0.3937
Feet	Meters	0.3048
Meters	Feet	3.2810
Yards	Meters	0.9144
Meters	Yards	1.0940
Miles	Kilometers	1.6090
Kilometers	Miles	0.6214
Acres	Hectares	0.4047
Hectares	Acres	2.4710
Gallons	Liters	4.5460
Liters	Gallons	0.2200
Ounces	Grams	28.35
Grams	Ounces	0.0353
Pounds	Grams	453.6
Grams	Pounds	0.0022
Pounds	Kilograms	0.4536
Kilograms	Pounds	2.205
Tons	Tonnes	1.0160
Tonnes	Tons	0.9842

long-sleeved clothing and high-factor sunscreen.
● Children's menus do exist in some restaurants, and knives and forks can always be provided. If your child does not take to Vietnamese food, most destinations have international restaurants and, if all else fails, there is always rice. Fruit and vegetables from markets will ensure that no one starves.
● Some hotels are more child-friendly than others. Good options include Ana Mandara, Nha Trang (▷ 248), the Furama Resort, Danang, and the Victoria Hotel Group.
● Many of the cities have playgrounds, although these are likely to be basic.

The Cao Dai Great Temple at Tay Ninh, near Ho Chi Minh City

● Neither children nor adults should drink the tap water in Vietnam. Bottled water is cheap and available everywhere. Some hotels supply it free of charge.
● Children should always be accompanied in the sea.
● Children receive reductions in the price of rail, bus and air travel (▷ 47–52).

PLACES OF WORSHIP
● Vietnam is mainly a Buddhist country (▷ 14–15).
● Mass is held in the Roman Catholic churches in the main towns in Vietnam, including St. Joseph's Cathedral (Hanoi), Dalat Cathedral, and Notre Dame Cathedral (Saigon).

PLANNING

CASH

- The unit of currency is the dong.
- Bills in circulation are in denominations of 200, 500, 1,000, 2,000, 5,000, 10,000, 20,000, 50,000, 100,000 and 500,000 dong.
- The 200, 500, 1,000, 2,000 and 5,000 dong bills are being phased out and replaced by coins.
- The 50,000d, 100,000d and 500,000d bills are now made of polymer to make them more durable and less easily counterfeited. They also have diamond markings to enable people with visually impairments to distinguish between them.
- Check the exchange rate closer to the time of your visit as rates can vary. The exchange rate at the time of writing was (approximately) US$1 = 16,300d; £1 = 31,200d, €1 = 21,100d.
- Since 2004, the value of the dong has stabilized and its rate of devaluation has slowed.
- You cannot bring dong into the country, so take US dollars

and/or travelers' checks and convert them when you are in Vietnam. You could also take a credit/debit card to use at an ATM.

- Any amount of foreign currency can be taken into or out of Vietnam, although amounts of more than US$3,000 must be declared on the customs form.

Even small denominations of dong come as bills

- Do not take dong out of the country—it is illegal and the cash cannot be converted overseas.
- It is quite difficult to convert dong back into US dollars even inside Vietnam.

CASH

The unit of currency in Vietnam is the dong. Banknotes are in denominations of **200, 500, 1,000, 2,000, 5,000, 10,000, 20,000, 50,000, 100,000 and 500,000** dong, although smaller denominations are being replaced by coins.

NAME	HEAD OFFICE ADDRESS	TELEPHONE
ANZ Bank	14 Le Thai To Street, Hanoi	tel 04-8258190
	Provides full banking services, including cash advances on credit cards,	
	2 percent commission on travelers' checks, 24-hour guarded ATMs.	
ANZ Bank	11 Me Linh Square, Saigon	tel 08-8232218
	2 percent commission charged on cashing travelers' checks into US$	
	or VND; ATM cashpoint.	
HSBC	235 Dong Khoi Street (facing Notre Dame Cathedral), Saigon	tel 08-8292288
	Provides all financial services, 2 percent commission on travelers' checks,	
	ATM cashpoint.	
Vietcombank	29 Ben Chuong Duong Street, Saigon	tel 08-8251317
	1.1 percent commission on travelers' checks, ATM cashpoint.	

- By law, shops should accept only dong, but in practice this is not enforced and dollars are accepted almost everywhere.
- ATMs are plentiful in Saigon and Hanoi and can also be found in other major visitor centers.
- ATMs are available at ANZ Bank in Hanoi and Saigon and at HSBC, Citibank and Vietcombank in Saigon. Many of the larger hotels have ATMs installed.
- Sapa does not have an ATM.
- It is best to travel with US dollars as a backup. Clean (that is, unmarked) US$100 bills receive the best rates. Bills that are dirty or slightly marked will be politely but firmly returned.
- Small US$ bills receive slightly lower rates.
- US$ can be changed in banks, in larger hotels and in gold or jewelry shops.
- Do not change money in the street or if approached by strangers.
- The best rates are offered by the banks (Vietcombank, in particular, offers good rates).
- Banks in the main towns also change other major currencies, including sterling, HK$, Thai baht, Swiss francs, euros, A$, S$, CAN$ and yen.
- Try to pay for everything in dong, not in US$. Prices are usually lower in dong, and in remote areas people may be unaware of the latest exchange rate. Also, to most Vietnamese 15,000d is a lot of money, while US$1 means nothing.
- VAT (IVA) of 10 percent and sales tax of 5 percent are added to some hotel and restaurant bills. These are non-refundable.
- www.oanda.com/converter/classic enables you to select a currency and convert it.

CREDIT CARDS

- These are increasingly widely accepted. Major credit cards taken are Visa, MasterCard, Amex and JCB.
- Large hotels, expensive restaurants and medical clinics invariably take credit cards, but there may be a surcharge of between 2.5 and 4.5 percent, depending upon the card that you use (Visa and MasterCard: 2.5 percent; Amex: 4.5 percent).

TRAVELERS' CHECKS

- Travelers' checks are best denominated in US$ and can be cashed only in banks in the major towns. A commission of 2 to 4 percent is payable if cashing into dollars, but not if you are converting them direct to dong. When cashing travelers' checks, take proof of purchase and your passport to the bank.

TIPPING

- Tipping varies widely. Vietnamese do not normally tip if eating in small family restaurants but may tip extravagantly in expensive bars. Foreigners normally leave the small change, and this is perfectly acceptable and appreciated. Big hotels and some restaurants add a 5 to 10 percent service charge and the government tax of 10 percent to the bill.

WIRING MONEY

- Western Union has hundreds of outlets in Vietnam, with transfers available in dong or

You will find ATMs in most major cities, but take cash as a backup

dollars. The principal agents are Asia Commercial Bank, Industrial and Commercial Bank and Vietnam Bank for Agriculture, and they are open during normal Monday to Friday banking hours. The offices for Saigon, Hanoi and Hue are as follows:

Agribank
28–30 Mac Thui Buoi, District 1,
Ho Chi Minh City
Tel 08-8231880
Open Mon–Fri 7.30am–4.30pm.

Industrial & Commercial Bank
37 Hang Bo Street,
Hoan Kiem District, Hanoi,
Tel 04-8285359
Open Mon–Fri 8am–4.30pm

Industrial & Commercial Bank
2A Le Qui Don Street, Hué
Tel 054-825857
Open Mon–Fri 7am–5pm

10 EVERYDAY ITEMS AND HOW MUCH THEY COST	
1 liter of bottled water	7,000–15,000d
Cup of coffee	5,000d
Bottle of beer	15,000d (in a shop); 20,000–30,000d (in a bar)
Ice cream	3,000–6,000d
Liter of fuel	7,100d
Bowl of *pho*	10,000–20,000d
Daily newspaper *(VN News)*	5,000d
Small baguette	5,000d
Coca-Cola	7,000d (shop)
Roll of camera film	25,000d

- Health care in Vietnam varies, with some very good private and government clinics and hospitals. There are Western hospitals in Hanoi and Saigon (▷ 268).
- You should see your doctor or travel clinic at least six weeks before your departure for general advice on travel risks, malaria and vaccinations.
- Make sure you have travel insurance, get a dental check, and know your blood group. If you suffer a long-term condition, such as diabetes or epilepsy, make sure someone knows or that you have a Medic Alert bracelet giving this information.
- Wear a shirt and hat for protection against the sun and put on plenty of sunscreen.

MALARIA

- Vietnam is a high-risk country.
- Symptoms can resemble an attack of influenza; you may feel lethargic and have a headache. In the worst cases, fits are followed by coma and death.
- All clinics in Vietnam can test for malaria quickly and reliably. If you come down with a fever, get tested as quickly as possible.
- Malaria exists in rural areas, but there is no risk in the Red River Delta, the coastal plains north of Nha Trang, Hanoi, Saigon, Danang, Nha Trang, Quy Nhon or Haiphong. But always check the latest advice before you travel and be careful as late changes to your itinerary may take you outside "safe" areas.
- Treatment is with drugs and may be oral or intravenous, depending on the seriousness of the infection.
- Remember ABCD: awareness (of whether the disease is present in your area), bite avoidance, chemoprophylaxis (use of chemicals to prevent disease), diagnosis.
- Prevention is best summarized as B and C: bite avoidance and chemoprophylaxis. Wear clothes that cover arms and legs and use insect repellents. Use a mosquito net dipped in permethrin as both a physical and chemical barrier at night.

VACCINATION CHART	
VACCINATION	**RECOMMENDED**
Polio	Yes, if none in last 10 years.
Tetanus	Yes, if none in last 10 years (five doses are enough for life).
Typhoid	Yes, if none in last three years.
Yellow fever	The disease does not exist in Vietnam. However, the authorities may wish to see a certificate if you have recently arrived from an endemic area in Africa or South America.
Rabies	Yes, if traveling to jungle and/or remote areas.
Hepatitis A	Yes, the disease can be caught easily from food/water.
Japanese encephalitis	May be advised for some areas, depending on the duration of the trip and proximity to rice-growing and pig-farming areas.
BCG	It is not known how much protection this vaccination gives the traveler against lung tuberculosis, but it is currently advised in the absence of any better alternative.

- Guard against malaria with the correct anti-malarials. Specialist advice is required as to which type to take; Malarone, Lariam (mefloquine) and doxycycline are available.

DENGUE FEVER

- Dengue fever is transmitted by mosquitoes that bite during the day, and can be contracted throughout Vietnam.
- It can cause a severe, flu-like illness, with fever, enlarged lymph glands, lethargy and muscle pains. Two or three days' illness are followed by a short period of recovery, then a second attack.
- Local children are prone to the much nastier hemorrhagic form of the disease, but this is rarely contracted by Westerners.
- The traveler's version of the disease is usually self-limiting and requires only rest and recuperation.
- Mosquito repellent

should be applied and limbs covered 24 hours a day.
- Check your accommodations for flowerpots and shallow pools of water, as these are where the dengue-carrying mosquitoes breed.

MOSQUITO REPELLENTS

- DEET (Di-ethyltoluamide) is the gold standard. Apply the repellent every four to six hours but more often if you are sweating heavily.
- If a non-DEET product is used, check who tested it. Validated products (tested at the London School of Hygiene and Tropical Medicine and the Centers for Disease Control and Prevention in Atlanta; www.cdc.gov) include Mosiguard, non-DEET Jungle Formula and non-DEET Autan.
- Citronella must be applied very frequently (hourly) to be effective.
- If you are a popular target for insect bites or develop lumps quite soon after being bitten, carry an Aspivenin kit. This pump suction device is available from many pharmacists and draws out some of the allergic materials to provide quick relief.

Accidents can happen on the best-planned vacation: Make sure you have adequate insurance

Be AIDS-aware: Health and safety billboards are everywhere

HEPATITIS

- Hepatitis—inflammation of the liver—can be contracted virally anywhere in Vietnam.
- The most obvious symptom is a yellowing of the skin or of the whites of the eyes; before this there may be itching and tiredness.
- Early on, depending on the type of hepatitis, a vaccine or immunoglobulin may reduce the duration of the illness.
- There are vaccines for hepatitis B (which is spread through blood and unprotected sex) and A. Unfortunately, there is no vaccine for hepatitis C, or the increasing list of other hepatitis viruses.

TUBERCULOSIS

- This disease is still a significant problem in Ho Chi Minh City and many other areas.
- Symptoms include coughing, tiredness, fever and lethargy.
- Have a BCG vaccination before you go and see a doctor early if you have a persistent cough, cough blood, have a fever or suffer unexplained weight loss.

SARS

- Each year there is the possibilty that avian flu or SARS might rear their heads. Check the latest news reports.
- If there is a problem in an area you are due to visit, seek expert advice.

DIARRHEA

- One survey found that up to 70 percent of travelers may suffer diarrhea during their trip. It should last only a short while, but if it lasts longer, or if there is blood or pain, get specialist medical attention.
- Try to prevent diarrhea by drinking only bottled water and avoiding ice cubes. Be wary of

- Visitors to Vietnam may be concerned about the effect of long-haul flights on their health. The most widely publicized concern is deep vein thrombosis, or DVT. Misleadingly called "economy class syndrome," DVT is the forming of a blood clot in the body's deep veins, particularly in the legs. The clot can move around the bloodstream and could be fatal.
- Those most at risk include the elderly, pregnant women and those using the contraceptive pill, smokers and people who are overweight. If you are at increased risk of DVT see your doctor before departing. Flying increases the likelihood of DVT because passengers are often seated in a cramped position for long periods of time and may become dehydrated.

To minimize risk:
Drink water (not alcohol)
Don't stay immobile for hours at a time
Stretch and exercise your legs periodically
Do wear elastic flight socks, which support veins and reduce the chances of a clot forming

EXERCISES

1 ANKLE ROTATIONS **2 CALF STRETCHES** **3 KNEE LIFTS**

Lift feet off the floor. Draw a circle with the toes, moving one foot clockwise and the other counterclockwise

Start with heel on the floor and point foot upward as high as you can. Then lift heels high, keeping balls of feet on the floor

Lift leg with knee bent while contracting your thigh muscle. Then straighten leg, pressing foot flat to the floor

Other health hazards for flyers are airborne diseases and bugs spread by the plane's air-conditioning system. These are largely unavoidable but if you have a serious medical condition seek advice from a doctor before flying.

salads (you don't know what they have been washed in), reheated foods, food that has been left out in the sun and unpasteurized dairy products.

LUNG FLUKE

- Avoid eating undercooked or raw crabs, as these contain a fluke (a flattened worm) that travels to the lungs.

SEXUAL HEALTH

- Unprotected sex can spread HIV, hepatitis B and C, gonorrhea (green discharge), chlamydia (nothing to see, but may cause

painful urination and later female infertility), painful recurrent herpes, syphilis and warts.
- The risk of disease is significantly decreased with the use of condoms.

PHARMACIES

- There are pharmacies in every town and they are increasingly better stocked.
- In larger cities, such as Hanoi, staff will often speak English.
- Be aware of counterfeit medicines and those past their sell-by date.

PLANNING

FURTHER INFORMATION

Centers for Disease Control and Prevention (USA)
www.cdc.gov
This US government site gives excellent advice on travel health and has useful disease maps and details of disease outbreaks.

World Health Organisation
www.who.int
The WHO site has links to the WHO Blue Book on travel advice, listing diseases in different regions of the world and vaccination schedules, and specifying countries with yellow fever vaccination certificate requirements and malarial risk.

Department of Health Travel Advice (UK)
www.dh.gov.uk

There are pharmacies in most major towns

Look for Health Advice for Travelers. Also available as a free booklet, the T6, from UK post offices. It lists the vaccine requirements for each country.

Medic Alert (UK)
www.medicalert.co.uk
The website of the foundation that produces bracelets and necklaces for those with existing medical problems. Write your key medical details on paper inside the bracelet.

Health Protection Agency (UK)
www.hpa.org.uk
Up-to-date malaria advice for travel around the world. Specific advice about the right drugs for each location and information for those who are pregnant, suffering from epilepsy or planning to travel with children.

Tropical Medicine Bureau (Eire)
www.tmb.ie
This Irish-based site has a good collection of general travel health information and disease risks.

HOSPITALS

Consultation rates vary but usually start at around US$40 for a consultation with a foreign doctor, and half that for a Vietnamese doctor.

HOSPITAL	ADDRESS	CONTACT
Hanoi		
Eye Hospital	85 Ba Trieu Street	04-8263966
Hanoi Family Medical Practice	109–112 Van Phuc	04-8430748
	24-hour medical service, including intensive care and dental care.	(09-0401919 24-hour emergency)
Hospital Bach Mai	Giai Phong Street	04-8693731
	English-speaking doctors. A dental service is also available.	
Huu Nghi (Friendship Hospital)	Tran Khanh Du Street	04-9722231
International Hospital	Phuong Mai, Dong Da	04-5771100, www.hfn.com.vn
International SOS	Central Building, 31 Hai Ba Trung Street	04-9340666
	Open 24 hours for emergencies, routine and medical evacuation. Dental service.	www.internationalsos.com
Ho Chi Minh City		
Cho Ray Hospital	201B Nguyen Chi Thanh Street, District 5	08-8554137
	The largest hospital, with 24-hour emergency care.	
Columbia Asia	1 No Trang Long Street, Quan Binh Thanh	08-8030678
(Gia Dinh International Clinic)	An American-run emergency clinic with medievac	(08-8238888 24-hour emergency)
	and general practice services.	www.columbiaasia.com
Columbia Asia	8 Alexandre de Rhodes Street	08-8238455
(Saigon International Clinic)	International doctors offering a full range of services.	(08-8238888 24-hour emergency)
		www.columbiaasia.com
Franco-Vietnamese Hospital	6 Nguyen Luong Bang, District 7, Saigon South	08-4113333 www.fvhospital.com
	This new and fully equipped hospital offers international	08-4113500
	medical care and is equipped to deal with emergency cases.	
Emergency Ambulance service		08-4113500
Ho Chi Minh City Family	Diamond Plaza, 34 Le Duan Street	08-8227848
Medical Practice	Well-equipped practice; emergency and evacuation	(09-13234911 24-hour emergency)
	service with Western doctors. Full range of services	www.doctorkot.com
	including tropical disease specialists and dental services.	
International Medical Center	1 Han Thuyen Street (facing the cathedral), District 1	08-8272366
	English-speaking French doctors.	
International SOS	65 Nguyen Du Street	08-8298424
	Comprehensive medical and dental service.	(08-8298520 24-hour emergency)
		www.internationalsos.com
Koseikai Dental Office	Saigon Tower, 29 Le Duan Street	08-8235918
	Japanese facilities with Japanese and Japanese-trained Vietnamese staff.	

PLANNING

FINDING HELP

Police	113
Fire	999
Ambulance	115

CRIME

● Bag- and jewelry-snatching is a common problem. Do not take any valuables on to the streets of Saigon. Possessions are safer in all but the most disreputable hotels than on the streets.

● Do not wear expensive jewelry or watches, or carry wallets, cellphones or handbags.

● Thieves work in teams in central Saigon, often with women carrying babies and begging as a decoy.

● Beware of people who obstruct your path (pushing a bicycle across the sidewalk is a common ruse) while your pockets are being emptied from behind.

● Take particular care in Nha Trang and Hanoi.

● Stick to tried and trusted cyclo drivers after dark or, better still, go by taxi. Never take a cyclo in a strange part of town after dark.

● If you are robbed, report the incident to the police for insurance purposes, but don't expect any further action.

● If you are arrested ask for consular assistance and English-speaking staff immediately.

Vietnamese police wear distinctive green uniforms

TRAVEL ADVISORIES

www.travel.state.gov/travel
The US State Department's continually updated travel advisories on its Travel Warnings and Consular Information Sheets page.
www.fco.gov.uk/travel
The UK Foreign and Commonwealth Office's travel warning section, which is regularly reviewed and updated.

SAFETY ISSUES

LANDMINES

● Unexploded ordnance is still a threat in some areas. Do not stray too far from the beaten track or unearth pieces of suspicious metal.

● The Technology Center for Bomb and Mine Disposal (BOMICO), a department of the Engineering Command of the Ministry of Defense, estimates that 7 to 8 percent of land is affected. It is thought that there are between 350,000 and 800,000 tons of war-era ordnance in the ground. All Vietnam's provinces are affected, but especially the DMZ and the south.

● According to the International Campaign to Ban Landmines, 66 people were killed in 2002 and 100 injured in mine/unexploded ordnance incidents. BOMICO estimates that 1,110 people die and 1,882 are injured every year. It is thought that between 1975 and the end of 2000, 38,849 had been killed and 65,852 injured.

HIV AND AIDS

● UNAIDS (the Joint United Nations Programme on HIV/AIDS) reports that while HIV incidence among the adult population is low (0.28 percent), rates could be as high as 65 percent among intravenous drug abusers, and sexual transmission is expected to become the dominant mode of HIV transmission in Vietnam in coming years.

● Between 40 and 50 new infections are reported every day in Vietnam according to www.unaids.org.vn.

● Like the other countries of Southeast Asia, Vietnam is thought to have the potential for "rapid increase" in the HIV/AIDS epidemic.

● The first reported case of AIDS was in 1990.

● Although 80,000 cases of HIV have so far been reported, it is believed that about 280,000 people, 2,500 of whom are children, will be living with HIV or AIDS by the end of 2007.

● In Dong Nai Province, where body art is fashionable, tattooing is believed to be a major cause of transmission of HIV.

● AIDS is found in all 61 of Vietnam's provinces. Urban and border regions have the highest incidence, topped by Quang Ninh Province, Haiphong and Saigon. Provinces such as Quang Binh and Quang Tri, in the center of the country, are least affected.

DRUGS

● Illegal drugs are common and inexpensive, and the use of hard drugs by Vietnamese is a rapidly growing problem, with a 400 percent increase in drug seizures over the previous year in 2001.

● It is not uncommon to see drug abusers injecting themselves in back alleys, but periodically bars and nightclubs are closed for a few weeks in response to the problem.

● Attitudes to traffickers are harsh; the death penalty is usually reserved for Vietnamese and other Asian carriers.

PLANNING

Vietnamese people are very friendly and will strike up conversations with visitors

CULTURAL ISSUES

Vietnam is remarkably relaxed and easygoing with regard to conventions, and it is rare to cause offence unwittingly. The main complaint Vietnamese have of foreigners is that some wear dirty and torn clothing. Backpackers come in for particularly severe criticism, and the term *tay ba lo* (Western backpacker) is a contemptuous one.

SOCIAL ETIQUETTE

● Shoes should be removed before entering temples and before going into people's houses.
● Modesty should be preserved, and excessive displays of bare flesh are not considered good form, particularly in temples and private houses.
● Shorts are fine for the beach and travelers' cafés but not for smart restaurants.
● Kissing and cuddling in public are likely to draw wide attention, not much of it favorable, but walking hand-in-hand is now accepted as a common, if slightly eccentric, Western habit.
● Hand-shaking among men is a standard greeting (often with both hands for added cordiality). Although Vietnamese women will consent to the process, it is often clear that they would prefer not to.
● The head is held by some to be sacred, and people would rather you didn't pat them on it, which amazingly some visitors do.
● Vietnamese who meet you for the first time will always ask how old you are, whether you

are married and whether you have children.
● Vietnamese names are written with the surname first, followed by the first name. Thus, Nguyen Minh is informally addressed not as Nguyen but as Minh.
● When addressing strangers of the same age, use *anh* (for a man) or *chi* (for a woman). When you know the first name use *anh* Minh, for example.
● When addressing your senior or someone of uncertain age, use *ông* for a man or *bà* for a woman.
● It is perfectly acceptable to address someone as Mr Minh or Ms Hanh, for example.

POLITICAL AND RELIGIOUS ACTIVITY

● Do not take photographs of military installations.
● Involvement in politics, possession of political material, business activities that have not been licensed by appropriate authorities or non sanctioned religious activities (including proselytizing) can result in detention.
● Sponsors of small, informal religious gatherings such as Bible-study groups in hotel rooms, as well as distributors of religious materials, have been detained, fined and expelled, according to the US State Department.
● Foreigners are free to attend Christian services. In Saigon, one or two services in the Notre Dame cathedral are in French and in English; in Protestant churches, found throughout the country, all services are in Vietnamese.

● Vietnam is predominantly a Buddhist country.
● Ancestor-worship is widely practiced and animism (the belief in, and worship of, the spirits of inanimate objects such as venerable trees, the land, mountains and so on) is widespread.

SLEEPING RULES

● Government restrictions limit the range of homestays and bed-and-breakfast accommodations. In a few places, such as the Mekong Delta and the northwest, some private homes are licensed to accept foreigners, but this tends to be at the discretion of the police.
● If you wish to stay at a friend's house, this is normally permitted, but your hosts will need to take your passport and arrival form to their local police station.
● You must always leave your passport with your hotel. This can make it difficult to rent motorcycles and reserve airline tickets, as a photocopy is not generally accepted. Explain your predicament to the hotel and promise to return the passport later.

SEXUAL ETIQUETTE

● Police and People's Committee regulations in some towns require a foreigner traveling with a Vietnamese spouse to bring a marriage certificate in order to share a hotel room.
● The age of consent in Vietnam is 18.
● There are rules and regulations relating to Vietnamese guests of the opposite sex being in your hotel room, though if the guest is your partner hotels are generally relaxed. However, in Hoi An and in international hotels in big cities, which are under police scrutiny, you will have to rent a second room.
● There are no legal restraints for two people of the same sex cohabitating in the same room.
● There are several bars in central Saigon popular with gay clients: www.utopia-asia.com is an Asian online resource for gays and lesbians. The site includes a list of scams and warnings in Vietnam as well as gay-friendly bars in Hanoi and Saigon.

PLANNING

COMMUNICATIONS

INTERNET
- Vietnam has a long way to go to catch up with nearby countries in terms of internet communication. The first wave of cybercafés was closed down by the authorities, and although e-mailing is now usually easy enough, access to the internet from within Vietnam is restricted (for example, the bbc.co.uk/news site can sometimes be blocked). Nevertheless, access has greatly improved, with broadband available in many places in Hanoi and Saigon and installed in some of the other main cities.
- Many large hotels offer broadband access.
- Many travelers' cafés in Hanoi and Saigon, and in other main towns, such as Sapa, Hué, Hoi An and Nha Trang, provide e-mail access, as do hotels and guesthouses.
- Rates for receiving, sending and printing e-mails have fallen as competition has spread, and are currently around 100d to 200d per minute in the two main cities (more in smaller places). Business centers in top hotels charge a lot more.

MAIL
- Generally, postal services are good. International aerograms take about two weeks in each direction. Every town has a post office, as does every district in every city, and provincial capitals have two general post offices: one for the province and one for the town.
- Post offices tend to keep long opening hours: daily 7am–9pm (smaller offices close for lunch).
- Postal deliveries are seven days a week and stop only on official national holidays.
- General post offices in the major cities can send parcels overseas and usually offer packing services for a small additional fee.
- To send letters and parcels from Vietnam costs: 100g airmail letter to Europe 46,800d, to the US 68,800d; 1kg surface parcel to Europe 136,400d, to the US 191,200d; postcard to Europe 8,000d, to the US 8,800d. Prices exclude 10 percent VAT.

The main post office in Ho Chi Minh City

Internet access is available at many Vietnamese hotels

USEFUL NUMBERS	
Vietnam international code	0084
Directory inquiries	116
Operator-assisted domestic long-distance calls	103
International directory inquiries	143
General information service	1080
Yellow pages	1081

- Outgoing packages are opened and the contents checked by the censor before being allowed out.
- Incoming parcels are rarely delivered to the door; a note is sent to summon you to the post office, where you must show your passport and pay a fee, before the parcel is produced and opened by customs officers.
- All major international courier companies have offices near the big general post offices.

- Post offices offer domestic telegram services, which can be very useful for getting messages to people who are not on the telephone. There is also an express mail service, EMS, which delivers letters or small packages the length of the country the following day.
- Post offices in Saigon, Hanoi, Hué, Hoi An, Nha Trang, Dalat and Danang provide poste restante facilities. Ask your correspondent to print your surname—for example, Chris ARNOLD, c/o Poste Restante, GPO, Hanoi.

TELEPHONE AND FAX
- All post offices can provide international telephone and fax services. The cost of calls has been greatly reduced, but some post offices and hotels will still charge a minimum of three minutes; hotels also

Cellphone usage is increasing in Vietnam

add their own surcharge. Note that you start paying for an overseas call from the moment you ring, even if the call is not answered.

● A one-minute call to the US costs about US$1.20 and to the UK US$1.50, 7am–11pm. Rates are reduced 11pm–7am: to the USA a minute costs US$1, to the UK US$1.20.

● If you dial 171 or 178 followed by 0 or 00 to make an international call, the cost is reduced again by approximately 30 percent.

● Local calls are inexpensive or even free of charge in some hotels.

● Most shops or cafés will let you call a local number for 2,000d: Look for the blue sign *"dien thoai cong cong"* (public telephone).

● To make a domestic call, dial 0 + area code + number.

● Equal tones followed by long pauses indicate that the telephone is ringing. Equal tones separated by equal pauses, or short pauses separated by short tones mean that the line is engaged.

● All towns and areas have telephone codes.

● Telephone numbers that begin with 091 or 090 are cellphone numbers.

● Sending a one-page fax abroad costs around US$2.25.

CELLPHONES
● Most cellphones with global roaming work in Vietnam, and coverage is improving. Every town tends to have quite a generous footprint of phone coverage.

● Calls on global roaming phones from within Vietnam are charged as international, so it may be cheaper to buy a pay-as-you-go SIM card from Vinaphone or Mobiphone (around 300,000d). Their offices are found near every big post office.

● Top-up cards (a minimum value of 100,000d) are available in plenty of places—just look for the sign.

OPENING TIMES AND TICKETS

DISCOUNT TRAVEL
● Discount travel is provided to those under 22 and over 60, primarily on Vietnam Airlines and on the train. Currently the discount applies to air tickets on the Saigon–Hanoi and Danang routes only. The ticket price from Saigon to Hanoi is US$99 instead of US$110. Tickets are valid for three months and must be booked seven days in advance. They are non-transferable and nonrefundable.

● Bus and car companies are less forthcoming with their discounts.

● Vietnam Airlines charges children under two 10 percent of the adult ticket price; those aged 2–12 must pay 75 percent of the adult ticket price.

● The railways allow children under five to travel free and charge 50 percent of the adult fare for those aged 5–10.

● The traveling café Open Tour bus tickets and tours are likewise free for children under two, but those aged 2–10 pay half the adult price.

NATIONAL HOLIDAYS	
January 1	(But not known as New Year's Day in Vietnam)
Late January–March	*Tet* (first to seventh day of the new lunar year)
February 3	Founding Anniversary of the Communist Party of Vietnam
April 30	Liberation Day of South Vietnam and Saigon
May 1	International Labor Day
May 19	Anniversary of the Birth of Ho Chi Minh; most state institutions shut, but the private sector carries on
September 2	National Day
September 3	President Ho Chi Minh's Anniversary

OPENING TIMES	
Banks	Mon–Fri 8 or 8.30 –4; some close 11–1.
Shops	Daily 8–8; some stay open a further hour or two, especially in visitor areas.
Supermarkets	Daily 8–8.
Offices	Mon–Fri 7.30–11.30, 1.30–4.30.
Museums and galleries	Times vary according to each place, but most are open all day, every day. Some are closed on Mondays.
Restaurants, cafés and bars	Daily from 7 or 8am; some open earlier. By law bars must close by midnight.
Churches	Open only during services; otherwise there may be a caretaker who will let you in.

PLANNING

TOURIST OFFICES

- The national tourist office is called Vietnam National Administration of Tourism: Vietnamtourism. Its role is to promote Vietnam as a tourist destination rather than provide tourist information.
- Visitors to its offices can find some information and maps but are more likely to be offered tours.
- Many of the 61 provinces in Vietnam have a branch office of the state-run tourist company. Some, such as Ho Chi Minh City's Saigontourist

(www.saigontourist.com), provide a useful source of information to their respective destinations.
- Good tourist information is also available from the many tour operators around the country (▷ 202–204); most are happy to offer advice as well as tours.
- Some hotels can provide tourist information, and arrange forward transportation, such as flights and bus tours.

The tourist office at Hanoi— happy to help

You can get tourist information in the most elaborate of places

STATE TOUR OPERATORS		
OFFICE	**ADDRESS**	**TELEPHONE/WEBSITE**
Ba Ria-Vung Tau Tourist Corporation	207 Vo Thi Sau Street	064-856445
Buon Me Thuot Daklak Tourist Office	Thang Loi Hotel, 3 Phan Chu Trinh Street	050-852108 **www.daklaktourist.com**
Can Tho Tourist	20 Hai Ba Trung Street	071-821852 **www.canthotourist.com.vn**
Cao Bang Tourist	Phong Lan Hotel, 83 Be Van Dan Street	026-852245
Cao Lanh Dong Thap Tourist Company	2 Doc Binh Kieu Street	067-855638
Dalat Tourist	35 Tran Hung Dao Street	063-822317
Danang Tourist Office	76 Hung Vuong Street	0511-821969
Ha Giang Tourist Company	Tran Hung Dao Street	019-867054
Haiphong Vietnamtourism	15 Le Dai Hanh Street	031-842669
Hanoi Vietnamtourism	80 Quan Su Street	04-9421061 **www.vietnamtourism.com**
Ho Chi Minh City Vietnamtourism	234 Nam Ky Khoi Nghia Street, District 1	08-9326776
Ho Chi Minh City Saigontourist	49 Le Thanh Ton Street, District 1	08-8298914
Hoi An Tourist Office	12 Phan Chu Trinh Street	0510-861276
Hué City Tourism	5 Ly Thuong Kiet Street	054-823577
Ninh Binh Tourism Administration	Tran Hung Dao Street	030-881958
Phan Rang Ninh Thuan Tourist	505 Thong Nhat Street	068-822722
Phan Thiet Binh Thuan Tourist	82 Trung Trac Street	062-816821
Pleiku Gia Lai Tourist Service Company	Hung Vuong Hotel, 215 Hung Vuong Street	059-824270
Tam Dao Tam Dao Tourism		0211-824213
Vinh Long-Cuu Long Tourist	1 Thang 5 Street	070-823616

Newspapers are also available in English

A selection of Vietnamese magazines

NEWSPAPERS
● The English-language daily *Vietnam News* (http://vietnamnews.vnagency.com.vn) is widely available and covers Vietnamese and foreign news selectively. It has especially good sports pages. The Sunday edition is worth reading for its cultural stories, and is particularly good on the traditions of ethnic minorities. Inside the back page of the *Vietnam News* is an excellent "What's on" section, recommended for visitors interested in cultural events in Hanoi and Saigon.
● The *Saigon Times Daily* (www.saigontimes.com.vn/daily) is more business-oriented.
● There are several weeklies, of which the *Vietnam Investment Review* is the best.
● The monthly *Vietnam Economic Times* (www.vneconomy.com.vn/eng) is very thorough and remains forthright in its views.
● The *Viet Nam News Agency* (www.vnagency.com.vn) is Vietnam's official news agency.
● The *Saigon Times* (www.saigontimesweekly.saigonnet.vn) has an interesting news summary with full listings of what's on.
● The *Saigon Today* network (www.saigontoday.net/index.asp) is a great round-up of local news, with photo galleries of events around town, stretching back for more than a year—an excellent way to get a real feel for Saigon.
● *The Guide* is a monthly leisure and tourism magazine, produced by the *Vietnam Economic Times*.

You can find it in major hotels, resorts, shops and restaurants in Vietnam's main cities and visitor centers, as well as on international flights (Vietnam Airlines, Cathay Pacific, Air France and Japan Airlines). It has interesting and useful stories on cultural and social issues, and on the life of expatriates in Vietnam. The extensive listings section is also useful.
● One- or two-day-old editions of the *Financial Times, International Tribune, USA Today, Le Figaro* and some weeklies, such as *The Economist, Time* and *Asiaweek*, are available in Saigon and Hanoi.

TELEVISION
● There is news in English on the TV once in the evening, mainly covering Party members' visits to factories, presentations of medals to Heroic Mothers and meetings of People's Committee personnel.
● All foreign films are dubbed over with a single monotone voice, except on cable TV, which is available in many hotels and features a full range of cable options—normally CNN, Star Sport, BBC World, HBO, Cinemax and Star Movies.

BOOKS
Books on the region
● *Travellers' Literary Companion to Southeast Asia* (Alastair Dingwall, 1994). Experts on Southeast Asian language and literature select extracts from novels and books by Western and regional writers. The extracts are brief, but give a good overview of what is available.

● *The Palaces of Southeast Asia: Architecture and Customs* (Jacques Dumarçay, 1991). A broad summary of palace art and architecture in both mainland and island Southeast Asia.
● *All the Wrong Places: Adrift in the Politics of the Pacific Rim* (James Fenton, 1988). British journalist James Fenton entertainingly recounts his experiences in Vietnam, Cambodia, the Philippines and Korea.
● *The Archaeology of Mainland Southeast Asia: From 10,000BC to the Fall of Angkor* (Charles Higham, 1989). Best summary of changing views of the archeology of the mainland.
● *A Field Guide to the Birds of Southeast Asia* (Ben F. King, M. W. Woodcock and E. C. Dickinson, 1975). Best regional guide to the birds of the area.
● *Western Impressions of Nature and Landscape in Southeast Asia* (Victor R. Savage, 1985). Based on a geography PhD thesis, this book is a mine of quotations and observations from Western travelers.
● *In Search of Southeast Asia: A Modern History* (D. J. Steinberg et al., 1987). The best standard history of the region, examining and assessing general processes of change and their impacts,

Read up on Vietnam before your visit to help you understand the country

Plenty of reading material at this newsstand in Danang

from the arrival of the Europeans in the region.

Art and archeology
● *Le Vietnam à Travers l'Architecture Coloniale* (Arnauld Le Brusq and Léonard de Selva, 1999). Available in French and German, but not in English. Chronicles the evolution of Vietnam's French colonial cities and describes the history of many of Vietnam's public buildings erected during French rule. Superbly illustrated with contemporary color photographs, archive pictures and plans.
● *Cham Sculpture in the Tourane Museum* (Henri Parmentier, with Paul Mus and Etienne Aymonier, 2001). Reprint of a classic 1922 text by Parmentier, who was responsible for assembling the Cham sculptures and after whom the museum in Danang was originally named.

Biography and autobiography
● *Ho Chi Minh: A Biographical Introduction* (Charles Fenn, 1973).
● *Ways of Escape* (Graham Greene, 1980) Autobiography covering Greene's 1950s Vietnam travels.
● *Prison Diary* (Ho Chi Minh, 1962, tr. Aileen Palmer). A collection of poems written by Ho while he was incarcerated in China in 1942. They record his prison experiences and his yearning for home.
● *Derailed in Uncle Ho's Victory Garden: Return to Vietnam and Cambodia* (Tim Page, 1995). War photojournalist Tim Page makes a return visit to Vietnam.

● *Following Ho Chi Minh: The Memoirs of a North Vietnamese Colonel* (Bui Tin, 1995). Autobiographical account of a North Vietnamese colonel's disillusionment with the Communist regime following Ho Chi Minh's death.

Culture
● *Customs and Culture of Vietnam* (Ann Caddell Crawford, 1966; out of print, though bootleg copies are available in Vietnam).

Economics, politics and development
● *Month of Pure Light: The Regreening of Vietnam* (Elizabeth Kemf, 1990). An account of the attempts to overcome the after-effects of US defoliation.
● *Vietnam: The Second Revolution* (Nicholas Nugent, 1996). A good summary of the main changes in Vietnam's economy and society.
● *Shadows and Wind: A View of Modern Vietnam* (Robert Templer, 1999). Templer was an Agence France Presse correspondent and this is his account of modern Vietnam and where it is headed. It is a downbeat picture of the country, one where bureaucratic inertia and political heavy-handedness constrain progress.
● *Vietnam at the Crossroads* (Michael C. Williams, 1992). A survey of recent political and economic reforms by a senior BBC World Service commentator; lucid and informed.
● *The Vietnam Wars 1945–1990* (Marilyn Young,

1991). Good account of the origins, development and aftermath of the Vietnam wars.

History
● *The Sacred Willow: Four Generations in the Life of a Vietnamese Family* (Mai Elliott, 1999). Recounts the history of Vietnam through the life of the Duong family from the 19th century to the tragedy of the boat people. Vietnam as seen through Vietnamese eyes.
● *The Deprat Affair: Ambition, Revenge and Deceit in French Indo-China* (Roger Osborne, 1999). The extraordinary story of Jacques Deprat, a brilliant young geologist, who may have been guilty of professional deceit. A useful insight into colonial society and mores in the first two decades of the 20th century.
● *The Vietnam Wars* (Justin Wintle, 1991). An examination of all Vietnam's many conflicts.

Novels
● *The Lover* (Marguerite Duras, 1984). The story of the illicit affair between an expat French woman and a Chinese man from Cholon in the 1930s.
● *The Quiet American* (Graham Greene, 1954). A remarkably prescient novel about America's experience in Vietnam, set in and around Saigon as the war between the French and the Viet Minh intensifies.
● *Saigon* (Anthony Grey, 1983). An entertaining novel covering events of the 20th century.
● *The Sorrow of War* (Bao Ninh, 1993). A wartime novel by a North Vietnamese soldier; a wonderful account of emotions during and after the war.

Travel and geography
● *The Voyage from London to Indochina* (Crosbie Garstin, 1928). Hilarious, irreverent account of a journey through Vietnam.
● *A Dragon Apparent: Travels in Cambodia, Laos and Vietnam* (Norman Lewis, 1951). One of the finest of all travel books. It details Lewis' account of his visit to Vietnam just a few years prior to the French defeat at Dien Bien Phu in 1954, and captures the twilight years of the Indochinese empire. He fraternizes with the French colonialist rulers and hitchhikes around in their transportation. His narrative reports encounters

Taking time out of sightseeing to catch up on the news

with these characters, with wildlife and with the *moi* (savages or slaves), as the French called the ethnic minorities living in the highlands.

● *The Great Railway Bazaar: By Train Through Asia* (Paul Theroux, 1975). Theroux's graphic account of one American's attempt to travel by rail between Saigon and Hué.

War in Vietnam

● *Hell in a Very Small Place: The Siege of Dien Bien Phu* (Bernard B. Fall, 1967).
● *The Last Valley: Dien Bien Phu and the French Defeat in Vietnam* (Martin Windrow, 2004). A detailed and highly readable account of this key 1954 battle.
● *Australia's Vietnam War* (Jeff Doyle, with Jeffrey Grey and Peter Pierce, 2002). Australia's role in, and motives for, joining the Vietnam War.
● *Fire in the Lake* (Francis Fitzgerald, 1972). A Pulitzer prize-winning, readable account of the US involvement.
● *Dispatches* (Michael Herr, 1977). An acclaimed account of the Vietnam War written by a correspondent who experienced the conflict firsthand.
● *American Tragedy: Kennedy, Johnson and the Origins of the Vietnam War* (David Kaiser, 1999). Based on recently opened archives; a penetrating insight into America's involvement in Vietnam.

Relaxing outside a bookstore

● *Vietnam: A History* (Stanley Karnow, 1983, revised 1991, second edition, 1997). A comprehensive and readable history.
● *The White House Years* (A. Henry Kissinger, 1979). The first volume of the memoirs of America's best-known diplomat covers the first Nixon term and ends with the Paris Peace Accord of 1973. *Years of Upheaval* (1982), covers the turbulent months from Kissinger's visit to Hanoi in February 1973 to Nixon's resignation in August 1974, and *Years of Renewal* (1998), the concluding volume, covers the end of the Vietnam war and collapse of the South.
● *Vietnam: A Reporter's War* (Hugh Lunn, 1985). Australian reporter Hugh Lunn's year in Vietnam with Reuters between 1967 and 1968, including an account of the Tet Offensive.
● *In Retrospect: The Tragedy and Lessons of Vietnam* (Robert S. McNamara and Brian Van de Mark, 1997). McNamara was US Secretary for Defense from 1961 to 1968 and this is his cathartic account of the war.
● *The Tunnels of Cu Chi* (Tom Mangold and John Penycate, 1985). A compelling account of

the building of the tunnels and of the Viet Cong who fought in them.
● *Chickenhawk* (Robert Mason, 1983). An excellent autobiography of a helicopter pilot.
● *The Human Stain* (Philip Roth, 2000). Not ostensibly about the Vietnam War at all, but it has an excellent account of American war veterans coming to terms with their traumas and with the country that shunned them.
● *A Bright Shining Lie* (Neil Sheehan, 1989). A meticulously researched 850-page account of the Vietnam War, based around the life of Lieutenant Colonel John Paul Vann.
● *Two Cities: Hanoi and Saigon* (Neil Sheehan, 1992). A short but fascinating book that tries to link the past with the present in a part autobiography, part travelog, part contemporary commentary.
● *River of Time* (Jon Swain, 1996). A gripping account by a war correspondent who speculates that American generals saw the war in Vietnam as a rehearsal for future conflict in Europe against the Red Army.
● *A Wavering Grace: A Vietnamese Family in War and*

Foreign-language magazines are available

Peace (Gavin Young, 1997). Young's account of the war in Vietnam, where he was a reporter, told through the lives of a Vietnamese family.
● *Vietnam Now: A Reporter Returns* (David Lamb, 2003). War reporter Lamb returns to journalism in Hanoi in 1997 and documents the social revolution since the end of the

war. All the more readable for presenting one of the few up-to-date accounts of contemporary Vietnam.

Vietnamese literature in English
● *The Tale of Kieu* (also known as *Truyen Kieu*) (Nguyen Du, 1983, translated by Huynh Sanh Thong). Early 19th-century

Vietnamese classic and, for many, the masterpiece of Vietnamese poetry. It is also published in Vietnam (in English) by the Foreign Languages Publishing House. It tells the story of a beautiful young woman and her doomed love affair with a soldier.

MAPS
● www.lib.utexas.edu
Click on the "map" button. Up-to-date maps of Asia showing relief, political boundaries and major towns.
● www.nationalgeographic.com
Click on the "map" button. National Geographic's cartographic division, which takes maps from their current atlas of the world.
● Vietnam maps can be bought in the UK from Stanfords, 12–14 Long Acre, London WC2E 9LP, tel 020 7836 1321, fax 020 7836 0189, www.stanfords.co.uk (branches in Bristol and Manchester).

USEFUL WEBSITES

www.asiasociety.org
Homepage of the Asia Society, with papers, reports and speeches, as well as nearly 1,000 links to what they consider to be the best educational, political and cultural sites on the web.

www.cpv.org.vn
The Communist Party of Vietnam's website is thorough, loyally supported (over 2 million hits) and slow.

www.fva.org
Free Vietnam Alliance is a movement with worldwide support campaigning for democracy in Vietnam.

www.hmongnet.org
Information on Hmong culture, history and language.

www.hrw.org
Human Rights Watch reports on police and military brutality against ethnic minorities in the Central Highlands and on the asylum-seekers who fled to Cambodia, as well as reporting on how Vietnam treats pro-democracy campaigners.

www.militaryvisions.com
A UK company with online military information and educational battle-site tours to Vietnam.

www.mofa.gov.vn
Ministry of Foreign Affairs website, with Vietnam's interpretation of world events in Vietnamese and English.

www.mrpumpy.net
For potential bicyclists, Mr Pumpy offers a full account of one route through the Mekong Delta and another through Laos to Vietnam. The routes are well explained and the pitfalls are highlighted.

www.pata.org
The Pacific Asia Travel Association has a useful news section arranged by country, with links to airlines and cruise lines, and some information on educational, environmental and other initiatives.

www.saigondaily.com
A good source of up-to-date information about Saigon and Vietnam. Also links to all relevant websites.

www.thingsasian.com
A huge online collection of historical, cultural and travelog articles.

www.unhcr.ch/cgi-bin/texis/vtx/home
The United Nations High Commission for Refugees (UNHCR) website has a series of country reports on human rights and other issues.

www.vdic.org.vn
Vietnam Development Information Center. This is a World Bank-sponsored site that has a number of informative papers on Vietnamese society and economy for downloading.

www.vietvet.org
The Vietnam Veterans Web ring offers a virtual visit and details of specialist veterans' tours to the country, including visits to battle sites and reports and diaries from recent visitors.

PLANNING

WORDS AND PHRASES

Outside Saigon, Hanoi, Hué, Hoi An, Nha Trang, Dalat and other visitor centers, language can be a problem for those who have no knowledge of Vietnamese, although you are likely to find a smattering of English wherever there are visitor services.

Vietnamese is not easy to pick up and pronunciation can sometimes present difficulties, but it is worth making an effort, and the Vietnamese are delighted when foreigners try to speak in their language.

● Vietnamese uses six tones and has 12 vowels and 27 consonants—pronunciation is varied by the use of diacritical marks.

● As in other tonal languages, one word can mean many things depending upon the tone used: "ma," for example, can mean horse, cheek, ghost, grave or rice seedling.

● Vietnamese is written in a Roman alphabet, so place and street names are recognizable.

● Vietnamese–English and English–Vietnamese dictionaries are inexpensive and widely available in most towns.

● English is the most useful foreign language; visitors can find themselves asked to clarify some point of pronunciation or grammar.

● French is still spoken by the more elderly and educated.

SOUNDS

TONAL SOUNDS
There are six tonal sounds in Vietnamese, which apply to a selection of vowels: a, e o and u. These tones depend on voice pitch and change in pitch. The mid tone is unmarked but other tones are represented by various additional characters. For instance, "á" indicates that the voice rises sharply from middle range; "ò'" indicates that the voice lowers from middle range, and "ô" tells the speaker to use a rising tone. The "ã" represents the voice starting low, rising sharply but broken by a stop, and the "ọ" starts low and drops even lower.

BASICS
yes	**da co**
no	**da khong**
please	**lam on/xin**
thank you	**cam on**
excuse me	**xin loi**
good night	**chuc anh/chi ngu ngon**

Where is the toilet?
Nha ve sinh o dau?

VOWEL SOUNDS
a	as in rather
ǎ	as in cut
â	as in hum
e	as in egg
ê	as in say
i	as in bin
y	as in be
o	as in saw
ô	as in so
ó	as in blur
u	as in rule
ư	as in put

CONSONANT SOUNDS
ch	as in child
-ch	as in eke (end position)
d	as in zip
đ	as in dad
g	as in gad
gi	as in zip
kh	as in king
ng	as in singer
nh	as in onion
ph	like an "f"
r	like a "z" in the North of the country
	like a "r" in the South
th	as in ten
tr	as in train
x	like an "s"

INTRODUCTIONS

hello or goodbye
xin chao

How are you?
Ong/ba khoe khong?

I'm fine, thanks
Cam on, toi khoe

What's your name?
Ong/ba ten la gi?

My name is...
Toi ten la...

How old are you?
Ong/ba bao nhieu tuoi?

Are you married?
Ahn/chi lap gia dinh chua?

Do you have children?
Ong/ba co con khong?

I'm glad to see you
Rat han hanh duoc gap

ong/ba

This is my wife/husband
Day la nhatoi

daughter
con gai

son
con trai

What is your job?
Ong/ba lam nghe gi?

PROFESSION
I'm a...	**Toi la**...
...doctor	...**bac si**
...nurse	...**y ta**
...teacher	...**giao vien**
...student	...**hoc sinh**
...engineer	...**ky su**
...journalist	...**nha bao**
...lawyer	...**luat su**
...secretary	...**thu ky**
...clerk	...**vien chuc van phong**
...worker	...**cong nhan**
...farmer	...**nong dan**
...scientist	...**khoa hoc gia**
...tourist	...**khach du lich**

NATIONALITY
Which country are you from?
Ong/ba la nguoi nuoc nao?

I am...	**Toi la nguoi**...
...American	...**My**
...Australian	...**Uc**
...Austrian	...**Ao**
...British	...**Anh**
...Chinese	...**Trung Quoc**
...Danish	...**Dan Mach**
...Dutch	...**Ha Lan**
...French	...**Phap**
...German	...**Duc**
...Indian	...**An Do**
...Irish	...**Ai Nhi Lan**
...Italian	...**Y**
...Japanese	...**Nhat**
...Norwegian	...**Na Uy**
...Swedish	**Thuy Dien**
...Swiss	...**Thuy Si**

GENERAL
emergency	**khan cap/cap cuu**
fire	**dam chay/lua**
flood	**lut/lu lut**
help	**giup/giup do**

MEDICAL
accident	**tai nan**
ambulance	**xe cuu thuong**
backache	**dau lung**
broken	**hu**
cut	**cat**
dentist	**nha si**
disease	**benh tat**
dizzy	**chong mat**
doctor	**bac si**

eye	**mat**
fever	**sot**
headache	**nhuc dau/dau dau**
hospital	**benh vien**
ill	**benh/om/dau**
injured	**bi thuong**
medicine	**thuoc**
nurse	**y ta**
pharmacy	**hieu thuoc tay**
sick	**benh/om/dau**

CONSULAR
consulate	**lanh su quan**
embassy	**su quan/toa dai su**

CRIME
arrest	**bat giam**
credit card	**the tin dung**
luggage	**hanh ly**
police officer	**canh sat**
police station	**tram canh sat**
robbed	**bi cuop**
traveler's checks	**ngan phieu du lich**
wallet	**vi/bop**

I want a ticket to...
Toi muon mot ve di...

How much is a ticket?
Bao nhieu tien mot ve?

return-ticket
ve khu hoi

one-way ticket
ve mot chieu

I want to go to...
Toi muon di den...

Is there a bus to Hanoi?
Co chuyen xe buyt di Ha Noi khong?

Does this bus go to Sapa?
Xe nay co di den Sapa khong?

When is the next train?
Chuyen xe lua ke tiep vao luc nao?

How long does the trip take?

Hanh trinh mat bao lau?

I want the next train to Hue
Toi muon mot chuyen tau som nhat di Hue

I want to go by express train
Toi muon mot chuyen tau toc hanh

What time does the train arrive?
Xe lua den luc may gio?

What time will the train depart?
Xe lua se khoi hanh luc may gio?

The train is late
Chuyen xe lua bi te

The train has been cancelled
Chuyen xe lua bi huy

USEFUL WORDS
airport	**phi truong**
boat	**thuyen**
bus station	**ben xe**
car	**xe hoi/oto**

church	**nha tho**
ferry	**pha**
ferry station	**ben pha**
flight	**chuyen bay**
market	**cho**
museum	**vien bao tang**
pagoda	**chua**
post office	**buu dien**
ship	**tau**
train	**xe lua/tau hoa**

DIRECTIONS
Where is the...?	**o dau**...?
railway station	**ga xe lua**
school	**truong hoc**
university	**truong dai hoc**
Could you show me the way to...?	
Ong/ba co the chi toi duong toi...?	
Is it far?	**Co xa khong?**
Is it near?	**Co gan khong?**
go straight	**di thang**
turn left	**queo/re trai**
turn right	**queo/re phai**
crossroads	**nga tu**
T-junction	**nga ba**
roundabout	**bung binh**

black	**den**
blue	**xanh da troi**
brown	**nau**
green	**xanh la cay**
gray	**xam**
orange	**cam**
pink	**hong**
purple	**tim**
red	**do**
white	**trang**
yellow	**vang**
color	**mau**
dark	**dam**
light	**nhat/lat**

1	**mot**	21	**hai muoi mot**
2	**hai**	30	**ba muoi**...etc
3	**ba**		
4	**bon**	100	**mot tram**
5	**nam**	101	**mot tram le**
6	**sau**		**mot**
7	**bay**		(or **mot tram**
8	**tam**		**mot**)
9	**chin**	200	**hai tram**...etc
10	**muoi/mot chuc**	1,000	**mot nghin/mot ngan**
11	**muoi mot**	10,000	**muoi nghin/**
12	**muoi hai**		**muoi ngan**
15	**muoi lam**...etc	100,000	**mot tram nghin**
20	**hai muoi**	1,000,000	**mot trieu**

morning	**buoi sang**	Tuesday	**thu ba**
noon	**trua**	Wednesday	**thu tu**
afternoon	**buoi chieu**	Thursday	**thu nam**
evening	**buoi toi**	Friday	**thu sau**
night	**ban dem**	Saturday	**thu bay**
day time	**ban ngay**	spring	**mua xuan**
today	**hom nay**	summer	**mua ha/he**
yesterday	**hom qua**	autumn	**mua thu**
tomorrow	**ngay mai**	winter	**mua dong**
day	**ngay**		
week	**tuan**	January	**thang gieng**
weekend	**cuoi tuan**	February	**thang hai**
month	**thang**	March	**thang ba**
year	**nam**	April	**thang tu**
		May	**thang nam**
one o'clock	**mot gio**	June	**thang sau**
two o'clock	**hai gio**	July	**thang bay**
three o'clock	**ba gio**	August	**thang tam**
four o'clock	**bon gio**...etc	September	**thang chin**
		October	**thang muoi**
Sunday	**chu nhat**	November	**thang muoi mot**
Monday	**thu hai**	December	**thang muoi hai**

RESTAURANTS

Can I have the menu please?
Xin cho toi xem thuc don?

I'm a vegetarian
Toi an chay

No chili, please
Xin dung cho ot

I'd like some rice
Toi muon mot it com

Do you have traditional food?
Co mon an truyen thong khong?

Do you have any special dishes?
Mon nao la dac san cua quan?

It's delicious
Rat ngon

I'm thirsty
Toi khat nuoc

Cold water, please
Cho toi xin mot coc nuoc lanh

No ice
khong da

Is the water safe to drink?
Nuoc uong co sach khong?

VIETNAMESE ADDRESSES

Large buildings with a single street number are usually subdivided 21A, 21B, 21C etc; some buildings may be further subdivided 21C1, 21C2, 21C3 and so on. So, if you are standing at 21 Hai Ba Trung Street and want number 31, it may be as far as two blocks away.

An oblique (/) in a number, as in 23/16 Dinh Tien Hoang Street, means that the address is to be found in a small side street (hem), in this case running off Dinh Tien Hoang Street by the side of No. 23; the house in question will probably be signed 23/16 rather than just 16. Usually, but by no means always, a hem will be quieter than the main street, and it may be worth looking at a guesthouse with an oblique number for that reason (especially in the Pham Ngu Lao area of Saigon).

An address sometimes contains the letter F followed by a number, as in F6; this is short for phuong (ward, a small administrative area). Q in an address stands for quan (district); this points you in the right general direction and is important in locating your destination, as a long street in Hanoi or Saigon may run through several quan. In suburban and rural areas districts are known as huyen—Huyen Nha Be, outside Saigon, for instance. Note that there are no zip codes (post codes) in Vietnam.

SHOPPING

I'd like to buy some clothes
Toi muon mua mot it quan ao

How much is it?
Gia bao nhieu?

It's too expensive
Mac qua

Can you lower the price?
Co bot khong?

Oh, it's still very expensive
O, van con mac lam

Is 10,000 dong OK?
10,000 dong, duoc khong?

Can I have a look?
Toi co the xem duoc khong?

Do you have one in a bigger

size?
Ong/ba co co lon hon khong?

Sorry, I don't like it
Rat tiec, toi khong thich

Do you have another one?
Ong/ba co cai khac khong?

I will take this one
Toi se mua cai nay

They don't/It doesn't fit me
No khong vua voi toi

It's too small
No nho qua

USEFUL SHOPPING WORDS

bag	**gio xach**	clothes	**quan ao**
book	**sach**	duty free	**mien thue**
cigarette	**thuoc la**	fabric	**vai**
		film (camera)	**phim**
		gas/petrol	**xang**
		handicraft	**do thu cong**
		hat	**non**
		jacket	**ao khoac**
		matches	**que diem**
		paintings	**tranh**
		pottery	**do gom**
		raincoat	**ao mua**
		razor	**dao cao**
		sandals	**dep**
		shampoo	**xa-phong goi dau**
		shoes	**giay**
		skirt	**vay dam**
		socks	**vo**
		souvenir	**do luu niem**
		supermarket	**sieu thi**
		t-shirt	**ao pun ngan tay**

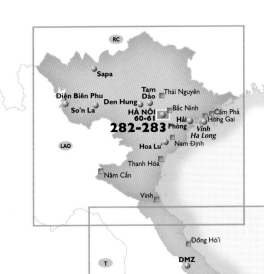

RC

Sapa

Tam Đảo
Điện Biên Phu
Den Hung
Thái Nguyên
So'n La
HÀ NỘI
60-61
Bắc Ninh
Cẩm Phả
282-283
Hải Phòng
Hồng Gai
Vịnh Ha Long
LAO
Hoa Lu'
Nam Định
Thanh Hóa
Nậm Cẩn
Vinh

Đồng Hớ'i

DMZ
T
Huê
Lang Chu Tich Hue
284-285
Đà Nẵng
Hội An
LAO
Mỹ So'n

Quy Nho'n

Tuy Hòa
Buôn Mê Thuột
K
Nha Trang
Đa Lat
286-287
Cao Dai
Dia Dao Củ Chi
Thú Dâu Môt
Châu Dốc
Hồ Chí Minh
Biên Hòa
Phan Thiết
Hà Tiên
130-131
Tân An
Đảo Phú Quô'c
Dong Thap Muoi
Mỹ Tho
Vũng Tàu
Vĩnh Long
Cân Tho'
Sóc Trăng
Cà Mau
Bac Liêu
Côn Đảo

282-287
0   60 km
0   40 miles

▬▬▬ National road
── Regional road
┄┄┄ Main road
┈┈┈ Minor road
─── Railway
▬▬▬ International boundary
──── Administrative region boundary
▦ Built-up area
■ City/Town
● Featured place of interest
● Other place of interest
✈ Airport
3143 ▲ Height in metres
⚓─ Port/Ferry route

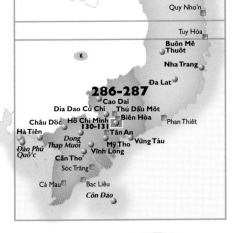

Maps

5

6

Nam
Un Res

Nong Han Res

Nam
Phung Res

592
Phu Pha Phüng ▲

7 Yasothon

Suwannaphum

Pha Nam Yoi NP

T

Ubon Ratchathani

Si Sa Ket

8

Khukhan

Phanom Dong Rak

Chuŏr Phnum Dãngrek

Stŏeng Srêng

9 Siêmréap

1146 ▲

Muang
Khammouan

U Thumphon

Xénô

Mukdahan   Savannakhet

Khemmarat

Amnat Charoer

Philbun Mangsahan

Warin Chamrap   Pakxé

*Shirinthorn
Res*

Champasak   Ban Nongsim

Phumsaron

Muang Không

Phumĭ Kâmpóng
Sralaun

306 ▲

Mekong

Banghiang

LAO

1588 ▲

Plateau

des

Bolovens

154

Tônle Kông

K

Tônle San

Stŏeng Trêng

*Tônle
Srepo*

Mekong

Kiém Ich   Lóc

HÀ TĨNH   Hà Tĩnh

Đại Lo'i   Khe   Cẩm Xuyên
Hu'o'ng Khê   Glao   Voi

2286 ▲   *Hô Kê*   Kỳ Anh Mỹ Ròn
Gó

Hg Lâm   Bâu Môn   Hg Lê

Hg Liên   *Mũi Độc*
Thanh Hóa   Rón
Khe Ve   Hòa Bình
Tyên Hóa
Lạc So'n
Xom Thôn   Lý Hòa
Ba Đồn   Bố Trạch
X Dõn   *15*
Dong Phong Nha   Cu Hoa
Phong Nha   **Đồng Hó'i**   Lệ
Nir
QUẢNG   B Ban   Đức Lập
BÌNH   Khe Cát
Bàn Xán
Cô Tràng
Tang Ky
Ban Hai
Cù Ba

1312 ▲   **DM**
Ta
Pu'ó'ng
Ban Naba   **Khe
Sanh**
Ban
Đồng

ACKNOWLEDGMENTS

Abbreviations for the credits are as follows:
AA = AA World Travel Library, t (top), b (bottom), c (centre), l (left),
r (right), bg (background)

UNDERSTANDING VIETNAM

4l, 4r AA/D Henley; 4cl, 4cr AA/J Holmes; 5l, 5r AA/D Henley; 5c, 5cr AA/J Holmes; 6bl, 6bc, 6br AA/D Henley; 7l, 7c, 7r AA/D Henley; 8cl, 8bl, 8c, 8cr AA/D Henley; 8tr, 8br AA/J Holmes; 9tl, 9cl AA/D Henley; 9cl Camargue Restaurant; 9bl Evason Hideaway at Ana Mandara; 9tr AA/J Holmes; 9cr AA/D Henley; 10l AA/J Holmes; 10tr, 10cbr AA/D Henley; 10ctr, 10br AA/J Holmes.

LIVING VIETNAM

11 AA/J Holmes, 12/13bg AA/D Henley; 12cl, 12bl, 12tl ,12c AA/D Henley; 12cr, 12tcl, 12tccl, 12tccr, 12tcr, 12tr AA/J Holmes; 13tl, 13c, 13b AA/J Holmes; 13tr, 13lc, 13rc AA/D Henley; 14/15bg AA/D Henley; 14tl, 14rc AA/D Henley; 14tr, 14lc, 14b AA/J Holmes; 15lc, 15tc, 15c, 15rc AA/D Henley; 15tr, 15rac AA/J Holmes; 16/17bg, 16br, 16tr, 16c AA/J Holmes; 16tl, 16bl AA/D Henley; 16lc AA/B Davies; 17tl, 17lc, 17c AA/J Holmes; 17tr AA/D Henley; 17b AA/B Davies; 18/19bg, 18tc AA/D Henley; 18/19t Catherine Karnow/CORBIS; 18tl, 18lc, 18bl, 18bc AA/J Holmes; 19tl AA/D Henley; 19tr, 19lc AA/J Holmes; 19cr © Bobby Chinn; 20/21bg, 20tl, 20tc, 20rc, 20b AA/D Henley; 20lc AA/J Holmes; 21tl, 21tr, 21lc AA/J Holmes; 21tc, 21b AA/D Henley; 22/3bg AA/D Henley; 22tl Warner Bros/The Kobal Collection; 22lc Zoetrope/United Artists/The Kobal Collection; 22b Paramount/The Kobal Collection/Vaughan, Stephen; 22tr MiraMax/Dimension Films/The Kobal Collection/Bray, Phil; 23tl EMI/Columbia/Warners/The Kobal Collection; 23tc United Artists/The Kobal Collection; 23tr Touchstone/The Kobal Collection; 23c © Sony Pictures/Everett (EVT)/Rex Features Ltd; 23tl AA/J Holmes; 24bg, 24lc AA/J Holmes; 24tc Steve Ratmer/CORBIS; 24tr Rex Features Ltd; 24c AA/D Henley.

THE STORY OF VIETNAM

25 AA/D Henley; 26/7bg, 26c, 26bc AA/J Holmes, 26/7, 26bl AA/D Henley; 27cl, 27c, 27cr CPA; 27bl, 27bc AA/D Henley; 27br AA/J Holmes; 28/9bg CPA; 28/9, 28c AA/D Henley; 28bl AA/J Holmes; 28bc, 28br CPA; 29lc, 29c, 29rc, 29bl, 29br CPA; 30bl AA/J Holmes; 30/1bg AA/J Holmes; 30br, 30c, 30cr CPA; 31bl AA/D Henley; 31tl, 31tc, 31tr, 31cl CPA; 31bc AA/J Holmes; 31br CPA; 32/3bg AA/D Henley; 32tl, 32cr AA/D Henley; 32bl, 32br CPA; 33tl, 33tc, 33tr, 33lc CPA; 33bl AA/D Henley; 33bc AA/J Holmes; 33br AA/D Henley; 34/5bg, 34/5 AA/J Holmes; 34bl AA/D Henley; 34bc, 34tr CPA; 35tl CPA; 35tr Bettmann/CORBIS; 35br CPA; 36/7bg AA/D Henley; 36tl, 36bl AA/D Henley; 36c Time cover 09-15-1967 of Nguyen Van Thieu (Photo by Time Life Pictures/Time Magazine, Copyright Time Inc./Time Life Pictures/Getty Images; 36br Zoetrope/United Artists/The Kobal Collection; 36cr CPA; 37tl Johnson Presidential Library noD-3007-16/CPA; 37tc CPA; 37tr AA/J Holmes; 37bl AA/C Sawyer; 37br CPA; 38bg, 38bc, 38tc AA/D Henley; 38br Reuters/CORBIS; 38bl AA/J Holmes.

ON THE MOVE

39 AA/J Holmes; 40t Digital Vision; 40c AA/D Henley; 41t Digital Vision; 41c AA/J Holmes; 42t AA/D Henley; 42c AA/J Holmes; 43t AA/D Henley; 43c AA/J Holmes; 44t AA/D Henley; 45t AA/D Henley; 45c AA/J Holmes; 46t AA/D Henley; 46cl, 46cr, 46b AA/J Holmes; 47t, 47c AA/D Henley; 48t, 48c, 48b AA/D Henley; 49t AA/D Henley; 49cl, 49cr AA/J Holmes; 50 Digital Vision; 51t Digital Vision; 51c AA/J Holmes; 52t Digital Vision 52cl, 52cr AA/J Holmes; 53t Digital Vision; 53b AA/J Holmes; 54t, 54c AA/J Holmes; 54b AA/D Henley; 55t AA/J Holmes; 55cl AA/D Henley; 56t, 56c AA/J Holmes.

THE SIGHTS

57 AA/D Henley; 59l AA/D Henley; 59r AA/J Holmes; 62tl, 62tc, 62tr AA/J Holmes; 62b AA/D Henley; 63t, 63r AA/D Henley; 64t, 64lc, 64c, 64rc, 64b AA/D Henley; 65 AA/D Henley; 65(insert) AA/J Holmes; 66l AA/D Henley; 66r AA/J Holmes; 67tl, 67tc, 67tr, 67b AA/D Henley; 68 AA/J Holmes; 69t AA/D Henley; 69l, 69c, 69r AA/J Holmes; 70 AA/D Henley; 71l, 71c, 71r, 71b AA/D Henley; 72/3 AA/D Henley; 72c AA/D Henley; 73r AA/J Holmes; 74tl, 74tr, 74bl AA/D Henley; 75 AA/D Henley; 76tl AA/J Holmes; 76tc, 76tr, 76b AA/D Henley; 77t, 77b AA/D Henley; 78tr, 78l AA/D Henley; 79tl AA/J Holmes; 79bc AA/D Henley; 81tl , 81tr AA/J Holmes; 81tc, 81br AA/D Henley; 82t AA/D Henley; 82lc AA/J Gocher; 83t AA/J Holmes; 83b AA/J Gocher; 84tl, 84tr, 84b AA/J Holmes; 85t, 85rc AA/J Holmes; 86t AA/D Henley; 86lc AA/J Holmes; 86c AA/D Henley; 86rc AA/J Gocher; 87 AA/J Holmes; 88l AA/D Henley; 88r AA/J Holmes; 89t AA/J Holmes; 89rc AA/J Gocher; 90t, 90b AA/D Henley; 91tl, 91tc AA/J Holmes; 91tr AA/D Henley; 92 AA/J Holmes; 93t, 93cl, 93c, 93rc AA/D Henley; 93b AA/ J Holmes; 94 AA/D Henley; 95l, 95r AA/D Henley; 95c AA/J Gocher; 96tl, 96tr, 96bl AA/D Henley; 97l AA/J Holmes; 97r AA/D Henley; 99l, 99r, 99lc AA/D Henley; 100/1 AA/D Henley; 100c AA/D Henley; 101 AA/D Henley; 102l AA/J Holmes; 102r Michelle Bennett/Lonely Planet Images; 103 AA/D Henley; 104t AA/J Holmes; 104lc, 104c, 104rc AA/D Henley; 105t, 105b AA/J Holmes; 106t AA/D Henley; 106c AA/J Holmes; 107lc AA/D Henley; 107c AA/J Holmes; 107rc, 107br AA/D Henley; 108t AA/D Henley; 108lc AA/J Holmes; 108b AA/ D Henley; 109 AA/J Holmes; 110 AA/J Holmes; 111 AA/J Holmes; 112/13 AA/J Holmes; 112lc AA/J Holmes; 113tr AA/D Henley; 113bl AA/J Holmes; 114/15 AA/D Henley; 114tl, 114lc, 114c AA/D Henley; 115r AA/J Holmes; 116tl, 116c, 116bl AA/J Holmes; 118t, 118c AA/D Henley; 119t, 119b AA/D Henley; 120t AA/D Henley; 120b AA/J Holmes; 121tc, 121br AA/D Henley; 122tl AA/J Holmes; 122tr AA/D Henley; 122bl AA/ J Holmes; 123t, 123r AA/J Holmes; 124t, 124r AA/J Holmes; 124l AA/ D Henley; 125 AA/D Henley; 126tl AA/D Henley; 126tc, 126tr, 126c AA/J Holmes; 128t AA/D Henley; 128b, 128c AA/J Holmes; 130 AA/D Henley; 131r AA/J Holmes; 131b AA/D Henley; 132t AA/J Holmes; 132l AA/D Henley; 133t AA/J Holmes; 133br AA/D Henley; 134l AA/J Holmes; 134r AA/D Henley; 135tl, 135tc, 135tr AA/D Henley; 135br AA/J Holmes; 136l, 136r AA/D Henley; 137t AA/D Henley; 137r AA/D Henley; 138tl, 138tr, 138cl AA/D Henley; 139tl AA/D Henley; 139tc, 139tr, 139br AA/D Henley; 140t, 140cl AA/D Henley; 141tl AA/K Paterson; 141tc, 141tr, 141bl AA/D Henley; 142t, 142l AA/D Henley; 144t, 144l, 144b AA/D Henley; 145t, 145cr AA/D Henley; 146t, 146cl, 146cr, 146b AA/D Henley; 147 AA/D Henley; 148l, 148r AA/D Henley; 149t, 149r AA/D Henley; 150tl, 150tr AA/D Henley; 151t AA/J Holmes; 151r AA/D Henley; 152t, 152l AA/D Henley; 153t, 153r AA/D Henley; 154l, 154r AA/D Henley; 155l, 155r AA/D Henley; 156t, 156l AA/D Henley.

WHAT TO DO

157 AA/D Henley; 158/9t AA/J Holmes; 158lc AA/D Henley; 158rc AA/J Holmes; 159rc AA/D Henley; 159lc AA/J Holmes; 160/1t AA/J Holmes; 160lc AA/D Henley; 160rc J Holmes; 161lc, 161rc AA/J Holmes; 162lc AA/J Holmes; 162rc AA; 162/3t AA/J Holmes; 163lc AA/D Henley; 163rc Café de la Poste, © Sofitel Hotels & Resorts; 164lc © Sofitel Hotels & Resorts; 164rc AA/J Holmes; 164/5t A/D Henley; 165lc AA/J Holmes; 165rc Furama Hotels & Resorts International; 166lc Furama Hotels & Resorts International; 166rc Evason Hideaway at Ana Mandara; 166/7t AA/D Henley; 166bl AA/D Henley; 167rc AA/J Holmes; 168/9t AA/J Holmes; 168c AA/D Henley; 169c AA/D Henley; 170/1t AA/J Holmes; 170c AA/J Holmes; 171c AA/D Henley; 172t AA/J Holmes; 173t AA/J Gocher; 173c AA/J Holmes; 174t AA/J Gocher; 175t AA/J Holmes; 175c AA/J Holmes; 176/7t AA/J Holmes; 176c Furama Hotels & Resorts International; 177c AA/J Holmes; 178/9t AA/J Holmes; 178c AA/D Henley; 179c AA/D Henley; 180t AA/J Holmes; 180c Ana Mandara; 181t AA/D Henley; 181c AA/D Henley; 182/3t

AA/D Henley; **182c** AA/D Henley; **183c** AA/D Henley; **184/5t** AA/D Henley; **184c** AA/J Holmes; **185c** AA/D Henley; **186c** Saigon Spa; **186t** AA/D Henley; **187c** AA/D Henley; **187t, 188c** and **188t** RAINBOW DIVERS: Nha Trang, Whale Island, Con Dao & Phu Quoc.

OUT AND ABOUT

189 AA/J Holmes; **191ct, 191cb** AA/D Henley; **192t, 192c** AA/D Henley; **193c, 193b** AA/D Henley; **194t, 194c** AA/D Henley; **195t, 195c, 195b** AA/D Henley; **196** AA/D Henley; **197t, 197c** AA/D Henley; **198t** AA/J Holmes; **198b** AA/D Henley; **199t, 199c** AA/D Henley; **199b** AA/J Holmes; **200t, 200c** AA/J Holmes; **201** C Boobbyer; **202** Carole Philp; **203** AA/D Henley; **204** AA/D Henley

EATING AND STAYING

205 AA/J Holmes; **206cl** ©Bobby Chinn; **206c, 206rc** AA/D Henley; **207lc, 207c** AA/D Henley; **207rc** AA/J Holmes; **208tc** AA/D Henley; **208lc, 208c, 208rc** AA/J Holmes; **209lc, 209c** AA/J Holmes; **209rc** AA/D Henley; **209b** AA/J Holmes; **210lc, 210c, 210rc, 210b** AA/D Henley; **211l** AA/D Henley; **211tr, 211br** ©Bobby Chinn; **212l** Brothers Restaurant; **212r** AA/D Henley; **231l** ©Hanoi Press Club; **213r** Highway4; **214tl** Highway4; **214tr** ©Hanoi Press Club; **215tc, 215bc** AA/D Henley; **215r** Tassili; **216tl** Bananastock; **216lc** AA/D Henley; **216tr, 216br** ©Hoa Sua School/Baguette & Chocolat; **216bc** AA/D Henley; **217** Red Dragon Pub; **218l** © Furama Hotels & Resorts International; **218r** © Sofitel Hotels & Resorts; **219tc** AA/D Henley; **219r** AA/D Henley; **220t, 220c, 220r** AA/D Henley; **221l** © Bamboo Village Resort; **221tc** © Coco Beach Resort; **221tr** Luna D'Autonno; **221bc** Ana Mandara; **222tc** © Sailing Club Vietnam; **222cr** Photodisc; **222bl** Photodisc; **222bc** © Sailing Club Vietnam; **223** Ashoka; **224** Café Latin; **225** Camargue; **227** © Furama Hotels & Resorts International; **228** AA/D Henley; **229l** Photodisc; **230tc, 230bc, 230tl** Victoria Hotels, Asia; **231br** AA/D Henley; **231tc** Tom's; **231cl** AA/J Holmes; **231bl** AA/D Henley; **231cr** © Bobby Chinn.

232l AA/D Henley; **232cl** AA/J Holmes; **232cr** AA/DHolmes; **232r** AA/J Holmes; **233l, 233cl** AA/D Henley; **233cr** © Sofitel Hotels & Resorts; **233r** AA/D Henley; **235tl, 235bl, 235c** AA/D Henley; **236** Hotel Nikko Hanoi; **237tc** © Sofitel Hotels & Resorts; **237r** Sunway Hotel; **238l, 238c, 238r** AA/D Henley; **239l, 239r** AA/D Henley; **240l** © Hoa Sua School/Baguette & Chocolat; **240c** AA/D Henley; **241** © Furama Hotels & Resorts International; **242** AA/J Holmes; **243tl, 243cl, 243bl** © Sofitel Hotels & Resorts; **243r** AA/D Henley; **242t, 242b** © Sofitel Hotels & Resorts; **243tl** © Sofitel Hotels & Resorts; **243bl** AA/J Holmes; **243r** AA/D Henley; **244l,** AA/D Henley; **244tr** Victoria Hotels, Asia; **245r, 245l** AA/D Henley; **246r** © Furama Hotels & Resorts International; **247l** © Coco Beach Resort; **247c** Full Moon Beach; **247r** © Sailing Club Vietnam; **248** Ana Mandara; **249c** Vin Pearl Resort; **249r** Evason Hideaway at Ana Mandara; **250tc** © Furama Hotels & Resorts International; **250br** AA/D Henley; **252tl, 252tc, 252tr** AA/D Henley; **252br** AA/J Holmes; **253tl, 253br, 253bc** AA/D Henley; **253bl** AA/J Holmes; **253tr** AA/D Henley; **b** AA/C Sawyer; **254bl** AA/D Henley; **255tl, 255tc, 255bc** Victoria Hotels, Asia; **256tc, 256bc** © Anoasis Beach Resort; **257bl, 257c, 257tr, 257tl** AA/D Henley; **258r** © Sammy Hotel; **258c** Petro House

PLANNING

259 AA/J Holmes; **260t** AA/J Holmes; **263** AA/J Holmes; **264t** AA/J Holmes; **264b** Currency information courtesy of MRI Bankers Guide to Foreign Currency, Houston, USA; **265** AA/D Henley; **266** AA/J Holmes; **267** AA/D Henley; **268** C Boobbyer; **269** AA/J Holmes; **270** AA/J Holmes; **271t** Photodisc; **271b** AA/D Henley; **272** AA/D Henley; **273t, 273b** AA/D Henley; **274tl, 274tr** AA/D Henley; **274b** AA/J Holmes; **275** AA/D Henley; **276tl** AA/J Holmes; **276br** AA/J Holmes; **277** AA/J Holmes.

Project editor
Becky Norris

Design work
Carole Philp, Jo Tapper

Picture research
Kathy Lockley, Carol Walker

Internal repro work
Susan Crowhurst, Ian Little, Michael Moody

Production
Helen Brown, Lyn Kirby

Mapping
Maps produced by the Cartography Department of AA Publishing

Main contributors
Susi Bailey, Claire Boobbyer, John Colet, Andrew Forbes, Aiden Glendinning, Carol Howland,
David Henley, Marie Lorimer

Copy editor
Nia Williams

Updater
David Henley/CPA Media

Revision Management
Bookwork Creative Associates Ltd

Published by AA Publishing, a trading name of Automobile Association Developments Limited,
whose registered office is Fanum House, Basing View, Basingstoke, Hampshire RG21 4EA, UK.
Registered number 1878835.

A CIP catalogue record for this book is available from the British Library.

ISBN-13: 978-0-7495-4632-8
ISBN-10: 0-7495-4632-8

Selected text supplied by Footprint Handbooks Limited © 2004

Key Guide is a registered trademark in Australia and is used under license.
Binding style with plastic section dividers by permission of AA Publishing.

Colour separation by Keenes
Printed and bound by Leo, China

Find out more about AA Publishing and the wide range of travel publications and services
the AA provides by visiting our website at www.theAA.com/travel

A03163
Maps in this title produced from:
mapping © MAIRDUMONT / Falk Verlag 2007
and map data © Footprint Handbooks Limited 2004

Relief map images supplied by Mountain High Maps® Copyright © 1993 Digital Wisdom, Inc
Weather chart statistics supplied by Weatherbase © Copyright 2004 Canty and Associates, LLC
Communicarta assistance with time chart gratefully acknowledged.

We believe the contents of this book are correct at the time of printing.
However, some details, particularly prices, opening times and telephone numbers
do change. We do not accept responsibility for any consequences arising from the use
of this book. This does not affect your statutory rights. We would be grateful if readers would
advise us of any inaccuracies they may encounter, or any suggestions they might like to make to
improve the book. There is a form provided at the back of the book for this purpose, or you can
email us at Keyguides@theaa.com

COVER PICTURE CREDITS

Front cover, top to bottom: Getty Images; AA/David Henley; AA David Henley; AA/David
Henley. Back cover: AA/Jim Holmes. Spine: Getty Images

Dear KeyGuide Reader

———————— ● ————————

Thank you for buying this KeyGuide. Your comments and opinions are very important to us, so please help us to improve our travel guides by taking a few minutes to complete this questionnaire.

You do not need a stamp (unless posted outside the UK). If you do not want to cut this page from your guide, then photocopy it or write your answers on a plain sheet of paper.

Send to: KeyGuide Editor, AA World Travel Guides
FREEPOST SCE 4598, Basingstoke RG21 4GY

Find out more about AA Publishing and the wide range of
travel publications the AA provides by visiting our website at
www.theAA.com/travel

ABOUT THIS GUIDE

Which KeyGuide did you buy? _____

Where did you buy it?_____

When? _ _ month/ _ _ year

Why did you choose this AA KeyGuide?
- ❏ Price ❏ AA Publication
- ❏ Used this series before; title _____
- ❏ Cover ❏ Other (please state) _____

Please let us know how helpful the following features of the guide were to you by circling the appropriate category: very helpful (**VH**), helpful (**H**) or little help (**LH**)

Size	**VH**	**H**	**LH**
Layout	**VH**	**H**	**LH**
Photos	**VH**	**H**	**LH**
Excursions	**VH**	**H**	**LH**
Entertainment	**VH**	**H**	**LH**
Hotels	**VH**	**H**	**LH**
Maps	**VH**	**H**	**LH**
Practical info	**VH**	**H**	**LH**
Restaurants	**VH**	**H**	**LH**
Shopping	**VH**	**H**	**LH**
Walks	**VH**	**H**	**LH**
Sights	**VH**	**H**	**LH**
Transport info	**VH**	**H**	**LH**

What was your favourite sight, attraction or feature listed in the guide?

Page _____ Please give your reason _____

_____

Which features in the guide could be changed or improved? Or are there any other comments you would like to make?

_____

_____

ABOUT YOU

Name (*Mr/Mrs/Ms*) _____

Address _____

_____

Postcode _____ Daytime tel nos _____

Email _____

Please *only* give us your mobile phone number/email if you wish to hear from us about other products and services from the AA and partners by text or mms.

Which age group are you in?
Under 25 ❏   25–34 ❏   35–44 ❏   45–54 ❏   55+ ❏

How many trips do you make a year?
Less than 1 ❏   1 ❏   2 ❏   3 or more ❏

ABOUT YOUR TRIP

Are you an AA member?   Yes ❏ No ❏

When did you book?   _ _ month/_ _ year

When did you travel?   _ _ month/_ _ year

Reason for your trip?   Business ❏ Leisure ❏

How many nights did you stay? _____

How did you travel?   Individual ❏ Couple ❏ Family ❏ Group ❏

Did you buy any other travel guides for your trip? _____

If yes, which ones? _____

_____

Thank you for taking the time to complete this questionnaire. Please send it to us as soon as possible, and remember, you do not need a stamp (*unless posted outside the UK*).

AA Travel Insurance call 0800 072 4168 or visit www.theaa.com

---

Titles in the KeyGuide series:
Australia, Barcelona, Britain, Brittany, Canada, China, Costa Rica, Croatia, Florence and Tuscany, France, Germany, Ireland, Italy, London, Mallorca, Mexico, New York, New Zealand, Normandy, Paris, Portugal, Prague, Provence and the Côte d'Azur, Rome, Scotland, South Africa, Spain, Thailand, Venice, Vietnam.
